DA

ELEVEN MORE
AMERICAN WOMEN POETS
IN THE 21ST CENTURY

The American Poets in the 21st Century Series

VOLUME 1

American Women Poets in the 21st Century:
Where Lyric Meets Language
   Claudia Rankine and Juliana Spahr, eds.

VOLUME 2

American Poets in the 21st Century:
The New Poetics
   Claudia Rankine and Lisa Sewell, eds.

VOLUME 3

Eleven More American Women Poets in the 21st Century:
Poetics across North America
   Claudia Rankine and Lisa Sewell, eds.

Eleven More
American Women Poets
in the 21st Century

Poetics across North America

Edited by

Claudia Rankine

and

Lisa Sewell

Wesleyan University Press · Middletown, Connecticut

Wesleyan University Press
Middletown CT 06459
www.wesleyan.edu/wespress
© 2012 by Wesleyan University Press
All rights reserved

Manufactured in the United States of America
Designed by Dennis Anderson and Scott Cahoon
Typeset in Sabon and The Sans Light by Passumpsic Publishing

Wesleyan University Press is a member of the
Green Press Initiative. The paper used in this book meets
their minimum requirement for recycled paper.

Library of Congress Cataloging-in-Publication Data
Eleven more American women poets in the 21st century:
poetics across North America / edited by Claudia Rankine
and Lisa Sewell.
      p. cm.—(Wesleyan poetry)
Includes bibliographical references and index.
ISBN 978-0-8195-7234-9 (cloth: alk. paper)—
ISBN 978-0-8195-7235-6 (pbk.: alk. paper)—
ISBN 978-0-8195-7236-3 (ebook)
1. American poetry—Women authors. 2. Women—United
States—Poetry. 3. American poetry—21st century. I. Rankine,
Claudia, 1963– II. Sewell, Lisa. III. Title: American women
poets in the twenty-first century.
PS589.E44 2012
811'.60809287—dc23   2011043613

5 4 3 2 1

Audio clips of many of the poems in this book
are available at the book's companion website:
www.wesleyan.edu/wespress/aptc3.

CONTENTS

Acknowledgments   xi

Introduction   1

MARY JO BANG   19

POEMS

From *The Eye Like A Strange Balloon*
High Art   19
Mrs. Autumn and Her Two Daughters   21
Untitled # 70 (Or, The Question of Remains)   22

From *Elegy*
Landscape with the Fall of Icarus   23
Words   24

From *The Bride of E*
And as in Alice   25
B Is for Beckett   26
C Is for Cher   26
In the Present and Probable Future   27

From the *Mrs. Dalloway* series
Opened and Shut   29

POETICS STATEMENT   30

ARTICULATIONS OF ARTIFICE IN THE WORK OF MARY JO BANG   34
by Karla Kelsey

LUCILLE CLIFTON   60

POEMS

From *Good Woman: Poems and a Memoir 1969–1980*
[the light that came to Lucille Clifton]   60

From *Quilting*
eve's version   61
lucifer speaks in his own voice   61

From *The Book of Light*
daughters   62
[won't you celebrate with me]   63
leda 1   64
leda 3   65

From *The Terrible Stories*
    telling our stories   65
From *Mercy*
    the river between us   65
From *Voices*
    sorrows   66
POETICS STATEMENT
Excerpts from an Interview with Charles Rowell   67
LUCILLE CLIFTON'S COMMUNAL "i"   68
  by Adrienne McCormick

KIMIKO HAHN   96

POEMS

From *Mosquito and Ant*
    Orchid Root   96
    Garnet   98
From *The Narrow Road to the Interior*
    Utica Station Dep.10:07 A.M. to N.Y. Penn Station   99
From *The Artist's Daughter*
    In Childhood   104
    Like Lavrinia   104
POETICS STATEMENT
Still *Writing the Body*   107
"I WANT TO GO WHERE THE HYSTERIC RESIDES"
Kimiko Hahn's Re-Articulation of the Feminine in Poetry   110
  by Zhou Xiaojing

CARLA HARRYMAN   127

POEMS

From *Baby*
    [Now. Word. Technology.]   127
    [Dark. Swat. Land.]   128
    [The. Open. Box.]   129
    [Baby. N. Baseball. Song.]   130
    [Wartime Surroundings.]   131
From *Adorno's Noise*
    [*consents to a few statements one knows ultimately
      to implicate murder*]   132
    [*it is difficult to write satire*]   134
    [*the opposite of slackness*]   135

POETICS STATEMENT
Siren 136

LISTENING IN ON CARLA HARRYMAN'S *BABY*
by Christine Hume 142

ERÍN MOURE 161

POEMS
From *O Cidadán*
document32 (inviolable) 161
document33 (arena) 162
Eleventh *Impermeable* of the Carthage of Harms 163
From *Little Theatres*
Theatre of the Confluence (A Carixa) 164
Theatre of the Stones that Ran (Fontao, 1943) 165
Theatre of the Millo Seco (Botos) 166
From *O Cadoiro*
[[T]he best woman i ever saw.] 167
[This night of liquid storms, high noon s dwelling] 168

POETICS STATEMENT
A Practice of Possibility, a Life in Languages 169

MOURE'S ABRASIONS 171
by Aaron Kunin

LAURA MULLEN 189

POEMS
From *The Surface* 189
From *The Tales of Horror*
(A Pretty Girl is Like a Melody) 191
From *After I Was Dead*
Secrets 193
35 ½ 195
From *Murmur* 197
From *Subject*
Circles 198

POETICS STATEMENT 200

LAURA MULLEN: THREATENED AS THREAT
Rethinking Gender and Genre 204
by Kass Fleisher

EILEEN MYLES 229

POEMS
Transitions 229
Snowflake 232
To My Class 234
Questions 237
Hi 239

POETICS STATEMENT 241
"WHEN WE'RE ALONE IN PUBLIC"
The Poetry of Eileen Myles 242
by Maggie Nelson

M. NOURBESE PHILIP 261

POEMS
From *She Tries Her Tongue; Her Silence Softly Breaks*
Discourse on the Logic of Language 262
From *Universal Grammar* 266
From *Zong!*
Os, Zong! #2 272
Zong! #4 273
Ferrum (excerpt) 274

POETICS STATEMENT
Ignoring Poetry (a work in progress) 279
THE LANGUAGE OF TRAUMA
Faith and Atheism in M. NourbeSe Philip's Poetry 283
by Dawn Lundy Martin

JOAN RETALLACK 308

POEMS
From *Errata Suite* 308
From *How to Do Things with Words*
The Woman in the Chinese Room 310
From *MONGRELISME* 313
From *MEMNOIR*
Curiosity and the Claim to Happiness 316
Lost Brief Case Conjecture 320

POETICS STATEMENT
Procedural Elegies: N Plus Zero 321
THE METHOD "IN *MEDIAS* MESS" 326
by Jena Osman

LISA ROBERTSON   352

POEMS

From *The Weather*
    Residence at C___   352
    Tuesday   353
    Residence at C___   356
    Saturday   356
From *Utopia (R's Boat)*
    [In the spring of 1979]   358

POETICS STATEMENT
Soft Architecture: A Manifesto   361

ABOUT SURFACE
Lisa Robertson's Poetics of Elegance   365
   by Sina Queyras

C. D. WRIGHT   386

POEMS

From *Steal Away*
    Floating Trees   386
    Privacy   388
From *Cooling Time*
    [only the crossing counts.]   389
    [elation washed over our absence toward everything
       in the increasing darkness]   389
From *One Big Self: An Investigation*
    Dear Prisoner,   390
    My Dear Conflicted Reader,   391
    Dear Child of God,   391
    [Mack trapped a spider]   392
From *Rising, Falling, Hovering*
    Re: Happiness, in pursuit thereof   392
    Like Having a Light at Your Back You Can't See
       but You Can Still Feel   393
    Like a Prisoner of Soft Words   394
    Like Something in His Handwriting   395
    Like Something Flying Backwards   396

POETICS STATEMENT
My American Scrawl   397

THE BORDER-CROSSING RELATIONAL POETRY OF C. D. WRIGHT   399
   by Suzanne Wise

Contributors   425

Index   431

Audio clips of many of the poems in this book
are available at the book's companion website:
www.wesleyan.edu/wespress.aptc3.

ACKNOWLEDGMENTS

The editors would like to thank Suzanna Tamminen for her support of this project. Many thanks as well to Laura Heinrich, Karen Garven, and especially Afton Woodward for invaluable editorial and administrative support. Permission to reprint copyrighted material has been obtained whenever possible. The editors gratefully acknowledge permission to reprint from the following sources:

Mary Jo Bang. "High Art," "Mrs. Autumn and Her Two Daughters," and "Untitled #70 (Or, The Question of Remains)" from *The Eye Like a Strange Balloon*, copyright © 2004 by Mary Jo Bang; "Landscape with the Fall of Icarus" from *Elegy*, copyright © 2007 by Mary Jo Bang; "And as in Alice," "B Is for Beckett," "C Is for Cher," "E Is Everywhere," and "In the Present and Probable Future" from *The Bride of E*, copyright © 2009 by Mary Jo Bang, are all reprinted with the permission of Graywolf Press, Minneapolis, MN, www.graywolfpress.org. "Opened and Shut" originally appeared in *Let's Say Yes* (Hand Held Editions, 2011) and is reprinted with the permission of the author and Hand Held Editions.

Excerpts from "The Role of Elegy," "Words," "Where Once," and "Landscape with the Fall of Icarus" from *Elegy*, copyright © 2007 by Mary Jo Bang, in Karla Kelsey's "Articulations of Artifice in the Work of Mary Jo Bang" are reprinted with the permission of Graywolf Press, Minneapolis, MN, www.graywolfpress.org.

Lucille Clifton. "the light that came to lucille clifton," "eve's version," "lucifer speaks in his own voice," "telling our stories," "the river between us," and "sorrows" from *The Collected Poems of Lucille Clifton*, copyright © 1980, 1991, 2004, 2008 by Lucille Clifton, are reprinted by permission of BOA Editions, Ltd., www.boaeditions.org. "daughters," "*won't you celebrate with me*," "leda 1," and "leda 3" from *The Book of Light*, copyright © 1993 by Lucille Clifton, are reprinted with the permission of Copper Canyon Press, www.coppercanyonpress.org.

Excerpts from "An Interview with Lucille Clifton," *Callaloo* 22:1 (1999), 56–72, copyright © 1999 by Charles H. Rowell, are reprinted with permission of the Johns Hopkins University Press.

Excerpts from "in the saying of," "Tuesday 9/11/01," and "Sunday morning 9/16/01" from *Mercy*, copyright © 2004 by Lucille Clifton; excerpt from "miss rosie" from *Good Woman: Poems and a Memoir 1969–1980*, copyright © 1987 by Lucille Clifton; excerpts from "the death of fred clifton," "shapeshifter poems,"

Book, copyright © 1999 by Laura Mullen, are reprinted by permission of Kelsey Street Press, www.kelsyst.com. "Secrets" and "35 ½" from *After I Was Dead*, copyright © 1999 by Laura Mullen, are reprinted by permission of the University of Georgia Press. Permission to use the excerpt from *Murmur*, copyright © 2007 by Laura Mullen, is granted by Futurepoem Books, www.futurepoem.com. "Circles" from *Subject*, copyright © 2005 by Laura Mullen, is reprinted by permission of the Regents of the University of California, published by University of California Press.

Excerpts from *The Tales of Horror: A Flip-Book*, copyright © 1999 by Laura Mullen, in Kass Fleisher's "Laura Mullen: Threatened as Threat" are reprinted by permission of Kelsey Street Press, www.kelsyst.com. Excerpts from poems in *Subject*, copyright © 2005 by Laura Mullen, in Fleisher's essay are reprinted by permission of the Regents of the University of California, published by University of California Press. Extracts from poems in *After I Was Dead*, copyright © 1999 by Laura Mullen, are reprinted by permission of the University of Georgia Press.

Eileen Myles. "Transitions," "Snowflake," "To My Class," "Questions," and "Hi" are used by permission of the author.

Maggie Nelson's "'When We're Alone in Public': The Poetry of Eileen Myles" is adapted from *Women, the New York School, and Other True Abstractions*, copyright © 2007 by Maggie Nelson, and is reprinted by permission of the University of Iowa Press.

M. NourbeSe Philip. Selections from *Zong!* are reprinted by permission of Wesleyan University Press.

Joan Retallack. "The Woman in the Chinese Room" from *How to Do Things with Words* (Sun & Moon Classics, 1998); excerpts from "MONGRELISME" from *MONGRELISME* (Paradigm Press, 1999); excerpts from "MEMNOIR" from *MEMNOIR* (The Post-Apollo Press, 2004); "Lost Briefcase Conjecture" and "N Plus Zero / A to Z" from *Procedural Elegies / Western Civ Cont'd /* (Roof Books, 2010) are reprinted by permission of the author.

Excerpts from "The Woman in the Chinese Room," "Scenes of Translation (from the translation)," "BE ING & NO TH' ING NESS: notes from the specific rim," and "AID/I/SAPPEARANCE" from *How to Do Things with Words*, copyright © 1998 by Joan Retallack, in Jena Osman's "The Method 'In *Medias* Mess'" are reprinted with the permission of Green Integer Books, Los Angeles, www.greeninteger.com. Extracts from "The Poethical Wager" from *The Poethical Wager* (University of California Press) by Joan Retallack, copyright © 2003, in Osman's essay are reprinted

ELEVEN MORE
AMERICAN WOMEN POETS
IN THE 21ST CENTURY

INTRODUCTION

Lisa Sewell

THIS ANTHOLOGY has come into being primarily in response to enthusiasm, even excitement about the current state of contemporary poetry in North America and, in particular, that portion being produced by women. It follows up on *American Women Poets in the 21st Century: Where Lyric Meets Language* (Wesleyan 2002), edited by Claudia Rankine and Juliana Spahr, which was inspired by the 1999 conference "Where Lyric Tradition Meets Language Poetry: Innovation in Contemporary Poetry by Women," though as Spahr notes in her introduction, it was not an actual proceedings of the conference.[1] The conference and the collection were explicitly interested in sparking a conversation across the ostensible divisions in contemporary poetry and in delineating an innovative meeting ground between lyric and avant-garde traditions. *Where Lyric Meets Language* contributed to the interrogation of these categories and also brought important critical and scholarly attention to the work of a range of contemporary women poets.[2] It is this second achievement that this new collection, *Eleven More American Women Poets in the 21st Century: Poetics Across North America*, will augment and advance, featuring the work of eleven more influential women poets: Mary Jo Bang, Lucille Clifton, Kimiko Hahn, Carla Harryman, Erín Moure, Laura Mullen, Eileen Myles, M. NourbeSe Philip, Joan Retallack, Lisa Robertson, and C. D. Wright. As with the first group, these writers have gained national and international reputations, and we hope to contribute to the scholarly and critical attention their work clearly merits.

We have followed the organization of the first collection, including poems and a poetics statement by each author, as well as a critical essay and bibliography, but this collection also looks beyond the parameters of the first, extending the geographic scope of the series, including several influential women poets from Canada. We have also been more eclectic in our choices, highlighting work that can clearly be located on either end of the spectrum between Language-oriented writing and the lyric tradition, as well as poets who trouble those categorical divisions. This is a variegated group to be sure, and we know we have created more gaps than we have filled. Each name evokes the name of another poet who could or should have been included—Fanny Howe, Alice Notley, Marilyn Chin, Rosemarie Waldrop, Jean Valentine—and we are already planning another volume that we hope will fill some of these gaps. But we also believe this anthology stands on its own in the breadth of its range and the intensity of its engagement with the world; the work collected here is richly representative, highlighting the ways women's writing reflects and revises current trends in American poetry. *Eleven More American Women Poets in the 21st Century: Poetics Across North America* does not aim to name a new, coherent community or school but to attend to women's writing in its various modes, its connectedness and difference, difficulty, and simplicity. Among the poems, statements, and essays are serendipitous juxtapositions and surprising connections but also real notes of dissonance and discord.

In the years since the publication of *Where Lyric Meets Language*, it has become more and more difficult to assign specific labels or rubrics to particular poets. As Stephen Burt suggests in the introduction to a collection of his reviews of contemporary poetry, "descriptions of poets in terms of schools or regions or first principles have rarely been less useful than they are now."[3] This development is especially well illustrated by the recent publication of the anthologies *Lyric Postmodernisms: An Anthology of Contemporary Innovative Poetries*, edited by Reginald Shepherd, and *American Hybrid*, edited by Cole Swensen and David St. John.[4] In her introduction, Swensen suggests that in contemporary poetry today, "idiosyncrasy rules to such a degree and differences are so numerous that distinct factions are hard, even impossible to pin down. Instead we find a thriving center of alterity."[5] Much of the work collected here also resists clear categorization, and many of these poets also appear in these other anthologies. But a narrative that situates all of these poets at the crossroads of hybridity would not account for Carla Harryman, who was instrumental in establishing the West Coast Language poetry movement during the 1970s, or for Lucille Clifton's plain-spoken but complex lyric "i," which remained consistent for more than thirty years.

While the nature of the lyric—can it be reclaimed from its masculinist origins, does it reflect a solipsistic retreat to interiority or a complex resistant engagement with the world—remains an ongoing concern for many of these writers, the paradox of a "thriving center of alterity" that Swensen identifies in hybrid poetry provides the strongest thread of connection. Whether alterity is explored through thematic or formal strategies, the drive to somehow enact, represent, or recognize radical, unassimilable difference informs a wide range of these poems, poetics statements, and essays. This drive takes various forms and moves in numerous directions, but it generally involves the interrogation of fixed boundaries—between genres, between genders, between bodies. Alterity here is founded in an ethics, which, following Emmanuel Levinas, resists the separation between "the one and the other": "Tout autre est tout autre [Every other one is every bit other]" is one of Levinas's most famous claims.[6] As Edith Wyschogrod explains:

traditional Western philosophy, including the work of Husserl and Heidegger, sustains a distinction between the one and the other. In empirical systems this distinction is retained as real; in idealistic systems it is rejected as illusory. But, Levinas argues, whether real or illusory, the distinction is always made and always rests upon the presupposition that it is constituted by a consciousness which discriminates. But the very possibility of incorporating the one and the other into a single point of view compromises the radical alterity, the "exteriority" of the other. Alterity which can be conjoined with or separated from the one by thought is not true alterity but part of what Levinas calls "the same." Radical otherness derives from a more primordial source. It can never be adequately thought for it lies beyond ontology. It is reflected in the world through the advent of other persons.[7]

In work as disparate as Carla Harryman's *Baby* and Mary Jo Bang's *Elegy*, that separation between "the one and the other" is indeed treated as illusory. As much of the work collected here suggests, poetic language can be a site of contradiction and a means for articulating multiple positions. By disparate routes, through a range of forms, the poets in this collection resist the binary of "the one" and "the other," gesturing toward what "can never be adequately thought." C. D. Wright notes in her poetics statement that although no three people can agree about what precisely poetry is, it "proposes an alternative perspective"; among these writers alternatives proliferate.

The most familiar route can be found in the theorization of identity. Even in work that seems to reside at the more expressive end of the spectrum, the autobiographical comes under scrutiny, whether the "i," as Lucille Clifton insists represents "both [her] Lucille and the me that stands for people who look like me and the me that is also human," or is reduced to what Joan Retallack has described as mere "point[s] of reference" among others, "part of an atmospheric exchange" instead of a "monological" expression.[8] Clifton's resistance to the stability of the lyric speaker is explicitly informed by her awareness of historically being positioned as the "other" in terms of gender and race, and a number of other writers—Kimiko Hahn, M. NourbeSe Philip—also explore and enact this awareness, though they also emphasize the ways language constitutes itself around a covered over or ignored alterity. And for a majority of the writers in this collection, it is through writing and the performativity that inheres in language that alterity can be approached. Through a range of formal strategies, Retallack, Bang, Philip, Moure, Harryman, and Mullen all foreground linguistic instability, insisting that the social space of language is never static but instead, as Moure suggests, is constantly "altered": "the body alters space, language alters space, languages alter space. Alter our mouths. Alter each other. In unpredictable ways." Multilingualism, mixing different languages within sentences, within words—what Joan Retallack terms "mongrelisme"—also destabilizes larger cultural ordering systems. The second, or third, language may be chosen—as in Moure's work and Hahn's—or imposed, but can be used to interrogate the effects of assimilation and colonialism, and to call attention to the ways language constitutes identity.

Resistance is also enacted through the interrogation of the boundaries between genres, including those that distinguish lyric and narrative, verse and prose, poetry and memoir, poetry and fiction. We can see this in Carla Harryman's prose poetry and Laura Mullen's lyric novels, in Bang's narrativizing lyrics and Hahn's hybrid forms that draw on multiple traditions (Chinese, Japanese, as well as European) and cannot be readily accounted for by any one culture. Moure, Philip, Robertson, and Retallack cross the boundaries of form, discourse, and genre within single works, producing hybrid texts, with implications for gendered boundaries as well. The urgency to at least gesture toward alterity, to attempt, successfully or not, to recognize "otherness" through syntax, form, or the problematization of subjectivity in some cases seems to have been made more urgent by the policies of the U.S. government during the first eight years of the new century. Wright's poems in *Rising, Falling, Hovering* incorporate responses to the U.S. occupation of Iraq; Bang's abecedarian *The Bride of E* tries to assess and catalog the "rueful apocalyptic drama" of post-9/11 America; and Moure explains that she wrote *Little Theatres* against the overriding background of "sorry rumblings of American public discourse" that eventually led to the invasion of Iraq.

Another thread that does not connect or appear in all of the work, but certainly signifies in several places, bright red, like a stop light, is a resistance to critical analysis itself, to readings that "unpack," assess, contextualize, and situate. As Sina Queyras notes, Lisa Robertson has long been associated with Canada's Kootenay School of Writing, which embraced "slogans" such as "we will not be understood," and as the Office for Soft Architecture, she created texts that "ma[de] no attempt to . . . [be] accessible or readable in a predictable sense, to anyone." Aaron Kunin describes a similar resistance in the work of Erín Moure as a "challenge to criticism," and Jena Osman notes that in reading Joan Retallack's work "expectations of interpretive analysis must be set aside so that the language can be approached on its own material terms: its sounds, rhythms, and associative paradoxes." This kind of resistance may be frustrating for the reader who is looking for stable ground from which to form an opinion, or a clear idea of what a work is "about." But it also provides a concrete experience of what it is like to encounter alterity in all of its inassimilable otherness.

It is worth noting that although this collection focuses on women's writing, these writers do not express a monolithic relationship to feminism.

Just as the volume depicts the wide variety of contemporary poetries, it is situated at the juncture and disjuncture between multiple and contradictory feminisms. While Clifton, Hahn, and Mullen are explicit about the influence of feminism on their poetics, in much of the work, feminism is implicit: an always already present jumping-off point. What is *essential* about gender in the work of many of these writers is the insistent investigation of the relationship *between* gender and language, and *between* gender and genre, that corresponds more with a third-wave (as opposed to post, or post-post) feminism that "can come to terms with . . . multiple, interpenetrating axes of identity," as Leslie Heywood and Jennifer Drake suggest in their introduction to *Third Wave Agenda: Being Feminist, Doing Feminism.*[9] Rather than being based in bodily experience, shared oppressions, and identity politics, the feminism evinced here reaches for a "reversible . . . intersubjective and dialogic model of interaction capable of evading the forced binarism of relativism or positivism."[10]

In her preface to *Contemporary Women's Poetry: Reading/Writing/Practice*, Isobel Armstrong emphasizes that this kind of resistance to the second wave concept of feminism is characteristic of both current women's writing and contemporary theory. Armstrong notes that for many women writers, and I would suggest that this is true for the writers collected here as well, "[the] self-conscious concern with multiple forms of language arises from a need not to be trapped inside the expressive self of the female subject, but the obligation *as a female subject*, to release the lyric 'I' from the trap of a narrow identity politics."[11] While some critics may question the need for yet another anthology that focuses on women's writing, the response to the first volume suggests that readers of all kinds are still hungry for critical efforts that situate women's poetry. We hope the risks of engaging in a project that highlights gender divisions are balanced by the positive effects of drawing attention to and providing critical perspectives on these writers, believing that it is possible to question and resist the binary oppositions that structure cultural understandings of gender while also recognizing that due to social and historical conditions, gender does make a difference. The work of the writers collected here presents a proliferation of identities and identifications alongside investigations of genre, the sentence, and the poetic line, claiming them as forms expansive and flexible enough to gesture toward and speak these new subjectivities.

THE POETRY of Mary Jo Bang, whose name serendipitously comes at the beginning of the alphabet, provides an apt starting point for this collection. It is serendipitous because her work brings many of the questions informing contemporary poetry into focus. The author of six books of poems, Bang has been exploring the alterity that informs lyric interiority since the beginning of her career, and though in much of her poetry "disjunction and abbreviation occupy the foreground," rather than claiming to invent a new lyric, she calls attention to the ways fracture and irresolution have always informed the lyric tradition. Highlighting her debts to previous works and to various predecessors, from Emily Dickinson and Virginia Woolf to Lewis Carroll, her work demonstrates the absorptive power but also exposes the suturing entailed in creating a unified speaker and poem. Bang's particular version of alterity involves an "othering" of the lyric speaker. As she explains in her poetics statement, she is interested in shifting away from the figure of the poet "plumbing the depths of her psyche" and has developed a number of strategies that allow her to operate at a remove from her materials. Theater, photography, and filmmaking are apt analogies to the approach Bang takes, but these poetic plays or films expose their sutures and break through the fourth wall to call attention to the artifice of each scene.

As she writes in "And as in Alice," from *The Bride of E*, "Alice cannot be in the poem, she says, because / She's only a metaphor for childhood / And a poem is a metaphor already." The poem is about Alice but also making poetry and about the fact that Lewis Carroll also called attention to the processes of imaginative making in his work. Even in her most apparently confessional, autobiographical work, *Elegy*, Bang blurs the boundary between bereft speaker and lost beloved object. Lyric identity is diffused among pronouns and subject positions, and as a whole the work insists that even at our most purely expressive moments, we are constructions in and of language. In her wide-ranging and deeply probing essay, "Articulations of Artifice in the Work of Mary Jo Bang," Karla Kelsey explores the various devices Bang employs to call attention to the hard work of fiction-making that creates the lyric poem. Kelsey suggests that by foregrounding "modes of representation, rather than the 'content' of what is represented." Bang's work explores and exploits "the tension between absorption in artifice and insistence upon recognizing the poem's construction." Focusing on Bang's reimagining of persona and ironic deployment of lofty and low symbolic figures, Kelsey suggests that by "turning into," instead of away from, the apparent disjunction between expressive and self-referential language, Bang creates a resonant and unique voice in the field of contemporary poetry. She also argues that by creating a body of work that articulates "the way in which lyric illusion functions," Bang posits that it is this very tension that has always already made the lyric a dynamic form.

It is with sadness but also pleasure that we include the work of Lucille Clifton in this anthology, a poet whose work also clearly demonstrates the dynamism of the lyric. Clifton's social and aesthetic poetic associations would seemingly make her the poet most invested in the conventional lyric:

woman who shines at the head
of my grandmother's bed,
brilliant woman, i like to think
you whispered into her ear
instructions. i like to think
you are the oddness in us

Her readily recognizable poems use accessible, transparent language and apparently treat the speaking subject as singular, stable, complete. But careful attention to the nuances of her work reveals a resistance to binary ordering systems that manifests in a flexible and mutable speaker. In her interview with Charles Rowell, she states: "either/or is not an African tradition. Both/and is tradition. I don't believe in either/or. I believe in both/and." Through speakers whose identifications are mobile and shifting—the "i" in a single poem can refer back to a persona but also to Clifton, and, she suggests, a shared identity based in community—she complicates the notion of a lyric subject, treating all her speakers as constructions in and of language.

In "Lucille Clifton's Communal 'i,'" Adrienne McCormick illuminates this unexplored aspect of Clifton's poetry, arguing that from early in her writing career, Clifton produced "a multi-layered communal 'i' . . . and a complex vision of lyric subjectivity as constructed, contingent, and communal." Focusing on work that ranges across Clifton's career—from the relatively early book, *Two-Headed Woman*, to her most recent, *Voices*—McCormick argues that Clifton is able to "bridge constituencies more often positioned in separate conversations" by committing herself to "both/and" thinking that is rooted in her inherited connection to African American traditions but also in her feminism. McCormick establishes the flexibility of Clifton's "communal i," demonstrating the instability of speakers in a wide range of poems, from poems in which the speaker is "Lucille Clifton," to those in which the speaker is clearly an "other."

Like Clifton, Kimiko Hahn explicitly identifies her work as feminist, titling her poetics statement "Still *Writing the Body*" and evoking feminist critics like Cixous and Irigaray as influences. Hahn strives for a poetry that rhythmically, sonically, and tonally evokes the corporeal *and* the emotional, which she understands as experienced viscerally, resisting the mind/body division that structures Western thought. In her poetics statement she expresses a determination "to draw the whole body back into the experience of writing and reading poetry." Hahn's work also crosses literary traditions and national borders. The bodily texts she creates are multivoiced collages, incorporating quotations from literary and critical writings, from Western and Asian traditions, and using Chinese and Japanese literary forms for inspiration. Hahn draws on and draws out the resistances that inhere in women's writings from earlier centuries, including the work of Japanese writers like Murasaki Shikibu's *Tale of the Genji* and Sei Shōnagon's "pillow book," both written during the Heian period (8th–12th century).[12] In "Orchid Root," Hahn writes, "I need to return to the Chinese women poets / The flat language / of pine and orchid" that can "instruct the senses" and teach the difference "between the Narcissus fragrance / and burning rubber." These poets also seem to teach Hahn to let the voice of the other, especially the Orientalized feminine other, haunt and inhabit her poems.

It is through this kind of haunting that Hahn evokes a gendered alterity and multiplicity in her work. In "'I Want to Go Where the Hysteric Resides': Kimiko Hahn's Re-Articulation of the Feminine in Poetry," Zhou Xiaojing focuses on poems that explore mother–daughter relationships, showing that Hahn redefines the feminine in terms that resist both Western masculinist discourse and the racism of cultural domination. Discussing works from both recent and older collections, Zhou argues that Hahn often speaks from the position of the radically "othered" feminine, specifically reclaiming the hysteric, a figure marginalized and maligned in phallocentric discourse. "Hahn posits an alternative way of knowing outside the gendered binary pairings such as mind/male versus body/female, and points to an alternative mother–daughter relationship outside of patriarchy and Orientalism." Despite Hahn's stated suspicions of the "cerebral" in contemporary poetry, Zhou finds that her work "enacts feminist theories" as "a method for investigating the female body and subjectivity" in order to inscribe the feminine outside of patriarchal and racial hierarchies. Through Zhou's careful reading, hysteria, in which the body speaks through symptoms, can be understood as productive instead of silencing, empowering instead of debilitating.

Resistance to the structuring functions of binary oppositions takes a more radical form in Carla Harryman's genre-blurring performative and performance-based poetry, though as with Hahn that resistance is also keenly connected to the body. In Harryman's work the connection to corporeality is foregrounded through the sheer physicality of the language, drawing attention to tone, the rhythms of speech patterns, repetition, and the ways sounds, syntax, and sentences accrue and "speak" to each other, as in this passage from *Baby*:

> Certain sounds rigid formulas thought. Attract futures stuck in happy land. Give me liberty or give me death had not history in baby's breath. But sound of force struck in her trunk. Here and then the beginning of baby's not. And not.

Since the 1970s, Harryman has been writing at the interstices between forms and between genres; she has also been involved in numerous collaborations, including projects with visual artists, musicians, in performances, and with other writers. Harryman is interested in polyvocality, and in all of her work binary oppositions are resisted on multiple levels: Subjects and objects achieve reciprocity; abstractions and corporeality are treated as equally substantive; chronology is undone; conventions of looking, speaking, listening, and hearing are denaturalized, as is gender.

In "Listening In on Carla Harryman's *Baby*," Christine Hume concentrates on Harryman's 2005 book *Baby* in order to explore an epistemology of listening that beautifully exemplifies Harryman's larger project. Drawing on theories of listening shaped by Roland Barthes, Adorno, Fred Moten, and others, Hume constructs a "primer" for reading Harryman, elaborating the multiple and contradictory forms of audition *Baby* evokes and outlining the ways the text "offers an acoustic space, a rich multidimensional resonant field of relations that allows simultaneity." Hume demonstrates that in *Baby*, listening—as an act/non-action—can gesture toward or at least evoke a reciprocal alterity, endowing listening "with the capacity to undo binary structures in the service of a relational model of identity." By emphasizing listening's Derridean lack of origins, as Hume notes, Harryman shows us that "we have always been listening."

Like Harryman, Erín Moure treats writing as theatrical, or as "theatral" as she puts it in her poetics statement. And her work too emphasizes sound, often reveling in the multivoiced chorus of sounds over and against, or alongside the words' meanings, thus expanding our sense of what it means to understand poetry. In an interview with Paulo da Costa, Moure explained: "We 'understand' poetry when it resonates with us, echoes with us, haunts us, piques our curiosity, compels us. That's what has value."[13] Much of her work calls attention to women writers, thinkers, and artists and to the gendered nature of meaning-making and language itself. In "document32 (inviolable)" from *O Cidadán*, she writes:

> How a woman wanting to write can be a *territorial* impossibility.
> . . . .
> Think of Ingeborg Bachmann in her hotel rooms. Her unsettled acts were noise's fissures. To see her as citizen is indeed to know *citizen* as repository of harm, where harm is gendered too. Myths of violability, inviolability, volatility, utility, lability played out. In wars, women are territories, and territories are *lieux de punition*.

But perhaps Moure's work is most explicitly feminist in its resistance to being categorized and named, and to absolute designations of any kind. Her poems incorporate multiple languages within sentences and even within words, and bear traces of the compositional process and her resistance to "definitive versions." This creates literal and figurative edges and unsmooth surfaces within works. In "Moure's Abrasions," Aaron Kunin suggests that Moure's resistant, unsmooth poetics evolve out of a simultaneous commitment to the intermingling, communal "flow" of multiple languages and to "the radical particularity of language." He charts several of the strategies she uses to create "new surfaces" in her poems and "stage" language, including a "proliferation" of proper names in and on her work (her name can appear in a range of spellings; she uses pseudonyms and homonyms); translation as a distinctive formal feature that results in the intermixing of languages within and between poems, within sentences and even words; and an interrogation of citizenship that does not depend on nation or language.

Along with her formal experimentation, Moure is also an intensely lyrical poet—a combination of attributes she shares with Laura Mullen. Over the course of her career, Mullen has pushed more and more at the surfaces of words, exploding and exposing the contradictions that inhere in traditional lyric forms and lyric subjectivity. The poems in *Subject*, her most recent book, express a simultaneous enchantment and disillusionment with poetic language and poetic form. Mullen works to achieve what Lyn Hejinian might refer to as a "radical openness" in her poems, preserving the multiple possibilities that inhere in language while also highlighting its limitations and coercive powers. In her poetics statement she writes that one of the central tenants of her work is "Accuracy," but an accuracy that:

> includes humility toward and respect for both the medium (language) and all that is NOT language, to try to find the words . . . for? toward? near? with . . . ? (In relation.) Words change the situation as they reposition us (we are part of the situation); spectators are also participants.

Her poetry and her prose reflect this awareness of what each new work evokes and erases, of what is written down and what is left out. Mullen's work also explores the limits of genre, publishing both poetry and fiction, and explicitly investigating the difference that inheres in each generic categorization. In "Laura Mullen: Threatened as Threat: Rethinking Gender and Genre," Kass Fleisher explores Mullen's interest in genre, claiming that it is inseparable from an interest in gender. Addressing both Mullen's poetry and her fiction, Fleischer argues that her "preoccupation with generic enforcement" is coupled to a desire to "dismantle social constructions of Woman by reconstructing the dual/duel she sees at play . . . in textual representations of women." In affecting this dismantling, Mullen is especially concerned with the ways dismantled women's bodies create the "fatal" center of interest in genre fiction such as the murder mystery and the romance.

Eileen Myles is perhaps better known as a poet, but like Mullen she explores multiple forms and has also published fiction. On the surface, her work seems closest to Clifton's, for she too develops personae in her work, including a persona named Eileen Myles, and like Clifton her language is straightforward, accessible, immediate. Her work is also strange and disorienting, using juxtaposition and accretion to shift within grammatical time frames ("sometimes / I'm driving / and I pressed / the button / to see who / called") and between pronouns within a poem or a series of lines, resulting in poems that move through time as well as space, and have the immediacy of thought. Myles claims that poetry "is recording," that her poems take place in "the moment," and it is this effect that links her to the New York School. Myles's work is also intensely performative, emphasizing the link between the physically present speaking/writing body and the written/spoken poem. The specific performativity in her work is connected to problems of visibility and invisibility, for as she acknowledges in her poetics statement, for a lesbian, visibility, even existence as anything but a joke, cannot be taken for granted.

In her essay "The Lesbian Poet," Myles describes her desire to address the specificity of the female body vis-à-vis menstruation, to "include the body, the woman's as I see it, to approach this blood as part of the score."[14] Myles's poems create a textual equivalent that can convey the specificity of what it is like to inhabit a particular desirous and desiring body, and in order to do so she emphasizes the performative, but in a way that is quite distinct from Harryman or Moure. As Maggie Nelson explains in "'When We're Alone in Public': The Poetry of Eileen Myles," Myles situates much of her work at the juncture between the "female personal and the public sector." In her work, Myles's use of markedly public speech foregrounds the privacy of the body; her "exhibitionistic" work entails questioning what precisely the female poet has to exhibit or expose. For Myles, like Hahn, the body is a sort of text, and an important part of her project is to bring the female body into the poem, to make "lack" flash and signify. While this may seem like an essentializing gesture along the lines of Cixous' *ecriture feminine*, Nelson argues that "Myles's 'proprioceptive' poetry has less to do with finding an essential mode of female expression than with scribing 'an economy, a metabolism or energy flow.'" Drawing on the (queer) theories of Judith Butler, Eve Kowalsky Sedgewick, and Monique Wittig, and in particular Sedgewick's thinking about queer performativity, Nelson charts the "insurrectionary" effects of Myles's "speech acts" in her poems, as well as her reimagining of the lyric speaker as both "personal" and performed.

The works of Canadian poet M. NourbeSe Philip are haunted by history, by untold stories and lost bodies, by lives that cannot be recovered because of the eradicating histories of colonialism and the African slave trade. Like Myles, Philip is interested in the speech act, but her work emphasizes the *impossibility* of speech for those of African descent, whose histories include the suppression of their native languages and the imposition of the colonizers' tongues. In works like *She Tries Her Tongue: Her Silence Slowly Breaks*, *Looking for Livingston*, and *Zong!*, Philip mines the juncture between silence and speech, invisibility and presence, attempting to depict both the erasure of specific lives and the possibility of a language that can gesture toward those absences. She engages and juxtaposes a range of texts, including legal documents, to point toward conflicting accounts and competing discourses as well as the excesses that inhere in all language. *Zong!*, Philip's most recent book, attempts to tell the story of the disastrous voyage of the slaveship *Zong*, whose captain had a large percentage of his "cargo" of 470 African slaves thrown overboard so that the owners could collect on their insurance. At the beginning of the "Notanda" section of the book, Philip writes: "There is no telling this story: it must be told." And it is the intersection of these impossible injunctions that *Zong!* unfolds and depicts.

"Discourse on the Logic of Language," from *She Tries Her Tongue*, also mines the interstices between speech and silence, both enacting and describing the impossibility of a "mother" tongue for those who inherit the oppressor's language:

> and english is
> my mother tongue
> is
> my father tongue
> is a foreign lan lan lang
> language
> l/anguish
>   anguish
> a foreign anguish
> is english—
> another tongue

As Dawn Lundy Martin suggests in "The Language of Trauma: Faith and Atheism in M. NourbeSe Philip's Poetry," in Philip's work, often "the speech attempt gets caught in the effort of speech, its impossibility in the wake of trauma, and circles back to language with variation." Focusing on *She Tries Her Tongue; Her Silence Softly Breaks* and *Zong!*, Martin engages theories of racial melancholia and post-traumatic stress to trace the ways Philip's work exposes the erased, invisible, or missing colonized bodies and stories, focusing on the ways the work "breaks down the mother tongue/foreign language to show the anguish beneath it, while simultaneously playing with its form and creating a 'new' language—a hybrid speak made recognizable from restructuring the old." Martin calls attention to the textual strategies Philip uses—including the fragmenting and fracturing of phrases and words, broken syntax, the use of repetition—to recover irrecoverable history, language, and bodies, or at least gesture toward that recovery while also enacting the futility of the attempt. She shows that ultimately Philip's text becomes the lost body "enact[ing] the trauma of disappearance, replaying it, and transferring the experience of trauma . . . [to] the bodies of those outside the text." As Martin notes, Philip allows the gaps in the stories—particularly in relationship to *Zong!*—into her texts, "occup[ying] the haunting absences as absences and mak[ing] them newly available for readers."

Like Philip's, Joan Retallack's work emphasizes surface difficulty and presents formidable challenges to the reader, as well as a resistant and transformative politics. Explicitly committed to "reciprocal alterity," Retallack combines chance-based methods of composition with a powerful sense of ethical responsibility. Her work uses the page as a field or canvas, calling attention to the typographical, to "other logically possible selves and worlds," and to the surprises that inhere in language—what she calls "wordswerve[s]." Over a twenty-year career, Retallack has continuously created texts that resist easy assessment and emphasize the real work of reading. She engages with the philosophy of Wittgenstein and Searle, but resists all totalizing assessments. Her work also bears the mark of her association with John Cage, and in particular the application of chance and procedure to making art. In her poetics statement, Retallack enacts her commitment to a procedural poethics—a term that infuses poetics with an explicitly ethical dimension—and also explores the reasons for her commitment to this mode. Procedures, she suggests, help us resist centers of the "self" and "official logics" but also importantly provide "instructions for how (even why) one is to go on." She strives to create a literature that "present[s] significant alternative sites for making meaning, potential locations for conceptual swerves."

In "The Method 'In *Medias* Mess,'" Jena Osman suggests that Retallack's work encourages, even demands, sustained awareness, a "durational attention" that can "lead to a wide-ranging and playful dialogue with the world." Focusing on several key works, including AFTERRIMAGES, *Mongrelisme*, *Memnoir*, and *Errata 5uite*, Osman argues that Retallack's procedural poethics allow her to connect art and life, but real life and a real world that is a "complicated, messy place," without reducing or totalizing that messiness and complication. Osman charts the various discourses—what she calls "messes"—Retallack engages with in her work, including the literary/philosophical and popular written "archive"; the (resisted) polyglot of languages in American culture; and digital media and technology. And despite the potential impossibility of doing so, for much of Retallack's work resists "stabilized interpretations," Osman delineates the methods in Retallack's work that "pry words loose from singular and definitive meanings . . . lead[ing[to . . . fluid acts of signification" and "swerves of discovery." Osman notes that the self and subjective experience are nevertheless not entirely absent from Retallack's work. Her poems "include a mixture of intuitive and procedural materials, each impacting the other." Autobiography is treated as one more "cultural material."

Retallack is well known for her important intervention in and contribution to feminist criticism, "Re: Thinking: Literary: Feminism," in which she rejects several feminist literary models, proffering instead a multiple, unintelligible, polylingual "experimental feminine" that can "*exercise* the power of the feminine" as constructed, "aesthetic behavior" and not as the "expression of female experience" (author's italics).[15] She calls for a literary feminism that reflects the "disruptively audible—if not immediately intelligible—swerve or real gender/genre trouble [that] is possible only if we recognize what has been the continual constituting presence of feminine forms in language."[16] Lisa Robertson's work seemingly responds to this call, building texts that reimagine subjectivity and pull that "continual constituting presence" of the feminine to the surface. Robertson often creates texts from other texts—in the case of *The Weather*, from accounts of cloud nomenclature, contemporary and early meteorological accounts of the weather in England, and neo-classical and romantic literature; in the case of *Rosseau's Boat*, from fifteen years of Robertson's own journals.[17] In these works, sentences borrowed from other texts are arranged to create new structures, building architecturally and drawing attention to the malleability of language, producing a "gestural plenitude" and "delusional space" that also gestures toward alterity.

Like many of the writers in this collection, Robertson's work rejects the ordering systems of genre divisions, moving within single works between lineated verse and prose. For Robertson, generic distinctions present limits and hazards that must be assessed and addressed, and like Laura Mullen, she links those dangers to the ideologies that control gender, and to women's absences, erasures, and silences. As she plaintively asks in "Tuesday," from *The Weather*:

> Where is our anger. And the shades darker than the plain part and darker at the top than the bottom. But darker at bottom than top. Days heap upon us. Where is Ti-Grace. But darker at the bottom than the top. Days heap upon us. Where is Christine. Broken on the word culture. But darker at the bottom than the top. Days heap upon us. Where is Valerie. Pulling the hard air into her lung. The life crumbles open. But darker at the bottom than the top. Days heap upon us. Where is Patty.

Here, sentences too "heap upon us," simultaneously evoking presence and absence. Such resistance to binary structuring can be located in many aspects of Robertson's work, including her insistent use of the plural pronoun. In her poetics statement, "Soft Architecture: A Manifesto," Robertson also employs the first person plural, writing, "We walked through the soft arcade. We became an architect."

This manifesto was issued by the Office for Soft Architecture (OSA), and as Sina Queyras observes in "About Surface: Lisa Robertson's Poetics of Elegance," in creating an office, Robertson "externalizes herself, creating not only an alter-ego but 'a space,' a built space" that is urban and inhabitable. As an office, Robertson asserts authority over those disciplines that have traditionally been the province of men—city planning, architecture, literary canon formation—and that have historically excluded women. Like Erín Moure, the OSA also insists on forms of mastery that do not master, and that include the domestic: interiors, sheets, curtains, clothing, soft fabric, malleable flesh. Focusing on three recent works, *The Weather*, *Occasional Work and Seven Walks from the Office for Soft Architecture*, and *Rousseau's Boat*, Queyras explores the multiple ways through attention to "surface" and an externalized poetic Robertson produces a complex, feminist poetics of "elegance" in which the poem is "a collaborative and inhabitable public space." As Queyras demonstrates, as an office for architecture, Robertson links the local to the global, calling attention to organic and mechanical forms, conducting a gendered "interrogation of surface," and building a new model of subjectivity that both revels in and disrupts the continuity and sheen of those surfaces.

The final poet in the collection is C. D. Wright, and her work provides an appropriate and provisional closing point. In her use of narrative structures, frequent use of transparent, vernacular language, and recourse to an "I" of lyric interiority, Wright's poetry circles back toward Lucille Clifton's. At the same time, her use of accretion, juxtaposition, and syntactical disruption can be linked to Language-influenced poets like Philip, Retallack, and Robertson, who precede her in this anthology. But Wright's work must be situated between lyric expression and Language poetry. This is partly because of the evolution of her work—which has moved from narrative forms to a more self-reflexive, materialist use of language—but it is also because Wright maintains explicit fidelity to both realms. Wright makes use of Language-based techniques of disruption and defamiliarization to call attention to the constructed nature of her poetry, but she also wants her poetry to clarify experience. As she writes in her poetics statement, "My American Scrawl," "Maybe poetry, the making of poetry, is not by definition a clarifying exercise, but it has a shot at it, as they say. It has a shot at the hyacinth light. And I really do want to communicate (by which I mean, pass it on) what little I have seen clearly (by which I do not mean, obviously seen)." In addition to writing at the divide between lyric and language, Wright troubles several other junctures as well—the line between body and word, between north and south, high and low culture, documentary and witness, objective and subjective—and quite crucially, like Robertson, Wright is insistent on the connections between the local and the global.

In "The Border-Crossing Relational Poetry of C. D. Wright," Suzanne Wise focuses on Wright's two most recent works, *One Big Self* and *Rising, Falling, Hovering*. She charts the "denaturalizing" strategies Wright evolves to create a poetry that formally and thematically resists totalizing gestures, that both draws our attention to things in their discrete specificity and recognizes commonalities and relatedness. Wise links Wright's crossing and questioning of geographical, class, and cultural boundaries to Edouard Glissant's theory of "A Poetics of Relation," demonstrating the various ways that her "border-crossing poetics" insist on a periphery that is the center and centers that line, the periphery. Glissant's poetics of relation, like Levinas's reciprocal alterity, resists the binary structuring of imperialism to depict a complex "multiple relationship with the Other." Wise also tracks the formal strategies Wright engages to further undergird her critique of American policies, domestic and international. In *Rising, Falling, Hovering*, she moves between long "hyperextended" sentences that forge connections between and among worlds that have been shattered and shorter lines that "demonstrate the snapping of syntax and logic under pressure to make sense of loss, grief, and a violent elsewhere." As Wise suggests, Wright is fully aware of her position of privilege in relationship to her subjects—inmates in Louisiana prisons in *One Big Self*, victims of U.S. imperialism and domestic neglect in *Rising, Falling, Hovering*—and is careful to evoke her own complicity in the systems of injustice she wishes to critique. But at the same time, through accretion and the use of juxtaposition without instruction, Wright is able "to reveal the complex realities of others." It is in this insistent depiction of those "complex realities" that Wright provides some relief from the dire situations she feels compelled to write about; as with Philip's work, we find a tentative beam of hope and light.

In 2007, poet and critic Jennifer Ashton published a review of three works that focus on women and "innovative" poetry, including the first volume of *American Women Poets in the 21st: Century: Where Lyric Meets Language*. Her assertion that "on a numerical level the problem of underrepresentation [of women's writing] has been corrected" led to a lively and important conversation—in print in the pages of the *Chicago Review* and *American Philology*, and online on Ron Silliman's blog and the Poetry Foundation's website—about how far women writers (and women in general) have or have not come, about how feminism currently signifies in the lives of a number of different writers, and about just how equitable the poetry world actually is and whether or not the "problem" had indeed been corrected.[18] No consensus was reached, but the outpouring of opinion, invective, and enthusiasm suggests that there is still plenty of interest in these issues. In creating this second volume devoted to women poets, we are responding to that interest and to the very enthusiastic reception of the first, and hope to add to the body of critical evaluation that is available, contributing to ongoing efforts to correct the historical exclusion of women's writing and women themselves from the literary tradition and calling attention to the ways women's writing reflects larger trends in the field. The work collected here confirms the ongoing "revisioning" of the lyric tradition Juliana Spahr identifies in her introduction to the first volume and the idea that "innovation" as a characteristic of women's writing can be aligned with both the expressive lyric and the experimental poem.[19] It also exposes readers to common threads of interest as well as absolute differences and demonstrates that whatever the "numbers," women are at the forefront of trends in contemporary poetry.

Audio clips of many of the poems in this book are available at the book's companion website: www.wesleyan.edu/wespress.aptc3.

NOTES

1. *American Women Poets in the 21st Century: Where Lyric Meets Language*, eds. Claudia Rankine and Juliana Spar (Middletown, CT: Wesleyan University Press, 2002), 1. Hereafter cited in the text as *Where Lyric Meets Language*.

2. A number of essay collections and anthologies that focus on innovative writing by women appeared during the first decade of the new century, including *We Who Love to Be Astonished: Experimental Women's Writing and Performance Poetics*, eds. Laura Hinton and Cynthia Hogue, (Tuscaloosa: University of Alabama Press, 2002), *Contemporary Women's Poetry: Reading/Writing/Practice*, eds. Alison Mark and Deryn Rees-Jones (New York: St. Martin's Press, 2000), and *Innovative Women Poets: An Anthology of Contemporary Poetry and Interviews*, eds. Elisabeth A. Frost and Cynthia Hogue (Iowa City: University of Iowa Press, 2006), as well as several scholarly studies including Elisabeth Frost, *The Feminist Avant-Garde in American Poetry* (Iowa City: University of Iowa Press, 2003) and Linda Kinnahan, *Lyric Interventions: Feminism Experimental Poetry and Contemporary Discourse* (Iowa City: University of Iowa Press, 2004).

3. Stephen Burt, *Close Calls with Nonsense: Reading New Poetry* (Saint Paul, MN: Graywolf, 2009), 6.

4. Reginald Shepherd, ed. *Lyric Postmodernisms: An Anthology of Contemporary Innovative Poetries* (Denver: Counterpath Press, 2008); *American Hybrid*, eds. Cole Swenson and David St. John (New York: W. W. Norton, 2009).

5. *American Hybrid*, xx.

6. Quoted in Edith Wyschogrod, "Language and Alterity in the Thought of Levinas," *Cambridge Companion to Emmanuel Levinas* (Cambridge: Cambridge University Press, 2006), 192.

7. Edith Wyschogrod, *Emmanuel Levinas: The Problem of Ethical Metaphysics* (New York: Fordham University Press, 2000), xxx.

8. Lucille Clifton and Charles H. Rowell, "An Interview with Lucille Clifton," *Callaloo* 22.1 (1999), 60; Redell Olsen, "An Interview With Joan Retallack," *How2*, 1, no. 6 (2001), www.scc.rutgers.edu.

9. *Third Wave Agenda: Being Feminist, Doing Feminism*, eds. Leslie Heywood and Jennifer Drake (Minneapolis: University of Minnesota Press, 1997), 3.

10. Nicky Marsh, *Democracy in Contemporary U.S. Women's Poetry* (London: Palgrave, 2007), 17.

11. Author's emphasis. Isobel Armstrong, preface to *Contemporary Women's Poetry: Reading/Writing/Practice*, xvii.

12. Hahn discusses these two works in "Pulse and Impulse: The *Zuihitsu*," in *The Grand Permission: New Writing on Poetics and Motherhood*, eds. Patricia Dienstfrey and Brenda Hillman (Middletown, CT: Wesleyan University Press, 2003), 75–81.

13. Paulo da Costa, "Dialogues and Polylogues: An Interview with Erin Mouré," www.paulodacosta.com/erinmour.htm.

14. Eileen Myles, *School of Fish* (Boston: Black Sparrow Books, 1997), 130.

15. Joan Retallack, *The Poethical Wager* (Berkeley: University of California Press, 2003), 134.

16. Ibid., 131.

17. Information about the evolution of these texts comes from "Lifted: An Interview with Lisa Robertson," *Chicago Review* 51/52 (2006): 38–54.

18. Jennifer Ashton, "Our Bodies, Our Poems," *American Literary History* 19 (2007), 213. See also Juliana Spahr and Stephanie Young's response to Ashton's essay, "Numbers Trouble," *Chicago Review* 53 (2007), 88–111; Ashton's response to Spahr and Young, "The Numbers Trouble with 'Numbers Trouble,'" ibid., 112–20; and Jennifer Scappettone's "Response to Jennifer Ashton, Bachelorettes, Even: Strategic Embodiment in Contemporary Experimentalism by Women," *Modern Philology* 105, no. 1 (2007), 178–84. See footnote 2 in Scappettone's essay for the web addresses of online blogs that also participate in this conversation.

19. Spahr, *American Women Poets in the 21st Century*, 6.

MARY JO BANG

FROM *The Eye Like a Strange Balloon*

High Art

There's a city outside
the mind. Another inside.
A mind full of something
becoming because.
A face too small for this red mouth. Look how

the line isn't a street anymore
but a track. Like that. The graveled
shroud of a train. I'm not usually like
this. A linkable Like arrives without its What.
Parks the car.

I remember the camera.
The clear click. The clean cutting off
of the instant. Good-bye, good-bye.
The slide in the sleeve.
This opening eye. Wanting to take

everything in, sequence after sequence.
The framed now that never ends ending;
the blue suit pulled from a pool
of aqua dreaming.
Not knowing why aside

from theory. Sexual configurations
of glamour. What is the scene?
What is the cover? The frozen waiting
for focus and drive.
Look, look, look. Art is what

looking takes you to. A red mouth
opening to say,
Don't look away.
I'm not usually like this.
The camera sliding by with its aperture

open. Form, repetition, constructs,
content, it happens. Here is the needle
that speeds the plot to the ambush.
It happens. The Whole Truth shading desire.
Atmospherics predominating

over drama. Chiaroscuro focused
on a point of desperation.
The recurrent dream of a catalog
of surprise revelations.
Having makes wanting

continue a darkness both familiar
and strange.
"What have you got there?"
"A translation of a story of a dream
world." The sequence of events exists.

Here, one; here two;
here, buckle; here shoe.
Now let there be sound.
Now let there be light.
Once there was this now.

Mrs. Autumn and Her Two Daughters

We live in an ocean
of white waiting to fall.
One of us is not like our mother and it's me. It's I.
My eyes are mostly closed.

My mother knows
how to make snow. We never see
our feet. Our skirts end in the oncoming frost.
My sister wears ermine. I have a narrow waist.

I no longer curl my hair. Why bother?
I love my sister but hate my mother
yet we're all of a piece.
Endless snipsnip. Ragged fragment.

We still live where you last left us—
between the palace where you keep your winter
and the summer garden of the ersatz emperor.
Did I hear you say China? If I did you are right.

We live atop the continent
that contains such poverty. Such pollution.
Such eerie beauty. Always a mountain.
Always a screen. White washes

over me. I do not act
like my mother. I lean farther.
What I make annihilates the mirror of China
but not the mountain.

Not the man walking away.
My mother says throw more snow but I can't
help thinking.
There is more to being than erasure.

You are wrong, she says. You don't wear your cape.

Untitled # 70 (Or, The Question of Remains)

The day she put on her glitz teardrops
and O Hon lip gloss,
ate an orange on an empty
and took the 8-train
to Grackleville, she met a man
climbing a narrow stairwell,
repeating to himself, This is all, this is all.
The music of a popular march played
in his head. This, he said, is all,
directing any further comment
to a longtime opposition blooming in his chest.
No, he said, to the offer
of a chaotic labyrinth of clouds,
devotion, rain, creatures of fables,
and opulent solitude.
Alone he entered the thicket
of empty situations, the rhetorical force
of conversation,
muttering as he went, This is all—

Apprentice to death. Toxic grace.
Terrible and beautiful repose.
Dismay and murkiest waters.
The blighted morning.
The coordinate night.
The sad fact of the pink glow
of Grackleville's late iridescence.

Landscape with the Fall of Icarus

How could I have failed you like this?
The narrator asks

The object. The object is a box
Of ashes. How could I not have saved you,

A boy made of bone and blood. A boy
Made of a mind. Of years. A hand

And paint on canvas. A marble carving.
How can I not reach where you are

And pull you back. How can I be
And you not. You're forever on the platform

Seeing the pattern of the train door closing.
Then the silver streak of me leaving.

What train was it? The number 6.
What day was it? Wednesday.

We had both admired the miniature mosaics
Stuck on the wall of the Met.

That car should be forever sealed in amber.
That dolorous day should be forever

Embedded in amber.
In garnet. In amber. In opal. In order

To keep going on. And how can it be
That this means nothing to anyone but me now.

Words

Parole. Mote in one's own eye. The deceit
That a lifetime is. I wasn't there
When something happened. Something

Happened. A chair was pushed out from a table.
Don't listen if you don't want to know
What happened, the Sergeant said. I don't want to know

The future as it's seen on that inked slip of paper
That says one has only now and no more.
It was fourth grade or fifth.

Or it was eighth grade or the grade up the side
Of the river or the ditch at the side of the road.
It was very steep. It's always been difficult.

Breath like a hollow rasp but almost silent.
A management that keeps one sane. A hand gliding
An iron over a piece of fabric.

Like skates, like a sewing stitch
Done to keep one's attention from wavering.
The self talking to a mirror.

All the doctors know that. The ones who see you lying
On a sofa. They know that there is a sound
In one's head. They know there is that deep

Relief from the waking state called sleep. How little else
They know unless you tell them. I tell them
I wish I could lie under the summer.

And as in Alice

Alice cannot be in the poem, she says, because
She's only a metaphor for childhood
And a poem is a metaphor already
So we'd only have a metaphor

Inside a metaphor. Do you see?
They all nod. They see. Except for the girl
With her head in the rabbit hole. From this vantage,
Her bum looks like the flattened backside

Of a black-and-white panda. She actually has one
In the crook of her arm.
Of course it's stuffed and not living.
Who would dare hold a real bear so near the outer ear?

She's wondering what possible harm might come to her
If she fell all the way down the dark she's looking through.
Would strange creatures sing songs
Where odd syllables came to a sibilant end at the end.

Perhaps the sounds would be a form of light hissing.
Like when a walrus blows air
Through two fractured front teeth. Perhaps it would
Take the form of a snake. But if a snake, it would need a tree.

Could she grow one from seed? Could one make a cat?
Make it sit on a branch and fade away again
The moment you told it that the rude noise it was hearing was
    rational thought
With an axe beating on the forest door.

B Is for Beckett

There is so little to say.

C Is for Cher

Culture miniature and clad as Cleopatra, she descends
A set of semicircular steps
Tiled in a geometric mosaic pattern

And there she finds the answer: everything
Changes depending on whether
You're up or down. Behind her,

A high-relief rectangle proscenium;
Beside her, whatever intrigued her last.
An unofficial fan leaps feverishly into action. At that,

She seems to multiply. History will be filled
With the shower of dots that will become her.
At that, she becomes. It's complex.

Through the glass she sees a pair of dazzling slippers.
At dinner her drink was called a Vladimir,
Hers was the plate that contained Washington oysters.

There she held a fork. There she was on a stage
Of discourse. Of course. Mickey Mouse comes over
And stops to stare. Cher is dressed in a long gold dress.

The sequins form stripes. "If I could turn back time."
She's singing. And Mickey in his red pants is acting
Like the goodwill minister to an enraptured world.

Mickey thinks. He turns the corner.
To the gift shop: ever open.
He buys retractable mother-of-pearl opera glasses

As a present. Yes, it's over. The present.
In which you discovered forward-thinking thought.

In the Present and Probable Future

Here we are viewing the land: waves of grave and grain.
That slight tremor? A house settling. A violent past walking
      through.

And over there, the burning deck. The political machine.
The inanimate come to life. The conventional flag wave.

Cormorants on pitched roofs watch the ship of state mandate
      folded
Twice over. *Many ingenious lovely things are gone.* This
      turbulence. This

Coming one-two march through a landscape created.
The dark relative against the brilliance of the last act

Of some staged production. The cast bows. A tape player click,
      click,
Clicks. Some kind of clock. A unit of measurement.

We wish ourselves back on the boat. Wish for the answer
To the question: When should we walk out

Of the theater into the night? When should we accept that life
      is only
An exaggerated form of special pleading, romanticized

Beyond saying into moon, stone, flock and trees?
What in the picture would you get rid of? The land that
        stretches back

To prehistoric times? Myriad islands? Ice caps and etcetera?
The atmosphere? The human body? All of the above?

All but the latter? You'd like to keep human as an aspect of the
        formula
But rid it of its grappling ambition to destroy? Good luck with
        that.

What does it mean to have a point of view? What does it mean
To have a notable achievement? To succeed in representing

The nuances of a determinate activity?
Listen, however events turn out, if we want we can continue
        to see

The image of the moon as an outburst of lyric, a vision of John
        Keats
And his friends, but we still have the battle to fight.

How many more days will be there? The unperceptive will
        be busy
Believing in magic: crop circles, the unmanipulated image,
        definitions

That defy definition. Others will take at face value the less
        favorable
Consequences of both cynicism and commercialization.

The latter will say the flock is simply an assemblage,
An obsessive presence looking down on the building where
        someone sits

Predicting the landslide rate. Long after we are gone
We can say we were here. We were working, wittingly or not,

Towards the eventual erosion of places ground down
And fought over, especially in the literal sense—exploitation

And industrial damage. Nothing is lost. If anything, we gain
Experience. There will be that unsullied moment, down to
                    the last

Detail, when the acquired interview and other quaint signs of
                    demise
Will speak about us to the flood and the fire.

FROM the *Mrs. Dalloway* series

Opened and Shut

She had prepared a looking-glass: hair, dress, thought,
sofa in the glow of dogs barking.

Beautifully close up. And once, flames
eating the edge of the sofa.

Her eyelashes blurred. Chin, nose, forehead, some lips.
The cheek. The glass looking first at one thing,
then another: nose, eyes, evening.

She sat looking at the map of her hands.
The window, the clock, her pulse.

The body was busy thinking, conjuring
the museum of a moment: emotion, scenes, people,
bags of treasures. Heaps of theories.

Theories to explain feeling the here and the back of the hand.
A theory allowed one thing after another.
First, dinner, then morning.

Her hand was the world.
To get to it she had to look at herself.

To get at the truth one would have to disregard
anything false. Yet the truth was intangible.

One eye on the horizon: a long indeterminable,
mere straightness, a few plants.
That indescribable purple.

Doors being opened. Visual impressions—
as if the eye were the brain, the body entering the house.

POETICS STATEMENT

THE DIVERSITY OF what is called poetry makes it near-impossible to make any general statement about it outside of perhaps noting that poetry, however it presents itself, usually emerges from a state of absorbed self-interestedness. Paradoxically, that very state of self-absorption, when it's intense, can produce an ecstatic state of unself-consciousness, what the Hungarian psychologist Mihaly Csikszentmihalyi has called "flow." This state can arise regardless of the type of poetry one is writing—traditional, avant-garde, it doesn't matter. It also occurs in rock climbers, dancers, painters, tennis players, and even in corporate CEOs. Writing poetry is only one of many types of activities that offer a single-minded immersion that has the potential to create a particularly pleasurable autotelic experience, an escapist state that T. S. Eliot wryly remarks on in his essay "Tradition and the Individual Talent": "Poetry is not a turning loose of emotion, but an escape from emotion; it is not the expression of personality, but an escape from personality. But, of course, only those who have personality and emotions know what it means to want to escape from these things."

When I attempt to isolate poetry from the long list of single-minded activities, and make a claim for poetry that will hold true regardless of the myriad forms it takes, I come up with this: poetry rests on the assumption that language is unstable—unstable because while it gestures toward both the material world and the world of interiority, it can never be either—just as the pipe in René Magritte's iconic painting *La trahison des images* (*The Treachery of Images*) will never be a real pipe. The painter has reminded us of that impossibility by writing "Ceci n'est pas une pipe" ("This is not a pipe") under the image of the pipe. Like René's painting, poetry, whatever else it does, has the potential to draw attention to the gap between the subject and the representation of it. Some poems make use of poetic strategies that have a long tradition of use (or are slight adaptations of traditional strategies) and others foreground an attempt to rearrange language in less traditional ways; either way, the poem exploits the innate instability of language. If the rearrangement is radically different from what has come before, we tend to think of these poems as "experimental."

Of course the clean edge of the new, any given moment's "experimental," is continually being corrupted; what is experimental in one moment drifts over time toward the center. Eliot's "Prufrock," flamboyantly outside the mainstream in its moment of publication, looks rather mainstream now. Stein, who in her day was more adamant at drawing attention to the unstable nature of language than Eliot, still appears less conventional than he does. Because certain aspects of Stein's poetry have been very intelligently deconstructed by scholars (especially by Marjorie Perloff, Ula Dydo, and Steven Meyer) and appropriated by L=A=N=G=U=A=G=E poets such as Lyn Hejinian and Susan Howe, and echoed in various Oulipian strategies, her writing now seems less unorthodox than it once did. At least it seems less unorthodox to many readers. There will always be readers who would prefer to exclude such radical experiments from the realm of poetry and reserve that nomenclature for poems that hold a mirror to the poems of the past (broken lines, a single identifiable speaker who assumes a pose that looks like the poet's, near-normative syntax, etc.). For those who feel that poetry, and all art, is best viewed as a means of provoking thoughts and raising questions, radical rearrangements that violate convention, such as Stein's, are fruitful provocations. These latter poets tend to have more of an anthropological neutrality about the forms a poem might take. For them poems are architectural interiors to be filled as they wish, to various effects. They appreciate that innovative poetic compositions will over time create texts that enlarge the domain of poetry, although these strange new poems sometimes require new ways of reading *and* a reconsideration of what constitutes a poem. Since nothing is off limits, those kinds of poets, and readers of the poetry they produce, eagerly await the next surprise, even if the next surprise is the poetry of boredom (see Kenneth Goldsmith's poetics statement, "Being Boring," in the 2007 edition of *American Poets in the 21st Century: The New Poetics*).

If it's difficult to make a general claim about poetry, it may be even more difficult to make a claim for one's own practice. While I don't consider my poems to be radical rearrangements of language, I'm always aware, while I'm writing them, that language is shifting. And I never lose sight of the fact that any "reality" that language gestures toward is artificial. To conceive of the poem as a stage and the speaker in it as *a character acting in a play* (instead of as a poet plumbing the depths of her psyche) provides me with a sense of remove. That sense of remove allows me to treat the poem as a constructed space, a set piece, where I can briefly animate a figure, allow it to speak or act, and afterward place it back in its dummy case. What occurs on the set, as well as the set design, can then gesture toward the conceptual. The poem can become a complex and unconsummated (thus, non-dictatorial) means of variously illustrating the abstract, or personifying values, or enacting ideas; a form of non-literal encoding.

Many of the compositional methods I'm drawn to in my own work, and in the work of others, fall under the rubric of *Ostrananie*—a Russian Formalist strategy named by Viktor Shklovsky in a 1916 essay entitled "Art as Technique." *Ostrananie* translates into English as "making strange." Strange in at least two senses: one, the estrangement through defamiliarization of the quotidian world, and the estrangement by dissociation of context from form. The hallmark of the strategy is a combination of collage and idiosyncrasy and the result is the creation of a neo-surrealist façade that can be informed in subtle ways by the political. This method asks the reader to surrender the need for completion and linearity and fathom the poem as if it's a record of the mind skipping. At the same time, every element in the poem is a clue to interconnectedness.

Disjunction and abbreviation occupy the foreground in many of these poems. Action and resolution are only hinted at, largely because completion would narrow the reach. Like Cindy Sherman's "Untitled Film Stills," this kind of poetry relies on constructed realities where a single frame is meant to evoke an entirety. The reader is asked to presume a possible context based on meager evidence—sometimes a single figure in a reduced setting with minimal props.

The very nature of thought is associative, and conjectural. Just as Sherman's photographs rely on the fact that viewers have their own experience of interiority and their own understanding of the material world, this kind of poetry assumes that both interiority and the real will be brought into play as the reader attempts to place the poetic image in a larger world. Depending on the situation that the scene gestures toward, the poem also has the potential for creating recognition on various subjective levels.

A certain degree of irony resides in the very idea that we attempt to expand on a partial narrative: What is that girl in Sherman's "Untitled Film Still #48" doing on that dark road at night? She's clearly headed for trou-

Cindy Sherman, *Untitled Film Still, 1979*, black and white photograph,
8 x 10 inches, 20.3 x 25.4 cm. Courtesy of the artist and Metro Pictures.

ble. Sherman is relying on the fact that we've seen that film, even if we
can't name it. The trope is so familiar, it's clichéd. We are invited to ex-
amine the trope *and* the ease with which we construct a well-worn nar-
rative around it. The very fact that the image is abbreviated has forced us
to engage in critical inquiry, even in the absence of a unified conceptual
apparatus. That's the game in my poems: What larger context(s) does the
image suggest? What possibilities does the language allow for? If Cher is
in a poem, if Mount Rushmore is, if there's a metal alloy ladder at the deep
end of a swimming pool, none of these is there arbitrarily but nor are their
uses delimited; each serves multiple purposes in the poem and readers will
intuit some but not all of what was in my mind when I placed them there
and will, of course—because reading is an interactive process—add their
own associations to mine. Any residual autobiographical connection gets
attenuated in the service of something larger (just as the use of the pipe in
Magritte's painting doesn't raise the question of whether Magritte is a pipe
smoker). Whatever the compounded total, the poem will be the product of
a moment's self-absorption, during which word games have been played in
the service of creating a world and simultaneously calling it into question.
The game is then sent out into the real world to be played by others.

ARTICULATIONS OF ARTIFICE IN THE WORK OF MARY JO BANG

Karla Kelsey

> Then I went home
> And wrote a script
> To follow where I got a free boat ride
> While taking pictures of pictures
> And all the pictures came out beautiful.[1]

A POET OF PERSONA, of film and stage metaphor, of persistent eye for visual detail—of insistence that we "look" and "look" once again[2]—Mary Jo Bang's six books turn on articulating the artifice of the lyric. Like the photographs of Cindy Sherman, an artist directly evoked in Bang's statement of poetics and in her ekphrastic poem "Untitled # 70 (Or, the Question of Remains)," Bang's work hinges on drawing attention to the dyadic nature of signs, the unpassable separation between signifier and signified that are separate elements, but also two sides of the same coin. Although each of Bang's books has a specific nature, in every project Bang conjures up surfaces, absorbing readers in vivid tableaux while exposing the constructed nature of imaginative objects.

The concept of the dyadic sign becomes particularly relevant when conceptual components are most submerged, as in media such as photography and language where the meaning of the sign is often mistakenly assumed to be a real-world referent. Artists such as Cindy Sherman and Mary Jo Bang problematize the impulse to fix meaning in this way. For example, when we look at any of Sherman's sixty-nine black-and-white photographs in her *Untitled Film Stills* series we first think we are looking at publicity pictures of an actress-in-character, taken from films made in the '60s and '70s. Here we see a blonde bombshell playing the role of a woman lounging in her bedroom, peignoir thrown open, eyes fluttered up to the ceiling ("Untitled Film Still #6"). In another an actress poses as the quintessential sexy librarian reaching for a book ("Untitled Film Still #13").[3] On first glance, we will assume that what the pictures "mean"—what they are "of"—is an actress caught in the act of posing in character. However, this is not the case. What is true of the photographs is that they all feature the artist herself, dressed up as the different female characters an actress from that era was most often asked to play. Understanding this reveals the extent to which the viewer's narrative about the blonde bombshell was not in the pictures themselves—for there was no blonde bombshell, merely an artist pretending to be someone else—but rather in the conceptual context we bring to our viewing. In addition, due to the fact that the photographs feature the artist herself, we are given to wonder who is literally behind the camera. As we look at the photographs we realize that we are assuming the point of view of somebody's gaze—but whose?

Sherman's work is unique because it draws us into a fantasy, asking us to indulge in the sensuous surface of images while, at the same time, complicating the way that they evoke meaning. Further, even when the method of the series is revealed, and we realize that we are looking at a commentary on the genre of film stills rather than at film stills themselves, their sensuous artifice continues to beckon: The woman in the photos still has wet, pouty lips, a coy glance as she turns to walk away. As we will see, Mary Jo Bang's work takes us through a very similar trajectory. There is always the lyric *and* attention to what constructs lyric surface—material language as well as mental image, association, response. Bang's poems, like Sherman's photographs, act as frames, embodying both signifier and signified, asking readers not only to engage with what is represented, but also to inspect each representation as something artfully constructed from multiple sources.

Such articulation of artifice defines Mary Jo Bang's position in the landscape of contemporary poetry, for, in many respects, a poet's relationship to lyric surface places him or her upon an ever-contentious continuum. On one end of the spectrum is the New Critical lyric, which values circumscribed utterance and the absorbent voice of a single, unified speaker overheard in the midst of an emotional moment.[4] Such work seeks to create a continuous dream of reading wherein the surface of language falls away and the reader becomes seeped in a moment of unmediated experience. Optimally, all of the poetic elements used in a single lyric—figurative language, diction, form, etc.—are crafted within the space of its emotional arc, feeding back into the central core of the poem. As such, the New Critical lyric is highly constructed but asks to be read as transparent window opening upon interior and exterior landscape rather than artificial—made—object.

On the other end of the spectrum, avant-garde writers have long been suspicious of such absorbent landscapes and repeatedly draw attention to the linguistic nature of the poetic object, outlining the construction of subjectivity and the objects, ideas, and emotions the poem articulates. Charles Bernstein's essay "Artifice of Absorption" characterizes such work as that which draws attention to artifice, rather than submerging it, through the use of "exaggeration, attention scattering, distraction, digression, interruptive, transgressive, undecorous, anticonventional, baroque, camp, decorative."[5] Work on this end of the spectrum draws attention to the impermeability of language, insisting that the experience of the poem is an experience of reading.

These divisions are, themselves, of course, artificial, for the lyric has always depended on the tension between absorption and attention to surface. Likewise, Bernstein insists that *all* poetics imply artifice, and he cites Helen Vendler, among others, to show that artifice is a recognized aspect of the tradition, even on the conservative end of the spectrum. He quotes Vendler's statement that "the symbolic strength of poetry consists in giving presence, through linguistic signs, to absent realities while insisting, by the very brilliance of poetic style, on the linguistic nature of its own being and the illusionistic character of its effects."[6] The crux of the issue is whether or not a poem admits to its artifice, and to what end. For the New Critical lyric, the exposure of artifice is considered artistic flaw. For the avant-garde writer, not to expose artifice is considered ethical flaw, and today's poetic climate is hyperconscious of this duality. As Susan Schultz has suggested, "Lyric poets (because there are always such) must find ways in which to accommodate the lyric to the actual world, where voice does not denote mastery so much as conflict, identity so much as its confusions and contradictions."[7]

If we take even the most basic definition of the lyric as a short poem—a poem short enough to be held in the mind—we will see that the genre itself admits contradiction, for regardless of how short a poem might be its multiple meanings happen simultaneously, eluding the grasp of the mind's moment. Take, for example, Bang's one-line poem "B Is for Beckett," from her most recent book *The Bride of E*. The poem reads, in its entirety: "There is so little to say."[8] On the one hand, this utterance can be held in the mind all at once. It is composed of only six words and it does not even require imagining a visual image. However, once we begin to think about the poem, the mind begins to trace ever-outward and the utterance shows itself to be uncontainable.

As we think through the poem, we see that the title of the poem rewrites the familiar alphabet instruction, "B is for ball," thus re-instructing us in the attachments of association, giving us an adult existential primer, a little glimpse of the way Bang's own mind associates. We toggle the "for" from "stands for" to "is for"—into a dedication. This poem, this B, is for Beckett. A whole page, one sentence, just for him. A whole page, just one sentence, feels apt: "There is so little to say," alone on the page as a poem, is so very Beckett that it might have been said by Beckett. But the phrase is also a response to the end of his play, *Ohio, Impromptu*, which finishes: "There is nothing left to tell."[9] Readers familiar with Bang's work, knowing that the title of her third book, *The Downstream Extremity of the Isle of Swans*, is lifted from *Ohio, Impromptu*, will feel additional resonance.

Thinking further and comparing the phrases now in our minds, the subtle difference between "telling" and "saying" crackles with significance. "Telling" connotes a relationship with a listener; "saying" has undertones of personal reservoir. Here there is a tremendous gap between there being "so little" to say and "nothing left" to tell. *Because* of Beckett's work, we have a little to say—not nothing. We have followed his direction, have gone on when we couldn't go on, and so, by his lead, he has, in some small part, delivered us from nothing. At the same time, we might take a different track with the poem, and come to the idea that because Beckett has said everything worth saying—has said most of what there is to say about existence—there is now "so little to say." All that is left is a linguistic shrug. A one-line poem to add to, to nod to, all that is Beckett.

I have spun this small poem out to great distance as model for the way Bang's work asks to be read and unfolded, cross-checked across books, both hers and others. From her first book to her most recent projects, the experience of Bang's work is visually and aurally sensual while being, at the same time, conceptual, for here the physical and the mental—the abstract and the concrete—are equal and necessary parts of the dyad of reading. As in "B Is for Beckett," the tension is between absence and presence, between the words articulated on the page and the ideas, connotations, associations, and references that come with their signification. This is stimulating territory, for once we enter the dream of the lyric, it seems that to both engage imagination in the work's "content" while bringing to the surface the constructed nature of its being, is an irreconcilable contradiction. But instead of turning away from such difficult questions and seeming contradictions, Mary Jo Bang's work thrives in such a space.

Bang engages this tension by transforming the New Critical speaker into persona and the representational dream of objects into strange, vivid signs that continue to come back across books. Familiar signs accrete new meanings as they work across texts: Mickey Mouse appears as a watch, a balloon, a character that speaks and dances. Lewis Carroll's Alice writes in her "Rite as Reign notebook," and later she refuses to appear in a poem. Needle-necked swans surface and swim under. Louise, from Bang's second book, *Louise in Love*, appears carrying a copy of *Mrs. Dalloway*, foreshadowing a current project of constructing poems out of Woolf's text. Rather than rejecting the lyric as a false thing, Bang turns into its façade, articulating the way in which lyric illusion functions. Her work ultimately shows that we owe the dynamism of the lyric to this tension—a tension that has necessarily always existed in its defining elements.

Indeed, Bang's headlong movement into absorption in artifice while at the same time revealing the poem's construction defines the way in which her work differs from many other writers working within the lyric tradition. This stance of lyric tension is rare in the contemporary landscape where, even though poets borrow from both lyric and experimental traditions, these two actions are often perceived as being mutually exclusive with mutually exclusive ends. As Bernstein notes, "if the artifice is recessed, the resulting textual transparency yields an apparent, if misleading content . . . if the artifice is foregrounded, there's a tendency to say that there is no content or meaning."[10] For the remainder of this essay I will focus on this aspect of lyric tension by concentrating on Bang's three most recent books—*The Eye Like a Strange Balloon*, *Elegy*, and *The Bride of E*—for these books foreground not only artifice, but the role that language plays in constructing the realities in which we absorb ourselves. However, because of the intertextual nature of Bang's work, it is important to set these volumes within the context of her first three books. To this end, I will briefly introduce the interplay of artifice and absorption in her early writing before looking at her more recent projects.

EVIDENT in Bang's first book, *Apology for Want*, are obsessions and gestures found throughout her work. There is a preoccupation with death, both overtly named and figured. There is obsession with the material, often textile-based details of life forged in the foundry of looking. Here we find high art along with the colloquial. There is the stall of silence at the edge of each line while, at the same time, enjambed sentences rush to fill the space with speech. There is the frank tone of a solitary voice, the sense of a real person speaking in language that here softens with longing, there sharpens with wit. And everywhere there are objects, of art and of everyday life, staring back at us, gleaming. However, out of all of Bang's books, *Apology for Want* most closely follows the conventions of the New Critical lyric and, therefore, pushes the artifice of each poem into the background whereas—in later work—she focuses on drawing attention to the surface. As a result of these conventions, in this first book the dream of the lyric is rarely disrupted—we are thoroughly absorbed. Nevertheless, within this smoothness we see the preoccupation with precise and particular imagery that prefigures Bang's work with the constructed nature of the art image in *The Eye Like a Strange Balloon*. In addition, *Apology for Want* recycles moments of its own imagery across different poems. This action prompts the reader to begin to see the poem-as-art-object, as something made with language, rather than as pure subjective utterance.

While *Apology for Want* lends itself to being read as the intimate thoughts of a single speaker, Bang's second book, *Louise in Love*, actively prohibits such approaches to reading by setting up a fictive scenario populated by highly artificial characters. The book revolves around Louise, a woman in love who both is and is not the actress Louise Brooks. She dresses and sighs with all of the accoutrements of a silent-era star, yet there is little to no context to Bang's character beyond what happens in each tableau-like scene, which prohibits us from reading this as historical work.

This status of being and not being a particular identity is fundamental to the mode of the book and the way in which Bang uses persona to foreground artifice. As soon as readers become comfortable with a particular notion of who and what Louise represents, Bang turns the figure, opening her up to other interpretations, asking us to see her—and her story—as a series of literary devices that fail to hold together into a singular speaker or a single, integrated subject. As Stephen Burt has suggested, in *Louise in Love,* such tactics of foregrounding artifice are not merely a fashionable response to contemporary cynicism about the rhetoric of love and beauty— about the rhetoric of self. Instead, artifice is the very tactic that "enables a love affair."[11] Rather than seeing Bang's insistence on artifice as something that she adds to her narrative like a voice-over or coloration of the real, Burt suggests that such artifice is part of the way we make it through everyday life.

The Downstream Extremity of the Isle of Swans, Bang's third book, takes this notion of artifice and deepens it beyond the realm of a love affair, into the gut of humanity's existential state. At the core of the book there is a realization that we can never know or see what goes on in another person's mind, and in this sense, we are always navigating a constructed experience, mediated by the other's presentation of self, and by our own assumptions. With this book, Bang unmoors her work from the safety of concrete, finite content and addresses concerns that—like those of her later projects—are much more abstract and foreground modes of representation, rather than the "content" of what is represented. For example, in *Downstream Extremity*, notions of the stage, acting, theater, and drama are developed and maintained, but without the anchor of the fictional background that they have in *Louise*. Instead of existing as part of a narrative world that more or less mirrors our own, these elements express the artifice implicit in our acts of figuring.

In addition to developing metaphors of film and theater that inform her subsequent work, *Downstream Extremity* develops two other tactics that are carried through Bang's later books. Heavy sound play, often in the form of alliteration as in the "picturesque—pretty pipers piped // against a backdrape of pineapple yellow" in the poem "The Beauties of Nature,"[12] draws our attention to extralexical aspects of poetic language that do not fold into traditional notions of semantic meaning. Such attention directs us to the material substance of language and the way that sound, as well as sense, works to hold a poem together. Allusion, the second tactic, here most noticeably ties the book to Beckett—but also to Shakespeare in a poem titled "It's Winter in the Eye, and Like Ophelia" and to Elizabeth Bishop (Bang's lines "the too-heavy hair, long with cool stars—pin pricks / in a watery bed sheet"[13] echo Bishop's poem "The Shampoo")— and to Wallace Stevens, clearly evoked in the lines "Who will catch the windmill's palm frond in a summer storm? / O the idea of order. It will be seen through."[14] These strategies mark Bang's increasing turn into the articulation of artifice, for they disrupt the careful New Critical illusion of a speaker overheard uttering the most private of individual thoughts. By performing such uttering in wrought, sound-heavy language that employs the figures of other writers, Bang throws the dynamics we assume to be true of the lyric into question.

PUBLISHED in 2004, *The Eye Like a Strange Balloon* consists entirely of ekphrastic poems, and the book moves through a select history of art including Sigmar Poke, Willem de Kooning, and Cindy Sherman. Organized in reverse chronological order, the book begins with a poem based on a 2003 work of art by Bruce Pearson and moves backward through time. The penultimate poem is based on an untitled first-century BC Samarian fragment. And, as if to completely fulfill the notion that "Art is what looking takes you to"—a phrase from the poem "High Art"—the last poem of the book reverses the process of ekphrastic making: Bang wrote "What Moonlight Will Do for Ruins," and then created her own piece of visual art after the poem.

In presenting us with representations of representations, *The Eye Like a Strange Balloon* operates as lyric cousin to Roland Barthes's *Camera Lucida*, a book of great importance to Bang. In this work, Barthes spins out the story of how we make photographs mean. Photography, like language, is a tricky medium because viewers, like readers, tend to equate the meaning of a photo with the figure that it represents, ignoring the art of the lens and the context of the photo's making and viewing. Like Barthes, Bang's book seeks to draw our attention to the lens. Traversing the visual landscape of Bang's book, we are struck by the many modes of invention that attach a thing to its representation, meaning to world and word.

Bang's study of the way narrative and thought attach to image dates back to her training as a visual artist. While working on a BA in photography in London, Bang became fascinated with the way in which, even in photojournalism, the relationship between image and narrative is constructed. As Bang relates, in one project she appropriated photographs from

> the Farm Security Administration in the 1930s, where you have people like Dorothy Lange and James Agee and Walker Evans going out and taking these so-called documentary photographs that have come to represent the "reality" of a particular era in a well-defined geographical region in America.[15]

She made changes to the original photographs (such as inserting Mickey Mouse into barren landscapes, or perching the Cheshire cat in a tree) and re-photographed them. Her impulse to do so came from learning that the original FSA photographers were sent out with scripts and told to take photos to match. When the scripts led to images that were too poverty-stricken to correlate with America's idea of itself, the government revised the scripts and asked for a more acceptably middle-class range of images. By inserting pop culture icons into such images, Bang asked her viewer to question the transparent frame they had been given, gesturing toward the fact that each act of looking is undergirded by narrative and idea.

The Eye Like a Strange Balloon operates directly within this lineage: The visual art behind the book serves less as palate of objects set out for description and more as objects that trigger lines of meditation, narrative, description, and association investigating the "how" of attachment. And while the work encompasses the ekphrastic tradition of representing in words what has been rendered on canvas, in marble, as tapestry, with projection, the book is always also interested in performing and questioning the ways in which such representation comes to be and mean. As Donna Stonecipher remarks in a review of the book,

> the poems . . . are full of eyes, mirrors, cameras, lenses, monocles, microscopes, and blind people. There are also repeated references to scenes, sequences, televisions, stages, operas, and films—all forms of constructed experience that the eye watches. The eye, therefore, is complicit in the artificializing of experience through its representation.[16]

The interest, here, is not to transparently render, but to carry across the sensation of looking and the act of mind as it connects. As such, *The Eye Like a Strange Balloon* works both within and against the mimetic assumption of ekphrastic work, mining the questions and beliefs that any viewer might hold about the artifice of representation.

We need only to look at the title of the collection to see these tensions at play. The phrase "The Eye Like a Strange Balloon" is a translation of part of the title of a painting by Odilon Redon—"L'oeil, comme un ballon bizarre se dirige vers l'infini." It is also the title of one of the poems of the book. As such, we begin with a complexed sign. In addition, the cover of the book does not reproduce the Redon painting; instead, the cover is a photograph of a girl in a red dress holding, in front of her face, a big, smiley-faced, yellow balloon. We see value placed on metaphor (the eye is likened to the balloon) and a curious absence of verb—it is easy to miss-see and mis-hear the title as "The eye is like a strange balloon" rather than the fragmented sentence, which leaves us wondering what the predicate of the sentence might be. Additionally, the visual pun of the cover images helps us to read "The Eye" as "the I"—the I as an ever-familiar emoticon-turned-balloon filled with air and masking the face. The "I" as a Redon painting, as a book of poems, as a poem, as a smiling simile waiting to be released into air.

This restless quality of engagement permeates the entire volume, marking the work as part of a contemporary, alternative tradition of ekphrastic writing. In an article about Cole Swensen's ekphrastic book *Try*, Lynn Keller outlines this tradition in terms that apply to *The Eye Like a Strange Balloon*. The conventions of ekphrastic writing have the writer stand at a distance from the work of art, creating a verbal representation of a visual work that represents an object in the world. In the alternative tradition Keller delineates, writers such as Swensen (and, I contend, Bang) re-vision the tradition by setting themselves inside and within the work of art—"living with the art," as Swensen says of her work.[17] In this way, such ekphrastic work is less about representing an object that is itself a representation, and more about exploring the abstract questions and connections that exist among and between modes of rendering.

One of the ways that Bang effects this task is by taking on the persona of figures depicted in the artwork, exploring the way in which narrative is constructed from fragments and is, itself, never complete. Bang's "Mrs. Autumn and Her Two Daughters," after Sigmar Polke's 1991 "Frau Herbst und ihre zwei Töchter," is one such work. As with other poems in the book, "Mrs. Autumn" takes its mode directly from the cues of the visual work. The painting asks for narrative, for it is dominated by a trio of black-and-white figures that are immediately recognizable as "Mrs. Autumn and Her Two Daughters." Dressed in Victorian garb, the women, perched on a cloud, are busy making snow. The mother and one of the daughters wear capes and wield oversized sheers, as the second, capeless daughter leans over the edge of the cloud, scattering snow. While there are other things going on in the painting (below the cloud is a miniature mountain, a man on a horse—and the figurative images are, themselves, layered over a background pattern), Polke draws our attention to this trio of women by placing them in the upper left hand corner of the pictorial plane—the place that Western "readers" go to automatically. The figures are much larger and darker than the sketch-like characters below and clearly center our experience.

If the figures in the painting aren't enough to inspire a narrative reading of the work, the painting's title attaches the image to the frame of a story. The trio is not just any trio, but forms a family portrait *sans* father. The mother is the only one with a proper name, and her name dubs her "wife" ("Mrs.") and gestures toward allegory ("Autumn"). The other two figures are undifferentiated from each other in the title (mere "Daughters") and look visually similar to each other. Thus, the triggering occasion for the narrative nature of the poem is twofold. The speaker of the poem immediately identifies herself as one of the daughters, and the course of the poem is spent in a struggle to voice differentiation: "My sister wears ermine. I have a narrow waist" and "I love my sister but hate my mother" and "One of us is not like our mother and it's me. It's I." [18] With subtle gestures, such as this moment of syntactical revision from "it's me" to the correct "It's I," Bang foregrounds the way in which language for identity creates identity.

In addition to the speaker's overt articulation of identity-making, the details of the poem foreground narrative invention rather than taking the existence of any given narrative for granted. In doing so, Bang suggests that our stories depend on the details we select for telling, and by comparing the visual image with Bang's poem we become aware of just how much is made in the act of looking. As Bang explains in an interview, "It turns out that the world is a fiction from the point of view of any written 'I' or 'you' or 'she.' It's a fiction because it is selective, and depending on what is selected, that becomes the story." [19] We see this at work in the poem, revealed in such moments as "We still live where you last left us—/ between the palace where you keep your winter / and the summer garden of the ersatz emperor." The speaker-daughter's address to an absent "you" (perhaps the father, perhaps the viewer) gestures outside the frame of the painting, but also gives us a context for the figures: "White washes // over me. I do not act / like my mother. I lean farther." Concrete detail becomes metaphor as we toggle back and forth between what is on canvas and what is said. As such, the poem comments on the formative properties of looking, of circumscribing oneself as object in a narrative-image-based field. In this way, the poem functions similarly to work done in *Louise in Love*: As a reader we are invited to fall in love with Louise, but we are also consistently reminded that she is an aesthetic object, a made work of fiction.

In contrast to the landscape of story present in "Mrs. Autumn," "High Art" is a poem of "Atmospherics predominating // over drama." [20] Instead of foregrounding the narrative of finding ourselves in the more-or-less fully formed images society throws at us, "High Art," written after the feature film by Lisa Cholodenko, foregrounds the messy, disjunctive constellation of action that results in these clean-seeming surfaces. The fact that Bang uses a movie to catalyze the poem makes sense: We go to see a movie and watch the plot unfold in a perfectly uniform pace of cause and effect. We also know, however, that such unfolding is an illusion. We know that the finished film links together shots that were taken in a much different sequence and then edited together to perform an arc. Scenes in the movie are likely re-shot and spliced together to provide the feeling of seamlessness. Music is added to give the work a texture of continuity—call it voice, call it "atmospherics." All of these processes are in service of creating a "city outside" the mind that matches another "inside"—inside the mind of the director, inside the mind of the viewer as image matches image in the darkened room of the theater.

Bang's poem thrives on articulating the fragments and the fragmentary nature of such becoming. While there are moments that speak to narrative ("I remember the camera. / The clear click"), cause is not followed up by effect and narrative is deeply submerged. Instead of working through a trajectory of plot, the poem articulates the path of images unfolding unto other images. Instead of working with narrative logic, connections are made by visual association and sound:

> A face too small for this red mouth. Look how

> the line isn't a street anymore
> but a track. Like that. The graveled
> shroud of a train. I'm not usually like
> this. A linkable Like arrives without its What.
> Parks the car.

One thread through this poem is visual and progresses by noticing similarity of shape in unconnected things: the line made by the mouth's lips becomes a line that was once a street but is now a track. This becomes a gravel shroud. Another thread tracks presence and absence: We see, in the mind, a street because we are told that it isn't there anymore. The way that "I am" is defined by being "not like / this." Linguistic play acts out the implied banter of "I'm not usually like this." "Like what?" is the expected response, but here we are told that the "what" is absent—but in its absence it is figured: "A linkable Like arrives without its What. / Parks the car." Here we have affirmation and acknowledgment that the comparison is not going to be fleshed out for us. Instead, we are given the presence of sound to pull us through the poem. Just as the visual line of flight takes off from the image of a mouth morphed into a street, a track, a gravel shroud, the long /ou/ sound of "mouth" and "how" is pulled through the "shroud" and subtly echoed by the long /ä/ repeated in "Parks the car." And then there is the /ī/ present in "line," "like," "I'm," "like," and (again) "like." Here, instead of being told or shown we are guided to *hear* the emphasis on comparison, so significant to the ekphrastic project, which necessarily asks such questions as: How does a film like "High Art" compare to life lived? Is it mimetic of the life, folding the construct of its making into the seamless possibility manufactured by a clever editor? In what way might a poem be "like" a film? In what way might they be like life?

While the poem certainly does not answer these questions, it gives guidance at its center. Here are stanzas five and six, which share the exact center of the poem:

> from theory. Sexual configurations
> of glamour. What is the scene?
> what is the cover? The frozen waiting
> for focus and drive.
> Look, look, look. Art is what

looking takes you to. A red mouth
opening to say,
Don't look away.
I'm not usually like this.
The camera sliding by with its aperture

At the heart of these central stanzas are the sentences "Look, look, look. Art is what // looking takes you to." Enjambed over the hinge of white space that separates and connects this centrally placed moment, here we have an anchor, not only for the surrounding poem, but for the book as a whole.

The moment teaches us how to read the poem, for even in isolation, the lines angle out in multiple directions. First, there is the semantic state of the sentences: "Look, look, look" is a command directed both to the speaker of the poem and to the reader, rendering the poem performative. Bang commands "look," and we have to realize that in some important sense, this is precisely what we are doing. To read is to look at letters on a page. To mouth the word "look," thrice, is to speak with the sound of an emphatic blink. It is also to look at images created in the mind's eye— and in the mind's "I." The second sentence is definitional: "Art is what"— suspended over the stanza's hinge of white space, we wait to be told the "what" that it is. The fact that art is a "what" rather than a who or how implies, perhaps, that all looking results in art and that all looking requires the constructive action embodied by art.

Such a combination of narrative and non-narrative modes is significant not only for providing a variety of models for the forms of "living with" art that ekphrastic poetry can provide, but also because it strikes at the heart of the tension between absorption in artifice and insistence upon recognizing a poem's construction. As Jonathan Culler notes in his essay "Why Lyric," the New Critical lyric—and its reception by critics—has encouraged us to think of the lyric in fundamentally narrative terms. He contends that this tradition conceives of the lyric as "a fictional imitation of the act of a speaker, and to interpret the lyric is to work out what sort of person is speaking, in what circumstances and with what attitude or, ideally, drama of attitudes."[21] Such handling of the lyric foregoes thinking about the artifice of language in lieu of a psychological interpretation that is more apt, Culler claims, to works of fiction. This mode of interpretation not only asks lyric to perform as a genre it is entirely unsuited to, but also ignores its fundamental, and traditional, differences from narrative:

Consider what the model of lyric as dramatic monologue misses: stress on the reconstruction of the dramatic situation deprives rhythm and sound patterning of any constitutive role (at best they reinforce or undercut meaning); it devalues intertextual relations, except when they can be assimilated to allusions made by the consciousness dramatized; and it ignores the characteristic extravagance of lyric, which frequently engages in speech acts without a known real-world counterpart.[22]

Culler ends his thoughts with a cry for criticism and pedagogy that revives a mode of study and teaching that foregrounds non-narrative aspects of the lyric, boldly asking us, in the end, to consider the lyric as something expansive enough to contain the absorption of narrative along with punctures of sound and allusion. Books such as Bang's *The Eye Like a Strange Balloon*, which so deftly navigate a range of such aspects, push us to see that such consideration is not only possible, but necessary.

IN MANY respects, *Elegy*, Bang's fifth book, comes as an anomaly in the trajectory formed by her work as it stretches from the circumscribed lyrics of *Apology for Want* to associative gestures, made in poems like "High Art," which continue into her most recent work. Written during the year after the death of her adult son from an accidental overdose, *Elegy* is framed as autobiographical—a framework that Bang refuses to place on her other books. The mask of the persona is taken off, language has been pared down, and the subject of the book is an immediately concrete object: how to contend with loss's grief and guilt, how to forge through the year of darkness that follows. However, if we are persuaded by Bernstein's argument that all acts of language imply artifice, we will read *Elegy* as both emotionally absorptive utterance *and* utterance constructed from the conventions of tradition. Reading the book as such renders the work no less genuine, and viewing it through the lens of Bang's relationship to artifice (rather than focusing solely on its devastating content) allows us to see the way *Elegy* resounds both apart from, and as part of, the trajectory of her work.

Elegy employs many familiar concerns and techniques born of earlier projects. In most respects, the list of themes from *Apology for Want* are revisited here. However, as we will see, those themes are layered with a heightened sense of what is at stake when we engage in representation, and it is not difficult to see this aspect as a development from the work of *The Eye Like a Strange Balloon*. While the mask of persona is off and the poems are spoken in propria persona, Bang still continues to complicate the notion of "speaker" by toggling back and forth between first and third person, rendering utterance now in the voice of "herself," now in the voice that sees itself as an overt object in the distance. Ophelia, Mickey, and Alice are returned to, but where these figures served to highlight the artificiality of visual construction in work such as *The Eye Like a Strange Balloon*, here they might read as contemporary mythological figures, in line with the elegiac tradition's incorporation of myth. Oftentimes the figures stand in as gateway figures between past and present, childhood and adulthood, fiction and reality. For example, in the poem "Don't," Alice appears not as a literary figure, but as a real girl who was turned, by an author, into a literary figure: "Remember the cat Lewis Carroll sent / To look in on Alice at least once a week / As she found what she found // Difficult to decipher. A gesture / Of sympathy, yes, yet nowhere could she find comfort."[23] As with other books, the majority of the poems employ stanzas of equal numbers of lines with heavy enjambment and variable line and sentence length. Theater and film imagery abounds—the phrase "On the screen at the back of the [her] mind" appears in two different poems, "Waiting"[24] and "Intractable, and Irreversible."[25] The poem "Blue Sky Elegy" gives us "The curtain comes down on the handcuffed one,"[26] and in "Enclosure" we get the statement "I can no more understand the world as a stage."[27] Moments of ironic tone resonate with familiarity, though here poems are absent of Bang's lighthearted play of wit. Comparison of moments such as, "For the ash in the box. The love of her life," from the poem "Intractable, and Irreversible,"[28] with lighter-hearted instances of irony evident in her other books allows such moments to doubly sound. The continuity of these gestures across projects—even in the midst of a life-changing event—implies that identity is composed of such action—that who we are depends on our techniques of figuring. As such, the articulations of *Elegy* are always imitations of the conventions of "elegy," and if we want to locate the author, we must look to the signature of gesture and to the way in which she inhabits the conventions—the artifice—of the elegiac mode.

As Peter Sacks outlines in *The English Elegy: Studies in the Genre from Spencer to Yeats*, elegy is "work"—by which he means both a literary product and, in the more dynamic sense, a working through of the grief experience.[29] The site of this work is the space between lived experience and the constructed artifice of language. Bang overtly recognizes this in her poem "The Role of Elegy" where she states that "The role of elegy is / To put a death mask on tragedy,"[30] for elegy is kin to tragedy. As tragedy moves an audience to experience physical and emotional catharsis, elegy moves its maker toward life beyond death. This movement resonates with remarks Bang has made about the necessity for writing these poems. Not intending them for publication, working on the poems literally carried her through grief's year.[31] It is interesting to note that such a stance is just as much a part of the tradition as its other conventions: poems of severe loss seem to require that their writers pen them *as if* it were only the act of writing that is at stake. Just as the elegiac poet must speak in propria persona, the poems must be a performance of not-wanting to perform.

These notions of speaker and intention are only two of many tools of artifice fundamental to elegy's catharsis: One of the central conventions of the elegiac genre is to transform the absent beloved into a symbol. And it is this symbol-making that allows the poem to do its life-work, for only after this transformation is grief accepted, allowing the one grieving to move on.[32] If we consider Mary Jo Bang as a poet of acceptance and resistance—a poet who creates with the tools of the lyric while revealing their artifice—it is this convention—the convention of symbolic figuring, of making artifice—that is most at issue in *Elegy*. Here we find the "enforced accommodation between the mourning self on the one hand and the very words of grief and fictions of consolation on the other."[33] Throughout *Elegy* we see this struggle between poet and material—the need to articulate and a reluctance to use prepackaged language of grief to create a stand-in for her son.

The stakes, here, are quite stunning. On the one hand, to write about the loss of the other is to necessarily render the other into language, fixing the other into a system of symbols, into an aesthetic object. By such fixing, the lost one can be kept, at least in image, as monument. And, according to the elegiac tradition, such fixture is essential for the one in grief to move on. On the other hand, such fixing is problematic, an "aestheticization"

> Of loss, of the unbearable
> Afterimage of the once material.
> To look for an imagined
>
> Consolidation of grief
> So we can all be finished
> Once and for all and genuinely shut up
> The cabinet of genuine particulars.[34]

Here we see a recognition that such consolation is only imaginary, as opposed to actual, in the service of "shutting up" the nagging voice of guilt and grief, of effacing any "genuine" particular that might still attach to the beloved.

"Landscape with the Fall of Icarus" squarely engages these problems of the aesthetic representation of the departed. The poem comes early in the book and illustrates techniques Bang uses to defray the cost of symbolism. In titling the poem after Breugel's painting, which is itself a representation of the story of Daedalus and his son, Bang overtly layers the experience of the poem with the artifice of representation: Bang's poem is ekphrastic of a painting that represents a myth that symbolizes both a son's hubris and a parent's failure to stop catastrophe. The poem begins with a blunt admission to such failure:

> How could I have failed you like this?
> The narrator asks
>
> The object. The object is a box
> Of ashes. How could I not have saved you,

A boy made of bone and blood. A boy
Made of a mind. Of years. A hand

And paint on canvas. A marble carving.
How can I not reach where you are

And pull you back. How can I be
And you not. You're forever on the platform[35]

In addition to its title, the poem directly addresses the act of art making by testing out the equation of "son equals art" with the phrases "A boy / Made of mind. Of years. A hand // And paint on canvas. A marble carving." However, this restless, fragmented listing action shows an inability—or an unwillingness—to settle on an aesthetic form. The poem ends with the desire that a "dolorous day" spent at the museum with her son be "Embedded in amber. / In garnet. In amber. In opal. In order // To keep going on." Here we see a desire to render life into art so as to preserve a last moment, gesturing toward the elegiac tradition of turning the departed into a symbol. However, it is important to note that it is the "dolorous day" that Bang seeks to immortalize in opal artifice—not her son.

Employed here, and evident in other poems, is the blunt, raw, description of the actual physical state of the son as "ash in a box." The relentless reduction and literalism of this phrase resists sentimentality and flies in the face of symbolization. Along these lines, throughout the book Bang takes care to never provide a physical description of her son and resists figuring him in general. We get small remnants such as articles of clothing: "Gray shirt, green pants"[36] and "Unchangeable: that shirt, those summer pants. // That beautiful face." Her son is allowed to speak in the poems, but words are air, echo chamber, and are not at risk for becoming stuck as symbolic figuration. Further, at one moment we think we will get a physical description, but the description folds into parody of symbol. The poem titled "Where Once" enjambs into the first line: "On the street, looking up, there you were" only to turn into the following line: "A single helium balloon, imagine / A flat-face mouse in Mylar."[37] Where we expected to come, at last, face to face with the son, we are given a Mickey Mouse balloon, a parody of a symbolic figure that is supposed, in the elegiac tradition, to take the place of the beloved.

Instead of objectifying her son, throughout *Elegy* Bang objectifies herself. In "Landscape with the Fall of Icarus," we see this in her reference to herself as "the narrator." Along with such gestures, throughout the book she refers to herself in the third person and often renders herself at a distance. In the poem "Intractable, and Irreversible" we get the phrase "I talk / But always to a mirror"[38] and in "Words" the mirror imagery continues with "The self talking to a mirror."[39] In "What Is So Frightening,"

Bang extends the distance implied by the mirror, doubling herself with the use of the third person and speaking of herself in the past tense, as if she is to herself only a distant memory: "There was / Someone like this before, she thought. // Upstanding, blank-faced, red-dressed. / Someone sitting in a box, defining herself / As one with roots."[40] This device reaches its deepest power at the heart of the book, where she figures herself with most distance. In the poem " 'In Order' Means Neat and Not Next" Bang writes, "She was sitting next to herself in a seat / . . . These are my footprints, she thought, / Looking at her feet, Mary Jo's in Mary Janes."[41] Here the distance is twofold; Bang not only figures herself in the third person, but presents this "she" in a moment of objectifying herself, of "sitting next to herself" and naming her feet "Mary Jo's in Mary Janes"—rather than owning them as part of her body.

In one sense we can take this objectification as Bang's desire to put herself in the place of her son—to have died in his place, saving him by taking on the solidity of the object in his name. There is also throughout *Elegy* an overt confession to a death wish—to become, herself, an object alongside her son. In "Words," Bang writes, "I tell them / I wish I could lie under the summer"[42] (note the resonance of Dickinson here), and in "What If" she states, "He'll be obedient and she'll be intractable / And dead. It's all they ever wanted."[43] These moments chart the severity of the emotional moment, and the pressures of refusing to complete the process of grief. Instead of completing the separation between living and dead, life and object, Bang pleads to be as he is, so as to continue on.

If *Elegy* resolves this struggle between the artifice necessary to the grief process and resistance to giving her son over to such surface, it is through the symbol of the poem itself. Here, "poem" is imbued with the act of connection that seeks to communicate across time and space, that seeks to communicate to the self as other as well as to the lost son. As such, the poem, only a symbol, but as such, an apt vehicle, becomes loaded with the weight of the grief process. By transforming the lived, literal mother-son connection, lost with the loss of the son, into a symbolic connection carried on through the body of the poem, Bang does not resolve her grief but navigates it into the arena of the lyric sign called "poem" and "mourning song" and "book" with the sparest of titles, bared bones.

The Bride of E, Bang's sixth book, radiates with what comes after the ends of things, obsessively illuminating the static space that opens after radical fracture. While the book returns to a more overt foregrounding of artifice, it gathers significant resonance if read as poetry that has traversed *Elegy*, for in this book Bang turns to the act of asking existential questions when the finish to the story, on both a personal and cultural level, is already known: "A blackout occurs and then we return to the routine: /

The inhumane blather on the screen."[44] This blackout might stand for the deathly puncture of post-modern theory to lyric transparency, the blow to the American psyche of security that was 9/11, the death of a loved one—any catastrophe that ensures nothing can return to its former state.

Here, among the ruins, Bang asks such questions as "What is there to say" and "What is there to do" now that the postmodern condition—the death of god, the death of the author, the death of lyric subjectivity—has negated the possibility of addressing the existential. The book serves less to answer such questions (for they are ultimately resistant) than to develop tactics for articulating the state of needing to ask. Deeply saturated with the impossibility of such loss, *The Bride of E* assumes a sensibility that seeks significance nevertheless, for as we have seen in "B Is for Beckett," "There is so little to say," a statement that recognizes both the paucity of our post-postmodern condition, and the necessity for pushing into that "little" and saying it. Here we find ourselves inside poems pushing us "forward, into the fog, driving a golf cart, / A tear in the corner of your eye produced / In spite of the ironically undercut temple of truth."[45]

In both form and content the book foregrounds language as vehicle for questioning and organizing thought in this landscape of after. In a space where the narrative of cause and effect has come under suspicion, the book is an abecedarian, arranged according to the alphabet. The titles of the poems are mostly definitional ("C Is for Cher," "B Is for Beckett," etc.), drawing attention to the way in which we are indoctrinated into meaning, for it would be difficult to find an adult who grew up in the United States without having spent his or her grammar school years learning that "A is for Apple," via a poster—featuring a brightly reddened apple—pinned to the schoolroom wall. By remembering the way we have been educated into language—through definition, memorization, and recitation—we can see that the concept of the dyadic sign is strictly banned (at least until college) and we are taught that a letter is part of a fundamental system wherein words equal objects out in the world. By employing this system and assigning more than one word to many letters in the alphabet (for example, "F Is for Forgetting" is followed by the titles "For Freud" and "For the Final Report"), Bang brings our attention to our own indoctrination and provides a method by which we might—through poetry—still manage to indoctrinate ourselves otherwise.

Further, Bang divides the book into two sections according to form. The first section, which at seventy-two pages takes the bulk of the eighty-five-page book, is composed of lineated verse and most often employs Bang's signature fixed-line stanza and heavy enjambment. The second section of the book is composed of five prose poems that feature a more autobiographical intonation than the rest of the work. And, although there is continuity in linguistic texture across sections, the division implies that different forms afford accentuation of different content. By dividing her book in this way, Bang proposes that prose—and the blur of image and sound run together without the advantage of the line break—is the texture of the private self in existential question. And, by giving this private self only a little more than ten pages, she invites us to question what constitutes the bulk of our being: the quotidian, communal realm of language that, though valenced by individual experience, is shared; or the private self? In many ways it is ironic that Bang gives the more public, socially oriented section the lineation conventional of the lyric, and the private self—so long the territory of the tradition—the form of prose.

This notion that contemporary existential crisis is not a private condition but one born and felt through the individual inextricably intertwined with the public discourse of language, again evokes Samuel Beckett—the master of continuing on when one cannot. In *The Theater of the Absurd*, Martin Esslin characterizes the way that such sensibility embodies the difficulty of language to express such a state, and his description, though of Beckett and of theater, is apt for the tensions Bang explores in the book:

> "anyone" who speaks is carried along by the logic of language and its articulation. Thus the writer who pits himself against the unsayable must use all his cunning so as not to say what the words make him say against his will, but to express instead what by their very nature they are designed to cover up: the uncertainty, the contradictory, the unthinkable.[46]

In response to such impossibility of expression, Bang relies on a cast of worn-out cultural icons, giving them lines of existential angst and questioning that can no longer be authentically asked. The book is populated with figures such as Mickey Mouse, Alice from Wonderland, Clark Kent, Jackie O, and Pee-Wee Herman. Accompanying them are Freud, Plato, Ophelia, Hamlet, and Eve, suggesting that icons of both high and low culture have been emptied of gravity but, as such, offer useful masks for articulating subjective searching that the poet cannot perform as herself. For example, in "C Is for Cher," one of the first poems written for the book, Bang has Cher and Mickey say things that a contemporary poet is unable to say without sounding saccharine. Cher enters the beginning of the poem:

> Culture miniature and clad as Cleopatra, she descends
> A set of semicircular steps
> Tiled in a geometric mosaic pattern
>
> And there she finds the answer: everything
> Changes depending on whether
> You're up or down. Behind her,
>
> A high-relief rectangle proscenium,
> Beside her, whatever intrigued her last.[47]

By setting the arrival at "the answer" in such a context, Bang is able to offer both a maxim that would sound unconvincing in an unmediated voice, and a critique of such (un)easy truths. Cher is clearly in the context of a stage set, and we cannot miss the irony of finding "the answer" in the mouth of Cher, made up as a faux Cleopatra, framed by a proscenium. Such answers may feel portentous in the moment, but are predestined to be discarded along with other things that "intrigued her last." The remarkable thing about such moments in Bang's work is that, while undercutting the seriousness of the answer, they don't negate the sense that such answers have a glimmer of wisdom: Things *do* change depending on whether you're up or down. Rather than casting such answers out as impossibly trivial, Bang layers the statement with the artificiality of cultural context, drawing attention to the way in which we are conditioned to trust and distrust such utterance.

Diving ever more deeply into the contemporary condition of postmodern artifice, Bang also navigates the problem of existential questioning by addressing the issue of language directly. For example, in "And as in Alice," Alice from Wonderland is redeployed, but this time she is rejected (or, rather, she absents herself from the poem) as an adequate symbol:

> Alice cannot be in the poem, she says, because
> She's only a metaphor for childhood
> And a poem is a metaphor already
> So we'd only have a metaphor
>
> Inside a metaphor. Do you see?
> They all nod. They see. Except for the girl
> With her head in the rabbit hole. . . .[48]

Here Bang marvelously and effectively navigates the problem of worn-out artifice. She deals with the issue directly: We know that Alice doesn't exist, that she is just a literary/cultural metaphor. Further, when we compare contemporary evocation of Alice with Carroll's complex philosophical and political landscape, we see how shallowly we evoke such symbols in contemporary culture. However, the fact that Alice has been such a reliable figure throughout Bang's work makes her refusal to appear have enormous impact. Alice was there in *The Eye Like a Strange Balloon*, shoring up the ruins of representation. In *Elegy*, she appears to remind both speaker and reader of the complicated literary tradition of turning children—one's own and others—into characters. Now, when we call on her again, she refuses to appear. She "cannot be in the poem." What does she mean, she cannot be in the poem? By using a specific figure, such as Alice—and a figure that the reader of Bang's work has history with—Bang is able to enact the intellectual and emotional impact of what, in the work of even the most inventive of postmodern theorists, comes across as speculative rather than felt.

The engine of this impact takes place most often in the form of unanswerable questions. In this way, the poems take up the tradition of the New Critical lyric, which foregrounds the concept of a speaker overheard, that is to say, of somebody speaking before a hidden audience. Take, for example, the poem "In the Present and Probable Future," a poem that begins with a bird's-eye view of things—"Here we are viewing the land: waves of grave and grain"—and arcs, over thirty lines later, into a post-apocalyptic moment where all that is left is "that unsullied moment, down to the last // Detail, when the acquired interview and other quaint signs of demise / Will speak about us to the flood and the fire."[49] With all of its beauty and stylization (such as the sentence "Cormorants on pitched roofs watch the ship of state mandate folded / twice over"), this is a speakerly poem that also encompasses colloquial phrases such as "Good luck with that," giving us the feeling of being talked to or of overhearing a grandiloquent monologue. However, it is important to note that the speaker, here, is not an "I" overheard but a "we." This punctures the domain of the New Critical lyric, so very centered around the individual, and asks that we reconsider what constitutes a speaker. Here the speaker is not so much an individual subjectivity, but the part of the self that engages in collective idea-making and action that is not separable from our modes of figuring—as the commonly used colloquial phrase "Good luck with that" proposes—but is part and parcel of it.

Furthermore, within this arc Bang asks sixteen questions ranging from "When should we accept that life is only / An exaggerated form of special pleading, romanticized // Beyond saying into moon, stone, flock and trees?" to "What does it mean to have a point of view? What does it mean / To have a notable achievement? To succeed in representing // The nuances of a determinate activity?"[50] Such questions encompass concerns that span from the generally existential to those that address the tradition of the lyric itself, for what is the New Critical lyric but success "in representing // The nuances of a determinate activity"—a "romanticized" "saying into moon, stone, flock and trees"? By commenting on the conventions of the poem from within the poem, Bang asks us to engage the poem as artifice while at the same time being swept up with the sincerity of its articulations: "Listen," the poet says, about halfway through the poem, "however events turn out, if we want we can continue to see // The image of the moon as an outburst of lyric, a vision of John Keats / And his friends, but we still have the battle to fight." Part of that battle, the poem contends, is seeing the moon not only as an outburst of lyric, but as an outburst that was constructed by a poetic tradition—and that is no less valuable for such a recognition, even though it asks us to remember that the moon we view is not only an object seen through a telescope, but also an image created with language.

BY foregrounding artifice, Bang not only mines tensions within the lyric tradition and between experimental and conventional notions of poem-making—but also foregrounds the tension between reading and writing. In many cases, Bang's attention to artifice asks the reader to be flexible and to do connective work, actively recognizing allusions across and beyond her books, recognizing that the poet stands, in most instances, just off-stage, channeling her voice through various masks. These actions of noticing, connecting, and questioning are demanded by the poems, and are principle ways in which these poems mean.

Increasing emphasis on engaging active readers leads to a question of where "the lyric," and its meaning, reside. Is the lyric in the poem itself, or is it in the eye of its beholder? Literary critics such as Paul de Man and Virginia Jackson propose that lyric is born in the process of reading. De Man takes this up as proof that there is no such thing as a lyric in and of itself, for, as he has famously stated, "no lyric can be read lyrically, nor can the object of a lyrical reading be itself a lyric."[51] Jackson arrives at similar ends by taking the opposite tactic and shows in her work on Emily Dickinson that "New Critical readings of texts like [Dickinson's] 'Further in Summer than the Birds' created an abstract personification in place of the historical person, and consequently created an abstract genre accessible to all persons educated to read lyrically."[52] Lyric, then, is a readerly, editorial lens, and we might more productively classify strategies of "lyric reading" rather than look for lyric in poetic works.

Far from opposing this idea, Bang's poetry renders these energies generative, not only by asking readers to engage in "lyric reading" that employs and challenges New Critical assumptions, but also by practicing a type of "lyric reading" that leaves lyric objects in her wake. Two recent projects that postdate *The Bride of E*—a "slant" translation of Dante's *Inferno* which will be published by Graywolf in 2012, and a series of poems that "write through" *Mrs. Dalloway*, using only the words from Woolf's text to construct new poems—extend Bang's investment in language-as-source, deriving new texts from other's works. For example, in "Opened and Shut," from the Dalloway series, we see Bang's heroine in a wholly different manner than we ever see Woolf's, despite the fact that Bang's poem is constructed of Woolf's words: "Beautifully close up. And once, flames / eating the edge of the sofa. // Her eyelashes blurred. Chin, nose, forehead, / some lips."[53] Here, again, Bang absorbs us into the moment of her poem: Engaged in a dream of imaginative looking, transfixed by the conflagration, we are led to wonder if the blurring figure is woman or doll. At the same time, we might marvel at the art of such a construct: How does Bang manage to excise and weld such a scene from the monument of Woolf's text? Such activity turns ever further into the material surface of language, exploring the way in which re-contextualization affects the sign, and the way in which attaching words to new signification overwrites, but does not efface, previous inscription. Indeed, here we are shown once again: Art is what looking takes us to.

NOTES TO CRITICAL ESSAY

1. Mary Jo Bang, *The Bride of E* (Minneapolis, MN: Graywolf Press, 2009), 5.

2. Mary Jo Bang, *The Eye Like a Strange Balloon* (New York: Grove Press, 2004), 12.

3. See Moma.org for images from 1997 exhibition, sponsored by Madonna, of Moma's collection of stills: www.moma.org/interactives/exhibitions/1997/Sherman (accessed May 30, 2010).

4. Northrop Frye, *Anatomy of Criticism* (New York, 1965), 249.

5. Charles Bernstein, "Artifice of Absorption," in *A Poetics* (Cambridge, MA: Harvard University Press, 1992), 29.

6. Helen Vendler, "Introduction to The Harvard Book of Contemporary American Poetry," quoted in Charles Bernstein, "Artifice of Absorption," in *A Poetics* (Cambridge, MA: Harvard University Press, 1992), 41.

7. Susan Schultz, " 'Called Null or Called Vocative': A Fate of Contemporary Lyric." *Talisman* 14 (1996): 70.

8. Bang, *The Bride of E*, 7.

9. Samuel Beckett, *Ohio Impromptu*, in *Three Plays* (New York: Grove Press, 1984),

10. Bernstein, "Artifice of Absorption," 10.

11. Stephen Burt, "My Name Is Henri," in *Close Calls with Nonsense* (Saint Paul, MN: Graywolf Press, 2009), 138.

12. Mary Jo Bang, *The Downstream Extremity of the Isle of Swans* (Athens: University of Georgia Press, 2004), 25.

13. Ibid., 12.

14. Ibid., 31.

15. Mary Jo Bang, "Interview with Mary Jo Bang" by Jennifer K. Dick. Poets.org, www.poets.org/m/dsp_poem.php?prmMID=19940 (accessed May 24, 2011).

16. Donna Stonecipher, review of *The Eye Like a Strange Balloon*. *Verse Magazine* online, http://versemag.blogspot.com/2006/02/new-review-of-mary-jo-bang.html (accessed May 23, 2010).

17. Kellery, Lyn, "Poems Living with Paintings: Cole Swensen's Ekphrastic Try." *Contemporary Literature* 46, no. 2 (summer 2005), 180.

18. Mary Jo Bang, *The Eye Like a Strange Balloon*, 25.

19. Mary Jo Bang, "Interview with Mary Jo Bang" by Jennifer K. Dick.

20. Mary Jo Bang, *The Eye Like a Strange Balloon*, 13.

21. Jonathan Culler, "Why Lyric?" *MLA* 123, no. 1 (2008), 201.

22. Ibid., 202.

23. Mary Jo Bang, *Elegy* (Saint Paul, MN: Graywolf Press, 2007), 35.

24. Ibid., 10.

25. Ibid., 51.

26. Ibid., 50.

27. Ibid., 21.

28. Ibid., 51.

29. Peter Sacks, *The English Elegy* (Baltimore, MD: Johns Hopkins University Press, 1985), 2.

30. Bang, *Elegy*, 63.

31. Personal correspondence.

32. Sacks, *English Elegy*, 5.

33. Ibid., 2.

34. Bang, *Elegy*, 63.

35. Ibid., 24.

36. Ibid., 10.

37. Ibid., 66.

38. Ibid., 51.

39. Ibid., 54.

40. Ibid., 15.

41. Ibid., 49.

42. Ibid., 54.

43. Ibid., 56.

44. Bang, *Elegy*, 15.

45. Ibid., 29.

46. Martin Esslin, *The Theater of the Absurd*, (New York: Vintage Books, 2004), 38.

47. Bang, *The Bride of E*, 9.

48. Ibid., 6.

49. Ibid., 46–47.

50. Ibid.

51. Paul de Man, "Anthropomorphism and Trope in the Lyric," in *The Rhetoric of Romanticism* (New York: Columbia University Press, 1984), 254.

52. Virginia Jackson, *Dickinson's Misery: A Theory of Lyric Reading* (Princeton, NJ: Princeton University Press, 2005), 100.

53. Mary Jo Bang, *Let's Say Yes* (New York: Handheld Editions, 2011).

BIBLIOGRAPHY

Books by Mary Jo Bang

Apology for Want. Hanover, NH: University Press of New England/Middlebury College Press, 1997.

Louise in Love. New York: Grove/Atlantic Press, 2001.

The Downstream Extremity of the Isle of Swans. Athens: University of Georgia Press, 2001.

The Eye Like a Strange Balloon. New York: Grove/Atlantic Press, 2004.

Elegy. St. Paul, MN: Graywolf Press, 2007.

The Bride of E. Saint Paul, MN: Graywolf Press, 2009.

Dante's Inferno: A New Version. Saint Paul, MN: Graywolf Press, 2012.

Chapbooks

Her Head in a Rabbit Hole. New York: Delirium Press, 2006.
Let's Say Yes. Brooklyn, NY: Handheld Editions, 2011.

Bilingual Editions

Elegia (Elegy), bilingual edition, Spanish/English, translation and prologue by Jaime Priede. Madrid, Spain: Bartleby Editores, 2010.
Eskapaden. Gedichte (Escapades: Poems), bilingual edition, German/English. Weisbaden, Germany: Lux Books, 2010.

Selected Interviews

With Susie DeFord, "Mary Jo Bang: The Bride of Alliteration," *Bomb Magazine*, October 5, 2009, www.bombsite.com (accessed May 27, 2010).
With Jennifer K. Dick, "The World Anew: Mary Jo Bang and Jennifer K. Dick in Conversation," *Verse* 22, no. 1 (2005).
With Vincent Guerra, "Mary Jo Bang: Interviewed by Vincent Guerra," *Southeast Review*, February 1, 2010.
With Jennifer Kronovet, "A Talk with Mary Jo Bang," *Stop Smiling Magazine*, no. 34 (March 2008).

Selected Criticism

Ashley, Renée. Review of *The Bride of E. Literary Review* 53, no. 3 (Spring 2010): 218–26.
Bar-Nadav, Hadara. "A Little Light: Mary Jo Bang and the State of the Elegy." *New Letters* 74, no. 4 (2008): 207.
Bar-Nadav, Hadara. "Sex with an Effigy." *American Book Review* 27, no. 1 (November/December 2005): 28–29.
Bendall, Molly. Review of *Louise in Love. Prairie Schooner* 77, no. 3 (Fall 2003): 185–88.
Biespiel, David. "Free-Verse Styles." *Sewanee Review* 111, no. 3 (Summer 2003): 470–79.
Burt, Stephen. "My Name Is Henri: Contemporary Poets Discover John Berryman." In *Close Calls with Nonsense: Reading New Poetry*. Saint Paul, MN: Graywolf Press, 2009: 129–43.
Cihlar, James. Review of *The Bride of E. Coldfront Magazine*, January 28, 2010, http://coldfrontmag.com/tag/mary-jo-bang (accessed May 28, 2010).
Etter, Carrie. "No Comfort." *Times Literary Supplement* (*TLS*) (London), March 6, 2009, 25.
Fischer, Barbara. "Object Relations." *Boston Review*, September/October 2005, http://bostonreview.net/BR30.5/fischer.php (accessed June 23, 2010).
Kelsey, Karla. Review of *The Bride of E. Constant Critic*, ConstantCritic.com, June 27, 2010, www.constantcritic.com/karla_kelsey/the-bride-of-e (accessed July 2, 2010).
Kirby, David. "Books in Brief Fiction & Poetry: 'Give Me Rapture and Bliss.'" *New York Times Book Review*, March 4, 2001, 23.

Neely, Mark. "Gestures Toward the Universe." *Jacket Magazine*, no. 16 (March 2002), www.jacketmagazine.com/16/neely.html (accessed July 2, 2010).

Orr, David. "In Memoriam." *New York Times Book Review*, March 30, 2008, 6.

Rauschenbusch, Stephanie. "Radical Originality." *American Book Review* 23 (July/August 2002): 18.

Sadoff, Ira. "Flat Death': Irretrievable Loss in Three Contemporary Poets." *Kenyon Review* 31, no. 3 (summer 2009): 188–99.

Solomon, Laura. Review of *Louise in Love*. *Verse* 18 (2001): 189–90.

Stonecipher, Donna. Review of *The Eye Like a Strange Balloon*. *Verse Magazine* (online edition), http://versemag.blogspot.com/2006/02/new-review-of-mary-jo-bang.html (accessed February 9, 2006).

Treseler, Heather. "Demeter's Song." *Notre Dame Review*, 26 (Summer/Fall 2008): 237–45.

LUCILLE CLIFTON

FROM *Good Woman: Poems and a Memoir 1969–1980*

the light that came to Lucille Clifton
came in a shift of knowing
when even her fondest sureties
faded away. it was the summer
she understood that she had not understood
and was not mistress even
of her own off eye. then
the man escaped throwing away his tie and
the children grew legs and started walking and
she could see the peril of an
unexamined life.
she closed her eyes, afraid to look for her
authenticity
but the light insists on itself in the world;
a voice from the nondead past started talking,
she closed her ears and it spelled out in her hand
"you might as well answer the door, my child,
the truth is furiously knocking."

eve's version

smooth talker
slides into my dreams
and fills them with apple
apple snug as my breast
in the palm of my hand
apple sleek apple sweet
and bright in my mouth

it is your own lush self
you hunger for
he whispers   lucifer
honey-tongue.

lucifer speaks in his own voice

sure as i am
of the seraphim
folding wing
so am i certain of a
graceful bed
and a soft caress
along my long belly
at endtime   it was
to be
i who was called son
if only of the morning
saw that some must
walk or all will crawl

so slithered into earth
and seized the serpent in
the animals   i became
the lord of snake for
adam and for eve
i   the only lucifer
light-bringer
created out of fire
illuminate i could
and so
illuminate i did

FROM *The Book of Light*

daughters

woman who shines at the head
of my grandmother's bed,
brilliant woman, i like to think
you whispered into her ear
instructions. i like to think
you are the oddness in us,
you are the arrow
that pierced our plain skin
and made us fancy women;
my wild witch gran, my magic mama,
and even these gaudy girls.
i like to think you gave us
extraordinary power and to
protect us, you became the name
we were cautioned to forget.

it is enough,
you must have murmured,
to remember that i was
and that you are. woman, i am
lucille, which stands for light,
daughter of thelma, daughter
of georgia, daughter of
dazzling you.

won't you celebrate with me
what i have shaped into
a kind of life? i had no model.
born in babylon
both nonwhite and woman
what did i see to be except myself?
i made it up
here on this bridge between
starshine and clay,
my one hand holding tight
my other hand; come celebrate
with me that everyday
something has tried to kill me
and has failed.

leda 1

there is nothing luminous
about this.
they took my children.
i live alone in the backside
of the village.
my mother moved
to another town. my father
follows me around the well,
his thick lips slavering,
and at night my dreams are full
of the cursing of me
fucking god fucking me.

leda 3

a personal note (re: visitations)
always pyrotechnics;
stars spinning into phalluses
of light, serpents promising
sweetness, their forked tongues
thick and erect, patriarchs of bird
exposing themselves in the air.
this skin is sick with loneliness.
You want what a man wants,
next time come as a man,
or don't come.

telling our stories

the fox came every evening to my door
asking for nothing. my fear
trapped me inside, hoping to dismiss her
but she sat till morning, waiting.

at dawn we would, each of us,
rise from our haunches, look through the glass
then walk away.

did she gather her village around her
and sing of the hairless moon face,
the trembling snout, the ignorant eyes?

child, i tell you now it was not
the animal blood i was hiding from,
it was the poet in her, the poet and
the terrible stories she could tell.

FROM *Mercy*

the river between us

in the river that your father fished
my father was baptized.   it was
their hunger that defined them,

one, a man who knew he could
feed himself if it all came down,
the other a man who knew he needed help.

this is about more than color. it is
about how we learn to see ourselves.
it is about geography and memory.

it is about being poor people
in america.   it is about my father
and yours and you and me and
the river that is between us.

FROM *Voices*

sorrows

who would believe them winged
who would believe they could be

beautiful   who would believe
they could fall so in love with mortals

that they would attach themselves
as scars attach and ride the skin

sometimes we hear them in our dreams
rattling their skulls   clicking

their bony fingers
they have heard me beseeching

as i whispered into my own
cupped hands   enough   not me again

but who can distinguish
one human voice

amid such choruses
of desire

POETICS STATEMENT

Excerpts from an Interview with Charles Rowell[1]

. . . A PERSON CAN, I hope, enjoy the poetry without knowing that I am
black or female. But it adds to their understanding if they do know it—
that is, that I am black and female. To me, that I am what I am is *all* of it;
all of what I am is relevant. Do you know what I mean?

All understandings of language involve more than the dictionary defini-
tion of a word. So the more one knows about who is using the word, the
more the reader brings to a fuller understanding of what is meant. Com-
munication involves not only definition but also nuance, sound, history,
baggage, culture, even generation and gender and race. A reader can relate
to a poem on some level, knowing little about the writer, but the more one
knows, the more one understands. Walt Whitman saying "i hear America
singing" made it necessary for Langston Hughes to remind, "I too sing
America," not so much because of what the writer might have understood
but because of what Langston Hughes guessed about the reader.

. . . I say to students all the time that either/or is not an African tradition.
Both/and is tradition. I don't believe in either/or. I believe in both/and. So
my "I" tends to be both me Lucille and the me that stands for people who
look like me, and the me that is also human, you know. I think if I distin-
guish anything, there's a distinction between what I look like on the out-
side and what somebody else does, and what we are on the inside. So it's
me as the outside and me as the inside. . . . What I'm writing is also history.
And some of it is the history of the inside of us; and some of it is the his-
tory of the outside.

Poetry is about more than logic. Poetry, it seems to me . . . comes from
both intellect and intuition. One doesn't separate oneself out. It's not ei-
ther/or; it's both/and again. And so if I write, I must write out of the whole
of what I am. . . . in writing poems, of course, I have to use my intellect.
But that's not all that I use. I use intuition. I even use fear, you know.

[Laughter] I try to use everything that I am. Now, in the academy—and I can talk about creative writing programs, I teach in them—one tends to think of poetry as not only an intellectual exercise but one that's just for the eyes. Does it look like a poem? Must be a poem. But I'm interested in other questions: Does it sound like a poem? Does it feel like a poem? Does it tell as much of the whole truth about being human as it can? Because the whole truth is that we're not all just our head and what we think. Logic is very useful; so is feeling.

LUCILLE CLIFTON'S COMMUNAL "i"

Adrienne McCormick

> who can distinguish
> one human voice
>
> amid such choruses
> of desire[1]

READING Lucille Clifton's work demands of her literary critics attention to four decades of poetic production, and to the cultural contexts of those decades. Her first book of poems, *Good Times*, was published in 1969, and her most recent, *Voices*, was published in 2008. Clifton's poems are fully engaged in her times, reflecting conversations with the Civil Rights and Black Arts movements; the movement of feminist poetries through issues relating to the body, sexuality, family, and revisionist mythmaking; shifting questions raised by confessional poetics and identity politics, multiculturalism, and critical race studies; environmentalist concerns manifested in environmental literature and ecofeminist thought; struggles with language, meaning, history, and subjectivity associated with African American postmodernity; and an abiding attention to spirituality as a force for change in contemporary society. Throughout these decades, Clifton has been publishing work that challenges conventional assumptions about the lyric subject. What Clifton produces throughout her career is a multilayered communal "i," rather than an authoritative, individual "I," and a complex vision of lyric subjectivity as constructed, contingent, and communal rather than essential, consistent, or coherent. In her poems, subjectivity is dispersed across first-, second-, and third-person pronouns, and her poems consistently explore what it means for an "i" to consider itself, its relations to others, and its ability to commune with those others. Thus, Clifton's work challenges contemporary readers to consider the complexities of a lyric "i" and to refuse the generalizations and dichotomies that too frequently characterize our understanding of it. Contemporary American poetry, for example, is often categorized into groups revealing either a refusal of a theoretically unsophisticated lyric "I," or an embrace of a simplistic lyric "I" denoting a fixed, coherent identity.[2] Arguing against such dichotomies, Kinereth Meyer argues that "the lyric I oscillates between 'breaking out' of the text's semantic topography and embedding itself within the same topography, identifying itself in language and losing itself in it like an object."[3] Clifton's lyric "i"—and it is always lower-case—reveals just such an oscillation, as she explores the abiding importance of the speaking voice—what Meyer terms "a ghost of orality"[4]—and the degree to which that voice and the self it is connected to are "made up"—signs of writing, figuration, and "the fictionality of the utterance."[5]

Indeed, Clifton's "i" does more than just move back and forth between these tendencies—toward speaking and writing, utterance and artifice—but crafts a multidirectional communal mode of articulation rooted in the both/and thinking that typifies feminist and African American ways of knowing. Rachel Blau DuPlessis argues for both/and vision as a key trait of feminist aesthetics, identifying it as "the end of the either/or dichotomized universe. . . . Structurally, such a writing might say different things, not settle on one, which is final."[6] What Clifton's work demands of her readers is a "geometry of knowing" that leaves simple categorizations behind, and seeks out the palimpsestic qualities of her work.[7] Clifton embraces both/and thinking—perhaps even both/and/and thinking—identifying it as not only feminist but profoundly rooted in her African American articulations as well, stating, "either/or is not an African tradition. Both/and is tradition. I don't believe in either/or. I believe in both/and."[8] What results is an approach to lyric subjectivity that refuses consistency or limitation. Clifton embraces neither a theoretically sanctioned articulation of lyric subjectivity, nor a consistently self-referential, confessional "I." She creates room for readers to move beyond binaries, and explore lyric subjectivity in a more particular manner. In the following, I first explore how Clifton's use of the poetic "i" is rooted in feminist, African American, and American multiethnic articulations of destabilized selves, and then provide readings of three ways in which she crafts a communal "i" and produces complex lyric subjectivities. First, I examine the "i" poems where she writes overtly as Lucille Clifton and explores "shifts in knowing" and contingent knowledges of self and family history as central to her complication of poetic subjectivity. Next, I explore her "other" personas—poems where she ostensibly inhabits the consciousness of the other, the most common way of complicating the poetic "i" by having it resonate both as poet/speaker and someone overtly named as other. These poems frequently include male others and Biblical personas, a key subcategory of "other" persona poems to which Clifton has returned throughout her career to probe the communal aspects of spiritual and artistic identities. Finally, I turn to the poems in which she moves beyond the communal voice to a voice that communes in a spiritual sense with nonhuman others, including animals and disembodied spirits, constantly undermining notions of poetic identity and self as rooted in individualism, fixity, or authority.

Clifton's Communal "i" and Feminist, African American, and Multiethnic Theorizing

One of Clifton's early readers, Alicia Ostriker, comments that women poets use an "I" that is not necessarily the abstract speaker that traditional, New Critical responses to poetry expect readers to assume: "When a woman poet today says 'I,' she is likely to mean herself. . . . It is the fact that the question of identity is a real one, for which the thinking woman has no answer, that turns her resolutely inward."[9] While using Ostriker's comment to explore a communal "I" may seem contradictory, her point is pertinent here for the manner in which she develops our understanding of the woman poet's "I" as a challenge to singular understandings and articulations of identity. In *Stealing the Language: The Emergence of Women's Poetry in America*, Ostriker qualifies the exploration of self in women's poetry, pointing out how women's articulations of self are frequently rooted in communal imaginings. Clifton's use of persona—mentioned only briefly in Ostriker's broad survey of American women poets—bears out many of Ostriker's observations and deserves further exploration from our vantage point today. Women's poetry, Ostriker argues, enacts "a subversion of the identification of self with ego as bounded form committed to preserving its boundaries, and begins to propose an alternative scheme of larger units wherein the self is plural, a spinning array of multiple selves." The female "I," Ostriker continues, can "perceive itself as composed of its parents, extended in its children, vitalized by powers of spiritual ancestresses, determined to identify with and redeem the defeated, and engaged in a communal drama denoted by the omnipresent 'we' of shared desire."[10] Clifton corroborates this concept, stating that "my 'I' tends to be both me Lucille and the me that stands for people who look like me, and the me that is also human."[11] Thus, Clifton's communal "i" has as one of its roots the multiple selves articulated in American women's poetry.

Clifton's exploration of a multiple poetic subjectivity is deeply informed by African American literary explorations of selfhood as well. African American thought has attended to the need for multiple articulations of the self since its origins, rich evidence of which we can see in the numerous explorations of signifying as a practice that draws attention to multiple modes of telling, speaking, or singing any story or narrative of the self.[12] Clifton's communal "i," her "we" speakers, her complex poetic subjects on the whole display a refusal of authority, fixity, and essence and embrace contingency, open-endedness, and fluidity. Indeed, in going beyond the familiar position of the singular voice, her poems refigure African American call-and-response oral structures, where the audience's presence determines the very possibility of articulation, demanding dialogic representations of self and validating communal ways of knowing over Western individualism. Finally, her poetry also embraces African American historiography and its roots in multiple, communal forms of telling stories about pasts too often lost to history, or devalued for their communal structures.

Clifton's communal "i" also engages with a broader dialogue regarding lyric and its articulations of the self in U.S. multiethnic poets who struggle with questions of identity, authenticity, and poetic subjectivity. Asian American poet John Yau writes: "I do not believe in the lyric I—the single modulating voice that names itself and others in an easily consumable narrative." But neither does he "subscribe to the death of the author, the postmodern belief that there is no self writing. That injunction is the most recent way for the academy to silence the Other, keep the Other from speaking and writing . . . I—the I writes—will not be spoken for."[13] Rather, Yau approaches writing as "a way of staying open to the flux. Writing as an attempt to hear the Other, the Others. Writing as a form of attention and responsibility."[14] Jeannine Thyreen-Mizingou positions Clifton in a cohort of contemporary American poets whose poems "assert responsibility for the other, as opposed to typical American individualization," and exhibit a paradigm that is rooted in grace and ethics and situated as part of a "plural discourse" that resists "monistic impulses."[15] Clifton's career consistently demonstrates the attention and responsibility to other voices that Yau emphasizes as central to the writing process, and the key role of a communal voice that Thyreen-Mizingou defines as crucial for contemporary American poets who question the limitations of American individualism at the turn of the 21st century.[16]

Having said this, though, it is important to also point out the dangers of stereotyping or essentializing any of the poetic tactics I refer to in the preceding and thus reproducing the very limiting approaches to poetic subjectivity that I seek to challenge. Through my argument, I do not mean to essentialize women poets or poets of color in any particular way as uniquely transcending self-referentiality or a naive "I" through political contexts, nor to posit conversely that "mainstream" poets writing with a self-referential "I" are all necessarily naive, uninteresting, or unsophisticated either. Rather, with this reading of Clifton, I seek to broaden the spectrum of what an "I" in contemporary poetry can mean, thus allowing us to complicate our thinking about lyric subjectivity more broadly.

Clifton's i

In the poems in which she refers to herself as Lucille Clifton—sometimes in the first person, and sometimes in the third—we see a vision of identity that is communal, produced in relations of power, and portrayed as specific and contingent. These poems reveal an approach to identity that neither celebrates a false coherence nor dismisses the "I" as a bankrupt literary convention. Beginning in her collection *Two-Headed Woman* (1980),[17] and most evident in *The Book of Light* (1993), Clifton has written poems that use a concept of "light"—a reference to new understandings—to question how she portrays and constructs her own identity. These poems frequently refer to light, since "Lucille" stands for light and for self-knowledge. The self-knowledge that Clifton constructs is not a fixed approach to her identity, but one that "reflects" its shifts, its multiple facets, its unsureness. The collection *Two-Headed Woman* begins with an untitled poem that links two-headedness with a "turning" toward the "light," to enable a different understanding of self and identity:

> following the Light
> see the sensational
> two-headed woman
> one face turned outward
> one face
> swiveling slowly in. (*GW*, 185)

Clifton's "two-headed woman" symbolizes the regenerativity of identity. The "two-headed woman's" slow turn marks the process by which Clifton begins to examine her identity as a black woman in a different way. In an untitled poem in the same collection, Clifton further characterizes this moment of turning by emphasizing how everything she once thought she knew about herself becomes unfamiliar:

> the light that came to Lucille Clifton
> came in a shift of knowing
> when even her fondest sureties
> faded away. it was the summer
> she understood that she had not understood
> and was not mistress even
> of her own off eye. (*GW*, 209)

The poem refers directly to the poet in the first line, but the identity the poem explores is not fixed or coherent. She writes of her self in the third person, and writes about the loss of "her fondest sureties." Clifton's poems theorize approaches to identity that require a "shift of knowing" from accepted, stereotypical concepts of identity that are usually rooted in the erasure of specific histories to an unknown, fearful, yet unavoidable search for new understandings of "authenticity." She describes her own experiences with this shift in the following lines from the same poem:

> she closed her eyes, afraid to look for her
> authenticity
> but the light insists on itself in the world;
> a voice from the nondead past started talking,
> she closed her ears and it spelled out in her hand
> "you might as well answer the door, my child,
> the truth is furiously knocking." (GW, 209)

The "light" signifies her "authenticity," but this is not a fixed authenticity. It springs from the "nondead past," another constant motif in Clifton's work. That past is the specific family history that lives in Clifton, which provides her the light by which she searches out her own sense of authenticity.[18] Rather than producing an essentialized understanding of self, Clifton emphasizes the contingency of self, a radical particularity that many feminist theorists have embraced in their refusal to adopt depoliticized, disempowered versions of the death of subjectivity. By extension, Clifton models a way of reading lyric subjectivity that defies the easy binaries that characterize discussions of lyric subjectivity.

Clifton redefines "authenticity" and considers the particularity of her self in several other poems in *The Book of Light*, ten of which address Clifton's ancestors, her personal growth in their "light," and her own children. These family history poems portray the family specificities that Clifton sees as particularly shaping her "authenticity." In "Daughters," Clifton records her maternal lineage from her great-grandmother, who was a midwife, to herself. She writes to her great-grandmother, "i like to think / you are the oddness in us" (13). Her unnamed great grandmother is portrayed as a source of strength for the manner in which she differentiates her "daughters" from others:

> i like to think you gave us
> extraordinary power and to
> protect us, you became the name
> we were cautioned to forget. (BL, 13)

Here Clifton shifts her approach, and in concluding the poem, does not name the great-grandmother she refers to—who shares her own name, Lucille. Not naming paradoxically allows for a more specific understanding of her—an empowering alternative for the racially marked speaker who is so often understood to speak for the entire race or ethnic group:

> it is enough,
> you must have murmured,
> to remember that i was
> and that you are. woman, i am
> lucille, which stands for light,
> daughter of thelma, daughter
> of georgia, daughter of
> dazzling you. (*BL*, 13)

Clifton insists on the presence and existence of the self—"i was," "you are," and "i am" weave through the lines—and yet, through their particularity, avoids essentializing identity as fixed or knowable by a single element, such as a name or an identifiable race. Family lineage is part of a magic weave of elements that produce the contingent presence that Clifton repeatedly summons. The phrase "i like to think" is repeated three times, and highlights the role of the speaker's/Clifton's knowing in producing the identity of her ancestor. This is not a definitive statement of identity, but a celebration of how identities are constructed in people's ways of knowing. The "truth" of the identity matters less than the power of Clifton's own thought about that identity, and its role in shaping her own thinking about herself. In her words, "What they call you is one thing. What you answer to is something else."[19]

Clifton concludes the section titled "reflection" with an untitled poem that asks her readers to "celebrate" the life and identity which she has constructed for herself: "won't you celebrate with me / what i have shaped into / a kind of life?" (*GW*, 25). These lines emphasize how what Clifton once referred to as her "authenticity" has become the life she herself "shaped" through poetry, family history, and her experiences as a black woman in the United States:

> i had no model.
> born in babylon
> both nonwhite and woman
> what did i see to be except myself?
> i made it up. (*BL*, 25)

The poem ends with Clifton celebrating her success at preserving the self she constructed, and asking the reader to celebrate that preservation:

> i made it up
> here on this bridge between
> starshine and clay,
> my one hand holding tight

my other hand; come celebrate
with me that everyday
something has tried to kill me
and has failed. (Ibid.)

In Clifton's formulation, making the self up out of her history and her op-
pression means both a reconceptualization of identity, and a "shift in know-
ing" that enables her very survival. This poem also highlights the degree to
which Clifton's "i" poems can also be read as persona poems. The poems
construct a self called Lucille Clifton, as much as a more traditional per-
sona poem constructs a self that is named as Other to Clifton/the poet.

The centrality of history to Clifton's poetic practice and to her construc-
tions of the communal "i" is evident in *Generations: A Memoir* as well,
and reveals Clifton again challenging rigid understandings of the self and
extending that challenge to understandings of history as narrowly reliant
upon verifiable facts. Clifton's project in the memoir is to explore the im-
brication of history, legend, lies, and truth, linking these to her understand-
ing of self. In one passage, Clifton asks her father about a story in which a
female ancestor of hers had killed a white man:

> Later I would ask my father for proof. Where are the records, Daddy? I
> would ask. The time may not be right and it may just be family legend or
> something. Somebody somewhere knows, he would say. And I would be dis-
> satisfied and fuss with Fred about fact and proof and history until he told
> me one day not to worry, that even the lies are true. In history, even the lies
> are true. (*GW*, 243)

Clifton at first seeks proof, but arrives at a more complex understanding
of how history is constituted through records and facts as well as through
knowledge that is marked as legend and lies. In questioning the need for
proof or fact, Clifton's work devalues traditional understandings of his-
tory rooted in empiricism and objectivity. As a statement, "In history, even
the lies are true" values the subjective telling, the lie, as a viable source of
historical knowledge. African American writers—and indeed, ethnic writ-
ers from many locations—add to the general emphasis upon subjectively
constructed histories a focus upon the politics of whose history gets re-
corded at all, demonstrating their awareness—shared with Walter Benja-
min—that "every image of the past that is not recognized by the present
as one of its own concerns threatens to disappear irretrievably."[20] Writing
against erasure and also against traditionally authorized modes of family
historiography, Clifton claims the lies as truth, destabilizing what counts
as "truth" and using her husband's words to validate multiple avenues to
reconstructing a narrative of the past.

This approach to history is closely linked to Clifton's approach to iden-
tity and the communal "i." One refrain throughout the memoir is "You

from Dahomey women" (*GW*, 253).[21] At one point, Clifton's father chastises her for saying "I'm from Dahomey women," by replying, "You don't even know where that is . . . You don't even know what it means" (*GW*, 250). Clifton realizes that he is right, and this made her inconsolable at the time. But the narrative of the memoir shows that she had constructed her own meaning out of being constantly told by her mother that she was "from Dahomey women." For Clifton, it meant freedom: "I'm going to write poems. I can do what I want to do! I'm from Dahomey women" (*GW*, 250). While her father makes her think she does not know what that means, she actually does because this is exactly the spirit in which her mother inculcates the young Clifton's links to Dahomey women. She wants her daughter to be proud, confident, and self-sufficient (*GW*, 232). Thus, Clifton's sense of herself as a Dahomey woman was accurate in the terms in which she meant it, though her claim was not factually based. Her identity is thus constructed as the family history is, through various kinds of subjective, contingent knowledges.

Clifton's Other Voices[22]

Clifton's persona poems also exhibit a communal sense of self, perhaps in a more overt manner. In these, her poetic "i" sits in tension with the other "I" created in the poem. These others are frequently male, and pull from Biblical characters, historical figures, and increasingly from popular culture in later work as well. In *Good Times* (1969), Clifton writes in the voices of tyrone, willie b, and her father. Clifton ends her interwoven persona poems on tyrone and willie b with two poems that exemplify the communal nature of identity in her imagining. Referring to himself throughout his poems as a "buffalo soldier," parlance for a courageous black youth, tyrone's last assertion in "tyrone (4)" reveals that his understanding of himself relies upon how others perceive him. After detailing several successful struggles of African Americans, tyrone remarks:

> they see the tear gas
> burn my buffalo soldier eyes
> they got to say
> Look yonder
> Tyrone
> Is (*GW*, 44)

"Tyrone" and "Is" are both capitalized in a rare showing of typographical authority, yet the name is always lower case in the poem titles. This sense of self comes from the speaker's perception that others (*"they* got to say") must recognize his bravery and survival. "Look yonder / Tyrone / Is" can be read as "there's Tyrone," but also as a statement of his being, his presence. The line breaks support the latter reading, with the emphasis placed upon his identity and his existence with "Tyrone" and "Is" comprising entire lines of the poem. Visually, however, the poem tapers to a point, in a manner that undercuts the surety of the statement. Tyrone needs his community to validate his sense of himself; Clifton creates for him a presence, and its authority (if we can call it that) is not individual but communal. His being is contingent upon community recognition and support.

"willie b (4)" ends on a similar note. Set in the civil strife of the 1960s, this persona recounts the exploits of a twelve-year-old boy who loves his mother deeply, and is involved in the rioting and activism around him. His final poem concludes, "look I am the one what burned down the dew drop inn / everybody say i'm a big boy for my age / me / willie b / son" (*GW* 45). We have another capital I, and an assertion of self that is again dependent upon community recognition. "Look" and "everybody say" project a sense of authority, but also reveal its absence. The lines repeat the first two lines of the poem, which feature the lower case "i": "i'm the one / what burned down the dew drop inn" (*GW* 45). The need for repetition also reveals his lack of an authoritative voice. The final three lines give three ways of reading willie b's identity, and thus the poem gives us another example—early in Clifton's career—of how she both asserts presence for those who have had little access to individual power and authority, and also shows how those assertions of self, severely qualified and contingent, are constructed in relations of power. The poems written in male voices—these are but two of many—lend rich layers to her exploration of the multiplicitous lyric "I" posited by Ostriker and claimed by multiethnic poets in many locations. Furthermore, the experiences recounted by tyrone and willie b provide access to specific African American histories, and the boys gain presence through their sense of having an audience that will validate their existence. They embody call-and-response oral structures through these poems, evoking a rich vein in African American cultural production. These are the complex layers of lyric subjectivity that belie the simple language found throughout Clifton's poetic oeuvre.

There is a great deal of situated presence and gender switching in Clifton's biblical persona poems as well. That Clifton takes on Biblical voices, and has done so throughout her career, testifies to the depth of her project, to refigure how we conceptualize speaking to and about, indeed communing with, our most sacred texts and ideas. Akasha Hull places Clifton's Biblical poems in the tradition of revisionist mythmaking theorized by Ostriker, who argues that poets use characters from myth, legend, and history "for altered ends."[23] Hull also points out the important context of African American spiritual traditions for Clifton's work with Biblical characters, and argues that Clifton humanizes, Africanizes, and eroticizes many of her characters, revealing the ordinary within the extraordinary, or "the human in the mythic, and the mythic in the human."[24]

These biblical persona poems reveal a consistent exploration of the complexities of the self. "What manner of man" comes from Clifton's David of Jerusalem poems, and begins with the question, "if i am not singing to myself / to whom then?" (*TS*, 69). These opening lines evoke the power of the "other" persona and the manner in which it allows the poet to speak as both the poet and as the other. Here, Clifton adopts David's "i," but clearly encapsulates the experience of the poet of the Psalms and thus the origins of poetry in song and lyric in the reference to "singing." The poem continues

> each sound, each word
> is a way of wondering that first
> brushed against me in the hills
> when i was an unshorn shepherd boy. (*TS*, 69)

The "way of wondering" is a classic Clifton phrase, revealing her frequent attention to how we come to know what we know as selves, poets, humans. Clifton comments on this poem in her interview with Charles Rowell, stating that David's story is interesting because of "the kinds of choices he had to make, or his lack of understanding of the idea that he was, after all, a poet and a dancer and an artist, and he was a great warrior. How to be both? I think that that's a dilemma . . . the result of a kind of either/or mentality."[25] This comment echoes her broader concern with articulating both/and sensibilities in an African American tradition. The concluding lines of the poem shift into the third person, with the "i" relegated to a parenthetical statement:

> how can this david love himself,
> be loved (i am singing and spinning now)
> if he stands in the tents of history
> bloody skull in one hand, harp in the other? (*TS*, 69)

The words in parentheses function as an aside to the reader, and can be interpreted as either in the voice of David or in the voice of the poet commenting on her own telling of this particular part of his story—which is also a part of her own wondering. The poem can be read as a mixture of "other" and "i" personas, starting in the voice of David and then shifting with the single line at the poem's center—"what is a man? what am i?"—into the poet's "i." The core of the poem is a question about self and identity, and circulates around Clifton's characteristic exploration of the multiple layers that produce any self.

Such a fluid, multilayered, communal understanding of self and identity can be seen in many of Clifton's Biblical personas. Ostriker points out that women revisionist poets challenge the validity of the "I," of any "I." Like the speaker in Adrienne Rich's "Diving Into the Wreck," whose discovery of her submerged self is a discovery that she is a "we" for whom even the distinction between subject and object dissolves, and like the multiple self of women's chant-poems, the heroines we find in women's revisionist mythology are more often fluid than solid.[26]

Hilary Holladay identifies the fluidity between Lucille and one of her most compelling Biblical personas, Lucifer. Referring to "Lucifer/Lucille," Holladay connects Lucifer as "light-bearer"—from the Latin name for the Morning Star/Venus[27]—to Lucille as light. Drawing from Bakhtin's work on dialogism, Holladay positions Clifton as creating a "complementary relationship between language and silence [that] parallels the relationship between the human and the divine. She uses grammar and syntax, moreover, to represent the plurality of the universe, the enfolding of the human within the divine."[28] In order to accomplish this, Holladay argues, Clifton "must assert her own presence within the persona of Lucifer," thus "suggesting that the concept of God, defined in terms of both unity and infinity, accommodates the multiplicity of men and women, just as the idea of Lucifer embraces the reality of Lucille."[29] Where Holladay reads Clifton's assertion of her presence within Lucifer in terms of the implications for theological understandings, I am more interested in what the linking of Lucille to Lucifer means in terms of crafting a communal lyric subjectivity. The series titled "brothers" concludes *The Book of Light*, and features a dialogue between Lucifer and a silent, listening God. In "how great Thou art," Clifton destabilizes a singular, unified concept of identity, even at the divine level. Addressing God, Lucifer claims that human desire "is You. all You, all You," creating a plural second-person (*BL*, 70). Written entirely in the second person, the poem asserts also that concepts of identity are shifting and multiple: "listen, You are beyond / even Your own understanding" (*BL*, 70). Lucifer continues, "that rib and rain and clay . . . is not what You believed / You were, / but it is what You are" (*BL*, 70). Written this way, the poem addresses the reader as well and models a communal understanding of self. Here, Lucifer articulates a version of God's identity that incorporates Adam and Eve: "the face, both he and she, / the odd ambition, the desire / to reach beyond the stars / is You. all You, all You" (*BL*, 70). Clifton's is a profoundly positive, liberating approach to self-understanding. It suggests possibility, fluidity, community. "all You, all You" functions as a call to an audience to hear, again echoing call-and-response traditions in African American spiritual traditions.

A communal self also appears in "as for myself," another poem in the Lucifer sequence. Holladay points out the elegance with which the title references both Lucille Clifton the poet and Lucifer the persona. The poem explores knowledge and understanding broadly, and reveals again Clifton's trademark questioning of identity. The poem begins,

> less snake than angel
> less angel than man
> how come i to this
> serpent's understanding? (*BL*, 71)

The remainder of the poem explores how Lucifer identifies with God and, through Eve and her ability to reproduce, with women generally. Using Lucifer's voice, Clifton draws from Hindu and African mythologies to present the snake as a regenerative symbol, and also to suggest the literal sense in which snakes can swallow their prey whole "to feel the living move" inside, as a woman would a fetus. Thus Lucifer is both Africanized and feminized—and ultimately not represented as a fixed entity (*BL*, 71). A pregnant woman challenges and complicates in a particularly gendered manner representations of the individual as consistent and impermeable. Lucifer identifies the power to reproduce as highly valued by God: "i too am blessed with / the one gift you cherish; to feel the living move in me / and to be unafraid" (*BL*, 71). By extension, Clifton values women's reproductivity and uses it here symbolically to evoke another version of a shifting, communal self.

In *Voices* (2008), Clifton begins her book with a series of poems again in the voices of others. The first, "marley was dead to begin with," quotes Charles Dickens's *A Christmas Carol*, but then proceeds to channel Bob Marley, the reggae singer and poet. Building upon the title, the opening lines reveal that the ghost of the poem is Bob Marley, as "in trenchtown and in babylon / the sound of marleys ghost / rose and began to fill the air" (*V*, 11). The poem's conclusion is most pertinent for reading the continuing presence of the communal "i" in Clifton's work. She evokes Marley's spirit as "alive again" in the "voices of his children":

> ziggy and i and i marley again
> standing and swaying
> everything gonna be alright
> little darling
> no woman   no cry (*V*, 11)

The first line of the final stanza repeats the "i" twice, evoking not only Clifton's long career of using the lower-case "i" to refer to herself in her poems but also Marley's Caribbean vernacular rooted in African language structures, a vernacular that collapses the self and other into a single term, "I." This vernacular is evident in the first four lines of Marley's "Redemption Song":

Old pirates, yes, they rob I;
Sold I to the merchant ships,
Minutes after they took I
From the bottomless pit.[30]

While Marley could be simply replacing the first-person singular object "me" with the first-person singular subject "i," when read in dialogue with Clifton's repetition, the poem also suggests an "i" that is not singular, but plural: "i" and "i," or "i" as "we/us." The song is clearly not only about what happened to one person, but to a large cohort of Africans during slavery, and Clifton's line "ziggy and i and i marley again" doubles the "I," suggesting not the singular self but an expression of self as communal, as "i" signals not just self but other as well.

The entire first section of *Voices* continues with poems titled "aunt jemima," "uncle ben," and "cream of wheat"—examining the abiding presence of racialization on the food shelves of any grocery store in the United States today—as well as "mataoka," which is subtitled "(actual name of Pocahontas)" and "witko," which is subtitled "aka crazy horse." Without even reading these last two poems, we notice once again the multiplicity— the multiple ways of naming or calling—within and surrounding individuals. Of these five poems, "uncle ben" and "witko" are in the third person, and the other three are persona poems in the first person. Throughout all of them, Clifton attends to the constructedness of identity and the layers of complexity surrounding poetic subjectivity. In "cream of wheat," the man from the box muses "what ever pictured me / then left me personless" (*V*, 14). The poem concludes not with an answer, but a question that is also a statement (given Clifton's refusal of punctuation):

> ben and jemima and me
> we pose and smile   i simmer   what
> is my name (*V*, 14)

Clifton's Communing "i"

Yet another approach that Clifton takes to the communal poetic "i" can be seen in her work, which examines not just a communal "i"—defined by its links to family and community—nor an "i" that speaks in the voices of others, but an "i" that communes with others. *The Oxford English Dictionary* defines the verb "to commune" in contemporary usage as "To talk together, converse," "To hold intimate (chiefly mental or spiritual) intercourse (*with*)," and also lists one obsolete usage as "To communicate verbally, tell, publish, report."[31] Clifton constructs numerous first person speakers that commune with nonhuman others. In these poems, Clifton constructs an "i" that communes with animals and the supernatural, for example, providing us with more facets to Clifton's exploration of complex identities and how they are constructed. Underlying all of these examples of communing is the African American tradition of call-and-response, with a voice demanding an audience in order to validate what it has to tell.

The fox poems in *The Terrible Stories* (1996) use the trope of shifting and turning that we saw in "the light that came to Lucille Clifton," which was written much earlier in Clifton's career, with the turns and shifts signaling fluid identities. While some of the fox poems describe a connection between Clifton and the fox and others describe their separateness, they consistently present the speaker communing with the fox as she explores their shared desire, creativity, and position as female beings. The fox poems riff on the slang for women as foxes, as sexy beings, and also explore the cunning and survival instincts of the fox from animal tales in African American oral and written traditions. Clifton claims this space for herself and the fox, positioning each of them as poets who have the power to tell stories. Storytelling assumes an audience, and the opening poem of the collection positions Clifton's poems as once again documenting communal interaction—the exchange between a teller and an auditor. The introductory poem to the collection, "telling our stories," ends with an address to an unidentified child as audience:

> child, i tell you now it was not
> the animal blood i was hiding from,
> it was the poet in her, the poet and
> the terrible stories she could tell. (*TS*, 9)

Again, we have an "i" telling a story to an audience, making sense of herself through a dialogue with another. Here, the poet fears that connection but in casting the fox as a poet reveals that she fears herself as much as she fears the fox.

In "the coming of fox," Clifton describes the fox in contrast to herself: "she sits in her safe shadow // silent as my skin bleeds / into long bright flags / of fur" (*TS*, 14). Becoming fox-like means becoming more animal, more sexual, more open to desire. Throughout the series, the fox represents the return of lost desire. We see this connection in "leaving fox":

> so many fuckless days and nights,
> only the solitary fox
> watching my window light
> barks her compassion. (*TS*, 16)

The poem then describes another of Clifton's signature transformative moments: "i move away from her eye . . . to a new place and check / for signs. so far / i am the only animal" (*TS*, 16). By this admonition, she has become animal like the fox, and open to her desires. The poem concludes:

"i will keep the door unlocked / until something human comes" (*TS*, 16). The final line suggests the possibility of communing with others, including sexual consummation. But in this poem, it remains only a possibility. The door is unlocked, but the speaker remains inside. The fox is always outside, and in her communing with the fox, Clifton/the speaker must consider a shifting bodily consciousness and what it means to be open to such changes. Rarely in Clifton's work do we get answers; rather, her style is characterized by questions. This emphasis upon asking is plain in "one year later," where the speaker asks what would have happened had she not remained indoors, and had instead sought a deeper communing with the fox: "what if, / then, / I had reared up baying, / and followed her off / into vixen country?" (*TS*, 17).

The poem "a dream of foxes" closes the fox series and reveals sexual desire giving way to a desire for safety. This poem is unusual in Clifton's body of work in that it lacks an identifiable speaker. The poem begins "in the dream of foxes," not "in *my* dream of foxes" (*TS*, 18). The dream parallels foxes with women, and imagines a place where women are safe:

> in the dream of foxes
> there is a field
> and a procession of women
> . . . .
> of honest women stepping
> without fear or guilt or shame
> safe through the generous fields. (*TS*, 18)

The absence of an "i" or a specific self as central in this poem expands its concern to a broader community of women, yet its connection to the previous fox poems in the series keeps it rooted to Clifton's "i" as it communes with the particular fox that she encounters and that inspired her to write these poems.[32] Clifton describes the process of writing as a way of continuing to hope, and of remaining connected to a community of readers. Envisioning safety for women is a central part of Clifton's poetic vision. Providing models of identity that extend from Clifton's own "i" to her other persona poems and even to poems where no "i" is present at all, her poetic oeuvre features a spectrum of ways of articulating a self, most often defined in communal relations with others, and frequently acknowledging the constructions of and constitutive shifts in identity that characterize any self's understanding.

This last poem in the fox series is interesting to contrast with Clifton's earlier shapeshifter series, in which she addresses her experiences with being sexually molested as a child. The Shapeshifter poems are likewise devoid of an identifiable "i" and address shifting identity in a bleaker sense than the fox poems do. Readers aware of Clifton's story know that she writes from her own childhood experiences in the shapeshifter series. The little girl in the poems is both Clifton and anyone who has experienced such abuse. In the fox poems, the speaker herself considers what it would be to change, to have a shift in identity that would involve embracing sexual desires. In the shapeshifter poems, the person who changes is the father. Clifton uses the werewolf myth to account for how any father could molest his daughter: "the moon when she rises / full / follows some men into themselves / and changes them there" (N, 77). When we read the fox series in light of the shapeshifter poems, we again see the range of approaches to shifting identities that Clifton's work reveals. In the fox poems, Clifton ends on a dream of safety for women. In these earlier poems, Clifton still seems to be searching for a way to address the experience of abuse, a way to get to a dream of safety. The second poem asks a series of questions, beginning with "who is there to protect her / from the hands of the father" and ending with "who   who   who   the owl / laments into the evening   who / will protect her   this   prettylittlegirl" (N, 78). Putting the question into the owl's lament, the empty spaces surrounding the words suggest silence, and a lack of response to the question called out to an unanswering audience. The final poem of the shapeshifter series brings the role of poetry into the exploration of abuse, and struggles with the role of the poem for the abused. Clifton casts the little girl as a poet, just as she did with the fox:

> the poem at the end of the world
> is the poem the little girl breathes
> into her pillow   the one
> she cannot tell   the one
> there is no one to hear (N, 80)

Cut off from an audience, from a community, the speaker/poet finds herself at the end of the world. Here, the little girl cannot find an audience for her poem, and thus sees no future for herself, no way to be. Clifton writes, "this poem / is a political poem   is a war poem   is a universal poem," expanding its concerns beyond her self to constitute an audience of others who have suffered abuse. But in the next line, she counters its universality, claiming "this poem / is about one human heart," and thus she again bridges the individual to the communal, and the communal to the individual experience as articulated in poetry (N, 80).

In *Voices*, Clifton includes four poems from the minds of animals. "horse prayer" and "raccoon prayer" insinuate themselves into the first-person thoughts of the horse and raccoon considering their lots in life and revealing—through prayers—the desires of each animal, the horse not to be subject to the two-leg and the raccoon seeking redemption in an afterlife without scavenging and uncleanness. Clearly, the prayers resonate for humans as well as animals, thus creating a communion between the two. The horse asks "why . . . when he declares himself / master / does he not understand my / neigh" (V, 15). "albino" similarly treats concerns that highlight a human/animal communing, as two women—one black, one white—encounter an albino stag, and yet it is the two women who are seen by the poem as different and other as the reader views them through the eyes of the stag:

> his pink eyes
> fixed
> on the joy
> of the black woman
> and the white one
> laughing together
> and he smiled
> at the sometime
> wonderfulness
> of other (V, 18)

Here, animal poems take Clifton into a place where redemptive laughter is possible, praise and thankfulness characterize the animal/divine interaction, and self/other commune in a moment of "wonderfulness." "dog's god" blesses the dog with "two-legs to feed him / and clean his waste" and the dog "spins and tumbles / in the passion / of his praise" (V, 17). The possibilities for communing here enter a different space than those we see in the earlier fox poems, and hearken back to the power of animal tales in African American literary history to provide alternative telling of all-too-human stories.

Clifton's *Mercy* (2004) extends her exploration of communal identity to the supernatural. The final series in the book is titled "the message from The Ones," twenty-three poems written in the second person. Choosing to name them "The Ones" rather than "the Others" demonstrates continuity between those giving the message and those receiving it, as opposed to the separation that naming them "the Others" would have implied. The Ones exhibit a communal "i" throughout, speaking as "we." They address the "you" in the series as someone with multiple names and identities as well: "we will call you / one eye / field of feeling / singing ear / quick hand" (*M*, 56). The next poem elaborates on the understanding of identity that The Ones articulate, which recognizes a lack of continuity in that "you":

> in the saying of
> you
> we will sometime
> be general
> and sometime
> particular

in the saying of we
we are we (*M*, 57)[33]

This "sometime . . . general" and "sometime / particular" you suggests the multiple "i" described by Clifton in her interview with Charles Rowell.[34] The reader is once again faced with both/and thinking and a series of poems rooted in a call-and-response format where a speaker or speakers directly address an audience. The ones speak directly to the silent "you" throughout, thus turning the speaker into the auditor who listens to the voices as they communicate to her, and positioning the reader as the "you" as well. The message they bring pertains to human interactions with other humans, human relations with the environment and the broader world around them, and human experiences with the spiritual world. The Ones speak in a communal and communing voice that brings a message of hope to the reader/auditor, and models change on a scale broader than the individual. The series emphasizes connections, and dissolves differences between people in a paradoxical statement of sameness; the poem begins "you are not / your brothers keeper / you are / your brother" (*M*, 68). Saying "you are your brother" implies "you are not yourself," or "you are not a self." The center of the poem includes a litany of others to whom The Ones of the poem connect the reader/auditor:

> the king is you
> the kike is you
> the honky is you
> the nigger is you
> the bitch is you
> the beauty is you
> the friend is you
> the enemy   oh (*M*, 68)

This collapse of identity is rooted in a Buddhist sensibility, where what we see is the sublimation of self, not the enshrinement of self that has been so often critiqued in contemporary American poetry. The sublimation of a singular self through its yoking to numerous other identities again refuses either/or ways of thinking, and invites a thoughtfulness, a fresh commitment, to living for connections with others through detachment from a fixed notion of self. Such Buddhist sensibilities are not completely new to Clifton's questionings, but resonate a great deal with her earlier chapbook, *Ten Oxherding Pictures*. First published in 1988, and then republished in *Callaloo* in 1999 and finally as the concluding series in her most recent publication *Voices* in 2008, the poems are based upon a series of pictures and poems from the 12th century that represent the Buddhist spiritual path; in the pictures, the ox is a metaphor for enlightenment. In "Seeing the Ox," Clifton writes:

```
not this me
not that me
now here where
no thing is defined
we are coming to the ox (V, 46)³⁵
```

The series concludes with the lines, "what is ox / ox is / what" (V, 54). Even the layers of publication history here suggest multiplicity and invite a sense of the path to enlightenment, or knowledge, as circular, not linear. In both "the message from The Ones" and "ten oxherding pictures," Clifton goes beyond shape shifting and beyond names to explore broader possibilities for understanding, for shifts in geometries of knowing. The worldview she creates in "the message from The Ones" emphasizes fluidity, and places value on all living things: "each leaf each heart has a place / irreplaceable / each is required to be" (M, 69). Each is required to be, but being is not essentialized, fixed, or knowable in a reductive, simplistic manner. Being is constructed, contingent. And best of all, "what has been made / can be unmade" (M, 74). The penultimate poem in the series focuses once again on the consistency of change, in imagining identity, consciousness, knowledge, and action. The poem continues with a reference to saints gendered as mothers, or mothers cast as saints, "hoping for children / nursed toward wholeness / holiness" (M, 74). The important word in this part of the poem is "toward." This is a moment of possibility in Clifton, where she urges a movement toward something, not an assertion of arrival or finitude. The poem concludes,

```
it is perhaps
a final chance

not the end of the world
of a world (M, 74)
```

The poem refuses to fix a single world with the article "the," but refers instead to the end of "a" world, suggesting the inevitability of another one that will replace it. Where "the poem at the end of the world" concludes the shapeshifter series on a note of inward-turning despair, this poem concludes on a note of infinite possibility. In communing with The Ones, the poem suggests, the listener opens up the possibility to grasp new ways of knowing, to be "wrapped in understanding" as The Ones are (M, 59). Clifton gives hints of what that understanding may entail, but in her characteristic manner, leaves it to her readers to fill in the blanks. One element of that understanding may pertain to a spirituality rooted in hope. Tiffany Eberle Kriner explores Clifton's use of prophecy—defined as both the articulation of "moral imperatives and predictive statements"—as central to a theology of hope (or eschatology).³⁶ Kriner argues that Clifton develops "an eschatological self, one that can balance a desire for future wholeness with ethical responsibility for the other by deferring stable identity."[37] The Ones are the antithesis of stable identity, and the notion of a "final chance" that they articulate through their prophetic voices exhibits Clifton's characteristic hopefulness. Thus, what Clifton achieves with the communal "we" throughout this series of poems is a call for a "geometry of knowing" that extends beyond knowing the self (in any simple sense) to understanding the complexity of any self and the need for more connection and communion among humans, and between humans and nonhumans, across differences in the world at large (*M*, 62).

In closing, I must note that while Clifton published "the message from The Ones" in *Mercy* in 2004, she began writing on The Ones much earlier. Holladay places the composition of "The Ones Who Talk," the original title for this series, near the same time as *An Ordinary Woman*, which was published in 1974, and *Two-Headed Woman*, in 1980.[38] What we have in retrospect is thirty years' worth of a poet making that which is too often seen as singular—the one, the "I," the self—into a plural entity—the Ones, a communal "i," collective subjectivities. In effect, Clifton's body of work asks us to see with collective eyes, to see beyond singular notions of the self. In his reading of Clifton's work, Mark Bernard White argues that we must approach her poetry with "an understanding of lyric as rhetorical discourse, functioning to teach and thereby to alter the consciousness of its audience."[39] What she teaches us is to be readers of the both/and, aware of the palimpsestic qualities within the text and, by extension, the self. Writing against Western notions of "absolute presence," "pure origin," and "true self" that are rooted in dualistic thinking, Trinh Minh-ha argues for an understanding of "multiple presence" found in the differences "*both between* and *within* entities"; she writes, "Not One, not two either. 'I' is, therefore, not a unified subject, a fixed identity, or that solid mass covered with layers of superficialities one has gradually to peel off before one can see its true face. 'I' is, itself, infinite layers."[40] In *Mercy*, Clifton includes a poem that asks why she writes the kinds of poems she writes, those with a particular rhetorical force layered beneath poems in observation of nature: "surely i am able to write poems / celebrating grass," the poem begins (*M*, 23). This poem speaks back to Gwendolyn Brooks's "love note / I: surely," part of the "Gay Chaps at the Bar" sonnet sequence published in *A Street in Bronzeville* in 1945.[41] The poem begins, "Surely you stay my certain own, you stay / my you."[42] The turn in Brooks' sonnet shifts away from certainty to disillusionment:

> Surely—But I am very off from that.
> From surely. From indeed. From the decent arrow
> That was my clean naïveté and my faith.

This morning men deliver wounds and death.
They will deliver death and wounds tomorrow.
And I doubt all. You. Or a violet. (*Blacks* 73)

Set against the backdrop of World War II, the poem is told in the voice of an African American soldier wondering whether his love remains true. The war has stripped him of his sureties, as the fight for freedoms in Europe rankled with those who lacked civil freedoms in the United States. But just as Clifton's fox poems revise her shapeshifter poems—the former dreaming of positive transformations where the latter are more tentative—Clifton's "surely" affirms the presence of multiple poems, multiple layers of meaning, where Brooks's poem doubts the power of the aesthetic ("a violet") to stand in conversation with the destruction of war. Clifton concludes her poem with a question:

surely   but whenever i begin
"the trees wave their knotted branches
and . . ." why
is there under that poem always
an other poem? (*M* 23)

She questions her method, asking why the other poem is always there, but both poems remain present, in dialogue with one another, the one enabling the other's presence. As readers and students of Clifton, we must learn to read all of her poems for the both/and that her communal, communing "i" entreats us to encounter.

NOTES TO POEMS AND POETICS STATEMENT

Lucille Clifton's poems were selected by Adrienne McCormick.

1. Charles H. Rowell, "An Interview with Lucille Clifton," *Callaloo* 22, no. 1 (1999): 56–72.

NOTES TO CRITICAL ESSAY

1. Lucille Clifton, "sorrows," *Voices* (Rochester: BOA, 2008), 25.
2. American poetry during the past four decades has been characterized by numerous rifts, perhaps most noticeably between the poetry mainstream and the vast proliferation of poets writing from identities marked by gendered, sexual, racial, ethnic and other cultural experiences. In *Opposing Poetries*, Hank Lazer examines the tensions between two verse cultures in the United States: one rooted in a transparent approach to the self and the lyric voice, to accessibility and a plainspoken style, and to traditional approaches to representation and poetic convention (what Charles Bernstein calls "official verse culture," or the verse produced in mainstream creative writing programs); the other committed to a refusal of the

traditional lyric I, to formal experimentation, and to representation that is linked with contemporary poststructuralist and postmodernist thought (Hank Lazer, *Opposing Poetries, Volume 1: Issues and Institutions,* Evanston: Northeastern University Press, 1996, 34). More specifically, these groups get separated into camps of lyric and Language poets, in a shorthand that oversimplifies many diverse practices within each of these monikers and tags those writing within the lyric form as "naive" for not refusing the lyric I, representational language, and poetic forms rooted in narrative and lyric conventions. Furthermore, poetry in general is seen as resistant or antithetical to theory in general and its attentions to language and deconstruction, fragmented subjectivities, and destabilized narratives of history and philosophy, for example. For more discussion on this issue, see John Koethe, "Contrary Impulses: The Tension between Poetry and Theory," *Critical Inquiry* 18 (Autumn 1991): 64–75.

3. Kinereth Meyer, "Speaking and Writing the Lyric 'I,'" *Genre* 22 (Summer 1989): 133.

4. Ibid., 132.

5. Ibid., 139. Meyer references the interdependence of speaking and writing in the lyric I through the essay, positioning them as analogous to "a ghost of orality," which articulates an actual speaking self and the negation of that self through trope or "figuration" as components of writing that signal the effacement of that self (129–49).

6. Rachel Blau DuPlessis, *The Pink Guitar: Writing as Feminist Practice* (New York, Routledge, 1990), 6.

7. Lucille Clifton, "in the geometry," *Mercy* (Rochester: BOA, 2004), 62.

8. Charles H. Rowell, "An Interview with Lucille Clifton." *Callaloo* 22, no. 1 (1999): 56–72. Literature Resource Center, http://galenet.galegroup.com (accessed November 20, 2007).

9. Alicia Ostriker, *Stealing the Language: The Emergence of Women's Poetry in America* (Boston: Beacon Press, 1986), 12.

10. Ostriker, *Stealing the Language,* 178.

11. Rowell, "An Interview with Lucille Clifton," 59.

12. The term "signifying" refers to Henry Louis Gates, Jr.'s formulation of it in *The Signifying Monkey: A Theory of Afro-American Literary Criticism* (1988), but more so to Wahneema Lubiano's usage, when she goes beyond Gates's approach to signifying as a mode of intertextuality to examine it as a practice more associated with "intratextual dynamism and the possible politics of a Signifyin(g) narrativity" (113n2), in "The Postmodernist Rag: Political Identity and the Vernacular in *Song of Solomon,*" in *New Essays on Song of Solomon,* ed. Valerie Smith (Cambridge, MA: Cambridge University Press, 1995), 93–116.

13. John Yau, "Between the Forest and Its Trees." *Amerasia Journal* 20, no. 3 (1994): 40.

14. Ibid., 41.

15. Jeannine Thyreen-Mizingou, "Grace and Ethics in Contemporary American Poetry: Resitua-ting the Other, the World, and the Self." *Religion and Literature* 32, no. 1 (Spring 2000): 67–97.

16. Thyreen-Mizingou's exploration of Clifton's communal voices differs from

mine in that she positions Clifton's exploration of selfhood as rooted in "union with the divine and in one's ethical response to the other" (68), whereas I explore Clifton's spiritual self as in dialogue with various other articulations of self in her body of work.

17. Clifton's first four poetry collections are republished in *Good Woman: Poems and a Memoir 1969–1980* (Rochester: BOA Editions, 1987), and all page numbers from poems in *Good Times* (1969), *Good News About the Earth* (1972), *An Ordinary Woman*, (1974), *Two-Headed Woman* (1980), and *Generations: A Memoir* (1976) are from this collection. I use the abbreviation *GW*, and will likewise shorten the titles of her other books as follows: *Next = N, The Book of Light = BL, The Terrible Stories = TS*, and *Mercy = M*.

18. See Akasha (Gloria) Hull, "Channeling the Ancestral Muse: Lucille Clifton and Dolores Kendrick," in *Female Subjects in Black and White: Race, Psychoanalysis, Feminism*, edited by Elizabeth Abel, Barbara Christian, and Helene Moglen (Berkeley: University of California Press, 1997), 330–48, for a discussion of the "Light" in this poem as a way of "designating Spirit" and an ability to hear the supernatural (347). Clifton acknowledges in an interview that her poems dealing with "light," her "shift in knowing," and the "nondead past" all refer to some extent to her ability to sense the presence and hear the voice of her dead mother, Thelma Sayles. My reading of Clifton's shift in knowing is more concerned with how she articulates poetic subjectivity and creates a multifaceted communal voice, whereas Hull explores the work as "salvific poetry" and as part of a process of writing that is rooted in "spirituality-based attentiveness" (347).

19. Bill Moyers, *Fooling with Words*, www.pbs.org/wnet/foolingwithwords/t_txtclifton.html, October 1, 2008.

20. Walter Benjamin, "Theses on the Philosophy of History," in *Illuminations*, ed. Hannah Arendt, (New York: Harcourt Brace Jovanovich, 1968), 255.

21. See also pages 232, 239, 245, 251, and 259.

22. First drafts of this essay were due before the publication of *Voices* in September 2008. The collection reveals Clifton's abiding concerns with persona and spiritual communing.

23. Ostriker, *Stealing the Language*, 212n Akasha (Gloria) Hull, "In Her Own Images: Lucille Clifton and the Bible," in *Dwelling in Possibility: Women Poets and Critics on Poetry*, ed. Yopie Prins and Maeera Shreiber (Ithaca, NY: Cornell University Press, 1997), 276.

24. Akasha (Gloria) Hull, "In Her Own Images: Lucille Clifton and the Bible," in *Dwelling in Possibility: Women Poets and Critics on Poetry*, ed. Yopie Prins and Maeera Shreiber (Ithaca, NY: Cornell University Press, 1997), 276, 280, 282. The latter reference comes from Clifton quoting a friend's response to her Biblical characters. See Clifton's comments in Rowell: "Someone once said to me that what they think I do is find the human in the mythic, and the mythic in the human." My concern with Clifton's biblical personas relates to creating communal voices, whereas Hull's work with these poems extends Ostriker's work on revisionist mythmaking to reveal how Clifton "succeeds at transforming the Bible from a patriarchal to an Afrocentric, feminist, sexual and broadly mystical text" (293).

25. Rowell, "An Interview with Lucille Clifton," 62.

26. Ostriker, *Stealing the Language*, 237.

27. Hull, "In Her Own Image," 289.

28. Holladay, *Wild Blessings*, 133.

29. Ibid., 133.

30. Bob Marley, "Redemption Song," LyricsFreak, www.lyricsfreak.com/b/bob+marley/redemption+song_20021829.html (accessed 19 March 2009).

31. *Oxford English Dictionary*. http://dictionary.oed.com.dbsearch.fredonia.edu (accessed August 17, 2008).

32. Clifton discusses the actual encounter with a fox that inspired her to write this series of poems in Rowell, "An Interview with Lucille Clifton."

33. Lucille Clifton, ["in the saying of"] from *Mercy*, copyright 2004 by Lucille Clifton. Reprinted with permission of BOA Editions, Ltd., www.boaeditions.org.

34. See Rowell, "An Interview with Lucille Clifton," 59.

35. Lucille Clifton, "Seeing the Ox," in *Ten Oxherding Pictures* (Santa Cruz, CA: Moving Parts Press, 1988). Reprinted in *Callaloo* 22, 1 (1999): 47–50. Reprinted in Lucille Clifton, *Voices* (Rochester, NY: BOA Editions, 2008), 41–54.

36. Tiffany Eberle Kriner, "Conjuring Hope in a Body: Lucille Clifton's Eschatology." *Christianity and Literature* 54, no. 2 (Winter 2005): 185.

37. Ibid., 187.

38. Holladay, *Wild Blessings*, 8.

39. Mark Bernard White, "Sharing the Living Light: Rhetorical, Poetic, and Social Identity in Lucille Clifton," *CLA Journal* 40, no. 3 (March 1997): 289.

40. Trinh T. Minh-ha, *Woman, Native, Other: Writing Postcoloniality and Feminism* (Bloomington: Indiana University Press, 1989), 90, 94.

41. Clifton also speaks back to Walt Whitman's *Leaves of Grass* here, a work she dialogues with in *Generations* as well. But Whitman's exploration of the relationship between self and other was rooted in celebration of self, and incorporation of other: "I CELEBRATE myself; / And what I assume you shall assume; / For every atom belonging to me, as good belongs to you" (13) or "I do not ask who you are . . . that is not important to me. / You can do nothing and be nothing but what I will infold you" (45), www.whitmanarchive.org/published/LG/1855/whole.html (accessed October 2, 2008).

42. Gwendolyn Brooks, *Blacks* (Chicago: Third World Press, 1994), 73. This collection reprints in full all of Brooks's work from 1945 to 1980, and selections from her work published between 1980 and 1986. "Gay Chaps at the Bar" was part of her first collection of poems, *A Street in Bronzeville*.

BIBLIOGRAPHY

Books by Lucille Clifton

POETRY

Good Times. New York: Random House, 1969.
Good News About the Earth. New York: Random House, 1972.
An Ordinary Woman. New York: Random House, 1974.
Two-Headed Woman. Amherst: University of Massachusetts Press, 1980.

Good Woman: Poems and a Memoir: 1969–1980. Brockport, NY: BOA Editions, 1987.

Next: New Poems. Brockport, NY: BOA Editions, 1987.

Ten Oxherding Pictures. Santa Cruz: Moving Parts Press, 1988. Reprinted in *Callaloo* 22, no. 1 (1999): 47–50. Also reprinted in full in *Voices*.

Quilting: Poems 1987–1990. Brockport, NY: BOA Editions, 1991.

The Book of Light. Port Townsend, WA: Copper Canyon, 1993.

The Terrible Stories. Brockport, NY: BOA Editions, 1996.

Blessing the Boats: New and Selected Poems. Rochester, NY: BOA Editions, 2000.

Mercy. Rochester, NY: BOA Editions, 2004.

Voices. Rochester, NY: BOA Editions, 2008.

MEMOIR

Generations: A Memoir. New York: Random House, 1976.

CHILDREN'S BOOKS

Some of the Days of Everett Anderson. New York: Holt, Rinehart and Winston, 1969.

The Black BC's. New York: Dutton, 1970.

Everett Anderson's Christmas Coming. New York: Holt, Rinehart and Winston, 1971.

All Us Come Cross the Water. New York: Holt, Rinehart and Winston, 1973.

The Boy Who Didn't Believe in Spring. New York: Dutton, 1973.

Don't You Remember? New York: Dutton, 1973.

Good, Says Jerome. New York: Dutton, 1973.

Everett Anderson's Year. New York: Holt, Rinehart and Winston, 1974.

The Times They Used to Be. New York: Holt, Rinehart and Winston, 1974.

My Brother Fine With Me. New York: Holt, Rinehart and Winston, 1975.

Everett Anderson's Friend. New York: Holt, Rinehart and Winston, 1976.

Three Wishes. New York: Viking, 1976.

Amifika. New York: Dutton, 1977.

Everett Anderson's 1 2 3. New York: Holt, Rinehart and Winston, 1977.

Everett Anderson's Nine Months Long. New York: Holt, Rinehart and Winston, 1978.

The Lucky Stone. New York: Delacorte, 1979.

My Friend Jacob. Coauthored by Thomas DiGrazia. New York: Dutton, 1980.

Here Is Another Bone to Pick with You. Minneapolis, MN: Toothpaste, 1981.

Sonora Beautiful. New York: Dutton, 1981.

Everett Anderson's Goodbye. New York: Holt, Rinehart and Winston, 1983.

Dear Creator: A Week of Poems for Young People and Their Teachers. New York: Doubleday, 1997.

One of the Problems of Everett Anderson. New York: Holt, 2001.

Selected Essays

"The Magic Mama." *Redbook*, November 1969, 18–19.

"The End of Love Is Death, the End of Death Is Love." *Atlantic*, March 1971, 65–67.

"Stories for Free Children: The Boy Who Didn't." *Ms.*, August 1973, 67.
"We Know This Place: Reaffirm Black's Sense of Being." *Essence*, July 1976, 53.
"If I Don't Know My Last Name, What Is the Meaning of My First?: *Roots*, the Saga of an American Family." *Ms.*, February 1977, 45.
"A Simple Language." In *Black Women Writers (1950–1980): A Critical Evaluation*, ed. Mari Evans. Garden City, NY: Anchor Press/Doubleday, 1984.

Selected Interviews

Bryant, Thema. "A Conversation with Lucille Clifton." *SAGE* 2, no. 1 (Spring 1985): 52.
Laing, E. K. "Making Each Word Count." *Christian Science Monitor* (February 5, 1988): B3.
Jordan, Shirley M. "Lucille Clifton." In *Broken Silences: Interviews with Black and White Women Writers*. New Brunswick, NJ: Rutgers University Press, 1993, 38–49.
Moyers, Bill. "Lucille Clifton." In *Language of Life: A Festival of Poets*. Garden City, NY: Doubleday, 1995, 81–95.
Holladay, Hilary. "No Ordinary Woman: An Interview with Lucille Clifton." "Poetry in America," special issue of *Poets & Writers Magazine* (April 1999): 30–35.
Kallet, Marilyn. "Doing What You Will Do: An Interview with Lucille Clifton." In *Sleeping with One Eye Open: Women Writers and the Art of Survival*. Athens: University of Georgia Press, 1999, 80–85.
Rowell, Charles H. "An Interview with Lucille Clifton," *Callaloo* 22, no. 1 (1999): 56–72.
Somers-Willet, Susan B. A. " 'A Music in Language': A Conversation with Lucille Clifton." *American Voice* 49 (Summer 1999): 73–92.
Glaser, Michael S. " 'I'd Like Not to Be a Stranger in the World': A Conversation/Interview with Lucille Clifton." *Antioch Review* 58, no. 3 (Summer 2000): 310–28.
Davis, Eisa. "Lucille Clifton and Sonia Sanchez: A Conversation." *Callaloo* 25, no. 4 (2002): 1038–74.
Pate, Alexs. "A Conversation with Lucille Clifton." *Black Renaissance Noire* 8, nos. 2–3 (Summer/Fall 2008): 12–17.

Selected Criticism

Annaporte-Easton, Jean. "Healing Our Wounds: The Direction of Difference in the Poetry of Lucille Clifton and Judith Johnston." *Mid-American Review* 14, no. 2 (1994): 78–87.
———. " 'She Has Made Herself Again': The Maternal Impulse as Poetry." *13th Moon: A Feminist Literary Magazine* 9, nos. 1–2 (1991): 116–35.
Hayes, Ned Dykstra. "Whole 'Alterity': Toward a Feminist A/Theology." In *Divine Aporia: Postmodern Conversations about the Other*, ed. John C. Hawley. Lewisburg, PA: Bucknell University Press, 2000, 173–87.
Holladay, Hilary. *Wild Blessings: The Poetry of Lucille Clifton*. Baton Rouge: Louisiana State University Press, 2004.

Hull, Akasha (Gloria). "Channeling the Ancestral Muse: Lucille Clifton and Dolores Kendrick." In *Female Subjects in Black and White: Race, Psychoanalysis, Feminism*, eds. Elizabeth Abel, Barbara Christian, and Helene Moglen. Berkeley: University of California Press, 1997, 330–48.

Hull, Akasha (Gloria). "In Her Own Images: Lucille Clifton and the Bible." In *Dwelling in Possibility: Women Poets and Critics on Poetry*, edited by Yopie Prins and Maeera Shreiber. Ithaca, NY: Cornell University Press, 1997, 273–95.

———. *Soul Talk: The New Spirituality of African American Women*. Rochester, VT: Inner Traditions, 2001.

Kriner, Tiffany Eberle. "Conjuring Hope in a Body: Lucille Clifton's Eschatology." *Christianity and Literature* 54, no. 2 (Winter 2005): 185–208.

Lazer, Hank. "Blackness Blessed: The Writings of Lucille Clifton." *Southern Review* 25, no. 3 (1989): 760–70.

Mance, Ajuan Maria. "Re-locating the Black Female Subject: The Landscape of the Body in the Poems of Lucille Clifton." In *Recovering the Black Female Body: Self-Representations by African American Women*, edited by Michael Bennett and Vanessa D. Dickerson. New Brunswick, NJ: Rutgers University Press, 2001, 123–40.

Ostriker, Alicia. "Kin and Kin: The Poetry of Lucille Clifton." *American Poetry Review* 22, no. 6 (1993): 41–48.

Raub, Bonnie. " 'The Light that Insists on Itself in the World': Lucille Clifton and African American Consciousness." *CLA Journal* 51, no. 4 (June 2008): 356–77.

Rushing, Andrea Benton. "Lucille Clifton: A Changing Voice for Changing Times." In *Coming to Light: American Women Poets in the Twentieth Century*, edited by Diane Wood Middlebrook and Marilyn Yalom. Ann Arbor: University of Michigan Press, 1985, 214–22.

Thyreen-Mizingou, Jeannine. "Grace and Ethics in Contemporary American Poetry: Resituating the Other, the World, and the Self." *Religion & Literature* 32, no. 1 (Spring 2000): 67–87.

Wall, Cheryl. "Sifting Legacies in Lucille Clifton's *Generations*." *Contemporary Literature* 40, no. 4 (Winter 1999): 552–74.

———. "Lucille Clifton: Defining What American Poetry Is." *Contemporary Literature* 46, no. 3 (2005): 541–43.

Waniek, Marilyn Nelson. "Black Silences, Black Songs." *Callaloo* 6, no. 1 (1983): 156–65.

White, Mark Bernard. "Sharing the Living Light: Rhetorical, Poetic, and Social Identity in Lucille Clifton." *CLA Journal* 40, issue 3 (March 1997): 289.

Whitley, Edward. " 'A Long Missing Part of Itself': Bringing Lucille Clifton's *Generations* into American Literature." *MELUS* 26, no. 2 (summer 2001): 47–64.

Worsham, Fabian Clements. "The Poetics of Matrilineage: Mothers and Daughters in the Poetry of African American Women, 1965–1985." In *Women of Color: Mother–Daughter Relationships in 20th Century Literature*, edited by Elizabeth Brown-Guillory. Austin: University of Texas Press, 1997, 117–21.

KIMIKO HAHN

FROM *Mosquito and Ant*

Orchid Root

correspondence to L

i.
Who thinks of the orchid root
but the horticulturalist
or the one now holding the shears
and a jar of water.
Who thinks of the soil
but the gardener when
even the scent of mulch completes the air
like light.

ii.
my hands smelling like tobacco
from his shirt which smelled of my hand lotion

iii.
I need to return to the Chinese women poets.
The flat language
of pine and orchid.
The clouds playing over the crescent moon.
Return to the coy lines
that advertise and contest.
The words weighted in object
as much as flight.
If there were a bridge outside my window

I would slip on silk slippers
the ones with a phoenix
and run across
to the sisters who know
how to instruct the senses:
when to know the difference
between the narcissus fragrance
and burning rubber.

iv.
Take—the anonymous courtesan
who wrote the lines:
My hairpins on your fallen jacket—
My stockings on your tiles—
My petals on your root—

v.
The women write poems to one another
to protest the man's inattention:
and they fall in love
consequently
as the honeysuckle climbs the fence
from one garden to the next,
its fragrance on the draft beneath the door.

vi.
PINE 杉
MAGPIE 鵲
CLOUD 雲

vii.
You and M can read classical Chinese
and I envy you both
like the bitch
I was raised to be:
haughty and self-effacing.
Always wanting.
Always evasive.

What saves me is knowing
if I don't want to write on something
there is nothing else to write.
This is what compels me
to locate the characters in *Matthew's.*

viiii.
the grass radicals—

ix.
Clearly I need the taste of plum
on my hands, my chin, his lips.
His. Mine. Plumb.

Garnet

i.
X wanted to present a gift
the husband would not detect
as inclination. Book bag.
Rhyming dictionary. Hand mirror.
I copied poems from *The Orchid Boat* for him.

ii.
You are the Empress Wu Tsu-T'ien
requesting her lover
examine her *pomegranate dress.*
I am as delighted as you.

iii.
Eating a bowl of raspberries
I imagine X sucking
on the beads of my garnet necklace—

iv.

She began as concubine to Empress T'ai then to his son, Emperor Kai, until he replaced his Empress with her. She ruled China from that moment. After his death and into old age she kept a male harem, concubines and courtier lovers. How do you feel about this?

v.

nipples the color of garnet

vi.

You advise, why dull a sharp point?
why flatten the crests? why
rinse out color? why douse what
the gut claims from the heart—

vii.

the *he* residing in the *she*

viii.

garnet hard as nipples—

FROM *The Narrow Road to the Interior*

Utica Station Dep.10:07 a.m. to N.Y. Penn Station

In the cavernous station, the train delayed for over an hour, I have watched a woman tend her newborn. She is tall, ties her hair back, has light dark skin and light, maybe green, eyes. Her baby is lighter; the man who picked up the ticket and kissed them, very black. I have watched her because her baby is so quiet. And I have not heard her voice.

On the train she sits one seat ahead and across the aisle. When the train brakes in Albany, the baby cries *ahh!* And she replies *ahh!* And I think, *just what I would do,* then feel miserable. *Was I* ever so attentive?

Placing one or the other child in the stroller, on the changing table, in a sassy seat, in the sandbox surrounded by plastic starfish and seahorses?

Stay. Come back.

She cradles the child, a boy by the blue; her rocking, syncopated with the train's chugging. Rain flecks the gray window. We pass a ditch of one hundred tires. A muddy lot of containers. Trees like sticks. A stray willow. We pass by the buds with such speed it could be late winter.

My heart is swollen, large as a newborn.

I do not want to return to their infancies. I would merely do the same: want to be in this notebook, not on the carpet covered with dolls. To be at the window waiting for their father, not swinging them in the park.

That was my mother—in the sandbox.

The farther south, the greener. Is it my imagination—or the proximity to the river?

I see a couple on a tiny jetty, holding a pink blanket.

My heart is swollen. As if a gland, not a muscle.

But I am wrong. There were stories I'd read and reread. *Mike Mulligan. The Runaway Bunny. Ping, the Duck.* If I read "a big word," I'd explain as if the explanation were part of the narrative: *private,* one's very own; *escape,* get away.

There were evenings where we ate a picnic dinner on the Columbia lawns while their father worked late. I remember because when a plane roared over us, I'd say *plane plane* and she would look up to watch it roar away.

One of my first tasks was to name things. Then it became her task. One daughter's then the next. We'd walk from apartment to park—*Pizza. Doggie. Car.*—naming things—*Daisy.*

Train. Bus. Firetruck.

It is so difficult to travel with an infant—the bags of plastic things. One's own pockets, weighted with keys and change. Maybe a magazine stuck in somewhere. Balancing a cup of coffee with one hand, steering the stroller with the other. The baby struggling to be held. Difficult pleasures.

Writing time, remote.

I told myself then, *I need to slow down*—as if picking lice off a child's head. As if reading a poem—instead of sniffing around for the self on some meridian.

Along this train ride down the Hudson, the tracks run so close to the water it is as if the water were the rails.

I wonder if there is clay along the river's edge—just as Barbara and I found clay in the brook behind her house. Or as my daughters dug into the sand for the red clay on Fire Island, our hands afterward, cinnabar-red.

Always, *Mommy needs to—   I need to—*

I look up from this notebook and see a tiny island with the shell of a castle—what is that? Is that how I've been a mother?

Dogwood blossoms, a cloud in the grove of branches.

A sail boat. A row boat.

The mother and infant sleep now, the boy like a cat on her chest. Or as if her heart rested on her sweater. I do recall that lovely pressure.

As we near the GWB, a tugboat towing a barge. Part of the bridge is wrapped in cloth. As if chilled.

I wish we didn't have to plunge into the tunnel.

Now forsythia. Now weeping cherry. I think of my mother—dead these past seven years—eight by Buddhist count.

The sudden brick landscape of Harlem. Then the tunnel, so now I see reflected in the window the boy who has been banging the seat, as if a sport. I need water to swallow an aspirin. I need to stretch.

My heart is swollen, as if—a hot water bottle!

The mother pats the baby. She begins to collect jackets for them both.

To put on an infant's jacket, I'd curl my own hand through the cuff and up the sleeve then pull her arm through. A tiny trick.

There was a difficult moment on a city bus: when I finally got the baby to stop stamping on the seat and sit down, the passenger behind me leaned forward and said, *You're a good mother.* I nearly wept.

Stay. Come back.

A mother with a fishing rod.

Looking for sensation on some meridian. In some station. Now speeding away from an acquaintance I might have asked, *shall I slip off my dress?* But I didn't. There was no urgency.

A mother with a plastic kite.

This is the difference: I don't find myself trailing a man around a room, screening gesture and tone.

This is the difference: I thought I was missing. Missing something.

As if a party balloon.

If my short hair didn't get so crushed I'd wear a baseball cap, too. (What would it say?)

Stay. Come back. Water. Pee-pee. You.

Before the tunnel—those dozen poles in the river— swollen and rotted from a long-vanished pier.

That's what the heart was—swollen—like a mother weeping for something. *A pier.*

Appear missing.

In Childhood

things don't die or remain damaged
but return: stumps grow back hands,
a head reconnects to a neck,
a whole corpse rises blushing and newly elastic.
Later this vision is not True:
the grandmother remains dead
not hibernating in a wolf's belly.
Or the blue parakeet does not return
from the little grave in the fern garden
though one may wake in the morning
thinking mother's call is the bird.
Or maybe the bird is with grandmother
inside light. Or grandmother was the bird
and is now the dog
gnawing on the chair leg.
Where do the gone things go
when the child is old enough
to walk herself to school,
her playmates already
pumping so high the swing hiccups?

Like Lavrinia

Like Lavrinia Merli, in 1890 in Majola, Mantua,
expired from hysteria and placed in a vault

on Thursday, July 3rd, where she regained consciousness,
tore at the graves clothes her peasant husband has just

smoothed around her seven-month pregnant belly,
and where she turned over and gave birth

but was not discovered until Saturday—
both mother and newborn then really dead;

like George Hefdecker of Erie, Pennsylvania,
a farmer, who upon suffering heart failure in 1891,

was temporarily buried until the purchase of a plot
and was unearthed four days later

with his fingers so bitten off his hands no longer looked human;

like Mr. Oppelt, a wealthy manufacturer in Rudenberg
whose vault, unsealed fifteen years after his death,

was found to contain a skeleton
seated in the corner, the coffin lid off;

like the gendarme in 1889, dead drunk on potato brandy,

whose banging in the coffin caused the sexton to bore holes

though the Frenchman had by then mutilated his head
in an effort to burst through and was fully deceased;

like the beggar turned up frozen

in a German village in 1807 and buried
only to be disinterred when a watchman detected

lamentations from the grave

although by that time he had indeed suffocated;
like them, yes, the air about my body dead

even in this abrupt consciousness.
                •
He sips his instant coffee black
and turns on 1010 WINS.
                •
He closes the door on the newly hung wallpaper

and the dishes soaking in sudsy gray gravy
for his nightly walk down Broadway

communing with Black hookers and White junkies.
He is looking for oxygen. I am the wife

under the fluorescent bathroom light

tweezing each hair around my sex.

It vaguely hurts. It reminds me that feeling
is not what I will get from him. It kills time

until "Miami Vice." Afterwards
the infant daughter will wake just as we lie down.

•

There are several reported happy endings.
Like the farm wife, Mrs. Sarseville, in 1891

who while milking cows saw beneath the floorboards

a nest of snakes and fell to the ground

then presumed dead by her physician and loved ones
until she sat upright in her coffin.

The daughter led the woman to the breakfast table
where she ate heartily. Ah!

It is amazing they are found ever.

POETICS STATEMENT
Still *Writing the Body*

COMING OF AGE during the civil rights era meant that, in my own writing, my female Eurasian body was a potential subject as opposed to someone else's object. It was a time when one could re-view something typically female, like intuition, as powerful rather than inconsequential. It was a thrilling moment full of exploration and discovery—and of course, *recovery*.

Although I had studied East Asian literature in graduate school, I was not exposed to much theory, literary or otherwise. So over the years I've haphazardly picked up and processed texts on my own. The French feminists in particular have had an abiding influence on me. I was intrigued by the idea of "writing the body" and the possibility of female expression ("express" as in expressing milk?). However, in my unsystematic search for a definition, I did not fully understand what such a text might look like—or sound or smell like for that matter.

Fast forward from that twenty-something to a fifty-something. I've arrived at an interpretation through two American poets: Emily Dickinson and Elizabeth Bishop. The content of their poetry is moving, and at the same time, their formal elements—diction, cadence, syntax, sound—are physically stirring. For example, in Bishop's "The Waiting Room," the body is literal content as the adult looks back at a common traumatic moment; meantime, the short lines and caesuras create a halting cadence and a halting means to make sense of this vertiginous realization. This recollection culminates in these lines: "[The waiting room] was sliding / beneath a big black wave, / another, and another." Similarly, the final lines in "First Death in Nova Scotia" display a delicate use of rhyme and assonance: go/ road/snow, tiny/lily, tiny/tight, clutch/shut up. Bishop has created a fabric of sounds that subtly wraps around the reader even as we proceed into snow. It is all the more gorgeous for the child's tone: "But how could Arthur go . . . ?"

Others have described her work in physical terms. In his anthology headnote, Michael Schmidt comments: "The enabling instrument in Bishop's poems is the syntax, . . . seemingly casual, barefoot. The effect is intimate, rapt, the voice always subject-defined, its repetitions and qualifications building towards a precise sense of that subject" (*The Great Modern Poets*, Quercus). Adrienne Rich in her essay on Bishop, "The Eye of the Outsider" (*Blood, Bread, and Poetry*, NY: W. W. Norton, 1983), wishes in part to address Bishop's "experience of outsider, closely—though not exclusively—linked with the essential outsiderhood of a lesbian identity." Here, too,

Rich includes physical terms: "the marvelous flexibility and sturdiness of her writing"; "'A Cold Spring' can be read as a record of a slow, deliberate, erotic unfolding"; "Bishop is difficult to quote from because her poems are so often hung on one long thread." Thread. *Fabric. Yes.*

Come to find out, not everyone is interested in poetry that is *moving*, emotionally and viscerally. But Emily Dickinson was: "If I feel physically as if the top of my head were taken off, I know it is a poem." Her own work is as physical as it is cerebral and her poetics keenly shape this reading experience. We feel the use of a hymnal structure with both nostalgic and lyrical resonances—the seductive slant rhyme—seductive because it is not obvious in the way perfect rhyme is obvious—the visual and breath pulsations rendered by her dashes. Heady stuff: "My Life had stood—a Loaded Gun—"

I NEED to interrupt myself here. I am reminded of my sister, Tomie Hahn—an enthomusicologist and performance artist—and how she describes her own work in *Sensational Knowledge: Embodying Culture through Japanese Dance* (Wesleyan University Press, 2007). On the surface, this association is obvious since the body is in actual motion, whereas a text is only physically moving when performed. But she combines the two in a way that reminds me of "writing the body." In her introduction she writes:

> "Know your body," headmaster Tachibana Hiroyo said during my dance lesson, as she gently drew her hand to her chest. In this fleeting moment she succinctly imparted a cultural sensibility, a Japanese way of knowing, that moved beyond these few words and gestures. Curious about my own understanding of such moments, and the embodiment of such sensibilities conveyed during lessons, I was drawn to research how culture is passed down, or embodied, through dance.

Here the body is more than a vehicle to perform gesture. It is *also* a text. The task of the teacher is to inscribe the lesson on the student's body in what Tomie calls "corporeal lessons." One might ask whether this isn't true of any dance instruction. Apparently not. She goes on to comment:

> As is generally known, philosophically, theory and practice are not separated in Japan—the mind and body are not considered to be separate entities but are instead regarded as interdependent. . . . Theory thus arises from practice. We embody the essence of theory when presence and thematic articulations of physical movements arise through practice.

Furthermore, because many of the dances are based on written narratives, the body realizes that story. It becomes a text expressing a text.

Such a pedagogical approach is as *sensational* as it is cerebral. While

Japanese culture has not taken on the more Puritanical elements in American cultures, the different sensibility does go against the Western grain, so to speak. The latter is more often than not a harsh vision committed to the rejection of the flesh (the flip side of our popular culture). As a psychologist friend says, "In the West we tend to experience things from the neck up." And a colleague of mine from the philosophy department has pointed out that Plato in his *Phaedo* actually praised philosophers for despising the body. Ironically, it seems that a lot of poetry today is reverting back to the West's anti-sensual bias—its fear and distrust of the flesh—by emphasizing the purely cerebral and conceptual. And this puzzles me.

I am determined to draw the whole body back into the experience of writing and reading poetry. (Not in a dogmatic manner although I have my obvious preoccupations.) For example, I teach poetry in an utterly simple way: to look at how repetition functions in a text, especially as an organizing principle. And, as I began to note before interrupting myself, any kind of repetition is bound to have an effect on the reader's body.

How do I consider repetition as a writer? One way to view these elements is texture—not a term used often. Jack Myers in *The Portable Poetry Workshop* (Wadsworth/Thomson, 2005) offers the following definition:

> *Texture* is the tactile aspect of poetry. One can't "touch" a poem, but the mind's inner senses can evoke a sense of how dense, cluttered, smooth, clear, rough, spiky, or forcefully paced the *aesthetic surface* of a poem (sonics, rhythm, imagery, lineation, typography, syntax, rhetorical devices, tropes, etc.) may be. Generally speaking, texture is composed of the elements of a poem that cannot be paraphrased—the aesthetic effect beyond semantic meaning—but which in and of themselves are "intelligences" or units of nonverbal meaning in the poem.

I like Myers's word "tactile" because, although he notes one cannot "touch" a poem, the word acknowledges how it exists in the physical world.

For myself, I am particularly interested in a dense or "rough" diction. Myers uses Van Gogh's "thick textures and saturated colors" as a visual example and compares his paintings to Gerard Manley Hopkins and Seamus Heaney texts. Here I return to Elizabeth Bishop: In "The Fish" (*The Complete Poems*, NY: Farrar, Straus and Giroux, 1980) she describes the skin as "speckled with barnacles, / fine rosettes of lime, / and infested / with tiny white sea-lice, / . . ." The rhyme as well as the rich repetition of *s*- and *t-sounds*, is thrilling. And because they are scattered, the sounds engage without obvious pattern. To my mind—which is my body—the sounds, *speck*, *rosettes*, *infest*, sound like that doily from one of her other famous poems. Like the texture of a doily.

In the course of preparing for this modest statement, I had the pleasure of looking through dusty volumes, most of them either on art *or* on art *and* politics. I recalled how my emerging writing identity so depended on the phrase "the personal is political." And I wonder if this now-cliché should be revived to include all the complex changes that have transpired over the decades; also to put into relief all the changes that have not taken place since institutions can change more swiftly than culture.

In my rummaging around for old textbooks I found *New French Feminisms* edited by Alein Marks and Isabelle de Courtivron (New York: Shocken Books, 1981). I was eager to see if I could locate, once and for all, a definition for "writing the body." I did not. But I reread a piece by Chantal Chawaf, "La chair linguistique [linguistic flesh]," and found this quote:

> [When I write] I move in close and what I see is enormous. I magnify the word with a close-up lens. I examine it at close range: it has its own way of being granulated, ruffled, wrinkled, gnarled, iridescent, sticky. . . . The corporality of language stirs up our sensuality, wakes it up, pulls it away from indifferent inertia.

I like that her words echo Myers's definition of "texture" as well as Dickinson's picture of poetic-combustion. I like that her words echo my sister's. And I like that the quote describes the work I love best, poetry expressed from body (by female and male writers, after all). What I aim and hope for is poetry that moves the reader. Away from *indifferent inertia—*

"I WANT TO GO WHERE THE HYSTERIC RESIDES"

Kimiko Hahn's Re-Articulation of the Feminine in Poetry[1]

Zhou Xiaojing

> Throughout history people have knocked their heads against the riddle of the nature of femininity—. . . Nor will *you* have escaped worrying over this problem—those of you who are men; to those of you who are women this will not apply—you are yourself the problem.   —SIGMUND FREUD, "Femininity"[2]

IN HIS INTRODUCTORY LECTURES on psychoanalysis, Freud reveals the impasse of a male-centered approach to female subjectivity and psychosexuality. Although Freud claims that the "nature of femininity" remains a "riddle" in his lecture "Femininity," he has in a way already defined it, for a phallocentric point of view on the feminine enigma is embedded in his remarks. Freud's statement about the nature of femininity positions man as the knowing subject, and woman as the object of knowledge to be mastered by the male subject. The cultural assumptions that inform Freud's lecture about the baffling "nature of femininity" have generated critical investigations in the feminine by feminists such as Luce Irigaray and Elizabeth Grosz, among others. In her explication of Luce Irigaray's feminist deconstruction of patriarchal discourses on femininity, Elizabeth Grosz observes that the challenge Irigaray poses entails two central themes: "that of the cultural debt to maternity, the creation of a means of representing the mother's relations to the child beyond the orbit of the symbolic father's authority; and that of adequately representing and constructing an autonomously conceived female sexuality, corporeality and morphology."[3] These two central themes underlie Kimiko Hahn's poetics and her sustained interrogation of mother–daughter relationships in her poems.

Since the publication of her first volume, *Air Pocket* (1989), Hahn has been exploring new ways for rearticulating the feminine, while enacting feminist theories in her poems as a method for investigating the female body and subjectivity. In her early poems collected in *Air Pocket* and her second volume, *Earshot* (1992), Hahn often examines the feminine mostly through autobiographical experiences of the mother–daughter relationship, and through women's experience as depicted in literature, especially in *The Tale of Genji*, with a focus on jealousy and rivalry among women whose relationships with one another are shaped by patriarchy. While the mother–daughter relationship continues to be a major subject in Hahn's later poems collected in *The Unbearable Heart* (1995), *Volatile* (1998), *Mosquito & Ant* (1999), *The Artist's Daughter* (2002), and *The Narrow Road to the Interior* (2006), it becomes more complex, as the mother figure begins to be associated with creativity and an alternative mode of knowing. This development parallels another in Hahn's intertextual dialogues and incorporations in her poems with writings by and about women. As her textual engagement with *The Tale of Genji* and other Japanese writings expands to include unconventional, innovative texts by women, such as *The Pillow Book* by Sei Shōnagon and verses by Chinese women written in *nu shu* (female script), this engagement becomes much more than an exploration of the feminine as a subject matter. In fact, both the language and form of Hahn's later poems become more oriented toward a feminine aesthetics. Since I have extensively discussed some of these aspects of Hahn's poetics elsewhere, I want to explore here some less examined poems by Hahn, with a focus on a prominent, yet seldom studied, feature of Hahn's poetry—a theorizing poetic performance as a rearticulation of the hysteric feminine defined by patriarchy and phallo(logo)centric discourse.[4]

For Asian Americans, however, to reclaim the feminine often involves confronting racism and Orientalism, which intersect sexism. Images of Asian femininity in the dominant media of the United States are fraught with Orientalist hyper-sexualization of Asian women as the exotic object of white male desire. Rearticulating the feminine for Asian Americans thus entails a critique of sexism and racism, as well as resistance to Eurocentric cultural domination. I would argue that Hahn's rearticulation of the feminine entails breaking away from gender norms defined by both patriarchy and Orientalism. To recognize and assert femininity, Grosz emphasizes, requires new ways of knowing and alternative modes of representation: "Recognizing feminine specificity implies seeing and developing other kinds of discourse, different forms of evaluation and new procedures for living in and reflecting on day-to-day life. . . . Different ways of knowing, different kinds of discourse, new methods and aspirations for language and knowledges need to be explored if women are to overcome their restrictive containment in patriarchal representation" (SS, 126). Hahn's poems articulate a subversive and creative femininity by engaging with psychoanalytical discourses, especially those developed by French feminist philosophers and psychoanalysts, and by drawing on women's cultures and literary traditions across national borders.

However, not enough critical attention has been given to Hahn's poetics of what might be called a corporeal femininity that refuses to be defined by gendered, raced hierarchies and heterosexual norms. Critics tend to emphasize the ways in which Hahn exposes Orientalist representations of Asian women. In her provocative psychoanalytical reading of Hahn's poems, Juliana Chang explores "how the Asian American female subject, as symbolized by the speaking subject" in Hahn's third volume *The Unbearable Heart*, "inhabits a melancholic position that signals a racial return of the national repressed."[5] Chang examines the racialization of the Asian American female in terms of the "oriental feminine," which operates as a "site of racial fantasy, desire, anxiety, and enjoyment" in the "national imaginary and symbolic" of the United States. At the same time, Chang argues that "the oriental feminine is the site not only of imaginary and symbolic fantasy, but also the site of the traumatic real" (241). The reality of Asian women's experience of racial discrimination and sexual exploration in Hahn's poems, Chang contends, critiques racism and sexism that are elided in the dominant media that perpetuate the myth of white men's erotic love relationships with Asian women. Nevertheless, femininity in the "oriental feminine" remains negative. In the "oriental feminine, which remains outside of modern history and modern subjectivity" (240), female subjugation is compounded by racial oppression and cultural subordination. As Chang states in concluding her article, "For the Asian American female subject of *The Unbearable Heart*, the oriental feminine is an object violently rendered other" (257).

Yet, in contrast to the abject Oriental feminine Chang locates in Hahn's work, Hahn also presents a subversive and creative femininity in *The Unbearable Heart*. In poems such as "The Hemisphere: Kuchuk Hanem," she interweaves lines from Edward Said's *Orientalism* and Flaubert's travel writing, *Flaubert in Egypt*, and juxtaposes them with Hanem's subversive speeches that are imagined by Hahn, and with Hahn's persona's memories of her mother, who is Japanese American. Countering the Oriental feminine, Hahn's persona asserts, "Woman's role as storyteller included creator and healer. My mother knew this, unconsciously."[6] This statement of the "woman's role" points to a femininity that breaks away from the "oriental feminine," resists normative femininity, and also refuses the inscrutability Freud ascribes to "femininity."[7] While defining the mother's roles as creator and healer through the daughter's voice, Hahn posits an alternative way of knowing outside the gendered binary pairings such as mind/male versus body/female, and points to an alternative mother–daughter relationship outside of patriarchy and Orientalism.

For Hahn, inscribing the feminine outside of patriarchal and racial hierarchies entails reinventing a poetic language and form that pose "questions about the outside, the absences, the silences of psychoanalysis, its repressions, disavowals, intolerable impulses, and wishes," as Grosz says of Luce Irigaray's writings (*JL*, 149). Hahn's poem "Translating Ancient Lines into the Vernacular," collected in her fifth volume *Mosquito & Ant*, is a salient example of her desire to investigate impulses and wishes that are repressed, disavowed, and deemed intolerable within patriarchal societies and discourses, and to rearticulate an alternative femininity outside phallo(logo)centric discourse. The title *Mosquito & Ant* refers to the material, inscriptive style of *nu shu* (female script)—a discrete script used exclusively by and among Chinese women in a rural area in southern China.[8] While evoking Asian women's autonomy and creativity, Hahn's poems in this collection emulate and reinvent Chinese and Japanese women's writings as a way of exploring women's experience, subjectivity, and desires through a feminine aesthetic. Hahn uses Chinese characters to mark new sections in the collection; She opens the second part of *Mosquito & Ant* with a page that is inscribed with the Chinese character for "Woman," and in the first poem in the section "Translating Ancient Lines into the Vernacular," she writes:

> I want to go where the hysteric resides,
> the spinning a child knows
> when she twirls around till air and earth
> are inebriated and she falls
> even bruises her knees even
> as a delightful lake of sandwich and milk rises—
> and she laughs so fully

the others laugh with her
or tell her:
now that's enough.[9]

The opening line, "I want to go where the hysteric resides," asserts a central theme that recurs in Hahn's seven books of poetry: the search for a female genealogy of culture, aesthetics, and poetic forms and languages that can reclaim women's body and subjectivity. By identifying the girl's spinning with "hysteria" commonly understood as "the feminine neurosis *par excellence*,"[10] Hahn simultaneously translates and redefines the meanings of hysteria as a defiant, rebellious gesture.

The girl's spinning and laughter convey a pleasure that is contagious to some and disturbing to others (as the authoritative voice, "*now that's enough*," suggests); they are a subversive allusion to Freud's definition of hysteria as a somatic expression of a psychical disorder and as the repression of female sexual desire that has been deemed unacceptable by patriarchal society. In *Studies on Hysteria*, Josef Breuer and Freud state: "*Hysterics suffer mainly from reminiscences.*"[11] For Freud and Breuer, hysteria results from the memories of traumas to which the hysteric is unable to react adequately and affectively through words, deeds, or tears. "The injured person's reaction to the trauma only exercises a completely 'cathartic' effect if it is an *adequate* reaction. . . . If the reaction is suppressed, the affect remains attached to the memory" (8). Thus, hysteria is a "psychical disorder" that is transformed "into purely somatic symptoms" (86). This somatic conversion of psychical repression, Freud suggests, signifies the hysteric's suppressed affection and sexual desire, which she is unable to articulate. In his analysis of an eighteen-year-old hysteric whom he calls "Dora" in "Fragment of an Analysis of a Case of Hysteria," Freud insists on regarding Dora's symptoms as " 'somatic compliance' which may afford the unconscious mental processes a physical outlet" of a morally inadmissible love and sexual desire for her own father and for Herr K., the husband of her father's mistress, Frau K., who used to be Dora's confidante and friend and with whom Dora was also supposed to be in love though somewhat unconsciously.[12] While these men are supposed to be the center of Dora's affection and desire, women are either dispensable (such as Dora's mother), or untrustworthy rivals (such as Frau K.). Dora's unconscious love for Frau K., Freud suggests, is secondary and is reinforced by displacement resulting from her suppressed unacceptable heterosexual desire. As he writes, "When, in a hysterical woman or girl, the sexual libido which is directed towards men has been energetically suppressed, it will regularly be found that the libido which is directed towards women has become vicariously reinforced and even to some extent conscious" ("Hysteria," 82). Despite his careful attention to numerous details of Dora's "human and social circumstances" ("Hysteria," 70), Freud overlooks other possible explanations for Dora's "somatic compliance."

Countering Freud's master narrative of female hysteria as a symptom of repression, Grosz argues that "Dora's hysterical symptoms can be seen as refusal rather than the expression of desire" (SS, 134). She notes that these symptoms "emerge after Herr K. has put her [Dora] in a compromising position (twice) where she is reduced to passive dependence on him—that is, where she demonstrates the attributes of 'normal femininity' " (SS, 134–35). Rather than regarding hysterical symptoms as the somatic conversion of repressed secret heterosexual desires, Grosz considers them "a corporeal discourse" through which the hysteric speaks her defiance:

> The hysteric thus attempts to "cope" with the demands and expectations of a male-dominated culture which relies on women's renunciation of their relations to other women, and of their unmediated relations of their own bodies and pleasures, by summoning up an apparently incapacitating "illness," which prevents her from giving satisfaction to men while satisfying herself in a compromise or symptomatic form. Here is a mode of defiance of patriarchy, not the site of its frustration. In this sense, the hysteric is a proto-feminist, . . . who, if she had access to the experiences of other women, may locate the problem in cultural expectations of femininity rather than in femininity itself. (SS, 135)

Refusing to erase the woman's agency as a subject, and situating Dora's symptoms in relation to an oppressive patriarchy, Grosz contends that "hysteria can be seen as the woman's rebellion against and rejection of the requirements of femininity (requirements which are humiliating for her insofar as they presume women's castration). It is a refusal rather than a repression of heterosexuality, and an attempt to return nostalgically to the pre-oedipal, homosexual desire for the mother" (SS, 134).

In a similar vein, Hélène Cixous and Catherine Clément in The Newly Born Woman relate the female hysteric to women's subjugated position in patriarchal society, and reinterpret hysteria as rebellion against the Law of the Father. At the same time, they connect the hysteric's rebellion against "cultural expectations of femininity" to the subversive roles of the sorceress and the witch. They regard the "feminine role" of the hysteric, the sorceress, and the witch as one that disrupts and disturbs the patriarchal and logocentric establishment "because the symptoms—the attacks—revolt and shake up the public, the group, the men, the others to whom they are exhibited. . . . The hysteric unties familiar bonds, introduces disorder into the well-regulated unfolding of everyday life, gives rise to magic in ostensible reason."[13] Emphasizing the "subversive weight" in "the return of the repressed" as embodied by the hysteric (9), Cixous and Clément seek to retell unsettling "women's stories" in which women are not merely victims, but active practitioners of an alternative way of knowing outside the symbolic order of patriarchy, as witches and sorceresses whose laughter is "frightening—like Medusa's laugh—petrifying and shattering constraint" (32). This is the kind of laughter that Hahn translates from "ancient lines" of sorceresses and witches "into the vernacular" through the girl who "laughs so fully / the others laugh with her / or tell her" to stop, and who spins so madly that she falls and is on the verge of vomiting, as "a delightful lake of sandwich and milk rises." Like the hysteric, this laughing, twirling, and vomiting girl resists the constraints imposed on her in defiance of propriety and authoritative discipline—"*now that's enough.*"

While concurring with feminist critics, David Eng explores further the social and political implications of hysteria for those who are socially constructed as the other. "As a mode of political resistance," Eng asserts, "hysteria signals the refusal of a female subject to occupy her proper place within a patriarchal society, her refusal to submit to dominant modes of identification, and her refusal to comply with conventional mores—a social . . . wandering from one's culturally assigned position."[14] In this regard, Eng notes the "double-edge status" of the hysteric, saying that "the hysterical condition calls attention to the social order's failure to discipline, regulate, coerce, or finally socialize its others into their proper social places." At the same time, "hysteria serves to exhume the disavowed, alternate, and buried stories of its sufferers"—the repressed histories of the excluded, undisciplined, and inassimilable others (*RC*, 176, 177).

These buried stories and repressed histories are precisely what Hahn seeks to exhume by going "where the hysteric resides" and "translating ancient lines into the vernacular." Her evocation and performance of the hysteric in her poems are at once subversive and innovative in constructing a female tradition of rebellion and creativity outside of Orientalist and patriarchal discourses such as Freud's master narratives about the nature of femininity. In her note to "Translating Ancient Lines into the Vernacular," Hahn writes that its title is triggered by a line from Cixous and Clément's book, "When the line is crossed, contagion is produced," in their discussion of the dissemination of the contagious "madness" of the witch as the "mother" of the hysteric (*MA*, 101). Thus by going "where the hysteric resides," Hahn explores an alternative site of knowledge and signifying tradition where the woman is "newly born" out of rebellious feminine texts and corporeal discourses that refuse women's proper places assigned by patriarchy, or defined by Orientalism.[15] As her persona in another poem, "Going Inside to Write," collected in her second volume, *Earshot*, says: "We garden with the knowledge of our bodies." And, in response to her father's call "from the far room," "she shouts: / I can't hear you. I can't / hear you."[16] The daughter's shouting back at the father to refuse his calls suggests that to reiterate the feminine outside the symbolic order of patriarchy entails simultaneously searching for a female genealogy and resisting the Father's interpellation and authority.

If femininity has been defined, prescribed, and inscribed by conventional practices and dominant discourses in a patriarchal society, it has to be recognized as such in order to be reclaimed and rearticulated. In seeking to accomplish this task, Hahn exposes the ways in which femininity is molded not only for male pleasure, but also for sustaining male domination. One of Hahn's early poems, "Dance Instructions for a Young Girl," collected in her first volume, *Air Pocket*, provides a striking contrast of femininity shaped by patriarchy to that of the hysteric model enacted in "Translating Ancient Lines into the Vernacular." The poem alludes to the fact that geishas were traditionally told to imitate male impersonators in Kabuki, a Japanese opera, in order to learn the art of femininity to please men:

> Stand: knees slightly
> bent, toes in *posed*
> *you watch the hawk over the river*
> *curve, until his voice*, shoulders back
> gently *overcome by Seiji's mouth*
> *against yours, the white breath*, and elbows
> close to your side. *The silk cords*
> *and sash crush your lungs* you are
> young—beautiful, and almost
> elegant. . . .[17]

Even though this young girl is beautiful, her beauty must be fashioned into an ideal feminine elegance through rigorous training by a male master whose poise, steps, and gestures the girl is required to imitate closely:

> Follow his flow
> of steps, a shallow stream between rocks
> *the carp. Seiji draws your han*
> *toward him or a stroke.*
> . . . .
>   Bow to him and the audience.
> When you straighten, his black and red lines
> against the white powder
> are drawn, as his gesture
> and step, perfectly. More perfectly *the weight*
> *of his chest* than your own, although his
> belongs to you, a woman. (*AP*, 12)

Rather than urging the novice geisha to achieve the feminine perfection modeled by the male master, the speaker protests on her behalf against the actor's appropriation of femininity, while exposing the compliance of that feminine ideal with patriarchy.

Since her first volume, Hahn has continuously investigated the formation of femininity and female subjectivity within patriarchy, by employing a psychoanalytical approach, especially in her references to the gender relationships in *The Tale of Genji* (*Genji monogatari* ca. 1000) by Murasaki Shikibu. Hahn's re-representation and analysis of the characters from *The Tale of Genji* in her poems form two lines of subversive inquiry—one exploring the ways in which idealized normative femininity is molded by patriarchy as embodied by Genji, the "shining" Prince, and the other investigating Genji's never-ending longing for his mother. While the first line of inquiry undermines the notion of femininity defined by gender norms, the second calls into question the Freudian notion about the formation of male subjectivity, in which the boy's abandonment or complete dismantlement of his Oedipus complex "in the most normal cases" leads to his attainment of "a severe super-ego" that gives man the "strength and independence" woman lacks ("Femininity," 357). Rather than representing Genji's pursuit of numerous women simply in terms of his attraction to apparently female beauty and artistic, intellectual cultivation, Hahn disrupts the centrality of the father–son relationship in the formation of the male subject by indicating that Genji's pursuit of numerous women is a displacement of his perpetual search for his mother, in poems such as "Comp. Lit." subtitled "after Murasaki Shikibu's *Genjimonogatari*" in *Earshot* and "Wisteria" included in *The Unbearable Heart* (18–25). Significantly, Hahn highlights the fact that in searching for his mother, Genji subjugates women and girls to objects of his desire, while also turning them into rivals for his attention and love: The "shining Prince" "locks" the girl "into womanhood"; "She grows to need him, / tolerate him and become the enemy / of all other women."[18] Countering this patriarchal constitution and subjugation of the feminine, Hahn's persona not only refuses to become dependent on man like Genji's women, but also refuses to switch her attachment from her mother to her father: "When I visit mother / I still want her / holding me in a blanket on a ship to Rome . . ." (*E*, 14).

Moreover, in these poems and many others, Hahn explores an alternative femininity, one that redefines motherhood and womanhood outside of patriarchy, and beyond the orbit of phallocentric privilege and authority. This reconceptualization and re-representation of femininity is embedded in the question her persona asks: "When does mother become a different symbol . . ." (*E*, 13). As a strategy for rejecting femininity that is compliant with patriarchy, Hahn stylistically mimics the hysteric by employing an apparently irrational, incoherent, and corporeal discourse of fragmentary utterances and disrupted narratives in many of her poems. At the same time, she incorporates women's cultures, stories, and writings into her poems as a way of reclaiming femininity and the mother–daughter bond. The last poem in her first volume, "Resistance: A Poem on Ikat Cloth," demonstrates Hahn's subversive "feminine" poetics, which deliberately resists Eurocentric English-language culture and the racial hegemony of white supremacy, as well as the privilege of heterosexual love. While the title alludes to an African textile technique of "resist-dying yarn before it is woven,"[19] the names of various locations in Indonesia, Japan, and Africa known for ikat are scattered throughout the poem, evoking the kind of "contagion" of a rebellious feminine culture that Cixous and Clément speak of. In this poem, Hahn interweaves fragments from the Japanese folk tale "*Shitakirisuzume*" ("The Tongue-Cut-Sparrow"), from *Tosanikki* (*The Tosa Diary*), a Japanese poetic diary written about 935 by Ki no Tsurayuki in a female persona, and from *To the Lighthouse* by Virginia Woolf. From these heterogeneous fragments among others, two different kinds of female relationships emerge—one marked by rivalry, vengeance, and isolation as indicated in the fragmentary speeches and the destructive rivalry between the female sparrow and the old woman in the Japanese folk tale; the other characterized by friendship, admiration, and affection as in the case of the daughter's love for her mother presented as personal memory. The daughter's sensuous, aesthetic memory of her mother with whom she "fell in love" "deeply as only a little girl could" (*Air Pocket* 60) at once evokes and undermines Freud's notion of the girl's inevitable turning away from and against her mother as she goes through the developmental stages of the "castration complex" and "envy for the penis" ("Femininity" 352). According to Freud, "the girl is driven out of her attachment to her mother through the influence of her envy for the penis. . . ," and her "hostility to her mother" intensifies as she enters the situation of the Oedipus complex ("Femininity," 357). Countering this account, and speaking to a "you" who can designate to both the self/speaker and others/reader, Hahn presents the adult female speaker's memory of falling in love with her mother deeply in such a way that it enacts what might be called "hysteria" as "an attempt to return nostalgically to the pre-oedipal, homosexual desire for the mother," to quote Grosz again.

Like her articulation of the girl's love for her mother, Hahn's use of a corporeal aesthetic in describing the mother–daughter relationship— "Pulling at your nipples / you dreamt of her body / that would become yours" (*AP*, 60)—not only undermines the Freudian definition and the Orientalist representation of femininity, but also asserts an alternative way of knowing and representing the feminine. In his analysis of Hahn's poems collected in *Mosquito & Ant*, Robert Grotjohn rightly notes that Hahn uses "autoeroticism" and "lesbian suggestion" to "construct" a feminist "return to her own body as a return to the maternal body, as simultaneously mother and daughter" throughout the volume.[20] Hahn enacts this return through auto-/homoeroticism and a corporeal feminist aesthetic that evokes the female hysteric and disturbs the propriety of phallogocentric discourse. The feminine in the female genealogy she constructs is uncontainable within patriarchal or Orientalist discourses, as her later poems demonstrate.

Apart from sensuous language, homoeroticism, and corporeal discourse, Hahn also employs metaphors and narratives to construct a female genealogy in poems such as "Daphne's Journal," which is collected in her sixth volume, *The Artist's Daughter*. Both the title and the content of the poem evoke the Greek myth about the river god Peneus's daughter, Daphne, who was pursued by the enamored Apollo, god of music and poetry. In flight, Daphne received help from other gods and was changed into a laurel tree, which became Apollo's favorite. Hence laurel wreaths were the traditional crowns for the finest classical poets and singers. Like the mythic Daphne, the Daphne in Hahn's poem is not attracted to but is rather repulsed by the enamored men, who try to impress her with their "poetic allusion." The poem begins with Daphne's actual and symbolic leaving of her father's house for the woods:

> The woods blacken the air and the already bloody soil, I can't see beyond some thickets even at noon. I love that blindness because then I hear every whisker and wing. And they, me. What sport.
> •
> The men at the house are jackasses with their poetic allusion. They think impressing father will impress me. Just the opposite.[21]

In contrast to the enchanting woods where Daphne has a sense of freedom and belonging, her father's house is constricting and empty to her, particularly when her mother has "abandon[ed] [her] in an exile from these hollow rooms" (*AD*, 59). While the dark woods and bloody soil evoke the disturbing unknown associated with witches, the house with "hollow rooms" where Daphne's father and the literary men converse evokes the established male-dominant canon, from which the mother is "exiled." But out there in the woods, Daphne can find her mother's presence: "I can taste her in the fragrance of the evergreens" (*AD*, 59). Daphne's leaving of the father's house for the woods, then, is another way of Hahn's going "where the hysteric resides," which is a poetic construction of a female genealogy through ways of knowing and articulating the feminine that refuses compliance with normative femininity established by patriarchy and Orientalism.

As she continues to reimagine and rearticulate femininity and the mother–daughter relationship, Hahn further expands her exploration of the social and political implications of women's traumatic experiences in terms of hysteric "somatic conversion," such as Cambodian women's loss of sight, resulting from their witness of the "killing fields." The hysteria of these women in Hahn's *zuihitsu*, "Blindside," "serves to exhume the disavowed, alternate, and buried stories of its sufferers" to quote David Eng's words again (*RC*, 177). Straddling prose and poetry, and as a miscellaneous genre which was originally developed outside the Japanese literary establishment and often identified with *The Pillow Book* written in the early eleventh century by the female writer Sei Shōnagon, the *zuihitsu* is a form of "refusal to comply with conventional mores," as Eng says of hysteria (*RC*, 174). Hahn's reinvention of the *zuihitsu* through collage juxtapositions of heterogeneous textual fragments in "Blindside," included in her fourth volume, *Volatile*, could be considered a poetic enactment of what Eng calls the hysteric's "double-edge status." This hysterical condition, which "calls attention to the social order's failure to discipline, regulate, coerce, or finally socialize its others into their proper social places," also serves to recover, make known the repressed or erased experiences of the hysteric (*RC*, 177), as the following juxtaposed fragments suggest:

> The women's psychosomatic blindness could be something I identify with. Not that I willfully do not see, but attempt to control the immediate.
> . . .
> The incidence of women turning what I will call mad in Asian American writings is very high: John Okada's *No-No Boy*, Milton Murayama's *All I Asking for Is My Body*, Maxine Hong Kingston's *Woman Warrior*, Hisaye Yamamoto's *17 Syllables*, Bharati Mukherjee's *Wife*, Wendy Law Yone's *The Coffin Tree*.
> . . .
> Of 170,000 Cambodian refugees living in the United States, half reside in Los Angeles. Local ophthalmologists noticed a high incidence of vision problems among those women who arrived in the 1980s fleeing Pol Pot's Khmer Rouge. Approximately 150 have lost all or most of their sight though there is nothing physically wrong with their eyes.
>
> The Khmer Rouge took Chhean Im's brother and sister away. They killed her father and another brother *before her eyes*.
>
> *During the day they would take people into a big meeting hall and beat them and beat them and we all sat in a circle and were made to watch.*
> . . .
> On learning of my work he tells me when nuns interviewed Koreans in Hiroshima after the bomb, the survivors *drew a blank*. When inadvertently questioned in Japanese, one began to wail and recall the horrors. Others could also recall it in Japanese, but not in their *mother tongue*.
> . . .
> The body protects the spirit just as the spirit protects the body.
> . . .
> *In 1919, Freud called this [physical] sacrifice "conversion disorder."*[22]

In association with the horror of Pol Pot's Khmer Rouge massacres, which caused the Cambodian women's psychosomatic blindness, Hahn calls the reader's attention to other historical and contemporary atrocities such as the atomic bombing of Nagasaki and Hiroshima, the sexual enslavement of Korean women by the Japanese military, the violence against Thai child prostitutes, the oppression of women by patriarchs, and the incarceration of Japanese Americans in concentration camps (*V*, 84–87).

As she urges the reader and herself to relate the women's traumatic pasts to the present, and to read the women's somatic "conversion disorder" as symptomatic of social problems, Hahn translates the Cambodian women's psychosomatic "blindness" into a corporeal discourse and articulates the resistant silence of the mad Japanese American woman in Hisaye Yamamoto's short story "Seventeen Syllables":

> the need to engage with a text so personally the text becomes one's own, becomes part of one's own experience, one's own vision in fact
>
> *hysterical blindness*
>
> My heart beats in my throat as if attempting speech.
>
> In "17 Syllables" the three visit a family whose mother has gone mad. Of course the protagonist's father in a jealous rage takes away his wife's only pleasure, writing haiku. Apart from revealing her own history to her daughter she is completely isolated. She can speak but she will not speak. (*V*, 86–87)

Like the female hysteric who "refuses heterosexual passivity and the sexual compliance with social norms by transferring sexual intensity and meaning onto her symptoms" (Grosz, *SS*, 134), the mother, who "has gone mad" and "will not speak," refuses to be compliant with patriarchal social norms, by transferring her protest into her silence. Similarly, Hahn resists the confinement of femininity in the masculine, phallocentric symbolic order, by translating women's experience into *"hysterical blindness"*—a version of "vision" of memories and imagination available only when she goes where "the hysteric resides." As her persona says: "When I shut my eyes I am exiled into my memories and imagination. I can only leave by admitting sight" (*V*, 88).

By seeking to "go where the hysteric resides" in her poetry, Hahn renders her poems symptomatic of women's memories, sufferings, pleasures, and protests. In their study of the female hysteric, Cixous and Clément contend, "The hysteric, whose body is transformed into a theatre for forgotten scenes, relives the past, bearing witness to a lost childhood that survives in suffering" (5). Like the hysteric, the psychosomatically blinded Cambodian women and the mad women in Asian American literature bear witness to losses, atrocities, and oppressions that refuse to be forgotten; their bodies are transformed into theatres for "forgotten scenes." In a way, Hahn's poems function like "theatres" in which "the return of the repressed" with its "subversive weight" is enacted, and through which an ongoing and open relationship with the past operates as a site for political activism and intervention, as well as a site for creative imagination and reinvention. By using psychoanalysis as a mode of interpretation of textual or psychosomatic "symptoms," as a device for the interrogation of knowledge, and as a strategy for making visible and heard the repressed, erased, and silenced, Hahn transforms the traumatic and the feminine into politically and aesthetically productive forces. In her poems, the hysterical "disorders" and "affective legacies of loss are mobilized for flashes of political hope," as David Eng and David Kazanjian have said of the politics of mourning in their discussion of recent scholarship in trauma studies.[23] In their preface to a collection of essays on loss, Eng and Kazanjian write that instead of attributing "a purely negative quality" to loss, the essays "apprehend it as productive rather than pathological, abundant rather than lacking, social rather than solipsistic, militant rather than reactionary." They emphasize the transformative effects of interpretation in the essays, which foreground the fact that losses "are laden with creative, political potential."[24] Hahn's poetry testifies to the creative, political potential of the actual and symbolic loss of the mother.

It is precisely by refusing to accept the Freudian notion of femininity in negative terms of "lack," or as object of male desire and knowledge, that Kimiko Hahn turns the feminine into abundant creative possibilities and political expressions through "Words that orbit the body / like a plea granted" (MA 55) and through "sentences that translate the bond between our body, her body, the body of our daughter."[25] Hahn's corporeal poetic strategy for rearticulating the feminine offers a possible solution to the question that Juliana Chang raises in her article: how to reinscribe femininity—the gendered and raced otherness—without reducing gender and cultural difference to the "norms" of patriarchal, Orientalist, or American hegemonic femininity? In exploring where the "hysteric resides," Hahn discovers that "Every time she speaks it is a leave-taking / of the sealed-off room she knew all along / toward a stew fragrant with fiction" (MA 80). In her poetry, the "riddle" of the Freudian femininity becomes subversive feminine "fiction" outside patriarchal, Orientalist, and Eurocentric norms and poetic forms.

NOTES TO CRITICAL ESSAY

1. I want to thank Dr. Wenxin Li and Dr. Cynthia Dobbs for their insightful comments on the draft of this essay during the early stage of its development. I am

indebted to my editors, Lisa Sewell and Claudia Rankine, for their constructive suggestions for revision.

2. Sigmund Freud, "Femininity," in *Freud on Women: A Reader*, ed. and intro. Elisabeth Young-Bruehl (New York: Norton, 1990), 342–43. All subsequent references to this lecture by Freud will appear as "Femininity" in the text.

3. Elizabeth Grosz, *Sexual Subversions: Three French Feminists* (St. Leonards, Australia: Allen & Unwin, 1989), 109. All subsequent references are to this edition and will appear as *SS* in the text.

4. For an extended discussion of Kimiko Hahn's intertextual incorporation and reinvention in her poems by engaging with Japanese and Chinese women's writings, see Zhou Xiaojing, "Kimiko Hahn: 'The Passion of Leaving Home,'" in *The Ethics and Poetics of Alterity in Asian American Poetry* (Iowa City: University of Iowa Press, 2006), 133–66.

5. Juliana Chang, "'I Cannot Find Her': The Oriental Feminine, Racial Melancholia, and Kimiko Hahn's *The Unbearable Heart*," *Meridians: Feminism, Race, Transnationalism* 4, no. 2 (2004): 239–40. All subsequent references to this work will appear in the text.

6. Kimiko Hahn, "The Hemisphere: Huchuk Hanem," in *The Unbearable Heart* (New York: Kaya, 1995), 60.

7. For extended discussion of "The Hemisphere: Huchuk Hanem," see Traise Yamamoto, 253–61; Zhou Xiaojing, "Two Hat Softeners," 182–85; and "Kimiko Hahn," 148–54.

8. Possibly originated during the Song Dynasty (960–1126), *nu shu* (female script) is known only by women, who used the language to correspond among themselves and to compose poems that they chanted during women's gatherings, wrote on fans, embroidered on decorative cloth, and collected into books. It was a custom for the women to have their books of poems in *nu shu* burned at their funerals. For more information about the language, see Gao Yinxian and Yi Nianhua, *Nu Shu: The Only Female Language in the World*, ed. Gong Zhebin (Taibei, Taiwan: Women's New Knowledge Foundation, 1990) [in Chinese].

9. Hahn, *Mosquito & Ant* (New York: Norton, 1999), 41. All subsequent references are to this edition and will appear as *MA* in the text.

10. Grosz's phrase in *Sexual Subversions*, 134.

11. Josef Breuber and Freud, *Studies on Hysteria*, trans. and ed. James Strachey with Anna Freud (New York: Basic Books, 1957), 7. All subsequent references are to this edition and will appear in the text.

12. Freud, "Selections from 'Fragment of an Analysis of a Case of Hysteria,'" in *Freud on Women: A Reader*, ed. Young-Bruehl, 72, 75, 84. All subsequent references to this work will appear as "Hysteria" in the text.

13. Hélène Cixous and Catherine Clément, *The Newly Born Woman*, trans. Betsy Wing, intro. Sandra M. Gilbert (Minneapolis: University of Minnesota Press, 1996), 5. All subsequent references are to this edition and will appear in the text.

14. David Eng, *Racial Castration: Managing Masculinity in Asian America* (Durham, NC: Duke University Press, 2001), 174. All subsequent references are to this edition and will appear as *RC* in the text.

15. For an insightful reading of the embodied subjectivity and language in Ki-

miko Hahn's poems, see Traise Yamamoto, *Masking Selves, Making Subjects: Japanese American Women, Identity, and the Body* (Berkeley: University of California Press, 1999), 236–61.

16. Hahn, *Earshot* (Brooklyn, NY: Hanging Loose Press, 1992), 16. All subsequent references are to this edition and will appear as *E* in the text.

17. Hahn, *Air Pocket* (Brooklyn, NY: Hanging Loose Press, 1989), 12. All subsequent references are to this edition and will appear as *AP* in the text.

18. "Comp. Lit.," in *Earshot*, 81.

19. See Kimiko Hahn's note to the title, in *Air Pocket*, p. 68.

20. Robert Grotjohn, "Kimiko Hahn's 'Interlingual Poetics' in *Mosquito and Ant*," *Transnational Asian American Literature: Sites and Transits*, ed. Shirley Geok-Lin Lim et al. (Philadelphia: Temple University Press, 2006), 230.

21. Hahn, *The Artist's Daughter* (New York: Norton, 2002), 58. All subsequent references are to this edition and appear as *AD* in the text.

22. Hahn, *Volatile* (Brooklyn, NY: Hanging Loose Press, 1998), 82–84. All subsequent references are to this edition and appear as *V* in the text.

23. David L. Eng and David Kazanjian, "Introduction: Mourning Remains," in *Loss: The Politics of Mourning*, ed. Eng and Kazanjian (Berkeley: University of California Press, 2003), 16.

24. Eng and Kazanjian, Preface, in *Loss: The Politics of Mourning*, ix.

25. Hahn incorporates this line, among others, from Luce Irigary in her poem "Responding to Light" in *Mosquito & Ant*, 79. See Irigary, *Sexes and Genealogies*, trans. Gillian C. Gill (New York: Columbia University Press, 1993), 18.

BIBLIOGRAPHY

Books by Kimiko Hahn

Air Pocket. Brooklyn, NY: Hanging Loose Press, 1989.
Earshot. Brooklyn, NY: Hanging Loose Press, 1992.
The Unbearable Heart. Brooklyn, NY: Kaya Production, 1995.
Volatile. Brooklyn, NY: Hanging Loose Press, 1998.
Mosquito & Ant. New York: Norton, 1999.
The Artist's Daughter. New York: Norton, 2002.
The Narrow Road to the Interior. New York: Norton, 2006.
Toxic Flora. New York: Norton, 2010.

Selected Interviews

Kalamaras, George. "To Adore a Fragment: An Interview with Kimiko Hahn." *Bloomsbury Review*, vol. 19, no. 2 (March–April 1999), 13–14.
Schlote, Christiane. "Mixing Aesthetics. A Poet's Cityscape: Kimiko Hahn." In *Voces de América/American Voices: Entrevistas a escritores americanos/Interviews with American Writers*, edited and introduced by Alonso Gallo and Laura P. Cádiz, Spain: Aduana Vieja, 2004, 541–59.
Sheck, Laurie. "Kimiko Hahn." *Bomb Magazine*, vol. 96 (summer 2006), 52–57.
Wiedewitsch, Adam. "A Careful Logic of Its Own: Order, Disorder, and Magic in

Poetry." An interview with Kimiko Hahn. *Teachers & Writers* (spring 2007), 3–11.

Selected Criticism

Chang, Juliana. " 'I Cannot Find Her': The Oriental Feminine, Racial Melancholia, and Kimiko Hahn's *The Unbearable Heart.*" *Meridians: Feminism, Race, Transnationalism*, vol. 4, no. 2 (2004), 239–60.

Grotjohn, Robert. "Kimiko Hahn's 'Interlingual Poetics' in *Mosquito and Ant.*" In *Transnational Asian American Literature: Sites and Transits*, edited by Shirley Geok-Lin Lim et al. Philadelphia: Temple University Press, 2006, 219–34.

Moscaliuc, Mihaela. "Unbecoming, a desperate homesickness / even at home: Kimiko Hahn and the Poetics of Exhumation." In *Orient and Orientalisms in U.S.-American Poetry and Poetics*, edited by Sabine Sielke and Christian Kloeckner. Berlin: Peter Lang, 2009, 329–53.

Tabios, Eileen. "Kimiko Hahn: Expressing Self and Desire, Even If One Must Writhe." In *Black Lightning: Poetry-In-Progress*, by Tabios. New York: Asian American Writers Workshop, 1998, 24–68.

Yamamoto, Traise. *Masking Selves, Making Subjects: Japanese American Women, Identity, and the Body*. Berkeley: University of California Press, 1999, 236–61.

Zhou, Xiaojing. "Breaking from Tradition: Experimental Poems by Four Contemporary Asian American Women Poets." *Revista Canaria de Estudios Ingleses*, vol. 37 (November 1998, A special issue on 20th-Century American Women Poets), 199–218.

———. "Two Hat Softeners 'In the Trade Confession': John Yau and Kimiko Hahn." In *Form and Transformation in Asian American Literature*, edited by Zhou Xiaojing and Samina Najmi. Seattle: University of Washington Press, 2005, 168–89.

———. "Kimiko Hahn: 'The Passion of Leaving Home.' " In *The Ethics and Poetics of Alterity in Asian American Poetry*. Iowa City: University of Iowa Press, 2006, 133–66.

CARLA HARRYMAN

FROM *Baby*

Now. Word. Technology.

These were words she would learn someday. In the meantime she was fire in the womb with a skirt. Then a shirt which she pulled up through a small door that people on the other side called a cervical opening. Oh hallowed name and jittery shirt. She listened to a tiger reading files. She wanted to know what a tiger looks like, first. Before she wanted to know what anything else looked like. Someone, had that someone known anything about what baby wanted, would have said authoritatively it's the sound of the parent's voice you anticipate desire and suck in all at once through those perfect mitten ears and translucent and batted at things pulled red then formed into conch spindles then later shielded by hands from undesirable noise. The tiger opened a file claiming, this is the beginning of a long story. Which is everything baby wanted except the shirt she rolled up and over and in and by with for her skirt. The corner of everything was smitten with attentiveness. The difference between a womb and a room lies in such corners of attentiveness. Or the technology of listening.

Dark. Swat. Land.

Flung into the tunnel of love, baby was nervous when anything bounced. Shirt, skirt, pie, belly. Mangled and trounced binoculars. This and that this. And that. Windows. And a window pulled toward the door with mighty arms sinking beneath the floor. Alice gravely hiccupping. Then sitting sitting and sitting. Sitting. For the four corners of the room subsided in the enormous hole. Movement was fear, a tiger, some kind of apple grinder breaking up asphalt. Caved in coughing. Land egg. Baby dream. Frothing. And E go. Certain sounds rigid formulas thought. Attract futures stuck in happy land. Give me liberty or give me death had not history in baby's breath. But sound of force struck in her trunk. Here and then beginning of baby's not. And not.

Baby.

Baby was a modernist. What is the feeling of freedom?

The. Open. Box.

Baby in another era was running from room to room with her arm thrust out and her finger bent in a peculiar position. She was making a splattering buzzing sound. A black fly in the form of baby! That ran splat right into the television set perched on a little stool. A stool baby had used only yesterday. Wha's 'at? asked baby, pointing at the TV screen. The tiger was there ready to whisper in her ear. It's a dungeon full of dirt. Oh, zee, zee, said baby in wonderment pulling at the knobs. Tiger realized too late baby liked dungeons full of dirt, especially when description poured spontaneously out of tiger's mouth. Baby loved the mouth of the tiger. Especially its sweaty lips. So the TV, it was black and white, went pop, on. Baby sat down on the floor with her entire hand in her mouth, her mouth sucking on the hand, four and five fingers. In and out. While nutty adults in miniature did all sorts of things talking in odd theatrical voices as if they were talking to air and air could listen. The air has huge ears, thought baby. She looked around all about her but could only feel the air brushing lightly against her cheeks in the interstitial world between now and then. In the meantime, the jackpot hobnobbing of the nitwits and sad sacks on television had vanished. In front of her was an emaciated child with huge ribs and a terrible listless look that frowned on baby's chubby face. Baby fearlessly batted at the TV screen. The baby's in the box. The baby's in the box! The baby's in the box! The box! Open the box now!

Baby. N. Baseball. Song.

Baby was going to sing and then sing twice. The song was later attenuated when there was nothing left to bring to the foreground of the forest, which had been the center of singing as baby experienced her lungs. Experience. Experience. She sang. She sang divided and then twice feeling the lungs of the forest as her own and then stepping back to observe herself as such phenomenon springing into readymade denomination from the head of an old god named Nietzsche. Or N. His name too had been clipped short like the song when she, growing tired and distracted, had less and less to bring forth as offering, as person, to the forest, which was transforming into high speed blur. Tings like notes left distinct prints in non-voiced ground near voiced air. These were things baby could not experience or express. She recuperated her energies and opened her mouth. She thought she was going to taste tings. Then she thought again and thus was thinking twice. The singing was attenuated, clipped short. Minor distractions delineated something back in the brain that her lips associated with sucking.

Baby's little body is a speedball. That's what someone remarked as she raced back and forth between the catcher's mound and home plate. Someone was watching her play. She is her own ball. This someone was laughing as baby flew into sky and ground.

Note.

There they were. The notes clipped. Short, spread out. Deathless and. Without design. Baby was trying to decide if she should let go the cry pressing up through her chest when the sound of children distracted her. Were they surrounding her? The children are coming. The children are coming. She sang. Wailed. Rolled into a speedball and proceeded on her back and forth diagonal course from h. plate to p. mound. Baby was not a team player. The shifting universe had narrowed to one demand: do not give up the strip of inside field. Singing, wailing, were trampled in the dust of a play that cut all others out.

Wartime Surroundings.

There were the surroundings baby had nibbled at. And the plum jam spilled on the surroundings. There were some larded bits of a piecrust baked for her quick while the giant pie for everybody baked and baked. Baby had heard the word nerve gas and thought that the kitchen smells were nerve gas. They made your nerves stand alert. Baby was running on the fuel of love, skidding to a halt at the kitchen door, then plunging back into the railthin kitchen with gusto until she reached some destination, which was erratically determined by the magnitude of her own physical force. The giant pie for everybody in the meantime was taking a long time to cook. What if it doesn't come out? she wanted to know. What if something is in there wrecking it? The anticipation was getting on her nerves. She wanted it to come out now. She had her plans, she was going to give that pie to the fat cats. She'd heard talking about those fat cats—out somewhere high rolling. Baby loved animals and wanted to feed the high rolling fat cats. She told the tiger she wanted to watch the fat cats eat pie and why didn't it hurry up. If you don't watch out, you'll be running for president. I hope the fat cats like pie, said baby. The tiger bit her lip and a tear rolled down her cheek, you're gonna break my heart. Well, you can have pie too—baby felt magnanimously toward tiger, who was as precise with a fork as she was spontaneous with a bag of sugar. What if I told you I was hoping to feed the pie to something scrawny and wild? asked tiger. There aren't any fat cats around here and that nerve gas, well, isn't really nerve gas. What you smell is a drop of fear sweetened by pie.

Smell. Of. Pie.

When baby grew up, the smell of pie would sometimes knock her out.

consents to a few statements one knows
ultimately to implicate murder
(A Score)

••••••• I have never seen a dead   confounding array of information

••••••• one a vast circular logic   two   we agreed to park it

••••••• three   each has been brought forward in the preceding statement
mental distance is necessary   I am serving in the Senate

••••••• It's buoyed our spirits   a road improvement plan
excuse it them, in times of peace

••••••• my sound mind's distance   having become a bit overbearingly
loud   no person pictured   one two three   brought forward
in the summons

••••••• dined is the precise sentence   designating a complete thought
whether   vegetarian   or   the poet suffered a word death
the outcome could not have been predicted   having become
reliant upon

••••••• other people stepped between   many saw it coming two persons
riveting   against our better judgment   the invasive species
was permitted to appear   in unprotected

••••••• blind spots   or cloture   osmosis one   vagrant two   crying
out loud three   each has been brought forward   in the future
site

••••• cite   lived there first "this is not prose"   still riveting Rosie became the symbol of unemployment   the constitution revels in formalities   I think I know what this document is trying to convey   what I was to it, without question   who it was to it, without question

••••• suffered a word death   knowing the literature   the dotted line they signed   I have never seen   a song with words intermixed such that all figures of speech borrow strikes from their roots   It is not that some grave responsibility awaits   It is not that this pleasure of   Where the accused stand waiting   It is not that this picture of

••••• Where the   was protected by   With   So that an appeal there not being   thus to be done now   actions are caused by chemicals   Leaving   the earth   for   a phrase:
      I had met her in the dark

*TO PERFORMERS: NOTE THAT DENSITY **INCREASES** TOWARD THE BOTTOM OF THE SCORE*

it is difficult to write satire
Lesson
The president was on top of me it's not what you think he was
trying to hurt me he didn't know that I had a vest on too that he
would have to try harder to get through he was pounding I was
scared but unreasonably and so my giggling mingled with fear
incredulity and true amusement the president wow was trying
to pow me this made him madder he was plowing in with a low
ball cut across the chest *I'm teaching you a lesson* his jaw was
relaxing that bewildered set in stone look of determination he
used for cameras relaxing a new expression was eeking through
showing another self more free less fake by a long shot glowing
but bitter "you'll never win you'll never beat me I'm stronger
than you" this was obvious whenever he let go his grip on my
shoulder even slightly I'd try to slide away from him he wanted
to *see me cry* he pinned me, whispered this in my ear, not *knock
me out* "the smug smile I'm gonna wipe it off your face" that's
what he was going for and for me to declare with sincerity I give
up you *are* going to be on top forever I've learned my lesson
just move off and I promise you'll never need your fists again
when you have completed your term I'll work in your library
file your papers escort researchers to the drawers where your
secret documents will be kept several decades hence and in the
meantime we can keep your wife's favorite poetry books in them
along with all the kind notes full of gratitude people have sent
you and the personal notes from leaders thanking you for your
hospitality and supporting your views on everything from—
well you know—staying the course we'll keep the notes in those
files until the keepers of state secrets let your truths slip out of
their vaults into your drawers full of dignity and proper views
and victory I'll call you whenever you like on a special line and
report on the most recent display of fan letters one floor down
in the presidential museum grand gallery—those tomes you had
missed out on reading when you were busy doing your duty
being obedient to the higher powers who had bestowed upon
you the protective armor we now both share.

the opposite of slackness
Orgasms
tis issue robbing pope sucking spear transit splash oops bore eye fro
eye hire harrow guarded leer trap fire slurry badge adage craze

speak speak speak engineer linger rotund dusty ust ust uh

hoe oat toe below spire rain stamen stick rat earth reeves heavy slob
oh sorrow mow

spot smear spot squashed stadium clinging pillar out hear a-rear
basting let low lyric violet storm

loaned honey nothing doing behind gravy train evil fell to slow en-
trance gained a billow in the random rain

never never adumbrate never fever scumbling punchable larynx snot
god sported inside mountain yawn swerve gliding dust to dust hard
shadow phase hammy maverick nut there scratching crevice hording
hot snow ocean bosses suds scribble which ways blacking

chancy chaos gouge loony brighter than tune

may may may may may may max may max may max ayax

razor ruby bird seared near her area reached piper ripping rail

low light lit little tick flea migrant sip pissy wit twill twill low will
piano frill label slain hero palo o opal laughing harrow barracuda
amour our radio crash

not on my time happy not on my time mad not on my time money
not on my time skin not on my time merry not on my time dig not
on my time fanny not on my time sorrow not on my time sand not
on my time sun not on my time moon not on my time hills not on
my time rivers not on my time rinse not on my time cloud not on
my time vapor not on my time film not on my time shame not on
my time hover not on my time blow not on my time sassy not on
my time slow not on my time honey not on my time more

defeat effete defeat effort defeat fort defeat eat eat de teat at art
faart or fete tete ear eat fete tete do to oat to o deaf effort fort ore
eee or taa tort or at eat taa tat or de de ten effete neat tete defeat

lulu lang loop bay bay bay rad hip hole cleave o decalogue boober
hover mine hammer am

bubble slumber pressure song cover over every wrong abridge my
sigh with over wing oh swim again beyond thy hand

points are reached at every point slimmed mirror prunes mere
mourning rave

POETICS STATEMENT

Siren[1]

Siren Diary
It is said that the Sirens knew everything that had happened in the past and
everything that was to happen in the future. Thankfully, I am not an ancient
Siren and do not possess their gift or curse of knowledge. Those who do and
will suffer, including you and I my sweet, are at the mercy of other forces be-
yond revelation. Still I wonder, what if I did know the future and could tell
you about it? That I saw a decrease of sunlight *west where I already was* and
an increase of drought and flooding like that occurring in the world today?
And what if we both saw the same thing as if reality were transparent and
no medium were necessary to transmit a vision? Or what if we collaborated
in constructing something, in words, that we both saw as if we were seeing
the same thing? With you speaking and I listening and me listening and you
speaking? If you saw what I was seeing, would it be more real? As if what
was envisioned were actually happening now? And what if we each shared
the same vision of the future already, in advance? Would this mutual sight
be convincing? Does not the messenger *author* of the future get in the way
of the message? The messenger may obstruct the vision she invokes by her
physical presence, voice, image, or symbolic stature. Or perhaps it's that the
person *behaved as if at the real death of a real girl*[2] complicates the text: see-
ing them together, person and text or you and me, qualifies an attachment
to either.

Detroit, August 5, 2009

An impending sense of catastrophe stops reverie, *me coated in sand*. A siren makes its way through traffic. My autonomic nervous system reacts. Before I can know it, I have scrambled onto the sidewalk, ducked under a tree limb, observed I'm in a crowd. What was that? Where was I *a cave in Cambodia* before? I continue on my way, a little more dazed than I had been just previous to the siren alarm. I can't get back to where I was before the sound, before I jumped off the roadway, before I noticed other people. Numbness or dazedness, a hovering sensation, that obstructs . . . what? The alert creature, the able-bodied soul, and *death* thought. I had been daydreaming in the middle of *I hate mythology*[3] the street. Then I forgot the town I was in: Detroit, Berlin, San Francisco, Red Hook, Ypsilanti?

Siren Diary
Notes with interruptions on "Adorno and the Siren":[4] Odysseus sheds copious tears during the blind Demodocus' song of the downfall of Troy at the table of Alcenous. The bard has brought the history of Odysseus' experience of the Trojan battle to life in song, and Odysseus responds hysterically, like a post-traumatic stress victim. He recuperates his masculinity (men don't cry) when he recounts his encounter with the Sirens; he shows he has *no way to revelation* learned how to control his hysteria, by lashing *there's location, attention, and tension*[5] himself to the mast to protect himself from the powerful allure of the Siren Song.

Sirens were half-bird, half human. They become identified in Adorno with *what about the animated things popping out of anything one notices*[6] the femme fatale. Yet reading with Adorno, this fixed "fatalistic" image reduces the Siren's capacity to operate within the circulatory system of music: their power comes before gender. The recovered "voice" in this system is a separating mechanism—the same as the bard's song—distinguishing "song from cry." It brings us to the "perennially" irresolute site between human and inhuman.[7]

I like Engh's argument but there is something wrong with her reading. She seems to forget, under the spell of *coots pattering on marshland* music, the prominence of storytelling, the medium with which Odysseus recovers his masculinity after he is undone by crying.

Red Hook, New York, July 19, 2009

The writer is figured between history and *now*. The writing *door to your Berkeley house, kitchen, workplace, yard carpeted in a tasty bitter lettuce* will be contradictory. It will reflect conditions of physical displacement and confusion between personal and public life. You will come upon sentences *these spirits move too quickly*[8] faltering or skipping *your platform shoes* around in paragraphs. You will find phrases interrupting the flow of the sentence. I am enlisting alienation effects without relinquishing the subject (my subjectivity) to the future's greater good. I am attempting to create an impression of a state of mind I was in thirty to forty years ago, something I had to get control of *I didn't choose to talk about no one to drive the car poetry* in order to write. I can still experience that feeling, alienated, but not alien to my subjective experience.

Call for a kind of resistance by the listener, and for mobilization and re-drafting as a producer . . .[9] I can not recall a time when *caught off guard* I did not imagine myself making something. As with certain female Romantics or Modernists, my actions and enthusiasms betrayed the pre-assigned role. When I encountered the reality of literature as dominated by male thought and lineage, I was a resistant listener, already mobilized as a producer. The producer's education included learning—going back hundreds of years—of the social resistance to her production.

Yet there was also a certain immobility entailed in this incommensurate producer, resistant-listener job. Although I did enthusiastically *returned to the bowels of the earth for renewal*[10] engage in it, I could not simply throw myself into the "cause for the advancement of radical literature" without also experiencing *you speculated about why more women poets did not* myself as distant from "literature," "cause," "radical."

I was split, alienated, and ambivalent. Why? There was something obdurate, not progressive *all brain dimmed to me* about certain modernisms that fascinated me in addition to horizons of promise and possibility. Conflict marked the encounter with a progressive future enlisting not only "constructivism" but something impossible, not unlike a monstrosity in a Kafka story.

Siren Diary
The Sirens had a will to travel. In the spirit of their having been granted wings, I offer the following dream:
   I was in India for a day. The first town I traveled to was happy and dull and in the next town I lost everything: wallet, passport, clothes, and a carved wooden trunk, an heirloom of mine (though I don't actually have any heirlooms). Or perhaps the heirloom belonged to you, who do have heirlooms. Not knowing whom the trunk belonged to placed me in a system between thieves and law abiders. The authorities, if there were any, were not interested in the trunk. People were kind to me and I found my way home, via air, in a day, where I was graciously, acceptingly embraced. Having left the West behind me willy-nilly, I took it with me, and could go no farther.
                                                                          Pittsburgh, July 5, 2009

In childhood, going west was going into ocean *as nervous system*. I associate the muffling effects of roaring surf to the pleasure I take in certain motile and disjointed sentences. A dream was a machine *frequent traveling and staying weeks and months elsewhere* made of words, with subjectivity's monkey wrench taking the machine apart and scrutinizing it as if it might be redrafted to the service of something else. I grew up in Costa Mesa, "the table by the sea."

Siren Diary
I find myself avoiding the problem of the Siren's seductive voice again. *The Classical Dictionary* states that the Sirens may have been companions to Persephone, that they begged for wings so that they could look for her when Hades snatched her away. Later, they *attribute the strange motion and inconsistent "behavior" of my sentences to an activity of memory* became monstrous and deformed, their wings clipped when they lost a singing contest to the muses. They sing of the past and future, as if they know it all, but their story seems ungrounded, made up. Their origins are speculative. Their situation, potent yet unanchored.[11]

In writing this, I imagine the Siren letting out a wail, like an ambulance in stuck traffic. But she turns on me, and says, "Shush your mouth."
Detroit, June 3, 2009

In a 1985 issue of *The Socialist Review*, I came upon what later became a famous feminist work, Donna Haraway's "Cyborg Manifesto: Science, Technology, and Feminism in the Late Twentieth Century." Having been disappointed by the agendas of socialist feminist groups I had fantasized participating in, I embraced Haraway's advocacy of irony, blasphemy, and global critique. Her manifesto combined *regardless of my absences and the anonymity of these 21st century suburbs* the right mix of laugher, mockery, and outrage.

"Autonomy never wins. *No objects, spaces, or boundaries, are sacred in themselves.*"[12]

Years later, in an ironic, melancholic, mood, while under the spell of Monique Wittig's essay "On the Social Contract" in *The Straight Mind*, I wrote about "the scale of minute resistance:"

The intention of the game is to invisibly shift history without the sources of the shift being identified and without the shift being understood as history. It will not be seen through an historical record or theory, but it nevertheless affects the outcome of the record or the theory without the recorders or theorizers knowing.[13]

Siren Diary
It is said that the Sirens lived on the rocks of an island among the strewn bones of men they have consumed. A more enlightened, scholarly vision observes them in Homer as more spirit than body. The corpses around them are .
there because the men refused to leave.

The Sirens are quixotic spirits *cross-dressing* of cultural imagination, which itself invokes, enlists, and critiques them as fixture, hallucination and projection. A Siren may be seductive *de-aestheticize the voice to show that women can possess more assertive, less predictable forms of vocality*[14] or grotesque, is hybrid, queer, or female depending on text and interpreter. An hallucinated Siren flies to Persephone too late. Catapulted from Hell, it swirls around the mast of a ship, seducing Odysseus by getting into his head: the condom does not protect him. An image on the internet shows Sirens in bathing suits up to their knees in water giving the camera the finger. Somewhere else, they stand in as barmaids on a lazy afternoon, filtered through the self-consciously sentimental gaze of a sorry on-looker.

Detroit, June 9, 2009

One day in the Fall of 1970, the Sirens got into my head and stayed there for quite some time. I was taking a course on Joyce's *Ulysses*, and the instructor had responded enthusiastically to my suggestion that I compose a work for flute, based on the first several pages of the Siren chapter. I told him that I experienced the text as a direct translation from language to music: he agreed. It wasn't simply the tunes Joyce borrowed for purposes of historical reference and compositional themes, it was the "thing in itself" that I understood *where the conscious part, the part played by words, is forgotten*[15] as musical. Although it took much of the fall quarter to compose the work and drum up the nerve to play it for the teacher in his office, writing it was not difficult. I was simply terrified by my own presumptuous ridiculousness in setting the god James Joyce to music with my meager musical skills. Ridiculous though I surely was, I much preferred thinking about the sound, phrasing, and patterning of the "lines" than thinking through the labyrinth of references and motifs referenced in the Sirens chapter.

I preferred to imagine the purpose of the Sirens chapter was its sound, or noise. The author's interpretive reading of his own work was the material *whereas the music nullifies all*[16] that transformed text to music. In other words, in a Kristevan sense, symbolic language became the matter of a semiotic event structured through musical forms. This "messed up my head," as John Olson the noise artist likes to put it, a circumstance I have always connected with "liveness" in art. It was not that I did not study or get the references, but rather that learning textual references seemed less consequential than the music, or noise of the text.

This experience rhymed dramatically with a comment Ronald Sukenick made in another class later that year *orange groves receding*, regarding W. H. Auden, an author whose works I knew. Auden's best works were written for sound not sense. This confirmed something I had begun to suspect, that writing *for* sense was a redundant and laborious affair. Writing *for* sense was analogous to responding to any question with the same set of responses, as if neither questions nor responses could change. Suken-ick was not merely a loyalist to sound, however; he was on the side of an "agonistic, sophistic, sophisticated, fluid, unpredictable, rhizomatic, affec-tive, inconsistent, and even contradictory, improvisation, and provisional" *rhetoric* "in its argument toward contingent resolution that can only be temporary."[17]

In her writing on opera, Catherine Clement critiques what appears to be exactly the kind of sound-focused response I had to the Sirens chapter in *Ulysses*. The musical sound, privileged over narrative representation, and unmoored from the meaning of language suppresses the violence done to the subject, whether woman or soldier, (or text), of operatic representation. In the 19th century opera, women sing themselves ecstatically to abjection and death while "the words do not bother him. But does he even know they exist? That is not certain. Nobody listens to the words, nobody pays any attention to them. . . . Words—just incidental!"[18]

Clement's critique reverses the feminist psychoanalytic gendering of non-symbolic, semiotic sound, assigning it not to the fullness of the mater-nal voice but to the masculine desire to efface the content of linguistic com-munication in order to retain power over the voice.

However, my resistance to the content in Joyce was, in a sense, the re-sistance to, or playful appropriation of, a structure of knowledge passed down by modernism's patriarchal imperatives. I can imagine that my ex-perience composing music for the Sirens helped provide an experience of composition that went directly into the "hybrid," or "new genre," writ-ing project I embarked on in the same year. I believe myself to have been thrilled that prose could be a poem that sounded like a score. This had both everything and nothing to do with gender.

Siren Diary
The song cacophony at one point will need a dream, or structure. Start anywhere:

I am returning from the East, possibly Croatia, to the West. The check-point is rather chaotic, with lots of miscellaneous personal things of travelers arrayed on long tables. I open my purse to find that none of my things are there: no wallet or identification. Instead a *segregated by color* mash of Ger-man receipts and American bills tumble around in it. It becomes understood that there are two identical purses, which are in turn identical to one I actu-ally own—a lightweight reversible brown pouch-shaped thing with a thin black shoulder strap, black lining and leopard print interior. Someone else has my purse and I have hers. It is apparent that I have the purse of someone who doesn't need a visa and can travel easily even in non-EU countries.

Birds circle a mast with the thick body lashed to it. They circle the light-houses, which I have visited up the coast of California and the Upper Pen-insula in Michigan. Memory is a cloud looking for a dune in a spot of sun,

sheltered from the wind. Voices travel too far. A pick-up on the distant road
returns their call. It is not meaning but sounds we make. In memory, the
ubiquitous fog is stepped around. Cool feet muscle through heavy sand. The
surf is uninviting but thrilling.

Berlin, May 22, 2009

LISTENING IN ON CARLA HARRYMAN'S *BABY*

Christine Hume

> "Let us leave theories there and return to here's hear."
>
> —JAMES JOYCE, *Finnegans Wake*

LANGUAGE IS FIRST entirely sonic to any baby; it begins pre-birth and
continues as a seamless part of the sensual world of infancy. Carla Har-
ryman's recent book of hybrid genre prose, *Baby*, creates a highly jocular,
edgy, and intellectual adventure out of sonic materiality. In this work, the
main character, baby, enacts a sophisticated pleasure of active, attentive lis-
tening: "The corner of everything was smitten with attentiveness. The dif-
ference between a womb and a room lies in such corners of attentiveness.
Or the technology of listening," ends the first paragraph of the book.[1] In
the womb and from the mother's womb, a baby's first and primary sense
is hearing. Hearing becomes listening there, and extends upon birth into
rooms and back into the body-cavities. Baby embodies the special intelli-
gence of audition, connecting internal and external worlds, not just as an
act of sensation, but as a fundamental mode of being that opposes long-
standing habits of perception, knowledge, and experience.

As Harryman takes up what Julia Kristeva calls the listener's respon-
sibility to "pluralize, pulverize, and musicate" what she hears,[2] baby's
concerns are emblematic of Harryman's obsession with language as per-
formance and performative language. Through three decades of books
and performances, the beginnings of language and self intermesh to create
new characters acting under the negative privilege of provisional existence.
As such, much of Harryman's work redresses perspectives and politics of
childhood. Child in *Memory Play*, Caesar in *Gardener of Stars*, Child in
Performing Objects Stationed in the Sub World, and the girl in "Fairy Tale"
from *There Never Was a Rose Without a Thorn* are strong examples of

non-adult characters that complicate normative notions of "childhood" and "character" itself. These sagacious, strong figures prepare us for the baby of *Baby* in the ways they both portray a non-adult status and embody motile concepts. Like baby, they suggest that certain kinds of meaning, knowledge, and experience can be delivered only through audition.

In all of Harryman's work, texts are meant to be heard and voiced; performances are extremely textual. Language's relationship to embodiment resounds as textual and oral economies in a singular corpus collide, reinforcing and inhibiting each other. Throughout her oeuvre, Harryman's characters use an "inward ear" to speak within hearing,[3] but they also hear voraciously (hundred-eared, over-hearing), from roving points of audition, both public and private. Focusing on *Baby*, this essay serves as a primer for the vividly multiple registers of listening that inform all of Harryman's work.

In *Baby*, listening relies not on stringing together singular voices in an unbroken sequence or in streamlining noise, but rather on trafficking in polyvocality. Harryman reinscribes listening with both somatic impact and ethical response. She endows listening with the capacity to undo binary structures in the service of a relational model of identity. By synthesizing two contradictory modes of audition, baby creates dialectical listening:

> The auditor, who we call baby, enjoyed both sensations: the sensation of being led into the surrounding comfort of a story, cradled as she was in the voice of the storyteller heralding the disappearance of the material world, and the sensation of abstraction, which required she situate herself within another kind of mental labyrinth, one that engaged the effects of the material world toward objective systems of thought. (13)

Listening is a cultural, rather than natural, practice, one that must be learned, and one with enormous social import. Listening informs *Baby*'s creation in every way, meshing internal and external worlds of the book. *Baby* springs forth via listening and in turn, asks that the reader engage it by listening as it triangulates with reading and speaking.

Recursive Listening

As a comedic counterpoint to dialectical listening, Harryman offers us TV listening: "While nutty adults in miniature did all sorts of things talking in odd theatrical voices as if they were talking to air and air could listen. The air has huge ears, thought baby" (35).

To be a listener is intrinsically to be located, it is *not* to be the air with ears. My term "dialectical listening" locates itself in fluent relation to the following modes of listening, some discovered, some appropriated, which encompass it. Dialectical listening rubs up against and sharpens itself on these channels of listening.

Mimetic listening: Mimetic activity occurs both in the production and the consumption of sounds. When speech has the power to conjure up and sustain in the listener previously heard speech—an aural grafting of past over present—we have mimetic listening. In practical terms, we learn to speak by listening, and what we hear is inevitably dictated by our experience of listening.[4] This kind of listening has both positive and negative value in *Baby*: On one hand, "all thinking *hears* the indelible imprint of survival" (italics mine, 24); on the other hand, it is akin to the "adult prison," an institutionalized listening that overhears "That baby is spoiled spoiled spoiled" (49), where the content (spoiled) indicates mimesis while the reiteration of that content highlights the colonizing process of mimesis. Mimetic listening might co-function with utopian listening—or what Roland Barthes calls listening *for*[5]—to create dialectical listening.

Negatively-capable listening: This might be an open quality of listening, the ability "to rest in uncertainties, Mysteries, doubts, without any irritable reaching after fact & reason," as John Keats put it, suggesting a practice equally creative and critical. The reader of *Baby* must feel comfortable with this kind of listening, but Harryman's text is demanding and requires some "reaching after." The ear must be protean enough to think-and-feel, wonder-and-anticipate, imagine-and-remember. If for Keats "Heard melodies are sweet, but those unheard / Are sweeter" ("Ode on a Grecian Urn"), Harryman tunes her ears everywhere at once, inward as well as outward, never overtly distinguishing "heard melodies" from "unheard" ones. In an interview, Harryman says that the "reticence to speak," which for my purposes I'm renaming "listening," "comes from having no comfortably identifiable place to speak from and the anxiety of the internal demand to invent a place to speak from."[6] In this model, listening dilates a physical space responsive to the spatiality of sound; for baby the spaces are womb, garden, woods, mountains, tomb, TV, underworld, and cave, which she "speechified to herself all the way out of . . ." (40). A cave stuffed with words is an ear or a mouth, where listening and speaking echo until they are all reverb.

Gestalt listening: Because listening is psychological (while hearing is physiological), we hear much more than we know or expect. Gestalt works from the assumption that the mind naturally perceives wholes out of incomplete information; gestalt listening is context-enriched and takes the relationality of listening as a given. This might also be termed "peripheral hearing" after Freud's concept of peripheral consciousness, a level of subconscious awareness such as subliminal perception, where we register information that comes below the threshold of awareness.[7] This includes registering half-heard or near-heard words, finishing elliptical statements or phrases, and recognition of a whole sound/idea based on a familiar part of that sound or idea. *Baby*'s half-oral, half-literary style, which privileges the unfinished, the unsaid, and the suggested, is a tribute to and validation of gestalt listening as a primary mode of communication. Three "cycles" in *Baby* emphasize orality as the language re-cycles and reprises a lyric feedback system inside an epic gesture. Gestalt listening often involves listening plurally, registering at least subconsciously multiple words and phrases at the same time. In Harryman's text this plurality leads to a seemingly unlimited extension of language, by association and echo: "The language had a force and baby's thoughts ran" (57).

Analytic listening: A term used in psychoanalysis, analytic listening intends to evaluate, decide, and recall as it maintains an open inquisitiveness and a deep connection with the speaker. Jean-Luc Nancy describes it as "being inclined toward affect and not just toward concept."[8] In *Baby*, analytic listening is evoked through telepathic listening and played to ironic effect: "The teenager told baby that she and her friends had been listening to her weird thoughts for a couple of hours and they recommended she just keep going on her way, back toward the exit" (39).

New analytic listening: Fred Moten coins this term to describe an amplification of both aspects of analytic listening that Nancy evokes. New analytic listening is an improvised listening "attuned to the ensemble of the work's organization and production, the ensemble of the politico-economic structure in which it is produced and the ensemble of the senses from which it springs and which it stimulates."[9] Moten says this kind of listening isn't a substitute for, but *is* seeing, *is* all the senses at once. Likewise, time's arrow points in all directions, contracted and condensed. New analytic listening involves multiplicity, hearing multiply and simultaneously in a resonance chamber. As she is fashioned by Harryman into a new status of person, baby calls for this new kind of listening with an extra metacognitive element. She is subject to and subject of constantly renuanced vocalities as well as the kind of synaesthetic listening that Moten attends. *Baby* engages a porousness between thought, gesture, and speech, and the capacity to effectively listen through every sense. Harryman puts Moten's theory into practice (as well as directly addresses it) by engulfing the reader in listening techniques.

Structural listening: Adorno's theory of structural listening is fundamentally applicable to Western instrumental music in the 19th and early 20th centuries, but it might relate loosely to any artwork. Structural listening describes the process wherein a listener follows and comprehends a musical concept, with all its integrated inner relationships and unfolding temporal situations, opposed to bytes of sound or what he calls "atomized listening" inherent in "regressive listening."[10] Adorno defines it best by example: "Structurally, one hears the first bar of a Beethoven symphonic movement only at the very moment when one hears the last bar."[11] *Baby* endorses the reciprocity that Adorno promotes between part and whole, thereby more fully realizing both. *Baby* also takes on a resistant listening in complex relation to a resistant object, thereby divorcing epistemology from the aggressiveness of appropriation and assimilation. "Give me liberty or give me death had not history in baby's breath. Here and then beginning of baby's not. And not" (12). Both dialectical listening and structural listening bear the mark of an antagonistic social totality; they show us what's wrong with standardized listening as a cultural habit full of consumerist compulsions. However, the hierarchies embedded in structural listening cannot translate into *Baby*. Nor do I see such a highly fragmented and elliptical text as *Baby* interested in laying claim to the autonomy principle critical to structural listening. *Baby* is in fact non-original, in that it suspends the concept of origin itself as a totalizing fallacy. Compare the following:

> HARRYMAN: "Adults acted like children acting like babies quite frequently themselves."
> ADORNO: "Regressive listeners behave like children." [12]
> HARRYMAN: "perfect mitten ears"
> ADORNO: "bad ears." [13]
> HARRYMAN: "The corner of everything was smitten with attentiveness."
> ADORNO: "Deconcentrated listening makes the perception of the whole impossible." [14]

Harryman might be strategically listening here as she viscerally rewires Adorno's ideas through multiple channels. To listen dialectically, as *Baby* shows us, is both to comprehend and to suspend comprehension, and not to dawdle in the shiny intensity of revelation.

Dialectical Listening

In *Baby*, dialectical listening refers to how (1) baby perceives the world (epistemology), (2) the reader perceives baby's world as interconnected, contradictory, and dynamic (ontology), as well as (3) Harryman's method of telling baby's story (discourse).

Dialectical listening lends speech nuance, correction, and flexibility. The aural/oral hauntings of writing participate with writing's reverberations in voice. By sublation, listening and speaking in *Baby* continually co-contaminate, cohabitate, and infinitely hybridize in a shifting and ongoing process of self-relation. Listening and hearing are specifically named in over a dozen places in this short text; baby is named "the auditor" (13) to tiger's story, yet the functions of storyteller and listener have already been complicated. For one, tiger's story is titled "How Baby Invented Allegory," implying that the object or listener is also the subject or speaker of the story (11). Through listening, baby intersubjectively answers back; thus *"listening speaks."* [15] In finding a negotiation between the value of speaking and listening, as each interpenetrates the other, Harryman's characters are not psychological portraits or personalities as much as they are rhetorical frames for the synaptic space between listening as a sensation and as an analytic process. Listening "between" requires synthesis and enables transcendence from formal dualism and monistic reductionism as it problematizes too-tidy symmetries and false alternatives embedded in an and/or system (baby or adult, male or female, self or other). Dialectical listening resolves ready-made binaries by suspending baby in a third kind of listening, where sensory life is present within imaginary life and vice versa; one is not suppressed underneath the crushing weight of the other; they intertwine and internest. Everyone in the text is bound by their listening, related by "ears and accumulation" (29).

Conversely, looking is associated with binding binaries; baby in fact "has a preinclination toward seeing things in pairs" (14). Listening, however, involves hearing much more than expected or wished for, because the "technology of listening" is not so easily shut down as that of the eyes, which can be closed or averted. Sound seems to hit the consciousness—with its mergings of perception and memory, intimacy and spectacle, self and other—much more directly than seeing, and in this way, *Baby* palpably credits readers with as much a will and a right to uncoerced, direct, fluid experience as baby herself. As a book, *Baby* primarily offers an acoustic space, a rich multidimensional, resonant field of relations that allows simultaneity, rather than a visual space, which tends to emphasize linearity, sequence, and point of view.

Listening and Identity

Baby's dialectical listening is what creates the conditions for her privileged provisionary status. Baby's status engages and renders the conventional problematic; conflicting values of "baby" (cultural and internal) exist in irresolvable contradiction. As a concept and character, she confronts the "sponge" theory of infants. Baby here is equally receptive and perceptive: "This is my drawing and I can go where I want . . ." (40). As "baby" invokes "regression" (20), "tantrum," "grabby," "surprise" (21), "havoc" (22) she is also seeking to introduce an ideal realization of identity, not to report an existing one. Yet it isn't until baby hears her appellation spoken with a "derogatory undertone" (40) for the first time that the hostile interpellation is capable of bouncing back against itself, thus blurring the territories of the psychological and the linguistic. Baby is a radical agent who has not become indoctrinated into the (ageist, sexist, racist) power structure of listening and speaking, has not swallowed the bifurcation pill, has not fully entered the "adult prison" of "either me or you" (40).

Baby is more of a nascent neither-nor; baby is a condition or state that anyone might slip into, and is therefore essentially nongendered. That baby is often entangled in clothes is indicative of her need to change them, to try on and cast off identities. Dialectical listening exposes contingencies of the conventional—no longer to be perceived as the way baby *is*, but as the way baby has been made to *seem*. The conditions (and incomprehensions) of baby, child, teenager, and adult replace the binary of gender as a primary epistemological system. By this means convention releases its claim to the transcendental. That is, through dialectical listening convention is denaturalized, and rendered profoundly social and situational. Just as gender is malleable, chronology is kicked out of a fixed and fetishized history in favor of a modulating status of being.

The unfinalizability of baby depends on the ensemble of committed (in both senses of the word) listeners around her. Tiger ("I"), a somewhat merged parental figure, caught in baby's internal life, appears "frantic to find baby" roughly midway through the book. Or has baby lost tiger?— either way is equally true. This comedic, archetypal scene is a send-up of autonomy and the unlocatability of baby on an epistemological and ontological level. "Someplace out there was the real, the reality principle, even reality and realism all tied up in a bundle. . . . That's where baby could be found. But 'I' I was left here in the imagination" (27–28). Tiger's insight is that subjectivity involves a play of multiple contexts. At the same time, Baby is not a "team player," in the game where to play is to "cut all others out" (47).

Listening and Utopia

Tiger's story enacts a form of subject-object reciprocity that lies at the heart of any imaginable form of social utopia. The improvisatory duet of baby and tiger recycles sounds and splinters digressions, both discursive and dramatic, familiar and farcical, in order to keep the text unfolding, to keep inventing worlds and possibilities. The sentence searches until it lands us somewhere more accurate, more desirable, more liberating: where "perched on pee" becomes "swelling in glee" (10) and taking up the "p" and "g," to become "primordial good" having "a sound: gee. The "g" in gee" becomes "Gee. Gee. Say it often enough and it'll put you to sleep. Sleep sleep" (11), which returns to "primordial goo" (13) which then becomes "primordial good, the derivative of goo" (14).

"Baby, what are you going to do?" (18).

The auditor (baby) makes decisions in order to meet stories—the heard —halfway. Focused, active audition takes what *is* and refashions it into what *might be*, a path to new knowledge and perception. With baby's ears full of her mother's litany, "I feel that I should do something. I feel like I should get out more I feel I could use some adult company I feel I've forgotten how to think," baby improvises a song out of its dominant grammar, paradoxically reducing the words and enlarging the meaning via rhythm: "I feel I feel I feel I feel I feel I feel I feel" set to *Row, Row, Row Your Boat* (49). Mother and baby cross-pollinate languages as they listen for the future. As baby listens out, she encounters what's possible through critique and recreation. The utopian potential that arises from the intersubjectivity of listening, where "I am listening" also means "listen to me." This assumed reciprocity overthrows implied power structures as it rattles the cages of desire and domination. Expressive-dynamic and rhythmic-spatial modes of listening[16]—that is, vocal and percussive aspects—function like subject and object here. The first mode generates the second, which penetrates the first. In the course of *Baby*, thoughts are listened to and overheard; internal noise is rendered transparent, democratized, amidst the surrounding sonic carnival. Likewise the reader becomes a listener as well; if Harryman's highly intricate and charged sound patterns do not compel the reader to read aloud and listen (to) herself, she will nonetheless inevitably hear it in the mental arena, where the semiotics of tone happens internally. The text must be equally heard and thought, each facilitating the other.

Baby is full of listening that gets recycled and revised, a constant generation and regeneration of stories, words, ideas, sounds out of which baby creates her world in a collaborative, comparative gesture. Many punctuationless passages in *Baby* reinforce orality, or the experience of listening and the inevitability of hearing as it organizes by sound—phrasal units, syntax, and repetition. Listen up: ". . . it's the sound of the parent's voice you anticipate desire and suck in all at once through those perfect mitten ears and translucent and batted at things pulled red then formed into conch spindles then later shielded by hands from undesirable noise" (7). This opening passage suggests that sound is material—translucent, batted, red. It also highlights the ear's shape internally and externally as important to the "technology of listening." Outside, the ears are mittens with shielding and batting qualities. In other words, the ear's ability to block out sound is as necessary as its ability to make contact with it and hit it around. Listening involves judgment, a process of selection in addition to an ability to decode obscured or transgressive sounds. Internally ears here are envisioned as conch shells, spiraling canals. Harryman exploits the fact that hearing happens digressively and circuitously and within our bones, muscles, and cavities; it circulates and echoes within us literally. Baby anticipates, desires, and sucks in the sound—listening is a force of creation, where desirable voice and undesirable noise chase each other around and around toward heterotopia.

Harryman highlights the intersubjective relation that conscious listening establishes between the subject (listener) and the object (composition), where both respond to history, which is itself (dialectically) intersubjective. Through the act of listening *to* and listening *for*, Harryman shows us language's best nature, its utopian character. Dialectical listening restores language's capacity to live within culture and history self-reflexively and with some measure of self-scrutiny.

Listening and Origins

In the opening passage, baby listens out for the parent's voice, which is the persistently previous sound; what she hears is tiger opening a file "claiming, this is the beginning of a long story," which later is the "The Beginning of a Long Story Titled How Baby Invented Allegory by the Tiger," which later is "not your typical mythic story about various atavistic gods in the form of animals and avatars seeming to take form from mud and mist" (13). Beginnings beget beginnings, which slip past and future into more beginnings. Baby herself has no name and so is nominally originless. Baby loses her original referent, but she is determined biologically and ideologically by parents, a family. She contests a taxonomic universe, not only because she parades assumed identities with playful authority and frightening celerity, but also because she cannot be kept separate. Alas, baby cannot be understood in the context of her genesis, but she cannot be understood outside it either.

Harryman's focus on the conceptual and epistemologic ramifications of listening asks us to reconsider notions of identity, origin, and autonomy. There is no nostalgia for origins here because there is no place or time where there was nothing to respond to, nothing to be responsible for. Origin's claim of no previousness intersects with autonomy's claim of no relation, crashing and collapsing both. "Baby" is a status unlikely to be anchored to identity via psychological assumptions about origin and causality, yet likely to be considered relationally. Harryman describes her distrust of autonomy in several publications; in "Wild Mothers" she says "autonomous impulses exist within a site of dialogue and disruption."[17] Listening, as she conceives it, exists by a negotiation between expectation and materiality, between imagination and perception, and between mishearing and selective hearing. There is always a prior listening even if it is thrown into the future via expectations. Listening is coextensive with speaking—each constructed by and instructed by the other, just as writing and reading are often conceptually indistinguishable: a quandary that suggests critical aporia.

Baby's listening attends to both irreducible phonetic parts and narrative such as allegory and origin story, challenging meaning on both mico and macro levels.[18] She listens out for her story and invents it as she goes. Sonic repetition metonymically suggests other words, other ways of meaning, in an "infinity under construction" (13). Consider phonic materiality that re-constitutes and rehears itself, that mishears and mischievously misleads:

> Baby heard the singer singing in my sin. Sin was a good word, fun to say and say wrong for sin and thin were close. Very close. Sin was halfway between thin and fin. Baby's friend Finn was sailing with the sharks but baby knew the difference between fin and Finnian, the formal name of Finn. Although sin sounded close to fin and thin, it was abstract. Baby didn't know the meaning of sin except as a sound associated with other sounds, sounds that meant things. Abstraction caused baby to babble in my thin fin in my fin sin Finnian's in thin fin's sin. Sin was nonsense, a kind of nonsense associated with things that made meaning. And so being in one's sin was being in everything and everything was the same as being in the world. Baby was in the world and it through sin, or singing. (52)

Voice is where language connects to fundamental vibrations and modalities of the body and universe; it is how baby explores the world's ongoing shift and shuffle. The myth of origin begins with sound but does not sound its beginnings—original sin or Nina Simone singing "Gin House Blues" ("stay away from me cos I'm in my sin"). In a passage this dense with repetition, the ear also starts to play, to re-nounce and repronounce. "In my sin" might be peripherally heard or misheard as "in my skin," especially after an initial invitation: "Sin was . . . fun to say and say wrong."[19] Our ears shadow and sharpen to sounds always already there; we listen historically, psychologically, physically, culturally. And we have always been listening.

Listening and Performativity

The language in Harryman's *Baby* is character and context, and as such, it performs relationships. Spoken language requires a listener, a co-partic-ipant. As a functionary of the necessary binary of communication I-and-you, tiger-and-baby agitate each other out of their exclusive roles. By its mobility, dialectical listening circulates, permutates, disaggregates the fixed network of speech roles. When tiger tells the allegory, baby performs it, she interrupts and dislodges it, but she also is the co-participant in the action, its subject and its co-creator. Dialectical listening is performative in several ways: it builds in recursion; it consistently draws our attention to spoken language and the sounds of language (we hear it); and it identifies with the other—the speaker—breaking the bondage of submissive or passive listening (it makes things happen). It also performs philosophical inquiry: "Pain isn't hurting she cries when nobody's listening" (57). Echoing the well-known proposition about a tree falling in the woods, Harry-man changes the terms to prioritize auditory instead of visual witness. In this case, Harryman also suggests the cathartic implications of being heard as well as the ethical responsibility of the listener. *Baby* suggests that it is not possible to imagine listening as an improvisational interface if we preserve "the old modes of listening: those of the believer, the disciple, and the patient."[20] Listening in the text is reflective and reflexive, often involving mutual transformation. What defines a fundamental aspect of the politicized domestic space that is *Baby*'s context is the embedded presence of others, an audience, and the necessity of cooperation and communication. Baby's listening performs fundamental connections: a fact made literal at one point when baby notices a ball of string—a string of words?—hanging from tiger's mouth: "She began to tug at the string. The string uncoiled easily." Baby then wraps each plant in the garden with string, "connecting them all to each other" (18). This scene recalls the tongue in Harryman's play *Performing Objects*, which becomes a ribbon wrapped around things on stage: an ensemble of listeners joined by a common tongue.[21]

Listening and Repetition

Baby is a catalogue of strategies and effects of repetition; prolific doubling in *Baby* is phonetic, auditory, imagistic, linguistic, and conceptual. Dualities, rhyming couplets, and dyads riddle the text, as do reiteration, and phonetic and linguistic echoes; yet "stable concepts" dissolve into "webs of knowledge systems." These systems take hold in the mind, which reproduced them in variations that indicated an "infinity under construction" (13). Thus the dialectic action of doubles ultimately breaks down the binary system; its perpetual splintering engenders ensembles that listeners must hear through. Doubling acts not as an antagonistic duality, but as a dynamic, developmental relationship *between* seeming pairs, investigating the interstices, and as that relationship resounds *outward*, collecting new relationships, new doublings on its way to finding new synthesis in a dialectical process. Repetition also builds in the recursive act of listening in much the same way Stein does with reading. It makes the act of listening a performance, to be rehearsed and replayed itself. Because sounds, words, and concepts happen twice, dialectical listening demands listening twice:

> Baby was going to sing and then sing twice. . . . Experience. Experience. She sang. She sang divided and then twice feeling the lungs of the forest as her own and then stepping back to observe herself as much phenomenon springing into readymade . . . She thought she was going to taste tings. Then she thought again and thus was thinking twice. (45)

Yet is it possible to listen to the same sound twice? As Barthes claims, we derive pleasure from repetition both by fulfillment of expectations (pattern) and from transgression of expectations (disruption of pattern); repetition suspends the listener in a state of anticipation. A rehearsed word gets wrenched into novel sense or nonsense—or more accurately, somewhere in limbo. A rehearsed word is made strange by the brute fact of its pre-presentation or because the planks have been yanked out of its context. Repetition doesn't promote sameness—the sound recomposes and decomposes; it refers, defers, and transfers; it exaggerates itself vertiginously. Recombinant propulsion and reiterative compulsion work not only for accrual of meaning and sparks of difference (Baraka's "the changing same"[22]), but also offer the possibility of slippages, mistakes, mishearings, failures of listening. Fruitful failure, or sound breaking itself out of its own return/resonance, might be thought of as a motivation for repetition. Repeated sounds are intrinsic to *Baby*'s humor: double meanings, negation, multiple uses of the same word, homophony, semantic shuffling brought on by eccentric inference—each highlights the aporia and insistent paradoxes in relationship between listening and speaking. Humor here is a meaningful discourse about the crisis of signification and the unbridgeable distances between the semantic, sensual, and semiotic. The constructed nature of listening—institutionalized listening—is freed up by repetition in *Baby*.

Listening and Silence

Baby associates silence with the "product of an unaffected poise" and the sagacity (22) of teenagers. On the penultimate page of the book, she learns how to silence parents and adults—something akin to swatting a fly —by agreeing with them when they least expect it. In both cases silence is a method of unsettling surprise. Often associated with origin, silence is never a precondition with Harryman. "In the beginning, there was nothing," Harryman mythologizes in "Fish Speech" from *There Never Was a Rose Without a Thorn*, ". . . Silence was neither dominant nor peaceful nor silent."[23] Likewise, in *Baby*, silence is just as ethically demanding and multiple as listening. When baby "doesn't want an imposition," she silences tiger by "sealing tiger's mouth with her wet tongue" (29). When "the other baby" abandons her, she does so by soothing her "with tongue and a special silence" (50); silence is always underneath the tongue, often the motivation for words, reflecting the paradoxical nature of consciousness. Harryman negotiates an undefined condition between sound and silence— speaking and listening—in a state of reciprocal struggle, never reconciled nor relieved. Intimacy and violence attend speech and silence; their rhythm opposes any instant of relief. They are, in Blanchot's phrase, a "torn unity," fueling communication: "The poet speaks by listening" and "likewise, he who listens, the 'reader,' is he by whom the work is spoken anew."[24] That is, meaning relies on ethical allegiance to listen dialectically.

The story frame of *Baby* becomes a fictional space that allows indirect experience of listening to someone else, creating a kind of auditory voyeurism. Baby, the auditor, is listening to tiger, but her listening is full of distractions and "noise" inherently faithful to the circumstances of the story. Though we are listening to the story of the story, we cannot absorb into the scene. We therefore experience our own absence from the scene. The listener cannot hear the story, but only its representation, and cannot hear the documentation, but rather only its transduction. Noting noisiness and disruptions, Joan Retallack characterizes Harryman's work as "full of the formal/verbal articulation of silence."[25] Noise is a powerful mechanism for establishing and reconfiguring subjectivity. Listening mimics language here in that it does not "replicate sciences of perspective as we've known them."[26] Instead, baby oscillates among quick scenes, sensory moments, analytic musings, and language sources outside herself, advocating a flexible and scattered ear. Even in virtual silence, there is anticipation, which holds final conclusion at bay. By keeping listening, *Baby* and its reader continue to explore multiplicity and blurred dimensions of communication. "If there had been silence, silence would have been pierced but the room was always humming" (42).

NOTES TO POETICS STATEMENT

1. My statement of poetics is an edited extract from "Siren," in *The Grand Piano 9* (Detroit, Mode A, 2009). *The Grand Piano* is a ten-volume collection of essays, composed as experiments in autobiography by ten writers associated with San Francisco language writing in the 1970s and 1980s. I have chosen to use segments of this essay in order to implicate and point to a history of collaboration throughout my writing life, even as the essay itself is a single-authored work. Additionally, the essay's concern with sound is related to Christine Hume's considerations of listening in her writing on *Baby*.

2. Bertholt Brecht, *Brecht on Theater*, trans. John Willett (New York, Hill & Wang, 1957), 95.

3. Carla Harryman, *Under the Bridge*, (San Francisco, This, 1980).

4. Barbara Engh, "Adorno and the Siren," in *Embodied Voices: Representing Female Vocality in Western Culture*, eds. Leslie C. Dunn and Nancy A. Jones (Cambridge, MA: Cambridge University Press, 1994), 133–35.

5. Ibid.

6. Ibid.

7. Ibid.

8. Catherine Clément, "Choosing Night," in *Syncope*, trans. Sally O'Driscoll and Deirdre M. Mahoney (Minneapolis: University of Minnesota, 1994), 31. This is an extract *these spirits move too quickly* from a critique of Cartesian tranquility.

9. Brecht, *Brecht on Theater*, 33.

10. Frances Boldereff, in *Charles Olson and Frances Boldereff: A Modern Cor-*

respondence, eds. Ralph Maud and Sharon Thesen (Middletown, CT: Wesleyan University Press, 1999), 416.

11. *The New Century Classical Handbook*, ed. Catherine B. Avery (New York: Appleton-Century-Crofts, 1962), 1014.

12. Carla Harryman, "Autonomy Speech," in *Animal Instincts* (1989), 111. The first lines of the essay incorporate nonattributed lines in italics from the opening of Haraway's essay.

13. "Meghom" in *There Never Was a Rose without a Thorn* (San Francisco: City Lights, 1995), 99.

14. Leslie C. Dunn and Nancy A. Jones, *Embodied Voices*, 4.

15. Caterine Clément, "Prelude," in *Opera or the Undoing of Women*, trans. Betsy Wing (Minneapolis: University of Minnesota Press, 1988), 16.

16. Ibid., 21.

17. Ronald Sukenick, *Narralogues: Truth in Fiction* (New York: SUNY, 2000), 1.

18. Ibid., 9.

NOTES TO CRITICAL ESSAY

1. Carla Harryman, *Baby* (New York: Adventures in Poetry, 2005), 7. Unless otherwise noted, all quotations from Harryman are from this work and cited in the text.

2. Julia Kristeva, *Revolution in Poetic Language*, trans. Margaret Waller (New York: Columbia University Press, 1984), 83.

3. The first half of this sentence paraphrases an observation made by Peter Quartermain, quoting Don Wellman, about John Donne, in "Sound Reading," *Close Listening: Poetry and the Performed Word*, ed. Charles Bernstein (New York: Oxford University Press, 1998), 224.

4. Jean-Luc Nancy speculates: "Perhaps we never *listen* to anything but the encoded, what is not yet framed in a system of signifying references, and we never *hear* anything but the already coded, which we decode." For further auscultation of listening, see Jean-Luc Nancy, *Listening*, trans. Charolette Mandell (New York: Fordham University Press, 2007), 36.

5. Roland Barthes, "On Listening," in *The Responsibility of Forms: Critical Essays on Art, Music, and Representation*, trans. Richard Howard (Berkeley: University of California Press, 1991), 247.

6. Carla Harryman, "Interview with Chris Tysh," in *Poetics Journal* 10 (June 1998): 216.

7. Sigmund Freud, *An Outline of Psycho-Analysis*, trans. James Strachey (New York: Norton, 1989), 187.

8. Nancy, *Listening*, 26.

9. Fred Moten, *In the Break: Aesthestics of the Black Radical Tradition* (Minneapolis: University of Minnesota Press, 2003), 67.

10. Atomized and regressive listening are the enemies of structural listening, according to Adorno. Among other things, both involve hearing merely a series of disconnected episodes. Adorno's typology articulates fundamental social impediments to the forms of listening and listeners whose ears are socially scarred. Theodor W.

Adorno, "The Radio Symphony" and "On the Fetish-Character in Music and the Regression of Listening," in *Essays on Music*, ed. Rihard Leppert, trans. Susan Gillespie (Berkley: University of California Press, 2002), 251–70, 288–317.

11. Ibid., 255.

12. Ibid., 307.

13. Ibid.

14. Ibid., 305.

15. Barthes, "On Listening," 150.

16. Adorno, "Radio Symphony," 197.

17. Carla Harryman, "Wild Mothers or 'Mom, Can I Show You My Leprechaun Trap,'" in *Moving Borders: Three Decades of Innovative Writing By Women*, ed. Mary Margaret Sloan (Jersey City, NJ: Talisman House, 1998), 689.

18. How to listen in doubly, with ears tuned, in Adorno's terms, to both atomized listening and structural listening? How does our attention unconsciously or unintentionally decide what's audible? How does it organize and hierarchize that information? How do we account for silences (taxonomized by Cage) and auditory habits of perception?

19. Indeed, and humorously, sin *is* meant to be wrong. This passage resonates with the last line of the book: "This religion of skin for which there was no titular value" (63), which brings us back to baby as the book's skin or title and the fallacy of origins. Nancy says, "Music is the art of making the outside of time return to every time, making return to every moment the beginning that listens to itself beginning and beginning again" (67).

20. Barthes, "On Listening," 152.

21. This connectivity might be figured as a Deleuzian assemblage where subject and object form a series of flows and intensities, linked in heterogeneous ways. Elizabeth Grosz understands orality as "creating linkages with other surfaces, other places, other objects or assemblages. The child's lips, for example, form connections (or in Deleuzian terms, machines, assemblages) with the breast or bottle." Elizabeth Grosz, *Volatile Bodies: Toward a Corporeal Feminism* (Bloomington: Indiana University Press, 1994), 116. It also revels in and resists the recurrent image in literature, art, and perfomance of a filled (and spilling) female mouth. Caryl Churchhill and David Lan's play *A Mouthful of Birds* features a female character who feels her mouth is stuffed with birds. By connecting orality with community, Harryman's image reclaims the common female character of chatterboxes and blather-mouths. In Harryman's "Architecture and Landscape of All Countries," Mom plays secret keys with a constant supply of horns and flutes: "Sometimes Mom would play a trumpet from her position at the mouth of the cave," which suggests a complex relation to orality and motherhood. *There Never Was a Rose Without a Thorn*, 44.

22. For more discussion, see Amiri [LeRoi Jones] Baraka, *The LeRoi Jones/ Amiri Baraka Reader*, ed. William J. Harris (New York: Thunder's Mouth Press, 1991).

23. Carla Harryman, "Fish Speech," in *There Never Was a Rose Without a Thorn* (San Francisco: City Lights Books, 1995), 41.

24. Maurice Blanchot, *The Space of Literature*, trans. Ann Smock (Lincoln: University of Nebraska Press, 1989), 226.

25. Joan Retallack, *Poetical Wager* (Berkley: University of California Press, 2003), 142.
26. Ibid., 143.

BIBLIOGRAPHY

Books by Carla Harryman

Percentage. Berkeley, CA: Tuumba Press, 1979.
Under the Bridge. San Francisco: This Press, 1980.
Property. Berkeley, CA: Tuumba Press, 1982.
The Middle. San Francisco: Gaz Press, 1983.
Vice. Hartford, CT: Potes and Poets Press, 1986.
Animal Instincts: Prose, Plays Essays. Berkeley, CA: This Press, 1989.
In the Mode Of. Tenerife, Canary Islands, Spain: Zasterle Press, 1992.
Memory Play. Oakland, CA: O Books, 1994.
There Never Was a Rose Without a Thorn. San Francisco: City Lights, 1995.
The Words: After Carl Sandburg's Rootabaga Stories and Jean-Paul Sartre. Berkeley, CA: O Books, 1999.
Dim Blue and Why Yell. New York: Belladonna, 2000.
Gardener of Stars. Berkeley, CA: Atelos, 2001.
Baby. New York: Adventures in Poetry, 2005.
The Grand Piano, volumes 1–9. With Rae Armantrout, Steve Benson, Lyn Hejinian, Tom Mandel, Ted Pearson, Bob Perleman, Kit Robinson, Ron Silliman, and Barrett Watten. Detroit: Mode A, 2006–2009.
Tourjours L'epine Es Sous La Rose. Trans. Martin Richet. Paris, France: Ikko, 2006.
Open Box. New York: Belladonna, 2007.
Adorno's Noise. New York and Chicago: Essay Press, 2008.

Edited Volumes

With eds. Amy Scholder and Avital Ronell. *Lust for Life: on the Writings of Kathy Acker*. New York and London: Verso, 2006.
Journal of Narrative Theory. Non/Narrative 41, no. 1 (Summer 2011).

Selected Prose

"Wild Mothers." In *Moving Borders: Three Decades of Innovative Writing by Women*. Ed. Mary Margaret Sloan. Jersey City, NJ: Talisman House, 1998, 688–94.
"Women's Writing: Hybrid Thoughts on Contingent Hierarchies and Reception." *How2*, 1.2 [online journal] (September 1999). www.asu.edu.
"Rules and Restraints in Women's Experimental Writing." In *We Who Love to Be Astonished: Women Experimenters and Performance Writing*. Eds. Cynthia Hogue and Laura Hinton. Tuscaloosa: University of Alabama Press, 2001, 116–24.

"Home in the Book of Daniel: Conversations on Theater and Community." *Trait* 2 (2002): 21–25.
"Site Sampling in Performing Objects Stationed in the Subworld." In *Additional Apparitions*. Eds. Keith Tuma and David Kennedy. Sheffield, UK: The Cherry on the Top Press, 2002, 157–71.
"The Ear of the Poet in the Mouth of the Performer." *How2* 2, no. 4 [online journal] (September 2003). www.asu.edu.
"The Nadja and Nanette of Gail Scott's Main Brides." In *Assembling Alternatives: Reading Postmodern Poetries Transnationally*. Ed. Romana Huk. Middletown, CT: Wesleyan University Press, 2003, 299–308.
"Parallel Play." In *The Grand Permission*. Eds. Patricia Dienstfry and Brenda Hillman. Middletown, CT: Wesleyan University Press, 2003, 121–34.
"Residues or Revolutions of the Language of Acker and Artaud." In *Devouring Institutions*. Ed. Michael Hardin. San Diego: SDSU Press, 2004, 157–66.
"The Mother of Us All." *How2* 2, no. 2 [online journal] (Spring 2004). www.asu.edu.
"How I Wrote Gardener of Stars." In *Biting the Error*. Eds. Robert Gluck, Gail Scott, and Megan Adams. Toronto: Coach House Press, 2004, 132–38.
"Acker Unformed." In *Lust for Life*. Eds. Amy Scholder, Carla Harryman, and Avital Ronell. New York and London: Verso, 2006, 35–44.
"Something Nation: Radical Spaces of Performance in Linton Kwesi Johnson and cris cheek." In *Diasporic Avant-gardes: Experimental Poetics and Cultural Displacement*. Eds. Carrie Noland and Barrett Watten. New York: Palgrave Macmillian, 2009, 207–24.

Selected Interviews

With Manuel Brito. *A Suite of Poetic Voices*. Santa Brigada, Spain: Kadle Books, 1994, 57–70.
With Megan Simpson. *Contemporary Literature* 37, no. 4 (Winter 1996): 511–32.
With Chris Tysh. *Poetics Journal: Knowledge* 10 (1998): 207–17.
With Laura Hinton. *Postmodern Culture* 16, no. 1 [online journal] (2006). http://pmc.iath.virginia.edu.
With Costinela Dragon. *Intersections. Intersections*. University of Bucharest (September 2009), www.american-studies.ro/issue.
With Sawako Nakayasu. *12 X 12: Conversations in 21st Century Poetics*. Eds. Christina Mengert and Joshua Marie Wilkinson. Iowa City: University of Iowa Press, 2009, 136–70.
With Rene Gladman. In *Reading Carla Harryman*. Curated by Laura Hinton. *How2* 3, no. 3 (2009). www.asu.edu.

Selected Criticism

Alystyre, Julian. "*There Never Was a Rose Without a Thorn.*" Review of *Contemporary Fiction* (1995): 153–54.
Bellamy, Dodie and Kevin Killian. Review of *In the Mode Of*. "Signals." *Small Press Traffic Newsletter* 15 (1992).
Bellamy, Dodie and Kevin Killian. Review of *Animal Instincts*. *Small Press Traffic Newsletter* 11 (1989).

Benson, Steve. Review of *Percentage*. *Poetry Flash* 82 (1982).

Brito, Manuel. "4 poetisas americanas." *Pagina* 63 (1996): 29–44.

Burt, Stephen. Review of *Baby*. *Rain Taxi* 10, no. 3 (Fall 2005): 32.

Campbell, Bruce. "But What Is an Adequate Vice to Limit the Liquid of This Voice?" Review of *Vice*. *Poetics Journal* (1991): 210–28.

Clifford, Pat. Review of *Adorno's Noise*. *Kaurab: A Bengali Poetry Webzine* 5 (March 2010). www.kaurab.com/english/books/adornos-noise.html.

Crawford, Lynn. Review of *Gardener of Stars*. *Detroit Metro Times* (March 20, 2002).

Davies, Alan. "The Next Sentence is Not a Death Sentence in" "Five Sound Minds" Review of *Adorno's Noise*. *Jacket* 39 (2010): http://jacketmagazine.com.

Davies, Alan. "Carla," *Writing* (1991).

Durgin, Patrick. "Matches, in Our Time." Review of *Adorno's Noise*. *Postmodern Culture* 19, no. 3 (May 2009). http://pmc.iath.virginia.edu.

Funston, Kenneth. Review of *Property*. *Los Angeles Times*, Aug. 15, 1982: K8.

Henning, Barbara. "Carla Harryman's *Memory Play*." *Poetry Project Newsletter* (1995): 28.

Hejinian, Lyn. "The *femme fatale* in the Schoolyard." In *The Grand Piano: Part 8*. Detroit: Mode A, 2009, 11–34.

Hinton, Laura. Curator. "Reading Carla Harryman." *How2* 3, no. 3 (2009). www.asu.edu.

Hofer, Jen, and Summi Kaipa. "On The Wide Road by Carla Harryman and Lyn Hejinian." *Tripwire* 3 (Summer 1999).

Lakoff, George. "On Whose Authority." Review of *The Middle*. *Poetry Flash* (1985).

Laurence, Patricia. Review of *Gardener of Stars*. *Review of Contemporary Fiction* (Summer 2002): 224–25.

Mannisto, Glen. "Shaping Ideas." Review of "Chairs of Words." *Metro Times*, March 19, 1998: 6.

Marsden, Helen. "Jellyfruits of Reason." *Craccum Arts* (1995): 15.

Martin, Steven Paul. "Carla Harryman: Mixing Genres." In *Open Form and the Feminine Imagination*. New York: Maisonneuve, 1989, 147–58.

Olsen, Redell. "Sites and (Human) Non-Sites of a (Sub) Urban World." In *Additional Apparitions: Poetry, Performance & Site Specificity*. Eds. David Kennedy and Keith Tuma. Sheffield, UK: Cherry on Top Press, 2002, 181–90.

Olsen, Redell. "Degrees of Liveness, Live and Electronic Subjects of Leslie Scalapino, Fiona, Templeton, and Carla Harryman." *How2* 1, no. 6 [online journal] (2001). www.asu.edu.

Robinson, Kit. Review of *Adorno's Noise*. *Rain Taxi* 14, no. 2 (Summer 2009): 20–21.

Scott, Gail. "Elixir for Thinking: Carla Harryman." Review of *There Never Was a Rose Without a Thorn*. *West Coast Line* 23, nos. 31–32 (Fall 1997).

Simpson, Megan. "Feminist Phenomenologies: Language as the Horizon of Encounter." In *Poetic Epistemologies: Gender and Knowing in Women's Language-Oriented Writing*. Albany, NY: SUNY Press, 2000, 145–62.

Stefans, Brian Kim. Review of *Gardener of Stars*. *A Little Review* [online].

Stroffolino, Chris. "Carla Harryman: An Introduction," and "Notes Toward a Harrymanian Reading of Shakespeare." In *Spin Cycle: Selected Essays and Reviews 1989–1999*. New York: Spuyten Duyvil, 2001, 132–61.

Wegner, Jonathan. Review of *Adorno's Noise*. *Make* 7 (Fall/Winter 2008–2009). http://makemag.com/review-adornos-noise/.

Williamson, Dustin. Review of *Baby*. *Poetry Project Newsletter* (February/March 2006): 27–28.

Wright, Laura. "Play in the Work of Carla Harryman," *Revista canaria des estudios ingleses* 37 (November 1998): 173–86.

ERÍN MOURE

document32 (inviolable)

When "my language" <u>fails</u>, only then can we detect signals that
harken to a porosity of borders or lability of zones. . . . (across
the entire electromagnetic spectrum, not just the visual. as in
planetary noise)

But first we have to suspend our need to see "identity" itself as
saturate signal (obliterating all "noise"), following Lispector

into a "not yet"—

How a woman wanting to write can be a *territorial* impossibility.
And *reading* (bodies or others) is itself always a kind of weak
signal communication, a process of tapping signals that scarcely
rise off the natural noise floor.

(the noise generated by a system within itself)

Think of Ingeborg Bachmann in her hotel rooms. Her unsettled
acts were noise's fissures. To see her as citizen is indeed to know
citizen as repository of harm, where harm is gendered too. Myths
of violability, inviolability, volatility, utility, lability played out. In
wars, women are territories, and territories are *lieux de punition.*

A César o que é de César. *(Bachmann in Rome.)*

"to interdepend" (Clarice says)

document33 (arena)

Perhaps it is "grief's" figure keeps one stuck in subjectivity
"irrevocably," gives *apparent* need for _essence_ to explain this
subjectivity. If so, fertile ground opens to totalitarianisms—for
totalitarianisms plead from essences. *Arena* here is *sand* too, thus
ground. Are essences debts? After so tiny a collection of attempts
forced her, have we played? To engage submissivity's power is
to extend or prolect the boundaries of "self" (the role of silence
in the piece). To move into a modality of the body other than
one based on boundary ethics. A modality *altogether other* than
subjectivity as essence

Traversal to innate connect -
- albeit source of

(grammar)   *beyond's economy*

in the *corpo cuerpo* those mountains and the view of Ribadeo
from the train

weeping (another woman in the car)

o meu corpus sanctus in which feelings erupt *whether I will them
or not*, says Aurèle Aoûtien

Eleventh *Impermeable* of the Carthage of Harms

an excerpt from Polybius, The Histories
(most of the wounded were those who went upon the bridge to help those injured in the first attack)

If there were emigrations
a small and bitter cloth

Immensitude of pulp from the oranges
cried out its colour

Flavour of almond in the mouth
your silk

A wager silk
a bitter flavour

Forgotten the screen she bent into the water
her arm a ghost beneath soft wool

A cistern opened by extrusive flow
its song diurnal water

your silk
your yellow almond silk

The city they had named her Carthage
somewhere south of "Oregonn"

A toll immense on lives was taken
for and against ablation of personal life

Wearing yellow trees a tear of light
against my amber

Those jackets a light does admit to breast or brean
her tear known against my amber.

AANOASNN

FROM *Little Theatres*

Theatre of the Confluence (A Carixa)

A little river and a big river
the story of the bronchials
Some of earth's heartbeat but not all

The water rose in the little river
and washed the big river away
Some of the lungs' telluric memory

The story of a river mouth
and a confluence
From such a place you can hear the river
or you can breathe
but you have to choose or it chooses you

If it chooses you you are an asthmatic
Now you can live here forever
You can sit under the oak leaves and feel wet spray

The big river and the little river
The story of breath in a meander

The big river and the little river
A little story of leaves the river swept away

Theatre of the Stones that Ran (Fontao, 1943)

At night in the valley of penedos erguidos
a glint of wolfram

the uncles' job at night
to touch the glint of wolfram

wolfram brought riches for all in Fontao
they all had jobs then in Fontao
even the prisoners worked in Fontao
the garrison eyed everyone

there was only the night left

The uncles mined the glint in the river course
and stood up in the water
at night they worked each with small hands of xeo
and stood up in the water
climbed out of the river with the wolfram

penedos erguidos
human uncles, tiny

and they ran

for M.I.

Theatre of the Millo Seco (Botos)

I am in the little field of my mother
Her field touches
oaks of the valley
and I touch the faces of my corn

Opening corn's faces
so that my hands touch its braille letters
The face of corn is all in braille
the corn wrote it

Fires will burn this evening
burn the dry husks of the corn
and I will learn to read
Sheep will wait by the trough
for they know corn's feature, corn's humility

corn's dichten

grain's

granite too

[T]he best woman i ever saw.
in faith of none better i did hear. is she that go[d]
made best appear. my lovely this the lov
liest of all i saw. of such high prais and
such good mind. in faith she is of all
best i ve ever seen and never heard of better.
And believe me that in truth she is
and will be the one. as ever she shall live
and any who will come to see and know her
i know well i can say that it is her.
Still more of her worth i will here sspeak
she is well loved but no other there is
who could love her as do i.
And such foul day i was born
For i love her greatly
for i crave her and see myself die
and see her not and such foul day i was born
but beg to go[d] to do as well to me as he to her
that he would grant me aid
to see her soon where i from her did part.

With better heart. Toward me.

du même auteur au début, marquant une indécision essentielle, privé et
parfois « secrèt », une inscription en forme, portrait d'amour, il n'importe
pas moins que, comme certains d'entre vous, il s'agit

CXVIII (139,1)
Dom Fernam Garcia Esgaraungha

This night of liquid storms, high noon s dwelling

Thi snigh tofliqu idstorms, highn oons~ duu ellin~
Can you follow me in the markings we call
words through such liquidity?

Liquidity s vault, that vault s over
all t brough near it
Pul sof rayn, epiphn ny?

*« Plus d'un, comme moi sans doute, écrivent pour n'avoir plus de
visage. »*
~~MFoucault~~ Cálgharii M.

[449] #504
Dom Dinis

POETICS STATEMENT

A practice of possibility, a life in languages

> "Le sujet . . . est la possibilité que la langue ne soit pas, n'ait pas
> lieu—ou, mieux, qu'elle n'ait lieu qu'à travers sa possibilité—de
> ne pas être, sa contingence."
> —G. AGAMBEN, *Ce qui reste d'Auschwitz*

I'VE BEEN WRITING for half my life in Montreal, in Québec, where one's own English is opened up and in constant motion. In daily life, French is the common, civic language, yet, contrary to what you hear, all is not simply English or French here. There is a *third* culture that rubs up against the borders of many cultures, that thrives in the midst of francophone culture itself. I am of this third culture. Of the culture of borders that leak. It is not a rare culture; neither is it one that clamors.[1] Perhaps because it is not "one." Writer/artist Daniel Canty has dubbed us "francomixophones." Yes, English is my mother tongue, but in me it is also a faulty tongue, has wobbles and errors in my mouth and head. And it is the philosophy of French, along with its theatre, feminism, politics of everyday, and ways of seeing that are most closely mine. As well, I exist in Galician. As foreign and not as foreign. For Galician, as my friends say, welcoming me into their language, belongs to those who love it.

Thinking, dreaming, living in other languages means for me that English is no longer a natural language. And the accent I bring back into English is an affect that creates fissures, joinings, alterations. The fact of thinking these questions in Galician and in Portuguese, *et en français*, affects my English when I translate my thoughts here in order to speak to you.

Language is social space, and in social spacings, embodiment and speech are both operative. The body alters space, language alters space, languages alter space. Alter our mouths. Alter each, each other. In unpredictable ways. Language—and learning another language, and another—alters the mouth, the body, the body's borders. And the body's capacity to understand.

If you read the work that results, it also alters your English, and your body. An affected language, an accented language, lives: it bears possibility.

The "globalization" or "making world" in which I see potentiality is one that admits and strengthens localities and pluralities, a plurality of localities, of nations, neither based nor congealed in myths of origin that operate by shutting others out, but which admit such myths as the heritage of all.

My books, I hope, enact that crossing of borders, leakages in borders, interpenetration (without absorption![2]) of forms that—paradoxically— make individual entities (countries, persons, communities) possible, even viable. Leakages in writings make writing possible. Leakages in languages, idioms, paradoxically, nourish individual languages so that they may thrive. In ways not rigid, not sealed, not marking strict identitarian limits of "outside" and "inside," but not losing identity either. My poems as a whole reflect, I think, that identity finds its stability in uncertainty, in the fluidity of limits, in the "not yet." This does not deny limits or nations, or the need for them; it just calls for a different way of viewing them, enacting them.

And I translate from my other languages into English. Translation itself has led me to think of the "I" as multiplied, fluid: *théâtrale*.

It was Fernando Pessoa, and my 2001 translation of his *O Guardador de Rebanhos*, a book from the previous century, that first beckoned me to think on the notion of theatre, and to think of place or site, even of the site of writing, of the moment of writing something down, as *théâtrale*, as subject or open to theatre, to a collective space/time.[3] It let me to examine, and jubilate in, Pessoa's superabundance of authors, of beings.

My notions of theatre, of community, of staging have been further amplified by reading and translating the gorgeous cacophonies of Galician poet Chus Pato. And by experiencing the interferences of the Elisa Sampedrín, in a realization that small theatres, and the language one does not yet recognize, may take us further than the big theatres of war and discourse (like the clash of civilizations) concocted for us in English by politicians. This Pessoa and Pato-inspired thinking gave me *Little Theatres*, the book of small noise, of words that sound like water. I wrote the book after *O Cidadán* came out in 2002, when English ached and weighed in me, for south of me, as autumn progressed, were the sorry rumblings of American public discourse beating the drum of English louder and louder till the very crescendo of language would deafen peace and lead inexorably to the theatres of war.[4]

At that point, I no longer wanted to write in the same language as the American leader. It seemed corrupt to me. I went away to a small country within another state, Galicia, whose indigenous culture was one that quietly resisted imperialism, whose climate was one of water, whose language even sounded like water to someone with ears too accustomed to English. I wanted to write a simple book, an antidote to the difficulties of *O Cidadán*, a book that, in the war-mongering around me and to the south of me, seemed out of date, drowned out. In my third language, Galician, where I am like a ten-year-old in words, I wrote. Later I translated the poems into English, and the translating brought me to write more in English, an English that welcomed Galician into it, in order to exist apart from big theatres.

This book, *Little Theatres*, pulled me further into that voice addressing not god or history (as big theatres do, i.e., the theatres of war) but another human. Because I could read Galician (and thus, with little difficulty, Portuguese), I went to Lisbon for two months to read the songbooks of the medieval troubadours of the northwest Iberian peninsula. In our age, when so many poets and critics lambaste lyric as if it were just an expression of "feeling" or of the inner states of an unquestioned and centered[5] subject, invoking lyric voice can seem at odds with current views of the subject's plurivocality, multiplicity. Yet in the work of the troubadours, lyric's "I" was not the "I" of romanticism—but théâtrale, a symptom, resolutely constructed. It was the I of Benveniste, of Agamben. What was it all about in 1050, in 1200, in Galician and Portuguese? And how has it been handed down to us? "Archive" itself is no innocent deposit or depository, as Derrida has noted.

I wanted simply to read the poems and see what happened in my own body and what I would write. Afterward, from my notebooks full of notes and words and phrases and reactions, I made poems, attributing each to the name of the troubadour closest in my notebook. Because of the attributions, the poems seem often to be translations, but they are only so in the sense that all reading and influence are always translation. The postface I wrote about the experience of working with those texts in O Cadoiro is available online at www.anansi.ca/ocadoiro/postface.

At the same time I finished translating Chus Pato's Charenton, and Pato's proliferation of subjects, subject positions, verb tenses, her intermingling of histories and racing trajectories, so théâtrale, was having further impacts on my poetry and on the possibilities for translation and poetry and collaboration that are happening now.

It's ongoing, really. When you read this, I will be somewhere else, for that is what a practice in language is, an elsewhere, a placing that involves a yet-to-come.

To echo Stéphane Mallarmé from Un coup de dés, a book published posthumously in 1914, its lines re-cited by Derrida as an epigraph in 1967—thus, continually archive, modified, inserted, volumnal, placed and "essentiellement lacunaire":

> "Le tout sans nouveauté
> qu'un espacement
> de la lecture"

MOURE'S ABRASIONS
Aaron Kunin

Names

The poet who is the subject of this essay has written under several names. On the covers of her books she may be called Erin Mouré, Erín Moure, or both. On the cover of the book *Sheep's Vigil by a Fervent Person* (2001), this name is given the Galician spelling Eirin Moure. So far these names are obviously variations on a theme. In the pages of *O Cadoiro* (2007), the name Cálgarii Mourii (also spelled Cálgharii M. and Cálgharij M.) is a little more difficult to recognize, but turns out to be a Latinized version of the same name, formed, like the name of a medieval scribe, by associating the poet's family with the place of her early life, Calgary. Only a few of the poems in *O Cadoiro* are attributed to this relatively familiar figure, and the attributions are disputed in notes and sometimes crossed out; other poems and fragments are said to be authored by a number of poets, singers, and dancers from the Galician-Portuguese songbooks of the late middle ages, such as María Pérez Balteira, María A. Soldadeira, and Meendinho M., or by poststructuralist thinkers such as Michel Foucault, Jean-Luc Nancy, and Giorgio Agamben, and, in disputed cases, some combination of the foregoing. Finally, in *Little Theatres* (2005), the title poems as well as a series of fragments alternately called "quotes" or "bits on little theatres" are attributed to someone named Elisa Sampedrín. The provenance of the "bits" is dubious; many of them are not writings or proper interviews but are "overheard" by stagehands or unnamed peripheral figures on a subway somewhere in Toronto. On the cover, only the "quotes" are attributed to Sampedrín; the poems are attributed to Erín Moure, about whom Sampedrín also contributes an ambiguous blurb: "Moure: where have I heard that name before? I thought she'd left. What on earth is she up to now?"

Where have I heard the name Moure? What is she up to? Good questions. A critical essay about a poet might begin by answering them, or might even assume the answers as givens. I am writing about a poet whose names proliferate as questions in her own work, so I begin by noting the proliferation, which is her first challenge to criticism.[1]

Heteronyms

Names are problems in many of Moure's books. In "The Acts," a series of theoretical prose meditations that concludes the collection *Furious* (1988), the speaker proposes "to try to move the force in language from the noun/verb centre," in order to get at "the Motion before the Name."[2] The problem seems to be that names are static. The solution is not to get rid of the names but to redistribute some of the powers of language to other parts of speech, such as prepositions, that are better equipped for moving the entire apparatus. In "Nureyev's Intercostals," a series of short lyrics from *Search Procedures* (1996), many of the names appear in quotation marks. " 'Clarice' 'Phyllis' // . . . 'Gail.' " "Quotes around a name," the speaker observes, pointing to what is already the most visible graphic intervention on the page.[3] The quotation marks indicate that someone else is speaking—

because, Michel Foucault might say, in this poem it matters who is speaking. Foucault asks the question (quoting a text by Beckett) "What does it matter who is speaking?" to interrupt what he calls "the author-function" that would assimilate texts to an author's project.[4] Instead of using a single name to activate the author-function and take responsibility for the poem's language, Moure's poem includes the names of several authors: Clarice is Clarice Lispector, Phyllis is Phyllis Webb, Gail is Gail Scott. The names appear inside rather than outside quotation marks, as though the authors were effects of speech rather than its source.

To take a final, admittedly extreme example, in "The Wittgenstein Letters to Mel Gibson's *Braveheart* (Skirting her a subject) (or *girls girls girls*)," from the collection *A Frame of the Book* (1999), the names of authors seem to be moving around on their own, without help from prepositions or punctuation. In lines that vaguely follow the cadences of lines by Rilke ("You must change your life") and Donne ("Go and catch a falling star"), a number of authors' names replace the substantives: "You must read your Frank O'Rilke now / . . . You must ask Norma Cole if she has read her Gertrude Rilke. / You must ask if you may call her Norma Rilke // Go and read your Norma Cole."[5] The proliferation of names does not undo the act of naming. Instead it suggests an enthusiastic participation in the author-function—so enthusiastic that it happens more than once. The problem with names, it turns out, is that there are not enough of them.

Why do we need more names? Traditionally, names are powerful in poetry. According to Horace, the work of poetry, particularly epideictic poetry, is to immortalize important persons by recording their names. Achilles dies in history, but his name, remembered in Homer's *Iliad*, isolates and preserves whatever is most valuable in him, granting him an artificial life in the form of the poem.[6] "I write their names in a verse," Yeats writes in "Easter, 1916," removing the Irish revolutionaries from the contingent reality of history and placing them in the absolute reality of poetry; in the same gesture, Yeats loudly congratulates himself on this deployment of his poetic powers.[7]

One device through which names multiply, which Moure learns from Fernando Pessoa, is the heteronym. Early in the twentieth century, Pessoa published poems under names that he called heteronyms (other names), as opposed to pseudonyms (fake names). Pessoa's heteronyms have distinct biographies, temperaments, and poetic values: Caeiro is a pagan, provincial outsider, but, from the perspective of the other heteronyms, a classical, foundational figure; Reis is a conservative, epigrammatic lyricist; and de Campos is a Romantic iconoclast. The concept of the heteronym might not appear to be very different from other modernist approaches to the demonic aspect of language. Ezra Pound, who abhors the implication that he might be speaking in his own voice, calls his poems "personae," a concept that he borrows from Robert Browning's dramatic monologues. The persona is a device for Pound to gain access to other voices, other uses of language, or even to translate from languages that he might not know well; it is also a shield that protects the poet from the demonic voices he summons.

There is no thought of protection for Pessoa. The heteronym is not a mask that he puts on but something he finds in himself. Of the appearance of Caeiro, he writes, "In me there appeared my master."[8] Moreover, unlike Pound, Pessoa does not resist speaking in his own voice: One of the heteronyms is named Fernando Pessoa. The heteronym represents a deep knowledge of how poetry makes artificial persons. When I read Pessoa's collection *O Guardador de Rebanhos* in Edwin Honig's English translation *The Keeper of Sheep*, the speaker is neither the fictional Alberto Caeiro nor the historical Pessoa nor the translator Honig. I am the speaker. The poem is a mold into which I pour myself; the poem allows me to make a new person, to think another person's thoughts, to speak with another voice, using the materials of myself.

"In me, there appeared my master."[9] This time I am quoting Moure's "Notes in Recollection" from *Sheep's Vigil by a Fervent Person*, a "transelation" of *O Guardador* from 2001. Moure's heteronyms could be thought of as adjuncts to the act of translation: When the poet writes in a different language, she becomes another person and requires a new name. However, in the case of *Sheep's Vigil*, the creation of the heteronym makes a shortcut between the Portuguese source and the English translation. When the master Caeiro appears in Eirin Moure, she is not translating from Caeiro or Pessoa. Instead, she reenacts the composition of the poems exactly as Pessoa wrote them, "in a sort of ecstasy," in words that are neither Pessoa's nor hers, but Caeiro's.

Languages

A second challenge to criticism, closely related to the act of translation in *Sheep's Vigil*, is Moure's use of multiple languages. She translates from French, Portuguese, and Galician into English, and writes directly in these languages within poems, sometimes combining several languages in the space of a line. Moure has a gift for languages, has a tendency to pick them up, and enjoys studying them. She has a special interest in languages that don't have very many speakers, such as Galician, "a language that belongs to those who love it," as she puts it in a lecture.[10] She has also done significant work as a literary translator. She is well known for her translations (with Robert Majzels) from the work of the Québécois writer Nicole Brossard; more recently she has been translating the work of the Galician writer Chus Pato. Early in her career, she worked for VIA Rail on the transcontinental train connecting Eastern and Western Canada, and used "Railway

French" as part of her job; since the 1980s, she has been based on Mon-tréal, where she lives and works mainly in French, and writes an English that incorporates a good deal of French, among other languages. In *O Ci-dadán*, the speaker describes the complexity of language use in Montréal, where her English is "a strange tongue (yet hegemonic)."[11] It makes sense to say that Moure's poetic language is formed by these circumstances.

Illuminating as it may be, this contextual account is not sufficient. After all, other poets are multilingual, incorporate translation into their work, and inhabit cosmopolitan cities, but no one else is writing books that re-semble Moure's. A contextual account fails to explain the curious attitude toward collecting languages that emerges when, for example, she picks up Edwin Honig's facing translation of *O Guardador de Rebanhos*:

> I looked at the verso side and realized: *I can read Portuguese.*
> Whoosh!
> It was as if studying Galician had created new neurons in my head.[12]

The suggestion of a neurological basis for language acquisition is impor-tant, although not especially a curiosity. Language is artificial, a learned activity, but it has organic effects. By studying a foreign language, Moure, like any student of languages, creates new tools for cognition. Similarly, in *O Cidadán*, she hypothesizes "that my thinking, because of (necessary) zone disequilibrium, may be 'French' thinking, even in English. // Which changes English."[13] French thinking occurs in English because the new way of thinking that French introduces isn't separate from the rest of the thinking organ. French, a second language, introduces not just concepts but "new neurons" into a brain whose first language is English, "which changes English."

But we haven't yet taken the final step: "*I can read Portuguese. //* Whoosh!" This is the curiosity, the process registered as "whoosh." What does this word, an onomatopoeia, mean exactly? It recurs and is objec-tified in the translations of Caeiro: "I bring the Universe to its *whoosh*, north of Vaughan Road."[14] In this poem, the speaker arrives at "whoosh," with the universe in tow, after a deliberate process of unlearning: "I try to shake off what I've learned, / Try to forget the method of remember-ing that was taught to me."[15] Finally she would unlearn even her name and heteronym, becoming pronoun, "I, *eu*, not Alberto or Eirin, / But a human animal." What would such a process of unlearning entail for lan-guage acquisition? Although "French thinking" simply can't be contained in French but spreads into English, "whoosh" makes all languages primary. In "whoosh," the spread of new neurons is not limited by what the brain already knows, as though, by studying Galician, one might unconsciously be studying all languages, because "language does not belong solely to its speakers, but to everyone."[16] Thus the process by which one acquires a second, third, or fourth language becomes as mysterious and apparently automatic as the process by which one came to speak a language at all.

The heteronyms share this curious attitude toward language. In one of her interview bits from *Little Theatres*, Sampedrín says: "It was hard at first seeing these languages take charge, even frightening a bit. Later we stepped into them like water."[17] Immersion is a method of intensive language instruction, but Sampedrín doesn't mean a course of study that isolates the learner in an atmosphere where only one language can be heard and spoken. The point of "stepped into them" is that the several languages flow together. Fluency is an attribute of the languages themselves, not of their speakers. The hardness of "at first" and the easiness of "later" both entail losing control to the flow of languages. The speaker in "The First Story of Latin (os araos)" makes the same comparison:

> The hunger we felt before entering the water.
> Latin was our language of birth, we
> spelled it: L.A.T.I.N.
> and it said *language* to us,
> we spelled our *language*.
>   Spoke this
> as if latin were water and we were entering its ocean
> with no turning around.[18]

Here learning a language does not look like a process in child development or a program in formal education. Instead, latin is a state of nature, "our language of birth."

The lowercase l signals that the word is not being used in its received senses. The speaker is not talking about the learned language of classical education, the ceremonial language of the Catholic church, or the local language of ancient Rome that becomes the lingua franca of an empire. Latin in this poem is a common noun, not a proper one, and it is used as a generic name for all languages, or perhaps an umbrella term for Romance languages: "it said *language* to us." Even the language of this poem, the vocabulary of which is predominantly English with some Galician words and phrases, is latin, since, the speaker claims, "I speak only latin."[19] If there's room for distinctions within this ocean of latin, they occur on a personal level: "my latin" is not the same as "your latin." Our communication thus entails a loss of someone's language: "In fact I am losing my latin for your latin."[20] At the personal level, the fluidity of language signals not its potential to submerge but its speed: "Ho! I'd better learn it quickly / before it moves on like water."[21] On one hand latin designates all languages, and on the other it designates the unique qualities of a person's voice. These are not incompatible alternatives: latin is a vast ocean in which all users of language swim, and it's made of small currents of personal usages.

"It's the way people use language makes me furious," Moure writes in "The Acts." "It takes us nowhere & makes me furious, that's all."[22] Her fury is directed against the divisions in culture: high culture, which is elitist, low culture ,which is anti-intellectual, and, most disingenuous of all, middlebrow culture, which pretends to adore common culture and intellect while tacitly insulting them. The title of the book in which this reflection appears, *Furious*, lends additional weight to the fury. The same word occurs in "Hooked," one of the lyric pieces in the first part of the collection, in a context that replaces anger with desire:

> light of late afternoon makes your eyes
> shine from any direction,
> as in those old paintings of saints
> whose eyes follow the viewer
> . . . .
> the small wound you bear because of my furious glances[23]

"Furious glances": the fury is predicated on an eyeline match charged with the mutual longing of two lovers in a community that might respond phobically to the spectacle of women embracing in public. Although not destructive—not actually applying an eraser to culture—the second species of fury nonetheless inflicts an almost paradoxically diminutive violence, leaving a "small wound" on the surface of the addressee. Which is it, then—the fury of destructive rage that would erase the cultural barriers supported by "the way people use language," or the fury of erotic longing that would close the distance between two bodies? The two meanings of furious, both underlined by the title, react against each other.

Starting with *Furious*, the distinctive formal feature in Moure's writing is a strange kind of translation. Her use of the word "furious" is an example. Each instance of fury has its own meaning. Moure seems to be saying: There are no repetitions, only translations. Elsewhere, whole poems translate one another. In the series with the running title "Pure Reason," there is a basic template for a poem that changes with the revolutionary introduction of a new speaker in each new iteration. In "Pure Reason: Science," animals used as test subjects for "diet soft drinks" take over both a radio broadcast and the poem: "As if you could dream like we dream and be cured, the animals say, / pushing back the announcer, / showing off into the microphone the cut scars / of our diet fantasy."[24] In "Pure Reason: Femininity," the women on the radio use the same template, "showing off into the microphone the cut scars / of obstetrics."[25]

The breakthrough poem in this practice of English-to-English translation appears to be "Three Versions." The poem lists diagnostic problems for an injured bird, and expands internally so that the third version contains the first version entirely, with the addition of new lines and new phrases within existing lines. All three end with a final metadiagnostic problem: "or if the poet has written with / or without discipline."[26] Moure tells the story of the composition of the poem in an interview: "When I was writing 'Three Versions,' I asked Gail [Scott], which one do you like? She read them and got really impatient with my question, saying, 'Why do you have to choose a definitive version?' That phrase of hers has echoed in my head since then. I think it's become woven into my practice over the years."[27]

The word translation itself becomes a problem in her writing. Moure describes the poems in her recent collection *O Cadoiro*, based in medieval cantigas, not as a translation of the cantigas but as a "fall" into them. (This is the etymology of the word *cadoiro*: "the place where falling is made.")[28] In *Sheep's Vigil*, which is laid out as a facing translation setting Caeiro's Portuguese alongside Moure's English, the word translation is not adequate, so she alters it by inserting an extra italicized syllable: "A Trans*e*lation," so that what is communicated in translation is a feeling of joy, "elation." In her "Notes in Recollection" she widens the insertion with a Portuguese spelling of her name: "Trans-eirin-elations." Then alters it again, truncating it this time: "Transcreations."[29]

I want to add another term to this vocabulary, a word that recurs unmodified throughout her recent books, resonant with metapoetic significance, which is "abrasion." In one of the key "Documents" in *O Cidadán*, the speaker wonders about the gender of citizenship: "And if O Cidadán is a girl (but grammar abrades here, vacates the girl *cidadán* already provided by grammar as *a cidadá*, removing her from the generic capacity to 'stand for'), a girl's arduous invitation to a girl, to inhabit/intersect her spaces."[30] What the speaker calls grammar's abrasion might also be described in the old-fashioned language of textual scholarship as a crux. That is to say, these lines open into multiple readings or versions, and the versions don't agree; they cross. The abrasion occurs when the masculine form *cidadán*, Galician for citizen, loses its final letter to become the feminine form of the word *cidadá*; Moure complicates the form *cidadán* by insisting on a woman inhabiting it. The insertion of the Galician word may also be abrasive to a sentence otherwise written in English (a language in which the gender of the citizen is unmarked).

Why should the languages abrade? Think of it like this. Moure is committed to the radical particularity of languages. The value of a language such as Galician is that it can say things that can't be said in any other language. At the same time, she is committed to a continuity, a flowing together of languages, "like water." "We had to speak all the languages," says Sampedrín in one of her bits in *Little Theatres*, "even the made-up ones."[31] They flow into one another, but they remain themselves. No repetition, only translations. Or, in other words, abrasion, the result of the inevitable contact between languages. When the languages touch, they irritate one another, a disturbance that may be arousing, exciting, or harmful.

The completely written surfaces of the poems in *O Cidadán*, covered with diagrams, arrows, and strike-throughs, show abundant evidence of abrasion between and within languages. In *Sheep's Vigil*, abrasion occurs in the process of translation. "I've got nothing to do with rhymes," Caeiro says in *Sheep's Vigil*. "Rarely / Are two trees equal."[32] This expression of the radical particularity of things—no equivalences, only translations—agrees with Caeiro's pagan animism. The title "Rhymes get on my nerves. Rarely," taken from the first line, disagrees slightly with the first line, and also with the Portuguese original, which has no title; later, a line that does not seem to correspond to anything on the Portuguese side manages to disagree with itself: "What do you think of those two trees [crossed out] rhymes?" The disagreement in this case concerns the problem of commensurability: the juxtaposition of the two words assumes it, and the strike-through refuses it. The poems are filled with these crossings-out and disagreements, showing all the work of their construction in the finished object.

Moure's translation, in which commensurables occur only "rarely," ends up looking very different from Honig's English translation, the book in which she first discovers that she can read Portuguese. Caeiro's "Rebanhos," Portuguese for "flocks," start out as sheep in *Sheep's Vigil*, but are quickly replaced by cats: "Hey, these are my sheep // I've got an entire flock of cats out my door now."[33] Probably the most remarkable disturbances on the English side are not the substitutions but the frequent overparticularizations. Although there are not many place names or proper names in the Portuguese poems, the English side includes frequent apparitions of Toronto, the city in which she writes the poems; Winnett, the street on which she lives and the creek that runs below it; and even the poet herself: "inside/outside is not Nature's predicament: / It's Eirin Moure's."[34] Once the process of translation creates a point of contact between languages, their mutual abrasion generates more and more particulars.

This process frequently continues beyond the passage into English: "Let's call a spade a spade, a star a star, creeks creeks and flowers—/ Well, let's call them *flores*."[35] The translation ends with a Portuguese word, in a flourish that has no corresponding line on the Portuguese side. The word *flores* is not used here as an eruption of color to give the poem a Portuguese flavor. Instead, as in the many lines where Moure transfers the Portuguese word *coisa* intact to the English side and then uses it in a doublet with the French word *chose* ("connect up each *chose* with a *coisa*"),[36] the process of translation has passed through English and into French, and finally back into Portuguese. Another poem is annoyed by intrusions from Rilke's elegies: "Beauty is the name of a terror which we can scarcely endure, / Oops, that's a poem by Rilke . . . They calmly disdain to destroy me, oh go away Rilke."[37] Similarly, in "Befallen II," a section from *O Cadoiro*, some of Moure's versions of cantigas are interlineated with doctored language from Derrida's *Mal d'archive*, printed on strips of paper and roughly sewn over the cantigas in brightly colored thread, with the seams and the ends of the thread showing. These sewn poems are shown in photofacsimile, so that they seem to add another surface to the page. The new surfaces are an obvious result of prolonged contact between languages. The poem continually translates into other languages and other poems, like a photographic image that has been developed without using a fixative agent, and so just keeps developing.

Citizens

The deliberate crossing of languages in Moure's writing eventually comes to allegorize the crossing of national borders. The three books that investigate persons, humans, and citizens (*Search Procedures* [1996], *A Frame of the Book* [1999], and *O Cidadán* [2001]) do not make citizenship depend solely on national identity. Citizenship in *O Cidadán* is "a seal or bond with the world, nothing to do with nation or origin."[38] In *Search Procedures*, the collection that initiates this investigation, the problem is not to limit citizens to one place but to understand how they move between places: "All my life I am beginning to account for / The fact of immigration."[39] Part of the moral Moure draws from the complicated situation of the English language in a Francophone community is that a stranger can be a citizen: "As foreign, to be, paradoxically but sensibly, part of the body politic."[40]

What happens to citizenship when Moure brackets nation and language? Her positive definitions are tentative and often take the form of counterfactuals or questions. Recall the speaker's question about the gender of citizenship: "*And what if O Cidadán were a girl.*"[41] This question challenges many of the foundational works of political theology, in which gender either is not a fact of citizenship or is assumed to be masculine. In Ernst Kantorowicz's study of kingship, *The King's Two Bodies*, the sovereign, as a living person, is given a mortal body; as a form of government, the sovereign also has an immortal body that is identified with the state.[42] The king is a specifically masculine form of government, although the immortal body of kingship can be effectively inhabited by a woman, as Elizabeth I of England and other rulers have demonstrated. In Hannah Arendt's idealized treatment of ancient Greek city-states, political life has no explicit gender and must be separated from social life (where gender makes a difference) to exist at all.[43] The social is parasitic on the political; in what Arendt views as the disaster of modernity, the confusion of the two makes political action impossible. In the Greek city-states, on the other hand, cit-

izens emerge from the "shadowy" social world of the household and be-
come visible and act freely by participating in forms of government.[44]

Moure's contribution to political theology is to make gender an irreduc-
ible fact of citizenship. The girlhood of the citizen both precedes nation-
building and extends past it, so that she can cross a national border and
survive, both stranger and citizen. The insistence that gender rather than
sovereignty is definitive puts Moure in conflict both with nationalist my-
thologies and with the poststructuralist political theory with which she is
in conversation. When she asks what would happen "if O Cidadán were a
girl," this question is intended as a corrective, discovering "the girl lost to
Derrida's Levinas," that is, lost both to Levinas's politics, which is charac-
terized by "blindness to women," and to Derrida's attempt to revise Levi-
nas's politics by including "the voice of women." Such a politics would be
condescending, or, at best, chivalrous; as Moure puts it, "Such generous
politic, ô, to usher into itself the voice of women!"[45]

Another contribution to political theology is a sense of vulnerability or
"risk," which is both a threat and a promise. Nations, like languages and
persons, have collapsible boundaries, and one of the possible functions of
these boundaries is to make others who cross them feel welcome on the
other side. This problematic is central to political theology, which is itself
a "border concept" marking a place where politics and religion come into
contact, as Julia Reinhard Lupton notes.[46] Here, again, Moure's speaker
ventures a definition in the form of a question: "Is the citizen a being who
risks harm?"[47] One of the four poetic subgenres in O Cidadán (along with
the notes and diagrams called "Documents," the erotic lyric addresses to
"Georgette," and a final "aleatory" subgenre) is the series of "Catalogues
of Harms." The positive examples of citizenship acts that emerge from
these catalogues tend to be those of border guards and consuls who, rather
than shield national borders, instead facilitate their crossing, such as Paul
Grüninger, who in 1938 forges documents to allow Austrian Jews fleeing
Nazism to enter Switzerland, and Portuguese consul de Sousa Mendes,
who in Bordeaux in 1940 issues visas on a grand scale, "working day and
night, signing papers for anyone who needed them, in his office and in his
car," to allow refugees from France to enter Portugal.[48] These exemplary
acts are Quixotic in the sense of self-defeating—in both cases, the individ-
uals are removed from the borders, disciplined, denied their pensions, and
only pardoned posthumously by later governments—but Moure insists
that Quixote, too, is a citizen, and neither he nor Grüninger, nor their deci-
sion to allow borders to let in rather than keep out, is "absurd."[49] In Search
Procedures, the exemplary act of the citizen is the Heimlich maneuver. "In
my life I will never invent anything as beautiful / & skilled. . . . What else is
there of any moral significance."[50] The beauty of the maneuver seems to be
partly its portability ("a skill you can carry anywhere"), and that its mo-

tion activates the organs involved in speech, albeit in an extreme situation in which "there is no use for poetry."

Faces

In her trilogy on the human, the person, and the citizen, and in other works, Moure subjects Emmanuel Levinas's ethics of face-to-face interaction to a playful critique. The first principle in Levinas's ethics is the recognition of the absolute, unbridgeable otherness of the other. The privileged site for the recognition of otherness is the other's vulnerable face.[51] (The words "recognition" and "interaction" are misleading, since Levinas ultimately denies their possibility.) The first principle is necessarily the last principle in his ethics. Where can you go from an experience of absolute otherness?

In *Little Theatres*, Elisa Sampedrín shows that there is somewhere else, by simply attributing a face to every thing in the universe:

> Boots are faces, a table is a face, the grass stem has an expression that is facial. When Levinas said "the face is not of the order of the seen," he was making the right connection, but backward. All of what is seen are faces.[52]

The work of the poet is to see the faces in things. In the series "Homages to Water," the speaker finds human forms in vegetables: The garlic bulb has tears without water, the cabbage leaves withdraw into themselves to meditate, and the onion is not just a face but a whole human head. In another series, corn becomes especially important both because it is an elemental material for making human bodies, and also because it has a human face: "I touch the faces of my corn // Opening corn's faces / so that my hands touch the braille letters."[53] The abstract face of the other adheres to a particular object, and multiplies on the segmented surface of the object, as each kernel of the corn acquires a face. The encounter with these faces is tactile and may even exclude the visual, as "braille" implies blindness. At the same time, touching is potentially aggressive. The speaker violates the integrity of the faces by offering to touch and possibly consume them.

In *O Cidadán*, Moure describes the encounter with the absolute otherness of the other's face as a condition of prosopagnosia, or face-blindness, a neurological disorder in which human faces are perceived indistinctly, without recognition. "To the prosopagnostic," she writes, "hair is emotional; 'faces are not.'"[54] People who can't recognize faces look to other cues, such as hair, to tell their friends and acquaintances apart. The quotation marks around the final clause draw attention to the adaptation of Gertrude Stein's discussion of emotion in writing in her *Lectures in America*: "Paragraphs are emotional; sentences are not."[55] Stein goes on to distinguish between "expressing" emotion and regulating or "limiting" it. She prefers the latter sense because it makes emotion an object for contemplation, analysis, and debate. Hair is emotional in this preferred sense. Just as paragraphs group and shape sentences, hair frames the face, limiting it. Which is to say that when faces are subject to a prohibition against recognition, hair acquires a face.

Theaters

In Michael Fried's art history, the task of art in modernity is to defeat theater. For Sampedrín, in *Little Theatres*, this task becomes the miniaturization of theater. What is the force of this dislocation?

Fried first made his argument in "Art and Objecthood," a polemical essay published in *Artforum* in 1967 that deplores the theatricality of minimalist art, which he persistently and unsympathetically calls "literalist" art.[56] The word "literalism" is a useful indicator of his objection to this art. In the most extreme gestures of minimalism, "what you see," as Frank Stella puts it, "is what you see." Thus there can be no organizing interaction between figure and ground, and viewers are left only with "what they see"; that is, they are left with the materials of the art and the experience of seeing them. Theatricality in this sense is not illusionism—quite the opposite. Minimalist works are theatrical in that they acknowledge their viewers, and perhaps play to them, or even intrude on them. The modernist art that Fried champions, on the other hand, creates illusions, transforms the materials, lifts them out of the literal situation in which they are viewed. However, although in "Art and Objecthood" theater is not a value, it takes on a much richer meaning when Fried pursues his argument across the long history of modern art; in later art historical writing, he describes paintings by Chardin and Courbet as compositions of small atoms of absorption and theater (where both terms are values, at least implicitly).[57]

This argument against the theatricality of art has a lot to do with poetry. For Fried, the defeat of theater could mean the lyricization of art. His notion of theater comes from John Stuart Mill's discussion of the isolation of the speaker in lyric. According to Mill, "eloquence is *heard*; poetry is *overheard*."[58] Unlike a politician or an actor playing to an audience, the speaker in a poem speaks without acknowledging that anyone may be listening.

With Pessoa's heteronyms, lyric becomes theatrical, but not in Fried's sense. I have argued that the notion of the heteronym is quite different from that of the persona, which conceptualizes the poem as dramatic monologue. Pessoa borrows something even more basic from the phenomenology of performance to understand the situation of the speaker in lyric: "The art of the actor consists in employing the author's drama in showing his acting ability upon it."[59] Pessoa is not performing for an audience as the heteronyms; he writes poems to become other persons. He is "the medium of the characters he himself created"—note that Pessoa speaks of his activity in the third person.[60] Readers of the poems will become the same medium.

Sometimes the theatrical element in *Little Theatres* seems to refer to an actual theatrical practice. Sampedrín uses a "proscenium," stages a play, collaborates with actors and "stagehands."[61] The littleness may designate physical scale or a poverty of means, as when Sampedrín says that she offers her audience "just that much gesture."[62] There's even a suggestion of the architectural in the series of poems entitled "Little Theatres," in that each poem is attached to a place, an idea, and in one case a date (e.g., "Theatre of the Stones That Ran [Fontao, 1943]"); the implication may be that the poem is dedicated to a small building where a performance once took place. Many of the poems in Moure's other collections are theatrical in Fried's sense. For example, some poems in *Search Procedures* include an ungenerous marginal commentary. Halfway through the book, after the fourth poem in the series "Anxiety," the author is "fired! There is an opening for a real poet in these pages."[63] The self-critique in "Paris nSleep" is more forgiving: "Maybe in another lifetime Mouré will smarten up. A good title might be 'Polishing Up the Abrasions.'"[64] The abrasions, which of course she never polishes, are theatrical in that they display their self-awareness as poems, and even supply the script for a cranky response.

The primary meaning of theater for Moure, as in Pessoa, is an interpretation of lyric: the poem as an opportunity to become another person, or, as Moure puts it in the postface to *O Cadoiro*, where she considers the writing of the medieval cantigas as an event in literary history, to "set aside God and history to turn toward . . . *another human.*"[65] The littleness is primarily a question of duration. In Sampedrín's theaters, "time has been stripped away."[66] This does not mean that the performance occurs outside of time, just that the time of the performance is "finite" and "small."[67] The performance takes place "in the time it takes to realize a missile is landing."[68] The poems refuse the ambition of lyric to get outside the passage of time, but nonetheless share in the resistance to time by occupying only the smallest possible cut from it. "The needles of the clock are cutting down the names of the hours."[69]

What time is it when the hours become nameless? At what scale does time reduce to the moment of realization that "a missile is landing"? This denuded time discloses a fact about lyric, which is that it has a theatrical aspect as well as a historical one. To conceptualize lyric as a little theater is to diminish its existence in history as part of an open sequence of solutions to a traditional formal problem. (Moure explores this intertextual aspect of lyric in *O Cadoiro*.) This denuded time also discloses a fact about theatrical performance, which is that its time is ahistorical and purely occasional. The scale of performances of shortest possible durations is outside of history but not outside of time, which is reduced to a discrete moment absolutely separate from other moments by an emptiness where time does not extend. In this sense, to quote another one of Sampedrín's bits, the little theaters really do "fill a space that film misses," which is to say that they occupy the space between scenes when there are no images and no objects.[70] The prohibition against bringing a working clock onstage is not, as in a casino, to avoid letting the audience notice how much time they have wasted in the space of the theater. It's because the poem is shaping time.

NOTES TO POETICS STATEMENT

1. Or, in my English, which is not American but Canadian: "clamours."

2. I think here of the national trope of my own country, Canada: the mosaic, rather than the American trope of the melting pot.

3. I use the French word in English to avoid what seems to be the dominant sense of the word "theatrical": exaggerated, false, unfelt. "Theatrical" seems to derive from "theatrics," and théâtrale," in contrast, from "theatre."

4. http://projects.publicintegrity.org/WarCard.

5. Or, in Canadian English, my English: "centred."

NOTES TO CRITICAL ESSAY

1. For convenience, because the purpose of this essay is to chart connections between books, I use the name Moure as a placeholder for most of the others. However, I observe a distinction between works authored by Moure and Sampedrín.

2. Erin Mouré, *Furious* (Toronto: House of Anansi, 1988), 94–95.

3. Erin Mouré, *Search Procedures* (Toronto: House of Anansi, 1996), 133.

4. Michel Foucault, "What Is an Author?" In *Language, Counter-Memory, Practice: Selected Essays and Interviews*, trans. Donald F. Bouchard and Sherry Simon (Ithaca, NY: Cornell University Press, 1977), 137.

5. Erin Mouré, *A Frame of the Book* (Toronto: House of Anansi, 1999), 118–19.

6. Horace, *The Odes and Epodes*, trans. C. E. Bennett (Cambridge, MA: Harvard University Press, 1947), 218. See Allen Grossman, "Summa Lyrica," *The Sighted Singer: Two Works on Poetry for Readers and Writers* (Baltimore, MD: Johns Hopkins University Press, 1992), 209–13.

7. William Butler Yeats, *Selected Poems and Three Plays* (New York: Collier, 1986).

8. Fernando Pessoa, *Always Astonished*, trans. Edwin Honig (San Francisco: City Lights Books, 1988), 9.

9. Eirin Moure, *Sheep's Vigil by a Fervent Person: A Transelation of Aiberto Caeiro/Fernando Pessoa's* O Guardador de Rebanos (Toronto: House of Anansi, 2001), viii.

10. "A practice of possibility, a life in languages," lecture delivered at Bangor, Wales, October 2007.

11. Erín Moure, *O Cidadán* (Toronto: House of Anansi, 2002), 82.

12. *Sheep's Vigil*, vii. Honig's translation is available in *Poems of Fernando Pessoa*, ed. and trans. Edwin Honig and Susan M. Brown (New York: Ecco, 1986), but Moure must be using a different edition because the cover of the book published by Ecco is green, not red.

13. Ibid., 75.

14. *Sheep's Vigil*, 115.

15. Ibid., 113.

16. *O Cidadán*, 59.

17. Erín Moure, *Little Theatres (Teatriños) or/ou Aturuxos Calados* (Toronto: House of Anansi, 2005), 37.

18. Ibid., 67.

19. Ibid., 71.

20. Ibid., 74.

21. Ibid., 73.

22. *Furious*, 86.

23. Ibid., 46–47.

24. Ibid., 21.

25. Ibid., 24.

26. Ibid., 75.

27. Pauline Butling and Susan Rudy, *Poets Talk: Conversations with Robert Kroetsch, Daphne Marlatt, Erin Mouré, Dionne Brand, Marie Annharte Baker, Jeff Derksen, and Fred Wah* (Edmonton: University of Alberta Press, 2005), 51.

28. Erin Moure, *O Cadoiro* (Toronto: House of Anansi, 2007), 133.

29. *Sheep's Vigil*, ix.

30. *O Cidadán*, 34.

31. *Little Theatres*, 37.

32. *Sheep's Vigil*, 47.

33. Ibid., 37.

34. Ibid., 75.

35. Ibid., 67.

36. Ibid., 111.

37. Ibid., 71.

38. *O Cidadán*, 9.

39. *Search Procedures*, 125.

40. *O Cidadán*, 84.

41. Ibid., 39.

42. Ernst Kantorowicz, *The King's Two Bodies: A Study in Mediaeval Political Theology* (Princeton, NJ: Princeton University Press, 1957).

43. Hannah Arendt, *The Human Condition* (Chicago: Chicago University Press, 1958), 22–78. On the difference between the political and the social, see Hanna Pitkin, *The Attack of the Blob: Hannah Arendt's Concept of the Social* (Chicago: Chicago University Press, 2000).

44. Arendt, 38.

45. *O Cidadán*, 39.

46. Julia Reinhard Lupton, *Citizen-Saints: Shakespeare and Political Theology* (Chicago: Chicago University Press, 2005), 4–5.

47. *O Cidadán*, 34.

48. Ibid., 98.

49. Ibid., 51.

50. *Search Procedures*, 42.

51. Emmanuel Levinas, *Totality and Infinity*, trans. Alphonso Lingis (Pittsburgh: Duquesne University Press, 1969). Moure also cites *Liberté et commandement* (St. Clément-la-Rivière: Fata Morgana, 1953). In *American Literature and the Free Market, 1945–2000* (New York: Cambridge University Press, 2010) Michael Clune describes Levinas's ethics as the endgame of the "recognition trope" whereby I am constituted as a subject through my recognition of you as an object. Clune documents and condemns the history through which recognition and Levinas's principled resistance to it have come to dominate political, moral, and aesthetic theory.

52. *Little Theatres*, 9.

53. Ibid., 30.

54. *O Cidadán*, 49.

55. Gertrude Stein, *Writings, 1932–1946*, eds. Catherine Stimpson and Harriet Chessman (New York: Library of America, 1998), 48.

56. Michael Fried, *Art and Objecthood: Essays and Reviews* (Chicago: Chicago University Press, 1998).

57. Michael Fried, *Absorption and Theatricality: Painting and Beholder in the Age of Diderot* (Chicago: Chicago University Press, 1988); *Courbet's Realism* (Chicago: Chicago University Press, 1992).

58. John Stuart Mill, "Thoughts on Poetry and Its Varieties," in *Autobiography and Literary Essays* (Toronto: University of Toronto Press, 1963), 345. For an interesting assessment of the "lyricization of criticism" following Mill, see Virginia Jackson, *Dickinson's Misery: A Theory of Lyric Reading* (Princeton, NJ: Princeton University Press, 2005).

59. Pessoa, *Always Astonished*, 52.

60. Ibid., 13.

61. *Little Theatres*, 38.

62. Ibid., 25.

63. *Search Procedures*, 61.

64. Ibid., 119.

65. *O Cadoiro*, 133.

66. *Little Theatres*, 41.

67. Ibid., 39.

68. Ibid., 43.

69. Ibid., 27.

70. Ibid., 37.

BIBLIOGRAPHY

Selected Books by Erín Moure

Empire, York Street. Toronto: Anansi, 1979.
Furious. Toronto: Anansi, 1988.
WSW. Montréal: Véhicule, 1989.
Sheepish Beauty, Civilian Love. Montréal: Véhicule, 1992.

The Green Word: Selected Poems. Toronto: Oxford University Press, 1994.
Search Procedures. Toronto: Anansi, 1996.
A Frame of the Book. Toronto: Anansi, 1999.
Pillage Laud. Toronto: Moveable Type, 1999; BookThug, 2011.
O Cidadán. Toronto: Anansi, 2002.
Little Theatres. Toronto: Anansi, 2005.
O Cadoiro. Toronto: Anansi, 2007.
Expeditions of a Chimaera. Co-authored with Oana Avasilichioaei. Toronto: Book-Thug, 2009.
O Resplandor. Toronto: Anansi, 2010.

Selected Translations

Pessoa, Fernando. *Sheep's Vigil by a Fervent Person*. Trans. Erín Moure. Toronto: Anansi, 2001.
Brossard, Nicole. *Museum of Bone and Water*. Trans. Erín Moure and Robert Majzels. Toronto: Anansi, 2003.
Brossard, Nicole. *Notebook of Roses and Civilization*. Trans. Erín Moure and Robert Majzels. Toronto: Anansi, 2007.
Pato, Chus. *Charenton*. Trans. Erín Moure. Exeter: Shearsman; Ottawa: Buschek-Books, 2007.
Ajens, Andrés. *Quase Flanders, Quase Extremadura*. Trans. Erín Moure. Victoria: La Mano Izquierda, 2008.
Pato, Chus. *Hordes of Writing*. Trans. Erín Moure. Exeter: Shearsman; Ottawa: BuschekBooks, 2007.

Selected Prose

Moure, Erín. *My Beloved Wager*. Edmonton: NeWest, 2009.

Selected Interviews

McCance, Dawne. "Crossings: An Interview with Erin Moure." *Mosaic*, vol. 36, 4 (2003), 1–16.
Butling, Pauline, and Susan Rudy. " 'Why Not Be Excessive': A Conversation with Erin Moure." In *Poets Talk*. Edmonton: University of Alberta Press, 2005, 43–61.

Selected Criticism

Carrière, Marie. "Erin Moure and the Spirit of Intersubjectivity." *Essays on Canadian Writing*, vol. 70 (2000), 64–80.
Dickson, Lisa. " 'Signals across Boundaries': Non-Congruence and Erin Moure's *Sheepish Beauty, Civilian Love*." *Canadian Literature*, vol. 155 (1997), 16–37.
Dopp, Jamie. " 'A Field of Potentialities': Reading Erin Moure." *Essays on Canadian Writing*, vol. 67 (1999), 261-87.
Moyes, Lianne. "Acts of Citizenship: Erin Moure's *O Cidadán* and the Limits of Worldliness." *Trans.Can.Lit: Resituating the Study of Canadian Literature*. Eds. Smaro Kamboureli and Roy Miki. Waterloo: Wilfrid Laurier University Press, 2007, 111–28.
Rudy, Susan. " 'What can atmosphere with / vocabularies delight?': Excessively Reading Erin Moure." In *Writing in Our Time: Canada's Radical Poetries in English (1957–2003)*. Eds. Pauline Butling and Susan Rudy. Waterloo: Wilfrid Laurier University Press, 2005, 205–216.

LAURA MULLEN

Sudden cold or the sudden sense of having been cold for a long
time

He said he was getting back some things that had been lost like
what

Love oh great looking out across the river he wouldn't meet my
eyes either

Something flashed up and fell back down into the water there
look no

I told him about the time I saw them feeding the crowd up out

Of the dark water of paler mouths opening closing like what

Getting the strength to say lost he was beautiful the play

Of that muscle I make you tense don't I just under the tan skin of
his jaw

I keep coming back to the surface that river your wrist I must
have

Pressing my mouth I can't look at your hands thinking of how
you

Touched me hurt you a lot love like what those memories

Saying you're wearing mallard colors after I chased to frighten

For no reason the ducks because I can't stand still enough If I
could

I would be so still you would think I would never hurt you

Screaming what was her last name what was her name

The wind-scarred surface of the water

What I'm not allowed to feel what I'm not allowed to say
pressing up

As though feeding my heart is everywhere under my skin

And rising up to the surface of the water clenching and
unclenching

The thick grey muscle the dense shoal of fish brought to just
beneath

The surface the grotesque bouquet of their rapidly blossoming
and

Shutting the crowd but as if behind glass so there was no sound

Of people screaming I feel helpless and cold saying please believe

I did not mean to hurt you you could say that to me too in
Orphée

The poet presses against the mirror which wavers like water
which lets him in

("A PRETTY GIRL IS LIKE A MELODY")

What might have been wind slamming the door shut. But No no no, you don't seem to understand, (fastening up the metal jaws of his capacious black satchel), this fantasy version he has created of you, this, if you will, *doppelgänger*, or double—which he has perfected in (need I remind you) your absence, no longer depends for its 'life' on your existence at all. Indeed, it might be best to admit at once that this intricate machinery (and here his open palm began its slow crawling towards me, the motion of some hard-shelled insect caught on its back, legs waving, accompanied by a distinctly audible ratchet-like noise, a ticking, as of some ancient clockworks) works, he went on, much better without you. What was it that stranded him there, repeating tonelessly—hand out in that timeless gesture—*without you . . . without you . . . without you . . . ?*

•

"I long for you."
Oh, yes,—that one:
I long for you.

"Yer rroses 'er suhrly coomin' along bonny *this* yeer, ma'm."
He tipped his hat. "What? Oh, yes . . ."—distractedly;
Looking out on what seemed to be a sea of blood.

(IL TUE SA FEMME . . .—
In the *nice-matin*: the story about a man
Who killed his wife—A COUPS DE ROULEAU DE MACHINE A
    ÉCRIRE:
"Il y a une mer du sang. . .")

Which lapped in sullen waves against what shore . . . .

This shore (my adored)—
See: sea-shore,—everything infected by
That metaphor . . . .

(Against which broke—in the *Times* and the *Voice*—
"Blood, used needles, sewage . . .":
That long hot summer.)

•

Squeezed out from these moments of time a few pieces of proof
that someone existed: "suddenly the stairs . . ."; "I do not think she
will be able to tell us what she's seen." A pause, "ever." Was there
anyone who, on the bridge, had had the time to see clearly how
the catastrophe—the impossibility of which had been so widely
advertised—would in fact occur? Obdurate heart of what white
unyielding . . . —why do you stay so far away? I sit here and spin these
stories about you (and then undo them, of course), this thin web of
lace I no sooner display the emptiness of than shred, pulling it quickly
back out on the ebb. And after all these ominous. These ominous.
These ominous rumors of.

•

She comes running up out of the darkness and past us, screaming.
There is the sound of a woman screaming and then we see her,
running down the sidewalk towards us and then through us; in
between us. She is wearing a white blouse and a short black skirt
and carrying something, what? I didn't notice, or don't remember.
It was late: after midnight; a street in Northern California in 1976,
in what was probably early spring, still cold. We stopped when
we first heard the screams and just stood there, "like statues,"
slightly apart from one another, and she brushed swiftly through
us as though we were invisible, as though it did not matter that
we were there (if we were there for her): we couldn't help her. It
was clear we couldn't help her (or I need to believe that?); it was
too late and whatever was behind her, (there was nothing behind
her, no one following her as she ran), it was much too late: there
was nothing anyone could do (and what good do I expect this to
do, now, showing how well I remember?): dark hair, her mouth

open, on her face the streetlight gleaming, the shine of tears. Even then we thought we made her up: out of our own distress, out of the unhappiness which filled us and about which we couldn't speak; we thought we made her up, we needed her so badly, we needed her there and so desperately needed her not to be real: for whatever had happened to her, broken loose upon and in her, to stay far away from us; to be no one's fault; not to have happened at all. We didn't believe she existed, we didn't want to believe. We wanted her even then to be something else we would never admit the existence of: she was the last piece of proof we needed, the last lost scrap of evidence the witnesses keep, to themselves. She was a special double-edged gift the night had given us, we thought; she was a test we had failed. She was a young woman running down a well-traveled street in the middle of the night screaming out of some pain we could not speak to or touch, who flashed between us, her face wet with tears and distorted, in her hands something . . . maybe her shoes? I think she may have been barefoot, or in her stockings—there was no sound of heels on concrete, as she came down heavily—and she was running, but her shuddering indrawn breaths were not for that, but because she was screaming, screams without words in them, just screaming, loud enough to hear from a distance as she came toward us, and in the distance, as she went away again, until the darkness and the silence took her back *as though she had never been.* . . .

FROM *After I Was Dead*

Secrets

    They were "warehousing" all the empty apartments here, and
        now
    The building echoes, empty, with the sound
    Of the roller as the painter paints
    The hallway, with the sound of the heels and toes

Of their shoes when they come to measure the windows,
Of their tap on the door when they tap on the door to come in
And measure the windows and take—sooner or later—
These windows I like so much away. The new ones,
I imagine, will be simpler and harder to open
From outside. They won't show me the outside
Cut into so many even pieces, each framed
In white . . .—I stopped there for a moment, held
Back (but you can't see it on the page), as if by bars.
When I saw that the easiest, best image—still—
For that was something I'd said before, used before; twice.
Now I can't be sure I'm being honest anymore. Or I have to
Let stand as the sign for being honest this effort to give it "all"
Away. Just the first effect of history. Having drinks
One night with my lover and a colleague the latter
Asked me how many men I thought I had slept with,
Right there, like that. We were drinking a lot and later I knew I,
    at least,
Was drinking too much. But I said I'd stopped
Counting a long time ago, and I meant it. And then he said
Roughly, and I said Forget it, and then he told us
How he counted the women up, at night, in the dark, like sheep.
His wife was away doing graduate work. What's the point of
    this,
What's the point of "all this"? Somewhere up there I was
    thinking—
It could have been the second line—*The need for money, the
need for sex*;
Something I'd decided not to say (I couldn't see how it fit)
Finally got said, or was being said the whole time, or came out.
    Not all
The apartments here are empty. There's someone living
Next door I've never seen I know is there because I've seen
The small bags of garbage he or she puts out in the hallway
When it's late, when it's too late to all the way out.
At the top of one bag the dried, curled-back-down-as-in-birth,
    dead

Ferns from a florist's arrangement stuck out, and a glass
Bottle. If I was ready to really look through it I bet I could
Tell you a lot about that person, I bet I could learn a lot
(But not as much as someone learned, whoever it was, hungry,
Who went through the garbage outside and found and ate the
    stale
Remains of my birthday cake, leaving behind the torn-open,
    empty box, not
As much as that . . .). *The need to eat* comes under the heading of
    money,
The need to know comes under the heading of sex. Are you
    reading this
To find out something? Did you find it out? It's been on the
    market for years,
But now that the building's been sold and they're making
    improvements
Those empty apartments must be worth a lot, or they ought to
Be able to ask a lot, to get a lot for those apartments
Whose doors swing open on brightly lit nothing to the curious
    touch.
Even in this section of the city the new disease has emptied out.

35 ½

Is this turning all too easily, too swiftly into
Language? A man keeps stepping out
From behind a banyan tree
Saying "Believe
It or not . . . . " Stopping. Starting over again. Stopping.

Of course there's a camera.

Of course there's a camera-
Man making it into
A movie, or trying: stopping

The speaker from stepping out
Of the frame, sending him back to "Believe . . . "
And the tree,
And the moving away from the tree.

What does the tree feel? What does the camera
Think about this? It's a fund-raising movie, "Believe
It or not, last year we were ranked in . . ." —
You don't want to hear this. I got out
Of there fast. "And so": the scene's stopped.

Incongruous, in a suit and a tie—stopped again
Mid-gesture, emphatic, between the tree's
Green and the lawn's—there's some guy walking out
Of a day in Spring (making a special pitch to the camera's
Potentially vast and yet intimate audience) and into
Something like timelessness. It's a matter of belief.
Or beliefs? That banyan's true, but hard to believe
In, in that dense cluster of trunks it hasn't stopped
Adding all those very slightly differing versions onto,
Like a news feed: tree, tree, tree, et cetera—
A dark mass of leaves above the whole business—the camera
Keeps running. *Don't worry, we can edit it out.*

I got out and I didn't get out . . . :
Like him I was getting paid to act like I believed
In what I was selling, only language was the camera
(So I was both of them) I couldn't stop—I couldn't stop
This I, I, I—turning into the tree
Now (do you *believe* that?), turning into

Something outside, stopped . . . .

Which goes on soliciting belief. For how long? O Tree,
O Camera. Just a couple of seconds turning into

I removed the plot. I wanted to hear what they were saying. It is not a Silent World at all, but—we are so distant—we come to think of it like that. I let go of character, working with some uneasy combination of roles, gestures, discourses. I faked the broken arm. Tried pretending I was a cop. Pulled out of context I waited to see how long the girls would try to maintain the fiction: we were just turning down the lonely dirt road because I'd remembered I'd forgotten . . . something. *This will just take a couple of minutes.* I thought the failure of the definitions would be more obvious: I was always surprised by their trust. Traces a jagged trajectory through an unstable setting, not intact, not

What happened to the previous

On that strip of exposed beach beside the highway long slender veils of semi-transparent wet mist tear, shiver, and reform in a shifting tableau of strange, half-remembered shapes. A thick smear of blood on the glass wall of the phone booth turns black in the glare of the

The corpse struggles to its knees, what you thought was the corpse, and—muttering to itself—starts scrubbing at the bloodstains. It's too late to offer to help her, clearly. She says, *Well, to tell you the truth*

The corpse sits up—what you thought was the corpse—and, with some difficulty, smooths away the possibly telltale footprints of her would be assassin (but the sand is so vague, who would even think to read them as "footprints"?) as far as she can reach with the arm he didn't break: a frown. She says *If you can't say anything* nice

Perched fussily on the living room couch (she'd opened a plastic garbage bag to sit on so as not to stain the upholstery), the corpse refuses to remove the bloody dress. I'm helping her clean her nails: she's afraid she might have caught a thread from his suit there, or some skin from his wrists. I've been trying to tell her she reads too many detective novels. She sighs. She doesn't like the tentative way I'm holding her fingers, she doesn't think I'm going deep enough. *Honestly*, she says, *do I have to do* everything

As though to say a few words. As though I didn't kill her. As if

Trying to make the technique itself as close to the ocean's as I could get it: going over and over the thing, saying it, taking it back, pushing it up as an instant's offering—at the tide line, script of seaweed, shells and stones, sand dollars, trash, foam scum. Written on the shifting stuff in the swift shine of the wet already vanished…; "Speaking," Levinas writes, "implies a possibility of breaking off and

"It's not you," she says, "it's your father. I can't believe that—in my condidtion—*I'm* the one who's going to have to find the knife," she shakes her head disgustedly, "and make sure he wiped

You: no tracks, no prints, no evidence / I: the cold reproach. Remember: the doors and windows are locked from the inside. (At this point I always like to ask the reader to

FROM *Subject*

Circles

(Breath cleared)
Window
        fluttered
Edges   fragile petal

Dust your touch
Would tear through

      caught in

Oh I see
(Through) you you
Said

       (O the snow the O
       Made for the gone
       Eye holes)

Oh they were so still, stilled, style
Oh they were
       such echoes

Spill
Beautiful each
In its box   labeled

Singing in the

We'd disappeared into
Laced our stiff
Bodies to each sorry
Try again window sill
Swinging perch in each
O
Singing their fool
Heads off thank you
Paper thin stutter there

Shrill each seeming
To sing how

Delightful

POETICS STATEMENT

ONE WORD is a lyric, two are a narrative. One word by itself, potential contexts in play, meanings "available," charged by association, suggestion, and unresolved possibility: an event, resonant with histories. Sound sounded, resounding. Two words, add to the above their relationship, and their order (a story—a power struggle). And if you change just one letter (lover, loser) . . . . My [politics] poetics involves attention to difference in the context of a heightened awareness of time, moving against inherited body / mind distinctions, in an effort to chart the involvement of thought in feeling and vice versa: embodied. Self and other are entangled, as are sound and silence. Exposures. Sudden uncertainty or a sudden glimpse of continuous uncertainty. Second takes, echoes, again the aslant encounter: I have a good memory, a fairly wide frame of reference, and a large capacity for error. And I can't touch type. Constant back and forth between mind and material, uneasy overlay and double (at least) exposure. Alienation and distance and the secret excess of process: lines scrawled on scraps of paper, in notebooks packed in boxes packed in closets on high shelves and forgotten files stored on the virtual "desktop," days or weeks of silence. "But you can't see it on the page": hesitations, avoidance, years between drafts and then

Tenets (IOS NEI?):
1) The poem should happen differently
   a) happen differently from what has preceded it
   b) happen differently from itself, each time it is read
2) Completed implications (form and content)
      where "completed" means deeply explored or suggestively complicated
3) Accuracy
      this idea includes humility toward and respect for both the medium (language) and all that is NOT language, to try to find the words . . . for? toward? near? with . . . ? (In relation.) Words change the situation as they reposition us (we are part of the situation); spectators are also participants

Note: Accuracy (which can and must be tested) not sincerity (which must be believed). Live it. To try to be true to complicated, unstable, and unevenly shared realities—that's "transparency." Art as intervention. The words for a house on fire—burning down: "fully involved structure." "You really have to turn yourself to ashes, otherwise it's just not worthwhile." (Joseph Beuys) "[T]his history of being rusted, being burned / rusting, being burned / the [*alval*?] [*bag*?] of of years / burned up, not down / burned off [*to*?] the for night" (Reginald Shepherd: poem in draft) "I was always aware of a possible silence falling / like the cover of a tomb . . ." (annotation by Louise Bourgeois for Roni Horn's *Wonderwater*). Cryptomnesia. . . .

DEMONST(E)RATION

"*By its impossible form, the monster bridges the gap between contraries in aesthetic defiance of the logical rule: it provides the third term, the copula, the mediation, between all those entities doomed, by logic and language, never to be joined.*" (Deformed Discourse)

In the laboratory secretly in the night stop there. In the laboratory out of the fragments of the dead and again halt. Entry in a journal, rem(a)inder, intimate: "July 24 [1816]: Write my story." *My* story: a slippage there. *Frankenstein.* To de-monstrate:[1] in the dead of night, alone in "my workshop of filthy creation" (a "cell, at the top of the house, . . . separated from all the other apartments")—living in my head—*now* I remember. One of the resurrection men[2] bangs a rusted shovel on the shut door, leaving a long streak of wet red clay. "Comparison and analysis need only the cadavers on the table; but interpretation is always producing parts of the body from its pockets, and fixing them in place." Origin one issue where—a "*collective* and *artificial* creature" which "cannot avail itself of the immense benefit of *totality*"—the body (of work) (and worker) disintegrates at the site of an alienated labor: "my heart often sickened at the work of my hands." "*Quel siecle a mains!*" "[D]isturbed," "the . . . secrets of the human frame" disturb a spectator: systems of articulation, of circulation (". . . yellow skin scarcely covered the work of muscles and arteries beneath"), "which should have remained hidden," reveal themselves and expose us. *Monstrum* the word widening the world: "*She is neither one nor two . . . She resists all adequate definition. Further, she has no 'proper' name. . . .*" Lost for a long moment beside the muddy puddle where you saw yourself for the first time and through borrowed eyes your own tears wept—wet to wet—long and always late by the dead author's lifted *montre*, warning that time decays beauties into "monstrous beings," while memory makes us each our own guest / (g)host. Acting out a strategy of identity on the unstable *Mer de Glace* language makes: "Ourself behind ourself, concealed / Should startle most—. . . ." But "series of . . . being" as series of erasures or *seriasure*, this particular "dreadful collection of memoranda" functions to engender forgetfulness (". . . a recipe not for memory but reminder"): this monster is re-membered in order to be dissolved in the same "darkness and distance" which swallows the text. Where we are recollected as, closing the book, "Not that": secured against otherness though "Decaying matter is so horrible a poison that certainly no aspects of the individual can provide protection." So much *about* the monster; what of the monstrous text? ("That I may reduce the monster to / Myself, and then may be myself. . . .") Scraps of flesh sutured awkwardly down around disparate purchases and thefts: a 'crazy' quilt. Well. Departing for parts unknown our fears are given deliciously terrible faces in the empty space at the curling edges of old maps, and though it turns out those ornate apparitions may have been drawn in part to protect the trade routes, one suspects a real horror of what resists definition also left its mark. And "how . . . [to] . . speak 'otherwise,' unless, perhaps, we can *make audible* that which agitates within us, suffers silently in the *holes of discourse*, in the unsaid, or in the non-sense." On the long silver table, gleaming faintly along their damp borders in the intermittent light, the pieces that don't belong together; what's under discussion here in part(s) is syntax. In its desire for a mate the monster "raises the frightening possibility of a new and uncontrollable signifying chain, one with unknown rules and grammar. . . ." Composition as de-composition: a series of positions where "A nice old chain is widening, it is absent, it is laid by." For life. The staggering progress of one for whom articulation is visibly thought. I remember her here who sat for her semblance: the Picasso portrait consisting "of multiple fragments...assembled under a new law" — *"But it doesn't look like me!"* *"Don't worry, it will."* "This shows the disorder, it does, it shows more likeness than anything else, it shows the single mind that directs an apple." We re(as)semble ourselves alone and out on the margins. "So the shape is there and the color and the outline and the miserable centre." Lurching toward you now with hands outstretched: to destroy? to embrace? "And I wished to exchange the ghastly image of my fancy for the realities around," the author of *Frankenstein* remembers, and the author of *Tender Buttons* remonstrates:

> Supposing there are bones. There are bones. When there are bones there is no supposing there are bones. There are bones and there is that consuming. The kindly way to feel separating is to have a space between. This shows a likeness.

The *Monster* of us all, as in what once started can't be stopped: confessing the self a collage repeated interventions momentarily normalize as narrative. In the "I"'s an incommensurable loneliness. Essayed. To *Picture Show*: "So come up to the lab / And see what's on the slab. . . ." Frankly, Stein:

> And how do you like what you are
> And how are you what you are
> And has this to do with the human mind.
> — "Identity a Poem"

GRAVE CITES:

Beckett, Samuel. *Proust.* New York: Grove, 1931.
Benjamin, Walter. "The Work of Art in the Age of Mechanical Reproduction." In *Il-luminations.* New York: Schocken Books, 1969.
Brooks, Peter. "Godlike Science / Unhallowed Arts." In *The Endurance of Franken-stein.* Berkeley: University of California Press, 1979.
Derrida, Jaques. *A Derrida Reader.* New York: Columbia University Press, 1991.
Derrida, Jaques. *La Carte Postale.* Paris: Flammarion, 1980.
Dickinson, Emily. *The Complete Poems.* Boston: Little, Brown.
Eliot, T. S. *Selected Prose.* New York: Harcourt Brace Jovanovich, 1975
Freud, Sigmund. "The Uncanny." In *Creativity and the Unconscious.* New York: Harper and Row, 1958.
Gauthier, Xaviere. "Is There Such a Thing As Women's Writing?" In *New French Feminisms.* New York: Schocken Books, 1981.
Irigaray, Luce. *This Sex Which Is Not One.* New York: Cornell University Press, 1985.
Kristeva, Julia. *Powers of Horror.* New York: Columbia University Press, 1982.
Moretti, Franco. *Signs Taken for Wonders.* London: Verso, 1983.
O'Brien, Richard, and Jim Sharman. *The Rocky Horror Picture Show.* 20th Cen-tury-Fox (England), 1975.
Plato. *Phaedrus.* Indianapolis, IN: Hackett, 1995
Poe, Edgar Allen. "The Short Story." In *The Portable Poe.* New York: Viking, 1945.
Rimbaud, Arthur. *Une Saison en Enfer & Le Bateau Ivre.* New York: New Direc-tions, 1945.
Shelley, Mary. *Frankenstein.* New York: St Martin's Press, Bedford Books, 1992.
Slaughter, Frank G. *Immortal Magyar/Semmelweis, the conqueror of childbed fever.* New York: Collier Books, 1961.
Stein, Gertrude. *A Stein Reader.* Evanston, IL: Northwestern University Press, 1993.
Stein, Gertrude. *Tender Buttons.* Los Angeles: Sun & Moon Classics.
Stevens, Wallace. *The Palm at the End of the Mind.* New York: Vintage, 1972.
Williams, David. *Deformed Discourse.* Montreal: McGill-Queen's University Press, 1996.

LAURA MULLEN: THREATENED AS THREAT
Rethinking Gender and Genre

Kass Fleisher

IN HER 2007 study of New York School, and "New York School-related," poets, Maggie Nelson notes that "Language writing is remarkable for being one of the first avant-garde movements with many—perhaps a majority—of female innovators, including luminaries such as Lyn Hejinian, Rae Armantrout, Harryette Mullen, and Leslie Scalapino" (xvii).[1] Nelson is highly conscious of the difficulties of aesthetic categories, and notes differences between, say, New York School and L=A=N=G=U=A=G=E writing, but adopts Eileen Myles's concept of these and other movements as being nonetheless of "one flow" of innovative aesthetics.

In her examination of gender- and sexuality-specific issues within this "flow," Nelson avers that "certain New York School tropes necessarily morph when their practitioners are women, whose historical relationship to detail, the personal, the local and the quotidian is somewhat overdetermined."[2] These categories, as well as those of masculine and feminine and the hierarchies that grow out of such categorizations, are coming undone thanks to the writers who inhabit this "flow," particularly women.

It's interesting for our purposes to note that the four Language-writing "luminaries" she lists have long resided in California, since, as it happens, Laura Mullen hails from northern California; Mullen has certainly been influenced by these four, and her work is situated at the very heart of this "flow." Consequently, I find myself less interested (as Nelson has to be) in what we call these various aesthetics—New York School-related, L/language, postmodernist, avant-garde, post-avant—than I am in the problematics Nelson has brought into focus. With regard to Mullen's work I hope to demonstrate her preoccupation with generic enforcement of cultural gender oppression—that is, the use of language, and language work, in the perpetuation of oppression.

In both her line-based poetry and her prose-based reworking of popular forms, Mullen dismantles social constructions of Woman by reconstructing the dual/duel she sees at play—a very dangerous play—in textual representations of women. Mullen demonstrates repeatedly that such popular forms as the mystery novel, whatever their mass appeal, are damaging to women socially, but her collapse of distinctions between poetry and prose, man and woman, fantasy and nightmare ultimately prove to be, as Nelson would have it, "a rich field from which to rethink, or re-experience," the problems of both gender and genre. Even as Mullen verifies that these popular forms are not simply good, clean fun but rather narrations of what we might call domestic violence—an elaboration of the quotidian that foregrounds its more harrowing underpinnings—she confirms that genre itself is complicit in this violence against women. All of her writing worries about(?) the ways in which conventional discourse reinforces conventional gender roles. Gender, then, *is* genre; genre *is* gender. For Mullen they are inextricably linked, and in coupling them she may have invented a problematic of her own.

I will pause here for a quick overview of the major works: Laura Mullen's first book, *The Surface*, was selected by the National Poetry Series in 1991. In 1999, the University of Georgia Press chose *After I Was Dead* for its Contemporary Poetry Series; that same year, Kelsey St. Press published *The Tales of Horror*. 2005 saw the release of *Subject* by University of California Press; and in 2007 *Murmur* was awarded Futurepoem's annual prize. (*The Tales of Horror* and *Murmur* are the first two prose, or poet's prose, entries of a soon-to-be-trilogy; as we go to press, the third is in progress.)[3]

While it is tempting to view Mullen's work to date as occupying two related but ultimately discrete categories—line-based poetry, as against her prosier deconstructions of pulp genre—I will argue that Mullen's poetry-based work both prefigures and rearticulates the concerns of her prose-based work. I regret dividing the "poetry" from the "prose" in my discussion here, feeling certain that Mullen herself would resist this, but do so for sake of clarity; because the "poetry" presented itself first, I will begin there and then turn to the "prose."

MULLEN'S work is always preoccupied with the impossibility of objectivity in textual representation, and of "detecting"—think the private detectives and fatal femmes of film noir—the solution to life's little, everyday horrors. If women's bodies can be identified only through the lens of suspect cultural practices, and if women have corresponding difficulty in establishing identities as such, then the author who attempts to render even provisional truths about these mysteriously recondite creatures will encounter a variety of challenges in articulating said truths. In one of the earliest commentaries on Mullen's work, a 1992 review of *The Surface*, David McDuff sees the collection as exemplifying the "bone-hard and often painful tension between language and reality." Indeed, this could serve as a description of all five of her books, provided the reality in question is understood as a social construct.

Mullen's interests in detection, so to speak, are prefigured in the early series "The Holmes Poems." In "A Case of Identity," for instance, she manages to marry gender to genre:

"I" or she at the church in white, waiting to make " 'fiction
With its conventionalities and foreseen conclusions [seem]
Most stale and unprofitable." [. . .]
[. . .] Don't you need someone
To catch you; to tell you who you are or were; to read
Your body back into the book-of-life where mismatched boots
Say you left the house in a hurry, not quite yourself? (*Surface* 9)

Women are frequently, in " 'fiction / With its conventionalities,' " "not quite
themselves," an autonomous self (should that exist) being impossible to
articulate in the context of such men as Sherlock, who will "solve" the
"myth[s]," who will "[find] this lady" (a "wife," as it happens) by dragging
one fountain or another (13). What Holmes will not and, in light of cir-
cumstantial evidence, *cannot* seek is the wife's identity—the identity of the
suborned. In a conversation with Cactus May, Mullen has said that poetry
"offered a space in which I could say some of what the world didn't seem
to allow me to say." Her alcoholic family "didn't fit into the narrative of a
normal happy family. . . . Poetry subverted that. It made space for leaps and
gaps which feels more true to how it is inside . . . thinking." If Holmes can't
see the victim through the dense fog of intellection, the victim is equally
unlikely to be able to say where/who she is.

Not surprisingly, then, in *The Surface* Mullen takes Narcissus as a pri-
mary theme, focusing on surfaces that more often than not are mirrors;
mirrors that more often than not are bodies of water; and the female bodies
made inscrutable by the shattering of such reflections. In a persistent sub-
text of the poems, there exists a glass that is not a looking glass, but *under*
which things are seen to exist. Water, mirrors, and that glass prove equally
threatening to women, often leaving the narrator and reader gasping for
air. In the title poem with which the book concludes, Mullen presents a tale
of unsettled lovers who witness a fish-feeding-frenzy in a river:

> The wind-scarred surface of the water
> What I'm not allowed to feel what I'm not allowed to say pressing up
> As though feeding my heart is everywhere under my skin
> And rising up to the surface of the water clenching and unclenching
> The thick grey muscle the dense shoal of fish brought to just beneath
> The surface the grotesque bouquet of their rapidly blossoming and
> Shutting the crowd but as if behind glass so there was no sound
> Of people screaming I feel helpless and cold saying please believe
> I did not mean to hurt you you could say that to me too in *Orphée*
> The poet presses against the mirror which wavers like water which lets
>   him in (68–69)

In Cocteau's 1950 film,[4] Orpheus pursues the Princess of Death to the Un-
derworld, stepping through mirror after mirror in the hopes of retriev-

ing his wife, Eurydice. Although the princess releases them—for Cocteau, through another mirror—ultimately Orpheus seals Eurydice's fate himself, taking a forbidden glance back at her through a rearview mirror. Mullen's poem foregrounds the idea that no surface or male gaze (as theorized in Laura Mulvey's classic essay, "Visual Pleasure and Narrative Cinema"[5]), accurately constitutes or safely permits a woman's existence. Silence attends the rise to the surface, mouth "clenching and unclenching"—there is no nourishment in glass; mirrored people screaming make no sound; she is "helpless" in the face of a lover's pain, which is mirrored by her own, except that hers goes unacknowledged ("I did not mean to hurt you you could say that to me too").

She is helpless against literary convention, as well, and lyric in particular, with which Mullen everywhere refuses to cooperate. The poem "Coloratura" is, for the most part, anything but an attempt at lyric timbre. The language of the poem is largely pedestrian ("The guy on the street you slept with you aren't speaking to you recognize / By his legs as in I'd know those legs anywhere") until Mullen begins her objection to the *bel canto* soprano technique popular in the Romantic era. To achieve this operatic style it was said that the vocalist should be able to sing without extinguishing a candle held before her mouth; lest we doubt the source of the allusion, the poet opposes *bel canto* directly: "The waitress blowing out the candles on the other tables" (39). The poem proceeds without a linguistic equivalent to the ornament of *coloratura*, addressing instead the conventions of the art form: ". . . the sun going down in that infected operatic / Red . . ."; "The intermittent jewel-like red light worse in the silence . . ." (40); ". . . I just can't help it the voice / Rises quavers falls and you just can't help but do the rest of it / Ordering all that chiffon and glitter and tulle . . ." (41). The poet speaks here directly to that which, for her, gives primary offense—the aggregate cultural artifices that make up the feminine—but saves particular frustration for the woman who adopts those artifices, becoming complicit in the suppression of the female voice: ". . . now that you've traded the pain of speaking / For the pain of keeping still evasive bright and full of interesting / Facts"). Mullen as poet does not evade the lyrical; the final stanza of "Sestina in Which My Grandmother Is Going Deaf" proclaims, "The shining edge / Of moon sails into the sky like a silver leaf, / As though the dark branches were words it didn't hear." Instead, this poet simply refuses to allow a poem to reside comfortably in that mode. The stanza concludes: "Is it so simple? Not to listen, is that release? / To go into silence alone, becoming that color, grey, / The way the drowned leave their names above water" (47). Silence, "keeping still": these are deadly practices.

As she toys irritably with operatic conventions, so Mullen confronts the pantoum in "Broken Pantoum for Three Voices (Only One of Which Is Love)." Instead of repeated lines, the only echo of the first quatrain we find in the second is a fraction of a word, "heavy." In stanza three the terms "undertow" and "believe" are repeated; in the fourth, "mirror" is reconfigured as "silver water"; and in the fifth we get another echo-fraction, "dark" (37–38). It is worth noting that a line composed of these terms might, for the conceptually inclined, sum up the themes of this book as a whole: heavy undertow / believe / mirror / silver water / dark. And so the pantoum finally resolves with this quatrain, which largely accomplishes as much:

> I am going to fill my pockets with stones,
> And walk into the blue of the water, the sky.
> And the weight of the body? *Now I believe you.* Rapt
> In the undertow, the snarling smiles of foam,
>   the teeth of the sea. (38)

It is worth asking, however, what Mullen achieves by calling this poem a pantoum (if "broken"); why use the term at all? (This is a question pertinent, in general, to many of the avant projects of the last half-century.) It seems clear that doing so aligns reader expectations, and indeed, dutifully, the reader searches for evidence of the promised form. A failure to detect evidence of the poem's professed formal model—or better, the effort to suss the nature of such formal "brokenness"—might encourage industrious readers to call into question the value of formalist form. And if Mullen is having, formally speaking, her own way, her final quatrain illuminates the threat the poet has been examining throughout the book entire, walking, as Virginia Woolf did, into "the teeth of the sea."

That is to say, Mullen illuminates the threat of the self to the self. Her second book, *After I Was Dead* (1999), continues with the themes of mirrors, water, self-construction, the conventions of composition, and threat:

> I had a sense of things as fragile,
> Myself as well;
> *Threatened*, but also
> Part of the threat. (Dead 17)

Mullen has described this work as (in part) an investigation into her suicide attempt at the age of fourteen. "My grandmother gave me a journal," she tells Cactus May. "Some brilliant insight on her part made her think that if I could write some of it down maybe I wouldn't take it out on myself, or extinguish myself." But the stanza just provided strongly suggests that the "fragile" self articulated here is more "*Threatened*" (emphasis hers) than threat, which is relegated to a merely "but also" (17). What is the source of the external threat, which apparently for this author once was internalized? Is there a boundary between external and internal ("*Not a skin, / Closed off*" [17]); and what is the nature of "writing it down" by way of not-extinguishing the self?

Mullen summarizes her intention: "The attention to beauty, to detail. Something / (Large) rotting away or wrong (waiting) / Underneath" (15). Everywhere we find obstacles to feeble attempts made by humans to (as we say) connect, and in this work Mullen indulges a lengthy scrutiny of place and of the architectures we ourselves build, but somehow cannot negotiate. In a series beginning with the poem "Structures," we attend to such oddities as ". . . 'those doorways / he found in Tibet.' / Which led into nothing and out of nothing." The loss of these places, their capacity to shelter, is intensely felt. *"Archways the sky showed through."* And, "Call me later. / Echoing off the invisible walls. / (Fear sets in.)" The use of end-stop in this poem, staccato lines with little enjambment, reinforces the abrupt disappointment of doors that lead only to sky, and to an outbreak of jitters. "(A little false, a little stiff with each other.) / (After.) (Before)" (23). Finally, "No marks on the body this time. / No clues" (25). In such empty spaces, in the context of such a lack of structural support, relationships happen "later" and "stiff[ly]," the self falters and exists only in scare-quotes: " 'I' the poor glue" (23); " 'I' the thin / ice on this river" (25). "I" becomes highly contingent under (*pace* Bowles) an unsheltering sky, as Mullen turns to still another art form (earlier it was opera; here, architecture) to demonstrate the failures of convention. Not only do the structures fail to function, but those failures expose the aggressions of patriarchal creators.

"In Baltimore, they painted / Bricks to resemble bricks" (26). The poem "Appearances" extends the architectural theme to the notion of having a public face. The ostensible topic of the poem is love:

> What I regret about that time
> Is how good I was at convincing
> Myself all I needed was the appearance
> Of love, which might—so it seemed in my deep
> Naïveté and cynicism—be all love was.
> Whatever love is, it isn't
> The thing I tried to will into being
> Back then: like an unbroken sleep,
> A smooth surface . . . . (27–28)

But the architectural metaphor allows the poet to address veneers that permit people and their environs "not to be, but to look / Other" (27). The surface trumps actual alterity every time; in Baltimore,

> There too, I hesitated
> Over the purchase of a deal
> Wardrobe with mirror, papered
> Over—I swear this—
> With what seemed to be
> A photograph of wood
> Veneer for a veneer. (26)

Papering mirror with wood—the narrator worries that the listener won't believe her ("I swear this")—and such is the degree of ridiculousness the narrator perceives in this situation. The effort claimed by maintaining the architecture that is the face we put on love—the narrator seems exhausted by it. Having returned to her more usual practice of enjambment, Mullen gives us a woman who "hesitated / Over" a wardrobe "papered / Over," but she's far more concerned by what's behind (*under*) this: ". . . an easily manipulated desire / To have things be other than they are" (27). Thus, the poet exposes the architecture of the production of the desiring-machine.[6]

As that nod toward Deleuze and Guattari would lead a reader to expect, Mullen takes this opportunity to comment on capitalist economies. The wardrobe sells for "Fifty dollars" in "one of the thrift / Stores, down by the water, / Where the change / Was counted out by hands that shook." The narrator is there "between the Salvation / Army and the projects; Church / Hospital and the porn theater" (26). Mullen is lingering in places that are not what they appear to be (one wonders how this accords with John Waters's Baltimore), and her attention splinters the putative norms and names of social architectures, her line breaks underscoring associated misdirections. Thrift *Stores* are not really for the thrifty; the *Army* provides little Salvation; the *Hospital* is not, let's be clear, a Church; all this "where the change"—isn't happening. The structures that stand immutable are the projects, and the porn theater, which is to say, the architecture necessary for the perpetuation of class- and gender-specific exploitation.

The buildings receiving the fake-brick facelifts, made of "chicken wire," "pulverized stone and concrete," are a mess. "Burnt out, falling down, boarded up, / Some of the houses seemed to have been / In a war. . . ." Why go to the trouble of make-believe renovation? "[T]o look / Other: more solid? More expensive? Older?" The cost of false renovation is further renovation:

> In the future
> Which arrived, whoever could afford the labor
> Blasted and chipped and scraped the false
> Front off: the word then was the weight of it
> Weakened the structure. (27)

Presumably, those who could not afford the labor would, in future, watch their homes fall down once more. Such is the price of trying to look "Other"; such is the price of grasping for false (upwardly mobile?) alterity.

And so it is both with love and composition. The poem concludes with a reference to Matisse's *The Pink Nude / Large Reclining Nude* (1935), which was

> [. . .] left to the city of Baltimore
> By the Cone sisters, who left, as well,

The record the artist kept—in a series
Of photographs—of all the other paintings
This one could have been and briefly was
(The subject shifting slightly in each frame
As though restless) . . . . (28)

Mullen's selection of Matisse here is perhaps apposite, and ironically so, in that Matisse claimed to need the relative calm of southern France in order to create his wildly colored Fauvist paintings; similarly, the production of appearances in "Appearances" may not be what it seems. Mullen's challenge to herself is to allow us to witness "In the worked-over, punctured canvas— / The traces of everything it took / To come to this" (28). On the one hand, "this" may amount to yet another, if more sophisticated, veneer; at the same time, "this" might at least gesture toward an "Up close" configuration of an unveneered, if you will—unclothed—woman. Is it possible to approximate an accurate representation of the unvarnished, the honestly naked (as John Berger would have it), "nude" female, one who seeks not unconditional love, but the requisite and untidy conditions of love?

In 2005, Mullen published *Subject*, which was released in the wake of work she was doing on the two genre-busting books (of which more later). It was welcomed, as Amy Newlove Schroeder put it, as "a funeral for subjectivity." Certainly *Subject* is more intently informed by Mullen's interim treatment of the horror and mystery genres; but, as is clear in the first lines of the first poem, "Wake," the "subject" is still the canvas, and what it took to come to this, and what is missing: "Widening line of light / What isn't inked" (1). Evincing a greater immersion in, and unsettling of, prose conventions than her first two poetry collections, Mullen's *Subject* registers, initially in lines, her abiding concern with the stubborn opacity of words, even or especially when we are most in need of clarity:

Tied she turned to watch her watch while waiting drenched
On the edge of a grave preoccupied by violent argument
What nostalgia I think this is praying (yes) *precisely*
Your hands at my throat (4)

Perhaps under threat of death, then, the poet turns quickly to prose in "Circles," a discussion of what many consider to be the beginning of a woman's life:

Drenched in white a screen of empty circles makes a wedding of expectations. There is nobody there is nobody home there is nobody there to home into nobody comes home is who to come to. What we have come to. A wide slide of perforations implies a scale of values vows are squeezed through. (5)

"That many of the poems present themselves as prose—i.e., appear as sentences—complicates [the subject] matters further," Susan Schultz writes, adding, "The wrenching paradoxes attendant to life and death, attraction and repulsion, and verse and a-verse typify Mullen's thinking."

Mullen's reworking of Gertrude Stein's famous remark about Oakland—"There is no there there" becoming "There is nobody there is nobody home there"—makes the obstacles between expression and reception, between writer and language, and writer and reader, more intimate. While certainly not a demonstration of unadulterated song, this prose-poem passage does not abandon prosodic pleasures. Witness the abundant assonance and smart use of repetition; nor is the passage devoid of sheer wordplay ("values vows"); elsewhere we find momentarily waltzing dactyls and other memorable feet. As "Circles" continues, the narrator addresses her general dismay at wedding rites ("Writing invitation after invitation and then again by hand every single thank you"), even as it signals the narrator's failure to fit into coupled culture: "And who invited you"; "No one is here right now to answer your call"; and finally, "Sorry there's no one available" (5). The woman seeking partner, the writer seeking reader—as with Schultz's already mentioned list of paradoxes (prose/poem, life/death, attraction/repulsion), what is complicated here is the nobody-there-ness, the absence, of (wedding?) reception.

Similarly, in "Late and Soon," Mullen's titular allusion to Wordsworth's memorable sonnet[7] might prepare us for a discussion of contemporary anomie, but as it turns out, the more tangible locus of the poem has once again to do with vagaries of love: "My love lying in the next room, in an in-between state: neither asleep nor awake" (10). Since there is some dispute, apparently, about precisely how awake he is, the word "lying" takes on two meanings. "We say the words have their own (light) life," the narrator notes (9).

The real target of "Late and Soon" is, however, not love, but love's more abstract and precarious destinations, which Mullen explores by figuring love as travel by train. She reworks Wordsworth's "we are out of tune": the train is "put in motion—according to a timetable. *According*, as in 'in' or 'out' of 'tune with'" (10). Her references to light entering through or obstructed by the train's windows suggest Wordsworth's "glimpses that would make me less forlorn." And interestingly, with its references to Proteus, Triton, and "The Sea that bares her bosom to the moon," Wordsworth's sonnet resonates with the water motif to which Mullen is herself so frequently drawn.

Further, the railway trope allows Mullen to address her bugbear, "The desire to *arrive* at a truth" (11), the primary obstacle to such an "arrival" being, again, language. "Choice and chance and the rules (their 'merciless' logic). (Having invented them, merciless—needing that lack?) So a single language or currency eases the necessity of recognizing value" (10). Having "put in motion" this "doubt"-ful relationship, the narrator fusses over its viability. A fight has been picked about how asleep he was, whether he should have been wakened. "*Wake up and smell the coffee*: now we're on the same page, or, you're on the right track." In a nod to Wordsworth's "getting and spending," she adds, "The Limited, The Express" (11).

In this way, the narrator arrives at her highly provisional truth. "Station, as versus stop." She has "Halted a progress or isolated a segment of, to examine." What she ends up with is "History. In the next room an empty bed and a silence. An initial lurch or tug in the direction designated as forward quickly smoothing out" (11). Designations are, here, arbitrarily arrived at according to "choice and chance and the rules." Here Mullen treats Wordsworth somewhat ironically, since, as he would have it, "It moves us not." Or as Schultz puts it, "forward direction denotes space and time, but not the steady progress of narrative, a progression Mullen refuses." Indeed, "movement," whether emotional, physical, or conceptual, is ambiguous at best in the work of a poet committed to resisting the literary conventions of narrative, and the cultural conventions of the feminine.

Subject continues to treat the concerns noted in the earlier collections, extending the discussions of threat, water, etc., but—perhaps in order to better explore the notion of subjectivity—a new motif emerges, that of windows, through which (as earlier) light and clarity pass with varying degrees of affect. In "Gift,"

> Now the sun explains the windows to
> themselves but all at once and
> flat [. . .]
> the tone impatient dismissive
> *A wi(n)dow is being dis-*
> *regarded*
> that special voice (13)

Later,

> The son explains the widow to herself but all at once and flatly (look
> you are
> flat   *broke*
> that special voice (13)

The equation of sun with son, and window with widow is a collapse that renders "explanation" oppressive. The sun explains the window, the son explains the widow, "to / themselves . . . the tone impatient dismissive . . . that special voice"; neither window (looked-through) nor widow (looked-through) possesses the autonomy of self-identity.

We should note that, in *Subject*, even as Mullen works more in prose, she also works with the page, which itself becomes a window of sorts. In another poem, "Frames," the doubled widow / window theme persists, but the structure of the page shifts (double-columned in this instance). After the husband's funeral, presumably, we begin with "Empty" and find a "Sign advertising distance."

Frame full of fragments   Window: snow (widow)

                                   Interior: obscuring view
Lines on face meaning   Of "empty" street [part] (16)

Into this obviously gendered experience of widowhood, Mullen mixes her protest against the 2000 U.S. presidential election, juxtaposing, in the first section of "Frames," the Vedantic concept of "linga sharira" (impermanent form or body) with "Frame: / A vote against uncertainty!" (17) The conflict between impermanence and certainty is clear enough, but this latter may also be a reference to economic game theoretics of the late 1990s that argued that citizens quite rationally practice vote-splitting (voting to elect members of both opposition parties to different positions) as a hedge against the risk of radical social change (of which more in a moment).[8] The second section of "Frames" depicts the infamous pictures of Palm Beach County officials examining the so-called "hanging chad":

> Held up to the light the light inscaped little new moon fingernail paring of if I changed can I burn my mind and read close edge where cuts slip onto floor under table tally when you're out out waiting it up as if to grasp but unsteady stack tilted in frame and pencil at counted twice then subtract "1 . . . the repose of 2 / . . . the foolishness of numbers [. . . .]" (18)

Having established that the election will be folded into the problem of disregarded widowhood, the third section of "Frames" contains three items, including a "Thought balloon: / 'Exploration' the American myth! / Silencing sequentially"; a horror: "*Swastika cuff link / Number tatooed on exposed wrist*"; and a question: "Caution: 'Will the Dead Speak?'" As always Mullen speaks for the dead, the pre-dead, and the after-dead:

> White raised scarification
> Evidence
> Of suicide attempts
> The hatching
> Of a text: *Held up to the light* (19)

The final section returns us to the "fully inked / Widow of the frantic to complete   One word" (20).

It is silence, from the grave and from the ballot box, but especially from the oppressed, that terrifies the poet more than anything—the incapacity to articulate need, desire, autonomy, and citizenship—the incapacity to *make* a clear "choice" for one side or the other ("yes no," the narrator complains [18] about our current social tendency toward purposeful political certainty, and thus our resistance to social change), our incapacity to fight "chance and rules" that are arbitrary and fail to hold up under enlightened examination, regardless of framing device. Mullen collapses here, as many feminists have, the personal with the political. Schultz writes: "Mullen ventures into and out of public and private spaces that we generally assume to be stable, plying and playing her words so as to reveal a core instability." In Mullen's universe it's small wonder that, given a citizenry of disregarded, dismissed, flat-broke widows, a peek through the glass house that is the United States government reveals, as game theorists predict, little more than constant hedging against the cessation of oppression.

Finally, *Subject*, in its obvious concern with subjectivity, turns more and more to the issue of text itself, and the relation of text to subject: "The difficulty (of reading) around someone else's (re)marks," Mullen writes in "Arose (Read as) A." The narrator describes the experience of reading marginalia, producing marginalia, text around text, marginalization long having served as a feminist metaphor for oppression. Again the allusion to Stein is productive, although this prose poem does not purport to unpack Stein's "Sacred Emily"[9] so much as rebut it. If Stein suggests that simply using the term "rose" brings to that text all of the rose's symbolic matter—no point in nattering on about it—Mullen suggests that no one reader will perceive all of the rose's sociohistorical functions. "Getting the reference only after somebody else pointed it out." It takes a village, then, to produce a true rose, and villages are, in our society, attended by (often patriarchal) hierarchies. "Penciled 'gag!' in the margin, responding to that stuff about the *half* or only *faintly formed* works that issue from the female imagination, with an exclamation point" (61).

As aforementioned, the typography in *Subject* reflects the poet's concern with textuality. Unlike Mullen's earlier collections, which are almost entirely flush-left, with each line capitalized, *Subject* chases the page, at times with those erratic columns, and at times by running text sideways. Blocks of prose text are mixed with broken lines. In "Assembly," she begins, "(Having finished with dimensions)   The 'fragile, voracious' [not to say 'love'] / line / as here lead" (83). The poet frequently interrupts herself with tab stops, as if unable to concede entirely that she is vulnerable to the fragility and voracity of the line (perhaps especially if it is a leaden "love" line). She does seem to be "finished with dimensions," finding possibilities on every page for three- and four-dimensional structures of topic, motif, line (or sentence), and voice (not to say narrative). "The incredibly responsive tracing around a white space *What* / is this?" the poet adds, after suspending the word "[deictic]" in brackets by itself at the bottom of a third column. *The Free Dictionary* gives us this definition of the term as used by linguists in adjectival form: "Of or relating to a word, the determination of whose referent is dependent on the context in which it is said or written."[10] In noun form, *Free Dictionary* has it as: "A deictic word, such as *I* or *there*." Little more is needed to summarize Mullen's prevailing occupations: White space too is fracture. There is no " 'I' " there, no " 'there' " there. (The sound/eye-specific allusion to "deitic" is productive as well—they who control "choice and chance and rules.")

As these concerns take on a formal, page-as-canvas representation in *Subject*, we get another deictic in the title of the final series of poems, titled "The Distance (This)," in its helplessly inarticulate "lines," such as:

Sonant	(interval)	(to keep)
Successive	A word for	
	The word for	(" ")
Another (87)		

What the inarticulation achieves is a representation of the challenges of articulation; the poet demonstrates suborned alterity, what it's like to be *subject to*.

Schultz expresses concern that "[s]ome [poems] are more effortful than effortless" and that "at times the poet asks too much of her materials, imposing rather than eliciting feelings." Here Schultz may be resisting that species of didacticism that some allege (unfairly, in my view) of Language writing; to revisit Maggie Nelson's what-to-call-the-"flow" challenge, Mullen is not strictly a Language poet, but, as Reginald Shepherd has pointed out on his blog, her work does at times demonstrate the "third-space" collapse of lyric and Language distinctions. I can offer anecdotally that I have myself heard leaders of the avant (or post-avant) (or "flowing") poetry community remark of Mullen's work that it's just "*too* difficult."

Rebecca Wolff, who has published Mullen's work in *Fence*, has said of post-avant writers that they "intentionally [blur] the distinction between 'difficulty' and 'accessibility,' preferring instead to address a continuum of utterance."[11] No one reader will experience the entire ambition of Mullen's poetry projects; as Schultz says, "The *subtexts*—those texts 'beneath' the text, which function as subjects—come from sources as various as Shakespeare, Toulouse-Lautrec, Leslie Scalapino, and 'The Signs of Right Thinking,' to say nothing of *Daily Lesson Plan in English* (1914)." No one reader will grasp every allusion (I missed the Scalapino myself), and no one reader will catch every play on words, just as no two readers will insert the same term into those empty quote marks in the stanza just shown.

Mullen does not abandon feeling and evocation, but she does insist that that which is evoked, that which is felt in a poem, is created by *words*, *words*, unreliable *words*. Mullen rarely lets the reader ignore the materiality of text, the conditions that give rise to her typescript. A line such as

"Sorry there's no one available" is quite affecting (it's also funny[12]); it also makes clear that the words we hear while stuck in contemporary, middle-class, phone-tree hell contain other implications and provocations. Mullen's concern as an artist is to point, literally *point*, this out. Through a rigorous interrogation of the self as embodied in language (langue and parole), she questions the capacity of words to serve as vehicles for things, ideas, relations. For Mullen, as is illuminated in " 'Gift' " and in " 'Frames,' " oppressive aspects of language conventions (" 'that special voice' ") operate similarly to oppressive social practices (" 'a text: *Held up to the light*' "). If her poems seem at times effortful, this perhaps serves to make present the poet in the poetry, to make conscious the work of the poet, the labor associated with creating effect and affect. Ultimately, what Mullen refuses to abandon is the role of intellect in art-making, and in, for that matter, *feeling*-making. Of the many binary oppositions her work seeks to undo, the head–heart divide may be the most resilient of them all, hence the one that draws her primary attention.

MULLEN'S poetry alternately prefigures and rearticulates her prose work; it's deceptive to separate Mullen's genre works from her poetry collections. For one thing, the thematic emphases are virtually identical; for another, as I have already suggested, the steps she takes toward undoing genre fiction in *The Tales of Horror* (1999) and *Murmur* (2007) clearly inform *Subject* (2005). It's also worth noting that Mullen's poetry collections are, like her prose works, quite specifically organized around thematic and structural progression. Her books are careful, conceptual wholes—concept albums, if you will. (Her uncollected published poems would make for a rather hefty volume, another indication that she writes into and through a specific concept for each collection.) I separate the discussion of the two modes only because the conceit of the genre works differs from that of the collections. As noted earlier, *Tales* and *Murmur* are the first and second installments of a trilogy planned by the author. The trilogy aims to unpack three popular genre forms that contribute a great deal, culturally, to defining the construct of woman: horror, mystery, and romance novels (and films). In light of the general (cultural) preference for prose narrative (as against poetry), it's entirely possible too that the trilogy will, in my view unfairly, comprise the dominant share of the poet's legacy.

The problem of what to call the genre works has plagued author, publisher, and reviewer alike. The author herself called *Tales* (while in progress) a novel, as well as a verse novel, and although the designation exists on neither the cover nor the spine, something that appears to be a subtitle resides on the cover page: "[A Flip-Book]." And in fact, the Library of Congress listing reads, *The Tales of Horror: A Flip-Book.*

Thus the hyperliterate Mullen leaves us wondering what we should make of this apparent auto-categorization. Flipping its pages, we see no animation, nothing like the 1868 kineograph by John Barnes Linnet, nothing like the German *Daumenkino* (thumb cinema), nothing like the tiny toys in boxes of Cracker Jack. But the back cover insists: "The tale is disassembled to offer alternate readings—as a story, as a flipbook [*sic*], and as a text scored for old and familiar voices." And perhaps it's true. Wikipedia puts it rather quite nicely: Flip books [*sic*—clearly there exists no consensus even on how best to punctuate the term] "rely on persistence of vision to create the illusion that continuous motion is being seen rather than a series of discontinuous images being exchanged in succession. Rather than 'reading' left to right, a viewer simply stares at the same location of the pictures in the flip book as the pages turn."

Tales most certainly relies on a persistence of a certain kind of vision; the reader must commit to seeking something like coherence despite the work's insistence that the motion of artifacts we might call gothic horror is quite dangerously discontinuous, having morphed over time to become more and more simplistically anti-woman. The work takes every opportunity to sever the illusion of historical continuity and to force us to stare repeatedly at the one thing in pulp horror that seems never to change: the body of the dead woman. What *Tales* will eventually teach us is that pulp horror isn't fun; it's a pulpish narration of violence against women.

Familiar themes emerge early. We meet Holmes, or his equivalent, confident in his experience and his capacity to arrive at truth, in "The Overture":

> The fruits of my past experiments the rather extensive if I may say so
> knowledge
> My endless researches had finally vouchsafed me in spite of which the
> truth
> Of the matter seemed to be that there was a point at which one could no
> longer say
> That one was entering but that one was now in the position of "having
> entered" (8)

Expertise—knowledge, mastery—will be a persistent foil in both *Tales* and *Murmur*; as Mullen herself has commented, "The women are so traumatized, they can't tell you what happened. And the men are too busy trying to master the details; they don't tell you anything" (Freeman).

Speaking of the women, we also meet the body, or the suggestion of the body, which is, as we've come to expect in Mullen's gambits, aligned with a body of water: "*Dark shape in its bed of rank weeds its entrance gaping but not I was wrong like that / Forever a shred of white lace at a broken window insisted on history.*" In this case the window will be associated with a widower, but we will examine these (social) structures "*that had been like that forever,"* this *"ancient house the abandoned house"* (8). Yet, as we know from history (if Gerda Lerner is correct[13]), social structures have not been anti-woman forever—and so we launch into the narrative-within-the-metanarrative that drives this study of the genre's conventions.

Since the conventional horror film is one of the genres under scrutiny here, one might be tempted to observe that Mullen breaks the narrative-within at the midpoint of the work, the midpoint being that plot-turning point in a Hollywood-formula screenplay that occurs precisely half-way through the film. Here we are in a scene from what could be any one of a hundred different films: "The ringing startled me out of sleep—the persistent ringing—and then a woman's voice (from beyond the grave)." The "he" of the scene, later shown writing, "lifted his pen from the paper [. . .] and gazed at her for a long moment before speaking, before breaking the silence, no, no, before he turned to the window and, looking out, let what seemed to be a long silence 'fall' between them" (56). Then, after a section break, one line: *"There was a series of high-pitched screams"* (57).

It is here that Mullen breaks the action to contemplate actual pulp horror novels—providing title, author, year (all of them locatable today on Amazon.com), and plot synopses of the sort one finds in back cover matter. Mullen provides four examples, all of them from the mid-eighties and all of them, the reader realizes, resonant with the themes and motifs Mullen presents. The summaries are cringe material:

> Kit Maitland's assignment to write an article about a Hudson River estate sale turns into a murder investigation, with Kit as the suspect. Additional complications occur when two men, Joris, her charming half-brother, and Simon, Kit's estranged husband, demand her loyalty. Her life depends on making the right choice. (57)

So cringe we do, but is there also—perhaps because this material comes so deeply embedded in Mullen's far more beautiful, far more stylistically ambitious work—a sense of readerly superiority? That only we lucky few can see through such an absurdly transparent use of language?—can see, that is, through the ideological ruse? Reginald Shepherd has written, "Only because of the backwardness of literature in comparison to music and visual art can self-appointed avant-gardistes still feel themselves in the forefront of artistic morality."[14] Certainly Mullen recruits the reader as partner in her critique of these artifacts, the cultural work they attempt, and their place in the "literary" marketplace. Reader and writer collapse into accomplices.

At any rate, the themes common to *Tales* and to these novels include a surface-level awareness of writing (a persistent theme in Stephen King's fiction), "estates" of the real sort, and the false agency implied in the notion that Kit must choose how to save her own life. (Someone else, presumably, possesses the agency not to threaten it in the first place.) It is impossible to know how many such novels from 1985 Mullen could have chosen, but her selection of these four is revealing. Aside from the preceding, which describes Isabelle Holland's *Flight of the Archangel*, Crowe's *Bloodrose House* features a home with rosebushes, and with secrets about its "former mistress," as we find in Mullen's tale. The title protagonist of Velda Johnston's *The Girl on the Beach* becomes "fascinated" with a man accused of killing his wife, and "decides to unmask the real killer"—her fascination serving, of course, to obliterate any "objectivity" she might bring to that cause. In Phyllis Whitney's *Dream of Orchids*, "Laurel's stepmother died in the family greenhouse, where exquisite orchids are grown. Laurel's discovery of the secret of the orchids puts her life in danger." This last strikes us as particularly nonsensical in that, surely, orchids are not killers of women. What secrets could orchids possibly harbor? The hint of a nefarious force beyond the greenhouse—what could it be?

A reading of the four synopses makes clear what the nefarious force must be: men. More specifically, men to which the heroines are related by blood or marriage; that is to say, family men. Men with access to the house. That which makes houses scary is—the man of the house. That which "complicates" a woman's domestic life is—the man of her house. Like some of the women in Mullen's poems, these heroines suffer difficulties with the social mandate to couple. Crowe's heroine is divorced. Holland's lead has a doubtless too-charming half-brother and an estranged husband. Johnson's girl-detective has just broken up with a fiancé and jumps from frying pan to fire, since her fascination is with a man who did twelve years for "killing his unfaithful wife." (Unfaithful. The wife's death was the wife's fault, then.) Whitney's victim has an estranged father and, like Cinderella, two stepsisters.

"The satin cushions," Mullen writes, returning to her own setting. "The bloodstains. The open window. And a sort of theme emerging [. . .]" (58). The theme goes something like this: The most dangerous place for a woman is her own home.

But before we leave this section, which Mullen titles (or pirates as) "FIC-TION DEPARTMENT / Book Notes / DAMSELS IN DISTRESS" (57), let us linger for a moment on the first entry. Crowe's heroine "goes to the English village of Yorkshire to complete research for a biography of Charlotte Brontë." This is Mullen's nod to the moment in history when the Gothic matured, when it ceased to be exoticization of anything but profoundly true love, and when it empowered women to pursue their own moral codes, as Jane Eyre does when she abandons Mr. Rochester and Thornfield Hall, not returning until she possesses her own financial means (more a gift of Brontë's plot, and evidence of the latter's personal convictions, than a realistic possibility in that day), and not until Rochester has been introduced to humility—by his wife. If Brontë's Thornfield is haunted, it is haunted not by ghosts or forces of the sort Ann Radcliffe might have indulged (supernatural forces that turn out to be flights of feminine fancy); it is haunted instead by a marriage made of commercial convenience. It is haunted by the financial exploitation of the West Indies by, among others, the British Empire. There is a madwoman in the attic, then, but (if you will) she has good reason to be mad, and if she doesn't herself have access to a happily-ever-after, at least she does some damage, and some perverse good, on her way out: She leaves Rochester in a condition that makes him Jane's equal. Jane has little to fear in her new home with the blinded, helpless Rochester.

Crucial here is the fact that Mullen selects four novels produced by women for this meta-burst into the trade marketplace. If the Gothic was tailored in Britain by Walpole in 1764 and pressed by M. G. Lewis (1794), and if Continental authors—male—subsequently joined in,[15] the English tradition tends to be thought a feminine one, with Radcliffe as Grande Dame and Austen's *Northanger Abbey* as early parody.

That said, the novels to which Mullen directs our attention, so that we may share in that superior cringe (as already mentioned), may have been composed by women, but via this coopted form the oppressed oppress (the threatened threaten), and their cumulative contemporary effect is the attenuation of the Gothic's earlier, socially transformative potential. Their effect, that is, is the *re*-placement of—the man in the house. Which is to say, there is little in these 1985 novels that challenge gender norms. In fact, Mullen ends *Tales* not in prose, but in poetry:

> And came to slowly, *"I don't,"*
> One hand held up against the glare,
> *"Remember."* Anything?
> What looks exchanged
> Above that slumped, white-shrouded
> Shape already blurring
> At the edges, losing
> Definition even as we watched?
> *"There were these . . ."*—
> One hand outflung, a gesture, empty—
> And then? *"And then*
> *Nothing."*

It is as if, having critiqued the gendered conventions of these novels (and their authoresses's complicity), *this* author collapses, finally, in a last gasp that could be represented only in lines.

Publisher's Weekly greeted *Tales* with encomia such as "brilliant" and "utterly original," as well as this: "Mullen swoops in and out of metaphor to poke fun at the gothic genre, and celebrate its astonishing versatility."

More insightfully, writing in the *Rocky Mountain Collegian*, Amy Freeland noted that *Tales* "uses stock elements from the horror genre to explore a reality that is sometimes more terrifying than the imagination. Physical violence and conformity to sexual roles are embedded just beneath the guise of a clichéd, humorous story."

But from that final murmur in *Tales*, that *"And then / Nothing"* in Mullen's travesty of the horror genre, we turn to *Murmur*, in which she takes her knife to the more recent, and correspondingly less storied, mystery genre. We have Poe, Doyle, Hammett, Chandler, films (and film noir) ranging from *M* to *Dial M for Murder* to *Blood Simple*, and Angela Lansbury refusing to age, damn her. But Mullen's primary concern, as usual, is the language of genre itself, and so readers are also provided with excursions into books like *Writing Mysteries: A Handbook by the Mystery Writers of America* (an Amazon.com search yields hundreds of such how-to-books). To draw our attention to the regimentation of the generic, Mullen cribs from, but also corrects, such texts: "there are very definite laws—unwritten perhaps, but ('if these walls could / speak') nonetheless / *or the color of the sky, at these angles, reflected back, interrupting what you might recognize* / binding, and every self-respecting concocter of literary mysteries lives up to" (93–94).

"Literary mysteries"? Evidently the modifier denotes some higher stylistic calling, Hammett's efforts presumably more durable than Lee Goldberg's, if not Patricia Highsmith's. Very much a genre ripe for flipping on its back, at any rate, its typically seamy underbelly nonetheless girded with binding laws, as above, the generic conventions that control both concocter and consumer. The iconography according to which such narratives customarily teem with nuances of sexuality and gender, articulating all manner of deviation from the norm, is all-too-often fashioned with malice aforethought, for both victim and reader:

> The truth of the problem must at all times be apparent—provided the reader is shrewd enough to see it. By this I mean that if the reader, after learning the explanation for the crime, should reread the book, he would see that the solution had, in a sense, been staring him in the face—that all the clues really pointed to the culprit—and that, if he had been as clever as the detective, he could have solved the mystery himself. (99)

What may seem to be a banal sample from the genre-enforcers (when served to us, as Mullen serves it, benignly decapitated) becomes ironic when juxtaposed against "Caught light in the wind-rippled surface of the water as though a green sequined dress" or "She dissolves and vanishes, disintegrates" (99). The attentive reader, treated by handbook conventions as something of a stooge, can certainly spot the clues (generic rule: dress, not pantsuit); and with subtle prompt can even hazard the denouement (body must wash up on shore). Meanwhile, the writer is the detective solving (according to the rules)—the mystery of reception? A crime? How can there be a crime with no agency? Perhaps the most dangerous "rule" of composing these artifacts is this one: "The motives for all crimes in detective novels should be personal." No stranger-danger for these folks, no, which will feel very familiar to women readers who know where to expect actual danger. But again, who is responsible, writer or reader? "It must reflect the reader's everyday experiences, and give him an outlet for his own repressed" (100)—

—*his* repression?

Here Mullen slams on the brakes. Once again the weapon, and quite possibly perpetrator, turns out to be language: "A Noun's Meant," as she calls it. Meant to what? *Murmur* quite loudly insists on interruption, disruption, eruption, struggle with expression—"Caught light . . . as though . . . dress" (line never finished). If we reread, we begin to see that the perp is the mysterious epicenter of this genre, and not simply in having committed a crime, but in having *authored* the crime. If the reader's empathic attention, like the writer's agency, is in some sense recruited by the detecting protagonist, then all three perps traffic in those aberrant social practices that complement stereotypes of victimhood.

Wait, though—don't we *all* traffic, however unwittingly, in aberrant social practices?

As with *Tales*, we're not quite sure which genre we have here, since again we suffer the odd line break:

> In the dream I speak to my wife.
> *For? At?* In my dream. In this
> Dream. Someone makes the thing
> Slow down, has time to worry
> About word choice. I think
> I cut her throat, though I couldn't
> Swear to it. (128)

Mullen's signature themes, motifs, and formal habits are all present here; additionally, her configuration of page-as-canvas congeals in *Murmur*. And here, finally, the poet simply refuses to solve the genre problem:

> You are reading
>   broken into
> What we see her seeing   what she sees (10)

Generic form is not the *predominant* issue, finally. It's worth repeating Mullen's remarks to Cactus May: "Poetry . . . made space for leaps and gaps which feels more true to how it is inside . . . thinking." For Mullen, language clearly mediates—indeed, is constitutive of—experience (and consciousness itself), and therefore is an abstraction (distortion) of reality, especially when the experience constituted is that of the perpetrator and not the victim.

Moreover, the reader has, by virtue of reading, "broken into," and is an intruder, as much as is the man sharing the victim's bed (thus, reader as perpetrator); and we note here how laws and conventions so often fail to penalize those who cut throats, if only symbolically (or, reader as trafficker in traditional literary conventions). Mullen reaffirms the dangers to women of men close-by in the penultimate movement of *Murmur*, with its fabulous pun on Benjamin, "L'Aura,"[16] and (as always with Mullen) its intertextual play. How could *Laura* Mullen *not* address Preminger's film?[17] The reader connects the dots between Preminger's stock characters and Mullen's exposure of same. We all but see Gene Tierney, the stunningly dressed, would-be stiff (costumes by Bonnie Cashin), and her dandy-confidant Clifton Webb the perp (as if fey men are more threatening to women than macho ones). "They rape she breaks into she starts / sharp acute right removes / The struggle of the sexes is the motor of history" (133). As for Dana Andrews, a man in love with a well-heeled fantasy, Mullen gives him voice, as well: "'I saved you, I was there just in time . . .'" (149). The conventions of the form empower the savior, disempower the saved, and empower the voyeur (viewer/reader)—assuming the voyeur identifies with the savior, or identifies with the victim but is willing to pretend that autonomy can be accessed through the savior, via the savior's infatuation with the (powerless) saved.

What defines the "struggle of the sexes" is the generic form that struggle takes, in stories told according to the rules of our most cherished oppositional pairs: the genders, the genres, life and death. Small Press Bookwatch aptly described *Murmur* as "a refractive perspective on space-time—amid the medley of infinite cosmic possibilities, the tale is told in such a manner that at one time or another everyone has committed the murder and everyone has been the victim." Robert Buckeye, writing in *The Review of Contemporary Fiction*, argues (tautologically?) that the work is a "reflexive metafiction." His choice of pronoun in the following ought perhaps to raise a penciled eyebrow: "The book always escapes its resolution. The writer stops writing it because he cannot make it 'Just This,' if even, by the end of the book, he no longer attempts to do so anymore. . . . [O]ne section tells us how to read murder mysteries, which is of no help at all."

What Buckeye misses—aside from the totality of the discussion of gender—is that our popular mystery books are, under Mullen's scrutiny, everyone's mysteries, "blurred into letters and then strange markings, lines, squiggles, which only faintly resembled writing." Eventually, "she got up . . . her empty hands held out as if she were reading her own palms or another element sliding invisibly over her uplifted hands, a text which changed at every instant, which never ceased moving, held open as if"—

—and so we end, again unfinished (151). Here the reader in/of the story goes to the edge of the sea to seek the tale written in the victim's own hand. And with that the oppositions collapse, endlessly mutable. As readers, text in fist, we are stiff and perp, sexed and sex, top and bottom, and all of the above.

As if there were words, as if words were not themselves a blur. As if it's poetry, prose, both, and neither—genre as ever-changing dynamic— it's immaterial, this material, so long as we grasp that readers are the ones who have to save the victim (themselves), not least by seeing through the enforcement of generically formed, formally reinforced misogyny.

In her work Mullen insists that we take nothing about language, about narrative, for granted. "It's not a story," a character writes in *Tales* (98). Hers is a voice that came out of the silence (possibly a shriek), and her chief determination seems to be the rescue of subjects from the *consensio* so often associated with *silentium*. This is an artist who insists upon her own palette, who eschews the easy, premixed codes of formal convention. As noted, oppositions turn upside down: the threatened exist as threat. The light of day can augur a nerve-wracking absence, while night can bring clarity—it's where things go bump, where things actually happen. Syntax is not, as is thought, a means to understanding; "*words fail*" (*Tales* 107); it presents the greatest obstacle to communication: having found a voice, the marginalized can only clank their chains and moan. Persuasion as such is only marginally possible: " 'language built us,' " so " 'language could tear us down' " (*Tales* 58). Image is of little use; the mirror is a dangerously distorted site, veneer on veneer. The only thing we know for certain is that error always accompanies locution, and that even the absence of words punctuates our frail attempts at making sense of things. As Mullen would have it, repeating John Cage's dictum: "*There's no such thing as silence*" (151).

NOTES TO POETICS STATEMENT

1. "De-monstration . . . transforms, it transforms itself, in its process rather than advancing a signifiable object of discourse." (Derrida, *La Carte Postale*)

2. A term for nineteenth-century body-snatchers—who stole from graves (or otherwise produced) bodies to sell for dissection and study by medical students.

NOTES TO CRITICAL ESSAY

1. Maggie Nelson, *Women, the New York School, and Other True Abstractions* (Iowa City: University of Iowa Press, 2007), xvii.

2. Ibid., xxiv.

3. Publishing information for Mullen's works is listed in the bibliography, as are citations for reviewers of the works.

4. *Orphée*. Dir. Jean Cocteau. Screenplay by Jean Cocteau. Andre Paulve Film, 1950.

5. Laura Mulvey, "Visual Pleasure and Narrative Cinema." *Screen* 16, no. 3 (Autumn 1975): 6–18.

6. Gilles Deleuze and Félix Guattari, *A Thousand Plateaus*, trans. Brian Massumi (Minneapolis: University of Minnesota Press, 1987).

7. William Wordsworth, "The World Is Too Much with Us." www.bartleby.com/145/ww317.html.

8. Mauricio Bugarin, "Vote Splitting As Insurance against Uncertainty." ideas.repec.org/p/wpa/wuwpga/9811001.html.

9. Gertrude Stein, "Sacred Emily." www.questia.com/PM.qst?a=0&d=6082895.

10. *The Free Dictionary by Farlex*. www.thefreedictionary.com/deictic.

11. Quoted in Reginald Shepherd, "On Laura Mullen." Reginald Shepherd's blog, http://reginaldshepherd.blogspot.com/2007/02/on-laura-mullen.html.

12. Few have commented on what a bitingly funny writer Mullen is. It's dangerous, and maybe a little disingenuous, for a critic or scholar to try to prove to her reader that a literary artifact is funny; take a "humorous" line out of context and it often falls flat. And no two funny bones are alike. It is, however (you simply must trust me), startlingly humorous in *The Tales of Horror* to turn the page from *"There was a series of high-pitched screams"* to "FICTION DEPARTMENT / Book Notes / DAMSELS IN DISTRESS"—and not quite so funny to return to "The satin cushions. The bloodstains. The open window." Thus is the humor not always "just" humor but also, crucially, revelation; why, for instance, is the notion of writing "fiction" about "damsels in distress" . . . funny?

There are droll, dry-witted moments aplenty in Mullen's oeuvre, but rather than belabor the point I will refer you instead to "Drive," in *After I Was Dead* ("[. . .] What's with this person / In front of me, I wonder, what's with this light. Shit" [30]) and to "The Squeaky Wheel" in *Subject* ("Squeaks. ('By'?) By definition! Like a mouse? Like a wheel (very). Greaseless? Graceless! How it squeaks *vis à vis* how we expected it to squeak. Or, "'Eeeek!'" [52]).

13. Gerda Lerner, *The Creation of Patriarchy* (New York: Oxford University Press, 1987).

14. Shepherd, http://reginaldshepherd.blogspot.com/2007/02/on-laura-mullen.html.

15. A typical reading list would include François Guillaume Ducray-Duminil, Gaston Leroux, Baculard d'Arnaud, Friedrich Schiller, and Christian Heinrich Spiess. See Eve Kosofsky Sedgwick, *The Coherence of Gothic Conventions* (New York, Metheun, 1986).

16. Walter Benjamin, in "The Work of Art in the Age of Mechanical Reproduction," wrote, "That which withers in the age of mechanical reproduction is the aura of the work of art." See www.marxists.org/reference/subject/philosophy/works/ge/benjamin.htm.

17. *Laura*. Dir. Otto Preminger. Screenplay by Jay Dratler, Samuel Hoffenstein, and Elizabeth Reinhardt. Twentieth Century-Fox, 1944. It's worth noting, since Mullen works not only at the level of intertext but at times at the level of intertext within intertext, the 1979 French film known in the United States as *Laura* (in

France, as *Les ombres de l'été*, or *Shades of the Summer*) by David Hamilton. The IMDB logline reads, "Sculptor Paul meets a former great love again after a long time—but is much more impressed by her 15 years old daughter Laura" (www .imdb.com/title/tt0079449).

BIBLIOGRAPHY

Books by Laura Mullen

The Surface. Urbana: University of Illinois Press, 1991.
After I Was Dead. Athens: University of Georgia Press, 1999.
Tales of Horror. Berkeley: Kelsey Street Press, 1999.
Subject. Berkeley: University of California Press, 2005.
Murmur. New York: Futurepoem Books, 2007.
Dark Archive. Berkeley: University of California Press, 2011.

Selected Prose

"His Father." In *Chick-Lit: On the Edge: New Womens Fiction Anthology.* Eds. Cris Mazza and Jeffrey DeShell. Normal, IL: FC2, 1995, 142–45.
"Demonst(e)ration." *American Book Review* 19, no. 6 (1998): 5.
"Active Magic." *Denver Quarterly* 34, no. 1 (1999): 105.
"The Poem." *Many Mountains Moving*, A Tribute to M. S. Merwin 4, no. 2 (2000): 120.
"Wearing It Out." In *Footnotes: On Shoes.* Eds. Shari Benstock and Suzanne Ferriss. New Brunswick, NJ: Rutgers University Press, 2001, 282–88.
"Torch Song (Prose Is a Prose Is a Prose)." In *Civil Disobediences: Poetics and Politics in Action.* Eds. Anne Waldman and Lisa Birman. Minneapolis: Coffee House Press, 2004, 440–46.
"Where It's at (I Got Two Tables and a Microphone)." In *The Iowa Anthology of New American Poetries.* Ed. Reginald Shepherd. Iowa City: University of Iowa Press, 2004, 161–75.
"English/History." In *Paraspheres: Extending beyond the Spheres of Literary and Genre Fiction: Fabulist and New Wave Fabulist Stories.* Richmond, CA: Omnidawn, 2006, 570–87.

Selected Interviews

With Cactus May. *The Nieve Roja Review* (Winter 1998/1999). http://nieveroja .colostate.edu/issue4/mullen_interview2.htm (accessed October 4, 2008).
With Amy Freeland. "CSU Professor Pens Gothic Poetry." *Rocky Mountain Collegian*, October 27, 1999. www.collegian.com/news/1999/10/27 (accessed October 4, 2008).
With Tod Marshall. *Range of the Possible: Conversations with Contemporary Poets.* Spokane: Eastern Washington University Press, 2002, 35–41.
With Colleen Fava. February 7, 2007, www.lauramullen.biz/work1.htm (accessed October 4, 2008).

Selected Criticism

Buckeye, Robert. Review of *Murmur*. *Review of Contemporary Fiction* 27, no. 3 (2007): 227.

Burke, Trina. *Cutbank*, 67 (2007): 168.

McCay, Mary. Review of *Murmur*. *The Times-Picayune*, May 6, 2007, www.nola .com/living/t-p/index.ssf?/base/living-o (accessed October 4, 2008).

McDuff, David. Review of *The Surface*. *Stand Magazine* (Spring 1992): 90–91.

Pretty Fakes. Review of *Murmur*. http://prettyfakes.com/?p=983 (accessed October 4, 2008).

Publisher's Weekly. Review of *The Tales of Horror*. August 30, 1999. http:// reginaldshepherd.blogspot.com/2007/02/on-laura-mullen.html (accessed October 4, 2008).

Small Press Bookwatch. Review of *Murmur*. August 1, 2007, www.publisher-sweekly.com/978-0-932716-48-4 (accessed June 6, 2011).

Wagner, Catherine. Review of *After I Was Dead*. *Interim* 18, nos. 1–2 (1999): 129.

White, Sam. Review of *After I Was Dead* and *The Tales of Horror*. *Boston Review* 25, no. 2 (2000): 62.

EILEEN MYLES

Transitions

sometimes
I'm driving
and I pressed
the button
to see who
called &
suddenly I'm
taking pictures.
Big dark
ones. He says
it's not about
where you sit
to make a
film
but I wasn't
taking a
picture
I was driving
it's black &

there's all
these lights
I'm strong
it's night
& I've

driven very
far

I keep hearing
the music
of the weekend
he says
it's not about
whether she & I
resume
it's how it goes
on
with me.

In my car
so long ago
I loved someone
who read me a poem
on the phone
about the car
of the day

you mean the
one I'm driving

and the fact that
she left it
on the phone
and that was new

she said I was overreacting

and that was too much
and we sent our messages
in light
and ack she hated
trees
I thought she's so
young cause
I like nature
now and her trunk

wrapped around
me one day
he licks my
arm my boy
& driving home I thought
if he dies
I will see his paw
in the sky
I am seeing it now
and she's always
home
going hwuh
and she said
I love our little
meeting I said

little

don't denigrate
my need to support

my need to say
that you *can*

I'm glad I'm
home it's wide
out there
we spoke about scaf-
folding
him fitting the
frame to the
eye
she's grown
I wanted to say
we laughed about
tang
and later on the
toilet

thought
about tango
and joan
L Tango Larkin
what's not technology
what's not seeing
an arm to say
I hold the
line   I hold
the day
I watch the snowflake
melting

Snowflake

There's no female
in my position

There's no man

wow
there's a raccoon
on the tail
of the plane
and there's
no one

seeing that now
but me

and there's no one close
enough right
in here
to see the
further
drawing

stripes or buildings
the bricks
of the world

I wonder
what I'll say about Sadie
and I wonder
if they are still
living in that
state
and if they hate
me for moving
her furniture
out and putting
it in storage

I walked past that restaurant
where I was so mad
I could have broke
the glass
I'm the only one in the mood to remember
this me living

and who threw
a snowball
against the
glass
and scared
me in my seat
so hot
with rage
why am I dry
freezing
I want to go
home

I saw a rose
in the heart

of the
year two thousand one
everything
turning
rose
dog head
a wheel of
love
but I was so mad

I locked it
up and took
the key and lived
for that moment
snowflake
I wasn't there
not even me
when she put
in the key
and it wouldn't
turn

To My Class

I'm trying
to figure
out what
kind of fucked
up flower
a reflection
is
when everything
dances
in a bowl
of aluminum
day's on

no extra
light
just the color
scheme
of the gym
& thinking
about that
the tile is that
exact
shade which
is not quite
white
they chose
it and it's
why the
feeling is not
exact

I've got
to lie
down
on the mat
to see
the frond
peeping
through
the
window
sitting up there's
too much
a bending plant
a grille
the whole
life of
the gym
not the tiny
crop

like sitting in a
Muslim
restaurant
and the cow
peeps in
like that

I'm trying to
sort
out a
few things
at this
exact
moment
in my life
something
more
marvelous
than a category
the body
place is
a thinking
place
a surprise
here
a day isn't
a bookshelf
unless it's
the endless
process
of
pulling one
down
and hours or
years
later
putting it back

up for
some other reason
among its
new friends
I don't really
need
glasses
to write
but I squint
and gradually
that grows
unfamiliar

Questions

I may
not have
the time
for all
of this
but A) I
enjoy the
slap of
my flipflops
on the stair
& though my
name is
not Roxanne
I remember
when I
would've liked
that like
a girl playing
witch in

her yard
with jars
& spider
webs & the
world was
misty. A)
almost took
it all.
Even if I'm
not Roxanne
I know
you liked
my voice
in the
dark &
I did too
B) Rabbits
like to be
up and around
at twilight
& dusk ex-
actly when
I get
scared
Did stripes
come from
any place
else in nature
but a changing
sky & a
sad parent
fills a
room & before
a child can
think she
feels it
too. C) The

Tree. There
was a moment
of light
before I
got in the
car. The
tree was
that green
that holds
up the
procession
of this.
It is the
world.
D) And now
I will drive
home. I
looked at
a lamppost
just for
a sec.
Could Eileen
ever be
Roxanne?
No.

Hi

for Steve Carey

You made me smell.
I didn't smell at
all before I met you
smells are pouring out of
my clothes, feet, my
socks my hair

this is gross
you've made me monstrous
and I love it
I knew a man who laughed
at himself
for being this way
stinking of love
it was what he was
a stinking factory of his love
lying there all day
going out to get a smoke
I'm the east coast version
of that
since I met you
since the era of my famous
resistance to you ended
it began like the wind
I am a window to the world
the mailman can see me
he waves; children out there playing
it's even this way when I'm out
there
except when I hold your hand
I want it; to be this exception
I've become
not a woman or man
The heart pumps
the man is dead and it's
spring
it's a smelly season
don't you think
the earth knows
the bugs are beginning to look
around
you're throwing your mother's
old stuff out
your friends are beginning

to understand
I want to show
mine something different
the ripples I've become
I'm influence
the way language changes
rocks heal & burn
meat stretches
your little round animal
face keeps coming around
the corner but
oh no now you're coming down
I'm looking up

POETICS STATEMENT

MY POEMS are comfortable with the idea that experience is a kind of knowing and that technology endlessly delivers new ways for us to describe how that knowing occurs. Putting a book together lately I remembered how I'd initially (like in the 70s) considered poetry a recording plain and simple. And now all these new forms of recording are amplifying and multiplying and frothing up the way I see. More and more the pleasure becomes how absolutely little I can do and still maintain a connection between this thought, this vista and that. The thrill for me is always the looming possibility of disconnection. The slim fact of the need to write at all instead of merely enjoying the hum. I have to add that as a female I consider myself living in a storm at sea. Inside our very intense relationships every woman I know struggles deeply. I read once that analysts in the twentieth century discovered that shell-shocked men in world war I resembled "neurotic" or "hysterical" women in ordinary time. From that I concluded that a woman exists in a constant state of war in this culture that still sees us as not quite human. I had considered focusing this statement on being queer but I actually think it stands up pretty well for all women, conventional or weird. Put two of us in a boat and it's just pretty hard to sail or paddle. Because of all the pressure inside and out. I think relationships between women, couples and groups of us are always occurring in a storm. The way this is definitely revealed in the larger culture (well I am getting queer now) is how everyone laughs when they hear the word lesbian. Try lesbian golfer, lesbian real estate agent, lesbian poet in a crowd and it always creates a roar. It's how people acknowledge that they know this thing is real. Their laughing discomfort. People are quickly laughing at the strangeness of women and so how can two women for example decide to have a life together. Why would anyone purport to live next to society and call that a life. Yet to do the ridiculous thing in writing or in living has to yield a wider truth in exchange for the estrangement. It's a new kind of energy, this impossible knowing *plus* the technology. You're on your own time now. Go ahead. That's what my work is all about.

"WHEN WE'RE ALONE IN PUBLIC"[1]

The Poetry of Eileen Myles

Maggie Nelson

OVER THE PAST thirty years, Eileen Myles has become a legendary and transformative figure in American literature and culture, by means of accomplishing two things. First, she has produced a prolific, explosive, expansive body of work that has established her as one of America's most important poets—one who has worked in and over the shimmering space between "lyric" and "language," fragment and narrative, the personal and the political, the minimal and the extravagant, the mundane and the mythic, the cerebral and the visceral, the particular and the universal, the powerless and the empowered. Second, by dint of her audacity, generosity, tenacity, and vision, she has also invented a completely new role for a female poet—and by extension, a female human being (indeed, any human being, should women ever be acknowledged as such a priori)—to inhabit in the public sphere. Certainly it is not every poet's duty, nor is it within every poet's field of desire or power, to invent or inhabit such a role. But when a poet manages to do so, as Myles has, it is a rare and lasting thing.

Some of the grounds for Myles's particularly insouciant form of poetic and political audacity can be located in her relationship to the so-called New York School. Over twenty years ago, Ted Berrigan called Myles "the last of the New York School poets," and the label stuck, in part because Myles never really chafed against it. When asked in a 2000 interview with poet Frances Richard if the appellation still resonated with her, Myles responded:

It depends on who asks. Once I was introduced at a reading by someone whom I thought of as a Language poet, and when they described me as "New York School"' I experienced it as a critique—like I was retro. But, yes, those were the writers (O'Hara, Ashbery, Koch, Guest) who woke me up, who gave me a sense of what an adventure being a poet could be . . . Ultimately, though, "New York School" just means I learned to be a poet in New York. As an aesthetic it means putting yourself in the middle of a place and being excited and stunned by it, and trying to make sense of it in your work.[2]

Myles here points out how the dimensions of a label are necessarily defined by a host of social contingencies: particular mentors, friendships, and other personal relations; specific aspects of a specific city; the contexts in which a term gets circulated—literally, who speaks it—and so on. Her ease with the label thus has much to do with her long-standing interest in the formation and power of aesthetic and social communities: "I move in groups," she explains to Richard.

Myles's presence on the New York School scene has also disallowed the all-important queerness of the New York School surreptitiously to slip into signifying only male homosexuality. Myles has audaciously championed the queerness of her predecessors and contemporaries, and labored tirelessly to record the "vivid and close-knit way of life" she has shared since the late '70s "with a number of dykes and fags, mostly artists." And while many critics interested in the New York School have been content to chart its lineage through the great but mostly straight cadre of writers such as Ted Berrigan, Charles North, Ron Padgett, David Shapiro, Tony Towle, Paul Violi, and others, Myles's interpretation summons a different, more anarchic roster—one that might also accommodate Kathy Acker, Dennis Cooper, Tim Dlugos, David Trinidad, and David Wojnarowicz, among others. Myles also consistently disallows the lethal breed of amnesia that ghosts the lesbian, especially the butch, body (whatever that might mean) by articulating (on the page) and actualizing (in performance) a poetry rooted in bodily presence, in the force and rhythm of her own particular body. "I think we all write our poems with our metabolism, our sexuality," she explains in "The Lesbian Poet." "[F]or me a poem has always been an imagined body of a sort, getting that down in time."[3]

Myles is not alone in emphasizing the link between the body and the poem. But where most poets and critics default to privileging orality, Myles's version keeps messier, more voracious bodily processes—such as the anal, the digestive, the hormonal (including the menstrual, the menopausal, and so on), the orgasmic, and the cellular—at center stage.[4] As she explains in her essay "The Lesbian Poet":

> My poem rumbles through it all, unbelievable, and as the month turns the poems get manic, crazy, weird, sullen and bloody, stay at home, the words I use narrate a female cycle, probably much more than a female orgasm. (. . .) It's my poetic dilemma, it seems. To include the body, the woman's as I see it, to approach this blood as part of the score. It should show up regularly in the culture's poems, this female conversation, because most of the poets who write bleed every month until they pass childbearing years. I'm waiting to watch the room change.[5]

This "female conversation" may sound like *écriture féminine*, but Myles's "proprioceptive" poetry has less to do with finding an essential mode of female expression than with scribing "an economy, a metabolism or energy flow" that is particularly hers. "If anything, my work is about being inside your body and taking your time and taking your space and telling it your own way," she says in an interview with Liz Galst in *The Boston Phoenix*, in reference to her book of autobiographical stories, *Chelsea Girls*. "And that's . . . important in terms of being a female and a lesbian—that you can take that time."[6]

Like the "visual diary" created by Nan Goldin's photographs, a major facet of Myles's work has been its construction of an ongoing "poetic documentary" of her life—a documentary in which certain primal scenes recur and get transformed via performance and repetition. One of these scenes is a reading she gave at St. Mark's (the Poetry Project at St. Mark's Church, New York City) in 1977, in which she "came out as a poet and a dyke maybe all in one reading." As she explains in "The Lesbian Poet," "It wasn't that I wasn't a poet before that [reading], but I'm addressing some kind of surge, a moving forward that happens at some points in a poet's life, so I mean I was all there, body and soul, after that."[7] Myles moved from Boston to New York in 1974, and she describes her first few years in New York as follows: "I was basically a cute girl in her twenties wanting to be a poet that all the guys would then try to fuck. I mean that was just the lay of the land. And be advised not to be a feminist, you know. And so I just sort of caroused around, and I drank a lot, too."[8] In the Richard interview, she elaborates further on this period:

> When I came to New York in the '70s, I didn't know I was a lesbian. I didn't want to come out. I was homophobic, or scared—I just didn't want to be a dyke. There wasn't a woman in that circle of poets, either, who could receive me and let me know I was heard. Alice Notley, who was married to Ted Berrigan, was there, and we were, and are, great friends, but she was a married woman and a mother and she was going to have a different life. . . . I made the model of what I needed there to be. I put lesbian content in the New York School poem because I wanted the poem to be there to receive me.[9]

Myles here gestures toward the paradoxical, almost mystical reciprocity of this process: The poem is there to receive you, yet you have to create the poem so that it can receive you. Myles's mastery of this process, both on and off the page, has been one of the most inspiring and culturally transformative aspects of her career to date.

The investigations that Judith Butler, Eve Kosofsky Sedgwick, and other theorists have done into queer performativity and the powers of language are also relevant here. In particular, Sedgwick's thinking about queer performativity makes heavy use of the linguistic philosophy of J. L. Austin—specifically, Austin's notion of the "performative utterance." Sedgwick is interested in "the implications for gender and sexuality of a tradition of philosophical thought concerning certain utterances that do not merely describe, but actually perform the actions they name: '*J'accuse*'; 'Be it resolved . . .'; 'I thee wed'; 'I apologize'; 'I dare you.'" Sedgwick sees this site of linguistic performativity as particularly rich and provocative because it represents "a place to reflect on ways in which language really can be said to produce effects: effects of identity, enforcement, seduction, challenge." [10] I can think of no other contemporary American poet who has wielded the power of the performative utterance as astutely and exhaustively as Myles.

New York School poets in general (with, perhaps, the notable exception of Barbara Guest) are known for their investment in speech. But Myles's exploration of the possibilities of linguistic utterance is of a different nature, as it has been shaped by her involvement with performance art and political activism. Though performative utterances can clearly take place in private ("I'm sorry," "I forgive you"), they proliferate in the public sphere. You can fight forever about whether or not your lover is really sorry, or whether or not you really forgive your parents, but to argue that a minister didn't really marry you, or that a judge didn't really sentence you, etc., opens up a whole different can of worms. That is to say: It brings in the question of social power, and of authorization.

Like Gertrude Stein, who famously set out to write "everybody's autobiography," or like Alice Notley, who insists that "[s]*omeone*, at this point, must take in hand the task of being everyone, & no one, as the first poets did," Myles habitually asserts an ambitious, all-encompassing, public role for herself as poet. "I would like to replace the poet with the whole human race," she recently wrote in her contributor's note to *The Best American Poetry 2002*. [11] In an essay entitled "How I Wrote Certain of My Poems" from her 1991 collection *Not Me*, Myles explains that she wants to address her culture—"some new, larger [culture] out there which I suspect exists"—by "making work which violates the hermetic nature of my own museum—as a friendly gesture towards the people who might recognize me. I mean exhibitionistic work, really." [12]

"Exhibitionism" is a particularly interesting concept when applied to or used by a woman, as its clinical meaning is "compulsive exposure of the sexual organs in public." Given that psychoanalytic schema typically figures the vagina as lack, the question of what, exactly, women can exhibit or "flash" necessarily invokes the spectacle of phallic appropriation. And it is precisely at this point of tension that Myles situates so much of her work, as to broadcast the "female personal in the public sector" is necessarily to impinge on male territory. In her interview with Foster, Myles explains the complexities of this impinging as follows:

> There's a privacy in public [that men have] that women do not have. . . . I'm really interested in public poetry and a private person's public nature. And I haven't found that a lot in women's work because it's not in women's lives. I mean it's kind of a fool's journey in a way, too, because I have the fate of a woman, that destiny. And so, much as I might like to move it over there, a lot of the reason my privacy will always be disturbed is that I am female.[13]

A "fool's journey" it may be, but Myles has used it to transform the boundaries of what kinds of claims on public space a female poet can make. "Although women are very visible as sexual beings, as social beings they are totally invisible, and as such must appear as little as possible, and always with some kind of excuse if they do so," Monique Wittig observes in *The Straight Mind*. "One only has to read interviews with outstanding women to hear them apologizing."[14] Myles's poems expressly avoid any such excuses or apologies. They also reject and transform any erasure of female anatomy and specificity by performing pussy-as-presence in both the private and public realms, as in her incantatory anthem that begins, "I always put my pussy / in the middle of trees," and goes on to assert: "I always put my lover's cunt / on the crest / of a wave / like a flag / that I can / pledge my / allegiance / to. This is my / country. Here, / when we're alone / in public."[15]

Myles would be the first to admit that this exhibitionist pose often stems from a lack of power—a lack of power that has as much to do with class as gender. This idea becomes vivid elsewhere in her novel *Cool For You*, when Myles describes the day when all the Harvard alums come back to town: "everyone was so happy and sometimes they had a golden son with them, and even outside you could hear the goony Harvard Band marching around the Square and when you rode along Memorial Drive they would be out there sculling and you could see it was their river and you were entirely fucked. Slam."[16] Myles often talks about how her Catholic school education worked together with her working-class background to drill into her the sense that she wasn't "something special." When she got to New York, she says she was consequently just "glad to be in the phone book."[17] "There's a lot of class stuff in the internal voice that says, 'Don't think you're so special,'" she explains. "In some ways my whole art impulse derives from saying, 'I know I'm not special.'"[18]

This impulse is complex. On the one hand, it has spurred Myles to a kind of self-mythologizing that stands in belligerent protest of this rebuke. On the other, it has led Myles to use this self-mythologizing to push beyond individual "specialness" and toward "replacing the poet with the whole human race" (another fool's journey, without a doubt). The title of the collection *Not Me* provides a condensed example of this paradox, as the phrase "not me" could be read as an intentionally unconvincing disavowal of the personal, or as the assertion of something patently true — i.e., that the collection is "not her," as representation is always incomplete, identity always in excess of its performance, and self always larger than language, no matter how "personal" the work. This paradox is also on display in Myles's many experiments with "mock-exaltation," as Patrick Durgin has put it: In "The Windsor Trail," she invents a "Lady Eileen"; in "Immanence," she aligns herself with god; in "The Poet," she is "the only saintly man in town"; in the opening poem of *School of Fish*, she is "The Troubadour"; elsewhere she casts herself as road warrior, shepherd, hunter, captain, and so on. These characterizations are not static dramatic personae, but rather momentary flashes of identification, mostly masculine, that glimmer throughout her work.

One of her most well-known poems in this vein is "An American Poem," which cannily performs being "somebody" and "nobody" at the same time. It begins:

> I was born in Boston in
> 1949. I never wanted
> this fact to be known, in
> fact I've spent the better
> half of my adult life
> trying to sweep my early
> years under the carpet
> and have a life that
> was clearly just mine
> and independent of
> the historic fate of
> my family. Can you
> imagine what it was
> like to be one of them,
> to be built like them,
> to talk like them
> to have the benefits
> of being born into such
> a wealthy and powerful
> American family.[19]

Autobiographical detail bleeds seamlessly into fictive conceit: Myles *was* born in Boston in 1949; it isn't until the line "a wealthy and powerful family," that one begins to catch on to the poem's ruse. The poem continues:

> . . . I hopped
> on an Amtrak to New
> York in the early
> '70s and I guess
> you could say
> my hidden years
> began. I thought
> Well I'll be a poet.
> What could be more
> foolish and obscure.
> I became a lesbian.
> Every woman in my
> family looks like
> a dyke but it's really
> stepping off the flag
> when you become one.
> While holding this ignominious
> pose I have seen and
> I have learned and
> I am beginning to think
> there is no escaping
> history. A woman I
> am currently having
> an affair with said
> you know you look
> like a Kennedy. I felt
> the blood rising in my
> cheeks. People have
> always laughed at
> my Boston accent
> confusing "large" for
> "lodge," "party"
> for "potty." But
> when this unsuspecting
> woman invoked for
> the first time my
> family name
> I knew the jig
> was up. Yes, I am,
> I am a Kennedy.[20]

The line "I am beginning to think / there is no escaping / history" takes on a particularly complex meaning here, in that the poem dramatizes a means of escape from her own personal history while it also fuses her story with the "historic fate" of the Kennedys, thus refusing to allow her "foolish and obscure" roots to be relegated to history's sidelines. As the poem goes on, its complexity thickens, as the speaker continues to posit herself as near-royalty slumming it as a poor poet and dyke, while she also *is* that poet and dyke, boldly asking her audience: "Am I the only / homosexual in this room / tonight. Am I the only / one whose friends have / died, are dying now." The oratorical grandiosity of the poem grows as it heads toward its final, climactic lines: "It is not normal for / me to be a Kennedy. / But I am no longer / ashamed, no longer / alone. I am not / alone tonight because / we are all Kennedys. / And I am your President."

The phrase "mock-exaltation" begins to seem inaccurate in light of such brazenness, as one of the most compelling aspects of Myles's posturing is how it eventually becomes indistinguishable from exaltation itself. The performative utterance "I am your President" is technically "infelicitous," to use Austin's term, in that Myles lacks the authorization or social power to make herself the President. But as Butler makes clear in *Excitable Speech*, not only is it "clearly possible to speak with authority *without* being authorized to speak," but also it is precisely this kind of "insurrectionary speech" that often brings about social transformation.[21] (For a nonverbal example of this phenomenon, Butler uses Rosa Parks: Parks had no authorization to hold her seat in the bus, but her assumption of the authority to do so sparked meaningful change.) Thus, while Myles may be a Kennedy imposter, the authority claimed by the poem ends up no sham. Further, this authority is more than poetical, and more than her own. "Shouldn't we all be Kennedys?," she asks her audience, before concluding triumphantly: "we are all Kennedys."

The opening of the short piece "Light Warrior" (in *Chelsea Girls*) makes related claims: "My name means Light Warrior when you bring it home to the present day through Latin and Gaelic. I am a significant person, maybe a saint, or larger than life. I hear that you judge a saint by her whole personality, not just her work. I'm beginning to see my work as my shadows, less and less necessary, done with less and less care."[22] "Light Warrior" appears, however, just stories away from "Popponesset," Myles's chilling, four-page account of getting gang-raped at a party at a beach house in Cape Cod while nearly unconscious from drinking. "A bunch of good-looking suburban guys, 18 or 19, same as me, who all owned cars, trashed me for two reasons: I was drunk, they didn't know me," she writes. The morning after, she wakes up alone, sick and "painfully numb." She walks down to the beach, where she writes her name in the sand with her toe. "EILEEN MYLES. Yes, that's who I am. I rubbed it out with my foot."[23] The "larger than life" celebration of her name in "Light Warrior" cannot be disentangled from the name written in the sand in a solitary act of survival and protest.

Myles's developing role as a "cult figure to generations of young, post-punk female writer-performers," as Holland Cotter put it in a 2001 profile of Myles in the *New York Times*,[24] stems in part from this dialectic, which balances a Stein-like conviction of her own genius and significance with a startling—indeed shameless—exploration of her powerlessness and shame. "I think the form of the novel gives dignity to my shame," she says in *Narrativity*,[25] in reference to *Cool For You*. "Sometimes I'm just ashamed to block the sun." A poem from *Skies*, "Inauguration Day," which corresponds to the controversial inauguration of George W. Bush in 2001, brings this shame into the public sphere, and transforms it with defiance: "you cannot insult / Me," the poem concludes. "I hold this sense of awe."[26] The sense of awe is hers inalienably, so to speak—the speaker holds it, contains it, a priori. But she also has to hold onto it, grasp it, protect it from that which might insult it. The poem thus becomes the container that the poet holds out as spectacle, offering, declaration, and potential agent of change.

"I've always thought a poet should think big, not small," Myles has said.[27] And in the United States, what could be bigger than the Presidency? In a blurring of art and activism that Allen Ginsberg pioneered in the '50s and '60s, and that feminist and conceptual artists hammered away at throughout the '70s, '80s, and early '90s, in 1992 Myles ran as an "openly-female," write-in candidate for President. In this context, the conceit of "An American Poem" collapses: The poem no longer just resembles or apes a Presidential campaign; it became a part of one. By this point in her career, Myles had published several books of poems, including *The Irony of the Leash* (1978), *A Fresh Young Voice from the Plains* (1981), and *Sappho's Boat* (1982). She had also written several plays and two books of prose, *Bread and Water* (1987) and *1969* (1989); edited the poetry magazine *dodgems* (1977–79); served for two years (1984–86) as the director of the Poetry Project; and performed extensively. ("In the '80s I remember a friend telling me he thought I was 'bringing Personism to performance.'"[28]) In 1990, she began touring a stage show called "Leaving New York." As the title suggests, around the time she turned forty, she was feeling "fed up" and ready to leave New York altogether. While touring, she was constantly "thinking of where I was performing and who I was performing for. Just regarding the public space as a political one, thinking what would be political for this particular group of people."[29] In the end, the experience brought her "to a whole new place with my art and my dealing with community." Instead of leaving the city, she had "one of those lightbulb experiences . . . I thought, I'm 40, I can run for president. I'm female, but I can run. I went down to the board of elections and looked into it and I found out the regulations for being a write-in candidate, so I did that for about a year and a half."[30]

Myles's run for president wildly amplified the personal-is-political formula. She describes the campaign experience as follows:

I toured 29 states, I fund-raised to continue the campaign. I was on MTV, *Interview* did a piece on me. If the point was to get attention, I could have gotten more. But I was sort of treating it like a performance artist doing duration, and my idea was, no matter what, I was going to run to the election. And I was going to run according to how I felt. Because a candidate never really tells you how they're feeling. And I thought I would be the candidate who did do that. My campaign was total disclosure, and I would endlessly disclose details about my life. It also enabled me to politicize personal poetry. Because it was all political, it was all personal. It was exhausting. It invaded every part of my life. You know, I'd go to a party, people would say, how's the campaign. I just could not get away from it. So I got a sense of how much, when you put something out there, it's really beyond your control. . . . Every public appearance I had, I would turn into a political opportunity. Every reading was a campaign opp, every performance, every panel. So I already had some [recognition] and it gave me more. Of course, interestingly, I did get more attention as a presidential candidate than I ever did as a poet. But the fact of the matter was, it was a poetic experience.[31]

Her candidacy didn't just politicize personal poetry; it also revealed something about the poetics of politics. What made it "a poetic experience" was the revelation that "when you put something out there, it's really beyond your control." In politics as in literature, rhetorical effects always exceed intention; they cannot be fully governed. This is the scandal of the speaking body, that "speech is always in some ways out of our control."[32] And the unpredictability of both poetry and politics designates them both as sites of potential transformation. That Myles wouldn't win the election was a foregone conclusion. But her candidacy was scandalous, not only in its spectacle of a broke, avant-garde, lesbian poet making a claim on phallic power, but also in her willingness to dedicate a period of her life to the production of unforeseeable effects.

In "Tradition and the Individual Talent," Eliot famously says that poetry ought to be an escape from personality and emotions. Less famous, however, is his next line: "But, of course, only those who have personality and emotions know what it means to want to escape from those things." In a weird echo of Eliot, Myles freely admits that she is "plagued with personal identity." But where Eliot advocates escape, Myles wants to venture into the heart of the storm, with all its attendant risks and shames. "The body always seems like the shame," she says in *Narrativity*. "The camera must cut away to the trees, the animal is telling too much." But Myles's camera will not cut away to the trees. The animal will not stop talking.

The Artaud epigraph that begins *Cool For You*—"*Jamais real, tojours vrai*"—sheds more light on Myles's particular approach to this first-person, talking body. The epigraph recalls the line that prefaces *Roland Barthes by Roland Barthes*: "*It must all be considered as if spoken by a character in a novel.*"[33] Myles's stance is similar, but more Pop: She likens her "I" to a character in a comic strip—a comic strip in which the figure "Eileen Myles" is necessary to carry the action from frame to frame, speaking in word-bubbles. "It's just that, for me, the pictures are invisible—the poem is purely the balloons, and the balloons are infinite." In creating this character, however, Myles does not fall back on any self-protective platitudes that hope to wedge a safe distance between speaker and self. And here we might recall the distinction Myles draws between her work and that of the first-generation New York School poets: "They would all assert that the poetry was not about them. It's about skimming the surface of the self. Using that facility to shape the poem. My dirty secret has always been that it's of course all about me." Not only is Myles unafraid of collapsing into the "dirty" realm of the overtly personal, but like Bernadette Mayer, John Ashbery, John Cage, and Andy Warhol, among others, she is also unafraid of collapsing into boredom. "My vehicle, my cartoon, coincided with say, Warhol and the soup can, or *Interview* magazine, these really boring interviews with people saying, 'Um.' I thought, 'Wow, boring. Great!' Warhol's movies, people just talking—pouring all that detail into poetry."[34]

Myles also sees the creation of the character "Eileen Myles" as a metonymic move, because, as she says, "instead of inventing some symbolic name for my narrator, I use a real piece of me." Myles thinks of metonym as a "filmmaker's term," and her embrace of it corresponds to her desire to move away from the "literariness" of poetry. "I experience writing poems as the chance to make a little movie," she says in her contributor's note in *The Best American Poetry 2002*. Her interest in meshing filmic devices with poetic tropes recalls the kinship that the first-generation New York School poets felt with Abstract Expressionist art. As James Schuyler once said to Myles, "I think anything that's all poetry is pretty boring, don't you babe?"[35] Myles regularly posits her speaker as a camera and the poem itself as a snapshot or collection of snapshots, complete with recurring "clicks": "used magazines, / poetry books on a blanket, click" ("Hot Night," *Not Me*); "I'm not a fool (click)" ("My Light," *Skies*); "this is a relationship / click / this is a relationship" ("Scribner's," *on my way*). This photography–poetry parallel saturates the collection *Skies*, as exemplified in the poem, "Where's ya camera," which opens: "That's so beautiful // framed by the wood stain / the sky stained palest orange / for only one moment // I must be precise / the tree is pure silhouette / pure black." The poet's job here is to turn the camera outward to the world and start shooting.

In describing what she sees, Myles often uses extremely plain language, and lets the principal artifice lie in the art of juxtaposition. Juxtaposition as a structuring principle has been plumbed throughout the twentieth century in the development of collage and montage aesthetics; Myles's contribution is an unprecious, increasingly abstract minimalism, propelled by a politicized nerve and relentlessly in pursuit of beauty, in all its simplicity and strangeness. As its title suggests, the poem "Writing" (from *Skies*) could be taken as a sort of manifesto for this technique:

Writing

I can
connect

any two
things

that's
god

teeny piece
of bandaid

little folded
piece
of bandaid

I ran
to the
bathroom

to see
my face

sometimes
I don't
want to

see my
face in

the mirror

sometimes
I can't
bear
my thoughts

sometimes
I can't
do anything

but that's
okay

bandaid
book
god

that's
right[36]

The nerve appears right from the start, as the poet feels, or flexes, her power—indeed, her godlike power—to "connect any two things." But just after proclaiming this power, a trip to the bathroom derails it: the shame of the body—here, of the face and the thoughts it reflects—is never far behind: "sometimes / I don't / want to / see my / face in // the mirror. // sometimes / I can't / bear / my thoughts." The poet talks herself away from this shame-spasm by remembering, or by performing, her poetic powers: "bandaid / book / god // that's right."

The movement of the poem—its swing from the power and pleasure of writing to an intense flash of self-contempt then back to power and pleasure—makes palpable the intimate relation that can exist between speech-making (particularly logorrheic speech, though not only that) and shame. For while "fast talk" can undoubtedly bring deep and voluptuous pleasures, as Silvan Tomkins has made clear, whenever one experiences a positive affect, such as interest, excitement, desire, or enjoyment, shame is almost always nearby, ready to jump in to reduce or inhibit the positive feeling. Sedgwick and Adam Frank explain this relationship succinctly in the introduction to their Tomkins reader, *Shame and Its Sisters*: "Without positive affect, there can be no shame: only a scene that offers you enjoyment or engages your interest can make you blush."[37] Thus the more deeply one invests in the pleasure of "fast talk," the more intense the accompanying shame may be.

For a writer, the stakes of this boundless excitement and boundless shame run especially high, as shame threatens to curtail speech. But even this curtailment need not shut the writer down entirely. "Shame is both an interruption and a further impediment to communication, which is itself communicated," Tomkins observes,[38] and in a sense Myles's prolific career relies on the latter part of this cycle. ("I find self-hate extremely motivating," she writes in an early poem from *Sappho's Boat*.[39]) Often Myles places herself in the very center of shame's sickening swirl and charts the action from its inside, as in this description of PMS in *Cool For You*:

> The whole world becomes my enemy. You start to go crazy. I know I do. I cry for myself. All alone. A life ruined. Tragic mistakes, things I repeat again and again in my head, trying to get right. Sometimes I can taste the thought of the thing I should have said, should have done. I'm so ashamed of myself. Bragging, raging, remaining quiet. Everyone I talk to has that edge in their voice. They pity me. I'm over. You can see it in my eyes. And you must leave

me forever. I can never forget what you've done. I didn't deserve this. I don't love you anymore. You had my body. I was completely open to you. It's taken me years to get this way. No one could touch me. They couldn't get through. I gave you such a gift. My cunt. And now we're through. And then I bleed.[40]

The blood breaks the spell, but for better or worse, the cycle will continue. In fact, this passage itself recycles sentiments expressed over a decade earlier in the poem, "Exploding the Spring Mystique": "I go home to my lover, who's of course / in her early 20s / A Younger Poet. There's a note on my pillow / *Sorry, Honey, you peaked. /* Arrrgh! I shriek at the heavens. (. . .) I collapse on my bed, a sexual and artistic homicide. / Though still breathing, and it is Spring."[41]

In her 2001 *New York Times* profile, Myles says: "There was something about my particular life—as a female, as a person prone to drug and alcohol abuse, as a lesbian—that I sensed was endangered. I had a feeling nobody would know what it was like if I didn't tell it." Reclamation in the face of endangerment is in fact a recurrent and far-reaching gesture in Myles's work, as the following excerpt from her interview with Richard suggests:

FR: So how do you address yourself to a contemporary avant-garde?

EM: I like the term. It's a little pedantic, but if I'm not that, what am I? "Experimental" has a much more tentative sound to me than "avant-garde." I always think of Bob Perelman saying that "experimental" sounded to him like you have some test tubes and a white lab coat and you might just blow up the science building. Bernadette Mayer always liked the word and used it.

FR: "Avant-garde" has that military connotation. You *meant* to blow up the science building.

EM: Yeah. You had to! It's like "queer." It's taking on a term of contempt and saying, "No, I'm proud to be avant-garde." I might feel the same way about the name "New York School."[42]

Myles knows that there exist no objective criteria for what constitutes a "real" avant-garde and what doesn't; she knows that imagining or articulating the possibilities of a movement, be it artistic or political, often goes a long ways toward consolidating one. When Myles came to New York in the early '70s and "put the lesbian content in the New York School poem," for example, she didn't know who or what, exactly, would be there to receive her vision. But as she explains in "My Intergeneration"[43] (here in reference to Sister Spit, the radical spoken-word group with whom Myles has toured nationally): "What was so great about meeting this bunch of punky girls twenty years later was that I was received. But I was received *later.*

It was like I had been talking to an imaginary tribe that then appeared, and that weirdly I even invented. Because when they saw my work they thought, 'Oh, I can do this.' I sort of created my own audience."

Myles's teaching—both in and out of schools—has also played a role in creating this audience and aesthetic community. In addition to her many stints at a variety of colleges and institutions (most recently, University of California at San Diego), throughout the 1990s, Myles regularly organized and led informal, unaffiliated writing workshops throughout New York City, usually taught out of an apartment or loft and advertised via word-of-mouth and flyers. These workshops—several of which I participated in—constructed a loose community of people (mostly women, but not all) who were fearlessly combining experimental writing practices with personal and political convictions. These workshops were not populated solely by poets, but rather by artists of all kinds, and provided a place for a younger generation of women, often newly arrived in the city, to meet and learn from slightly or significantly older artists who had already been working in New York for some time.[44] Such an environment provided the grounds for a casual form of "affidamento," a term Italian feminists use to describe "a relationship of trust between two women, in which the younger asks the elder to help her obtain something she desires," as Myles explains in "The Lesbian Poet."[45]

For Myles, sustained and active disobedience to categories in a publishing world increasingly obsessed with explanatory delimitations is yet another form of resistance: "I think literary categories are false," she explains to Laurie Weeks in *index* magazine. "They belong to the marketplace and the academy. It's the obedience issue that I'm saying fuck you to, the scholar or the editor trying to trap the writer like a little bug under the cup of 'poetry' or 'prose.'" Myles has blessedly continued this "fuck you" trajectory, creating a steady stream of work that refuses taming or entrapment. This body of work recently or imminently includes the libretto for *Hell*, an internationally toured opera (with music by Michael Webster); a book of poems titled *Sorry, Tree*; a collection of nonfiction writing titled *The Importance of Being Iceland* (2009); an appropriately large *Selected Poems*; and *The Inferno: A Poet's Novel*, an epic autobiographical novel that chronicles "the hell of being a female poet," and that will undoubtedly stand as one of the most raucous, joyful, and innovative accounts of what it meant to become a writer in America in the twentieth century. In her statement for this anthology, Myles says: "My poems are dedicated to the idea that experience is a kind of knowing and that technology is endlessly delivering us new ways to describe how that knowing occurs." Given this dedication, Myles will undoubtedly remain both a rambling scout and a fearless leader of such describing and knowing well into the twenty-first century.

1. This entry is an abridged version of a chapter called " 'When We're Alone in Public': The Metabolic Work of Eileen Myles," from Maggie Nelson, *Women, the New York School, and Other True Abstractions* (Iowa City: University of Iowa Press, 2007).

2. Frances Richard, "Never Real, Always True: An Interview with Eileen Myles," *Provincetown Arts* (2000), 24.

3. Eileen Myles, *School of Fish* (Santa Rosa: Black Sparrow Press, 1997), 124.

4. The writer/dancer Deborah Hay is the only artist I know of to elaborate explicitly on this "cellular" idea—see her book *my body, the buddhist* (Middletown, CT: Wesleyan University Press, 2000), in which she describes her body as her "53-trillion celled teacher," and her dance practice as the observation of "cellular consciousness." Muriel Rukeyser also insisted that her poetry came from her female body in a more expansive way—see Kate Daniels's preface to Rukeyser's *Out of Silence: Selected Poems*, in which Daniels reports that Rukeyser once told Cynthia Ozick at a 1976 panel, "You, Cynthia, write from the mind, but I write from the body, a female body" (xv).

5. Myles, *School of Fish*, 130.

6. Liz Galst, "Interview with Eileen Myles," *The Boston Phoenix* (July 1994).

7. Myles, *School of Fish*, 123–24.

8. See Myles's interview with Edward Foster in Edward Foster, *Poetry and Poetics: A New Millennium* (Jersey City, NJ: Talisman, 2000), 54.

9. Richard, "Never Real, Always True," 26.

10. Eve Sedgwick, *Tendencies* (Durham, NC: Duke University Press, 1993), 11.

11. Eileen Myles, "Contributor's Note." In *The Best American Poetry 2002*. Ed. Robert Creeley (New York: Scribner, 2002), 255.

12. Myles, *Not Me* (New York: Semiotext(e), 1991), 202.

13. Foster, *Poetry and Poetics*, 60.

14. Monique Wittig, *The Straight Mind and Other Essays* (Boston: Beacon Press, 1992), 8.

15. Myles, *Maxfield Parrish: Early and New Poems* (Santa Rosa, CA: Black Sparrow Press, 1995), 48.

16. Myles, *Cool For You* (New York: Soft Skull Press, 2000), 10.

17. Foster, *Poetry and Poetics*, 55.

18. Richard, "Never Real, Always True," 29.

19. Myles, *Not Me*, 13.

20. Ibid, 14-15.

21. Judith Butler, *Excitable Speech: A Politics of the Performative* (New York: Routledge, 1997), 157.

22. Myles, *Chelsea Girls*, 35.

23. Ibid, 190.

24. Holland Cotter, "Poetry Soaked in the Personal and Political." *New York Times*, May 30, 2001, E1/5.

25. Myles, "Long and Social." *Narrativity*, no. 2 (December 2001), online at www.sfsu.edu~newlit/narrativity/issue_two/myles.html.

26. Myles, *Skies* (Santa Rosa, CA: Black Sparrow Press, 2001), 204.

27. Richard, "Never Real, Always True," 26.

28. Ibid.

29. See Patrick Durgin, entry on Eileen Myles in *Dictionary of Literary Biography*, vol. 193: *American Poets Since World War II*, ed. Joseph Conte (Farmington Hills, MI: The Gale Group, 1998), 203–12.

30. Ibid.

31. See the interview conducted by Michelle Alb for the Naropa Summer Writing Program, summer 1998, online at http://www.naropa.edu/swp/myles.html.

32. Butler, *Excitable Speech*, 155.

33. The links to Artaud and Barthes are no accident, in that Myles's autobiographical writing may bear more kinship with European traditions of experimental "life writing" than with the American "tell-all" memoir. See Chris Kraus, "Review of *Cool For You*," *The Nation* (January 1, 2001), www.thenation.com/doc/20010101/kraus, in which she smartly distinguishes between the sort of life writing practiced by Acker and Myles and the more traditional forms of the American "memoir," especially what Kraus calls the "Female Madness Tale."

34. Richard, "Never Real, Always True," 29.

35. Ibid, 28.

36. Myles, *Skies*, 80–81.

37. See Silvan Tomkins, *Shame and Its Sisters*. Eds. Eve Kosofsky Sedgwick and Adam Frank (Durham, NC: Duke University Press, 1995), 22.

38. Ibid., 135.

39. Myles, *Maxfield Parrish*, 142.

40. Myles, *Cool For You*, 89.

41. Myles, *Maxfield Parrish*, 144.

42. Richard, "Never Real, Always True," 27.

43. Myles, "My Intergeneration." *Village Voice* (June 2000), 75.

44. Idiosyncratic genius abounded in these workshops—and here I'm thinking of people such as Annie Iobst and Lucy Sexton, who performed as the duo Dancenoise; screenwriter/playwright/fiction writer Laurie Weeks; video artist Cecilia Dougherty; artist/boxer Nancy Brooks Brody; rock musicians Anne Kugler and Cynthia Nelson; art writer Nathan Kernan; painter Jennie Portnof; photographer Shannon Ebner; artist/restaurateur Tanya Rynd; and countless others.

45. Myles, *School of Fish*, 130.

BIBLIOGRAPHY

Books by Eileen Myles

PROSE

Chelsea Girls. Santa Rosa, CA: Black Sparrow Press, 1994.

Cool For You. New York: Soft Skull Press, 2000.

The Importance of Being Iceland: Travel Essays in Art. Cambridge, MA: Semiotext(e), 2009.

SELECTED POETRY
Not Me. Cambridge, MA: Semiotext(e), 1991.
Maxfield Parrish: Early and New Poems. Santa Rosa, CA: Black Sparrow Press, 1995.
School of Fish. Santa Rosa, CA: Black Sparrow Press, 1997.
on my way. Cambridge, MA: Faux Press, 2001.
Skies. Santa Rosa, CA: Black Sparrow Press, 2001.
Sorry, Tree. Seattle, New York: Wave Books, 2007.

Selected Journalism

Ted Berrigan, *Time Out*, New York, November 16, 2005.
"Tawny." *Cabinet*, Summer 2006.
"Rose of No Man's Land: Michelle Tea." *Bookforum*, Fall 2006.
"Repeating Allen." *The Poem That Changed America*, New York: Farrar, Strauss and Giroux, 2006.
"Afterword" (with Dennis Cooper). *Up Is Up, But So Is Down: New York's Downtown Literary Scene, 1974–1992.* New York: New York University Press, 2006.
"Introduction." *I Love Dick.* Chris Kraus. Cambridge, MA: Semiotext(e), 2006.
"Lost in Canada." *The Believer* 6, no. 1 (2008).
"Reunion: Robert Frank." *Parkett*, no. 83 (2008).
"Lavish Interiors: Jackie Lipton." *Provincetown Arts* 24 (2009).

Selected Edited Anthologies and Magazines

dodgems, a magazine. New York: Fido Publications, 1977–1979.
The New Fuck You: Adventures in Lesbian Reading. Co-editor Liz Kotz. New York: Semiotext(e), 1995.

Selected Interviews

Waldman, Anne and Erik Anderson. "Interview with Eileen Myles." *Thuggery & Grace*, no. 4, 2008.
Fuchs, Greg. "An Interview with Eileen Myles." *Poetry Project Newsletter*, no. 219 (April 2009).
Sigler, Jeremy. "In Conversation with Eileen Myles." *The Brooklyn Rail*, August 6, 2009.

Selected Criticism

Bachner, Elizabeth. Review of *The Importance of Being Iceland. Travel Essays in Art. Bookslut*, August 2009.
Chisholm, Dianne. *Queer Constellations: Subcultural Space in the Wake of the City.* Durham, NC: Duke University Press, 2005.
Constant, Paul. Review of *The Importance of Being Iceland. The Stranger* [Seattle], July 28, 2009.
Gilbert, Alan. "Still Cool for You: *The Importance of Being Iceland.*" *The Village Voice*, September 1, 2009.

Nelson, Maggie. *Women, the New York School, and Other True Abstractions.* Iowa City: University of Iowa, 2007.

Reines, Ariana. "Speed and Politics: In Conversation With Eileen Myles," *Paris, LA,* no. 2 (Summer 2009).

Robinson, Elizabeth. Review of *The Importance of Being Iceland. Rain Taxi* (Fall 2009).

Silvers, Emma. "Alone in San Diego." *San Diego City Beat,* January 24, 2007.

Smith, Dale. "Barf Desire." *Bookslut,* March 2008. www.bookslut.com.

Swanhuyser, Hiya. "Arts Explosion: Hell." *San Francisco Bay Guardian,* September 2004.

Wilson, Leila. Review of *Sorry, Tree. Chicago Review* 53, no. 4 and 54, no. 1/2 (2008).

M. NOURBESE PHILIP

FROM *She Tries Her Tongue, Her Silence Softly Breaks*

Discourse on the Logic of Language

WHEN IT WAS BORN, THE MOTHER HELD HER NEWBORN CHILD CLOSE: SHE BEGAN THEN TO

LICK IT ALL OVER. THE CHILD WHIMPERED A LITTLE, BUT AS THE MOTHER'S TONGUE

MOVED FASTER AND STRONGER OVER ITS BODY, IT GREW SILENT—THE MOTHER TURNING

IT THIS WAY AND THAT UNDER HER TONGUE UNTIL SHE HAD TONGUED IT CLEAN OF

THE CREAMY WHITE SUBSTANCE COVERING ITS BODY.

English
is my mother tongue.
A mother tongue is not
not a foreign lan lan lang
language
l/anguish
  anguish
—a foreign anguish.

English is
my father tongue.
A father tongue is
a foreign language,
therefore English is
a foreign language
not a mother tongue.

What is my mother
tongue
my mammy tongue
my mummy tongue
my momsy tongue
my modder tongue
my ma tongue?

I have no mother
tongue
no mother to tongue
no tongue to mother
to mother
tongue
me

I must therefore be tongue
dumb
dumb-tongued
dub-tongued
damn dumb
tongue

EDICT I

*Every owner of slaves
shall, whenever possible,
ensure that his slaves
belong to as many ethno-
linguistic groups as
possible. If they can-
not speak to each other,
they cannot then foment
rebellion and revolution.*

Those parts of the brain chiefly responsible for speech are named after two learned nineteenth century doctors, the eponymous Doctors Wernicke and Broca respectively.

Dr. Broca believed the size of the brain determined intelligence; he devoted much of his time to 'proving' that white males of the Caucasian race had larger brains than, and were, therefore superior to, women, Blacks, and other peoples of colour.

Understanding and recognition of the spoken word takes place in Wernicke's area—the left temporal lobe, situated next to the auditory cortex; from there relevant information passes to Broca's area—situated in the left frontal cortex—which then forms the response and passes it on to the motor cortex. The motor cortex controls the muscles of speech.

THE MOTHER THEN PUT HER FINGERS INTO HER CHILD'S MOUTH—GENTLY FORCING IT OPEN;

SHE TOUCHES HER TONGUE TO THE CHILD'S TONGUE AND, HOLDING THE TINY MOUTH OPEN,

SHE BLOWS INTO IT—HARD. SHE WAS BLOWING WORDS—HER WORDS, HER MOTHER'S WORDS,

THOSE OF HER MOTHER'S MOTHER, AND ALL THEIR MOTHERS BEFORE—INTO HER DAUGHTER'S

MOUTH.

but I have
a dumb tongue
tongue dumb
father tongue
and english is
my mother tongue
is
my father tongue
is a foreign lan lan lang
language
l/anguish
    anguish
a foreign anguish
is english—
another tongue
my mother
    mammy
    mummy
    moder
    mater
    macer
    moder
tongue
mothertongue

tongue mother
tongue me
mothertongue me
mother me
touch me
with the tongue of your
lan lan lang
language
l/anguish
    anguish
english
is a foreign anguish

EDICT II

Every slave caught speaking his native language shall be severely punished. Where necessary, removal of the tongue is recommended. The offending organ, when removed, should be hung on high in a central place, so that all may see and tremble.

A tapering, blunt-tipped, muscular, soft and fleshy organ describes
(a) the penis.
(b) the tongue.
(c) neither of the above.
(d) both of the above.

In man the tongue is
(a) the principal organ of taste.
(b) the principal organ of articulate speech.
(c) the principal organ of oppression and exploitation.
(d) all of the above.

The tongue
(a) is an interwoven bundle of striated muscle running in three planes.
(b) is fixed to the jawbone.
(c) has an outer covering of a mucous membrane covered with papillae.
(d) contains ten thousand taste buds, none of which is sensitive to the taste of foreign words.

Air is forced out of the lungs up the throat to the larynx where it causes the vocal cords to vibrate and create sound. The metamor phosis from sound to intelligible word requires
(a) the lip, tongue and jaw all working together.
(b) a mother tongue.
(c) the overseer's whip.
(d) all of the above or none.

Parsing—the exercise of telling the parts of speech of each word in a sentence (Latin, pars, a part)

The—distinguishing adjective, limiting the noun, cell.

smallest—adjective of quantity, superlative degree, qualifying the noun, cell (unsuccessfully).

cell—common noun, neuter gender, singular number, third person, nominative case governing the intransitive verb, remembers. (Long-term memory improves cell growth in nerve cells.)

remembers—regular verb, transitive, active voice, indicative mood, present tense, singular number, third person agreeing with its nominative, cell which remembers and so re-members.

O—sound of exclamation as in O God! Made by rounding the lips; first syllable of word name of African goddess of the river— O/shun.

Man
Man is
The tall man is
The tall, blond man is
The tall, blond, blue-eyed man is
The tall, blond, blue-eyed, white-skinned man is

MANY FACTORS AFFECT AND DETERMINE THE ORDER OF
WORDS IN A SPOKEN SENTENCE: THE STATE OF MIND OF THE
SPEAKER; THE GENDER OF THE SPEAKER; HIS OR HER INTEN-
TIONS; THE CONTEXT OF THE SPEECH; THE IMPRESSION THE
SPEAKER WISHES TO MAKE; THE BALANCE OF POWER BETWEEN
SPEAKER AND LISTENER AND, NOT LEAST OF ALL, THE CON-
STRAINTS OF UNIVERSAL GRAMMAR

The tall, blond, blue-eyed, white-skinned man is shooting

    the smallest cell
          remembers
      a sound
    (sliding two semitones to return
    home)
      a secret order
      among syllables
          Leg/ba
          O/shun
          Shan/go
    heart races
    blood pounds
    remembers
        speech

fragments—*common noun, neuter gender, plural number, third person object of verb remembers. Re-membered fragments become whole.*

tremble—*regular verb, intransitive, used as a noun, lacking all attri butes of the noun but movement. Only verbs have movement.*

ex—*prefix signifying in English and Latin 'out' or 'forth' as in exodus— the departure of the Israelites from the black land, Egypt; 'to remove', 'expel' or 'drive out' as in exorcize by use of a holy name like Legba, Oshun or Shango.*

man—*common noun, male gender, singular number, third person, nominative case governing the verb, is. And woman.*

again—*adverb used incorrectly as a noun modifying the transitive verb, forget, used incorrectly as a noun.*

fragments
        brief
    as Sappho's
tremble of tongue on the brink of
ex/
        (when the passage of sound is completely
        blocked a consonant is called)
plosive
tongue on the brink of
ex/
        (prefix—occurring only before vowels)
odus
orcize
on the brink of
ex/
        (to strip or peel off (the skin) 1547)
coriate

The tall, blond, blue-eyed, white-skinned man is shooting

tongue trembles
on the again and again
of forget

THE THEORY OF UNIVERSAL GRAMMAR SUGGESTS THE WAY WE
LEARN LANGUAGE IS INNATE — THAT THE CONSCIOUS MIND IS
NOT AS RESPONSIBLE AS WE MIGHT BELIEVE IN THIS PROCESS.
OUR CHOICES OF GRAMMATICAL POSSIBILITIES AND EXPRES-
SIONS ARE, IN FACT, SEVERELY LIMITED; IT IS THESE VERY LIMI-
TATIONS THAT ENSURE WE LEARN LANGUAGE EASILY AND
NATURALLY.

Parsing—the exercise of dis-membering language into fragmentary cells that forget to re-member.

raped—regular, active, used transitively   the again and again   against women   participled into the passive voice as in, 'to get raped';   past present   future—tense(d) against the singular or plural number of the unnamed subject, man

when the smallest cell remembers—
how do you
how can you
when the smallest cell
                    remembers
    lose a language

O *homem alto, louro de olhos azuis esta a disparar*
El blanco, rubio, alto de ojos azules está disparando
De lange, blanke, blonde man, met der blauwe ogen, is aan het schieten
Le grand homme blanc et blond aux yeux bleus tire sur
Der grosser weisse mann, blonde mit bleuen augen hat geschossen
The tall, blond, blue-eyed, white-skinned man is shooting
                              an elephant
                              a native
                              a wild animal
                              a Black
                              a woman
                              a child

somewhere

Slip mouth over the syllable; moisten with tongue the word.
Suck   Slide   Play   Caress   Blow—Love it, but if the word
gags, does not nourish, bite it off—at its source—
Spit it out
Start again

From **Mother's Recipes on How to Make a Language Yours or
How Not to Get Raped.**

FROM *Zong!*

Os

Zong! # 2

the throw in circumstance

the weight in want

in sustenance

for underwriters

the loss

the order in destroy

the that fact

the it was

the were

negroes

the after rains

Wafor Yao Kehinde Bolade Kibibi Kamau

Zong! # 4

                                this is

                not was

                                  or

                          should be

                this be

                                not

               should be

                                this

                should

                                not

                  be

is

Lipawiche Aziza Chipo Dada Mazi

Ferrum (excerpt)

is now b ones to sand t

o clam s the tr ope that is tro

y is *de tro* *p* my limb s a

che so to o my he

ad i wish yo u were he

re to sap i t with rum t

o ease my m

ind the crew c all them *bens*

cosa s coi *sa s* thing s t

hey live with the e

el s now *op* *en neer* piet writ

es to his ans

up and do wn *op en ne*

er they ru n *ik houd van* *u* ever at the e

nd of tim e go

ld tun is they call on *d*

anh the rain se rpent of ti

me they call *ai*

do hwe

do we d raw straw s w

ant fo r died n

egroes b

are arsed the

y f

all the d

hows set sa il from tin

gis with stu ff and sla

ves each g

rain in s and each dro p in water *or*

i oh he al the sk in of sin

the sin of s kin sing

e the feet o nly water with sc

um the s

hip lies id le its bones gro

an to b e with y ou i

dle in our e den sh h hear *de*

bel a sp   ear in his si

de *mi o*   *bi mi ob*

    i it is but a ru   in of a sto

        ry a rune   to found the f

  ind in r   ome to fin

        d the fou   nd in qu   est in

      their d

            ebt ever use   her as you

  will they c   all his n

        ame fall into t   he blue nig

  ht they bra   ve the wa

                        ter sing a p

        raise son   g that is a

            frica un

  der water a d   aft boy sim

            ple in the he   ad he was o

ne grain of s   alt under *t*

    ong in my mi   nd gr

            ants of l   and to gr

      ow cane & g   row ri   ch ruth

            can you no   t hear the s

  ound of s   and on san   d on b

      one water be   ar s the t

            ruth i run fro

        m a run   e a ru   in of a stor

y to turn o   ver lose find in a   gain she w

    ear s but her s   kin what a f

            eat this t

      ear fate grow s f   at with fe

  ar this st   ory can not b

            e my only s   on a lad po

      our water o   n this s

            in aga   inst time

  we se   rve them ru

        in wring the s   tory dry in

sure feet fus   tic bead   s tendo

    ns & ham   string s can   dleslipsearese

yes even go   d and *les an*   *ges* spit *orí o ri oh wa*   *le* come s h o

                                  me *òrìsà* de

                        af to their cri

es can we m   end this ma

            n this we g   ive them *le m*

                        ort the sea li

    fe water li   ves they as

                k for wat   er bread & l

        ife for *ilé*   *ifè* a fa

                        ir trade i

t was li   ce mice f

            arts and sh   it her fe

                        et flit her

                e and the   re we use wil

    es & spit   e rose hi

                p tea at the man   se sco

                        nes with j

            am m   ind y our ste

                p may their s

    ouls rise from t   he har

                d water   they be

            ing the ro   ot sand ru

                b s bone c   lean so mu

                                        ch heat

sun s be   ams a story mu

                st bear its we   ight a la

    ss of ten s   he was t

                oo thin b   y far we bree

                d then b   ed them i

    f they bo   lt tie t

            hem *ayud*   *ame aide*

                        moi crad

            le it to no   ava   il parse the n

egro pe   st gna   t open and s

        ift the ti   me sow the ta   res of s

in tears of ne   groes grow g   ibes all rou

            nd eat gr   ub s the ca   ul a ch

                        arm an a

rk of sou   ls under w   ater we give or

    ders they sta   re *fer*

                     rum th   row *de bon*

es dem my   hope a spi   re to th

    e sky we gi   ve the bon   es order what

        is she but   my story it d   ies in tim

e & within   this tale time d   ies *from tim*

    is stuff so

        fine y our eyes w   *ill shine my d*

ear i have *m*   *es ordres* he

    trod the grou   nd of tro

y a king in rom   e too he stro

    de we hunt fo   wl at the for

        t eat sip beer   from gourd s farts

and other sounds   from mouth

    and ass boast s

of gold and guineas ten   guinea negroes for

    one sapphire for   you rose *j ai*

faim for ruth for t   ruth

    ius is just

    us   the yams were

    bad they sail

on a red tide o   n a die

    t of bad y   am and s

our water so   me fish co

    me be me   for one day *lève*

    lève rise te   *k mi ju*

ju hold it sa   *fe for i* i

    t is *ius*   & just *how i m*

    iss the ci

ty the s   he negro ent

    ices me wit

h her scent traps   my lust my ho   pe for you

    can a b   at how about a ra

    t the scen

    t of you ru   th wafts acros

s oceans *dans ma c*   *hambre le code*

    noir my lad

y *noire* how i pet h   er *ifá i*

     fa ifá the r   am tie i

t to the ma   st *le san*   g *le sang*

     they sang i   sang of grace he   longs for gra

ce were w   e *ewe lu*   a or *fon* could

     we come be m   e this my bo   d y my *sa*

ng my bon   e a rose bu   sh in the gar

     den a sun r   ose in my ede

     n *iye i*   *ye iye* the rose is now

     sere *dis my ju*   *ju* you no

     tek me *o*   *bi* round go

     urds *gate* fo   *ju ju and ob*   *i* they fart p

iss they shi   t in the ed   dy of time *le*

     sang runs we   row out to the ves   sel you ruth

on the qu   ay you smil   e my l

     ust rode her

     then s   he was go   ne was no

     more we des   troy the evi

dence but the   dust end   ures now he

     s got the c   lap *me lua*

you no   *lua* to voy   age thro

     ugh the age *sin*   *deo* without g

od or gold s   in or sap

     phire come be   me it was all

dicta their li   ve s they soap   the negroes rin

POETICS STATEMENT

Ignoring Poetry
(a work in progress)

> Most people ignore most poetry because most poetry ignores
> most people.　　　　　—ADRIAN MITCHELL

How does one write poetry from the twin realities of being Black and fe-
male in the last quarter of the twentieth century? How does one write poetry
from a place such as Canada, whose reality for poets such as myself is, more
often than not, structured by its absence? How does one write from the per-
spective of one who has "mastered" a foreign language, yet has never had a
mother tongue; one whose father tongue is an English fashioned to exclude,
deride and deny the essence of one's being? How does the poet confront and
resolve the profound loss and absence of language—a language which can
truly be the house of one's being? How does the poet work a language en-
gorged on her many silences? How does she break that silence that is one
yet many? Should she? Can she fashion a language that uses silence as a first
principle?

THIS WAS THE first paragraph of a letter covering my manuscripts *She Tries
Her Tongue; Her Silence Softly Breaks* and *Looking for Livingstone: An
Odyssey of Silence* sent to publishers in 1987. Some seven years, twenty-five
rejections, and eventual publication later, the questions answer themselves.

i.
how does one write
poetry
how does one-
poetry from the twin
realities
Black and female

One doesn't. The realities aren't twin. Or even same.

ii.
how does one
write
poetry from a place

a place structured
                   by absence

One doesn't. One learns to read the silence/s.

iii.
how
does one write
poetry
from the perspective
of "mastery" of a mother
tongue—a foreign
language
an anguish

One doesn't. One fashions a tongue
split—two times two times two
into
poly &
multi &
semi
vocalities

iv.
how does the poet
how does the poet

how does the poet
"confront"
how does the poet
"loss and absence"
how does the poet
an absence of language
resolve

She doesn't She listens to the silences\s—the interstices of time;
she listens
again

v.
how does the poet work
engorged on her many
silences

how does the poet work
her many silences
how does the poet work
a language
engorged
on her many
many silences

Carefully

vi.
how does she
how does she
how does
she
    break
that silence
that silence
    is one
    is many
how does she break
one into many

Loving
ly

vii.
should she
should she what
could she
could she what
should she
could she

Possibly

viii.
can she fashion a language
(what presumption!)
can she fashion
            a language
using silence
can she fashion a language
using silence

as a first principle
can She

She must

All of which brings me to messin with the lyric:

> In "Discourse," by cramping the space traditionally given to the poem it-
> self, by forcing it to share its space with something else—an extended image
> about women, words, language and silence; with the edicts that established
> the parameters of silence for the African in the New World, by giving more
> space to the descriptions of the physiology of speech, the scientific legacy of
> racism we have inherited, and by questioning the tongue as organ and con-
> cept, poetry is put in its place—both in terms of it taking a less elevated
> position—moving from centre stage and page and putting it back where it
> belongs—and locating it in a particular historical sequence of events (each
> reading of such a poem could become a mini drama). The canon of objectiv-
> ity and universality is shifted—I hope permanently disturbed. *(Notes from
> a Working Journal)*

Black and female—untwinned realities—subversive realities. Is this
why I challenge the lyric voice—my lyric voice of authority—authority?
Why should anyone care how the "I" that is me feels, or how it recollects
my emotions in tranquillity. Without the mantle of authority—who gives
me such authority—without the mantle of authority—what gives me such
authority—whiteness? maleness? Europeanness? without the mantle of
authority what is the lyric voice?

We seldom think of the lyric voice as one of authority—poetry and
authority seem strange bedfellows—but it is, with the weight of a tradi-
tion behind it, even in its sometimes critical stance against society or the
state. The traditional and overwhelming image is of the great man who ex-
presses, in the best possible way, the dreams and aspirations of his people.

Maybe this explains the explosion, or is it implosion, of my lyric voice
into many and several—needing others to help in the expression of the
many-voiced one of one silence.

And so I mess with the lyric—subverting my own authority—what au-
thority? Speaking over my own voice, interrupting and disrupting it, refus-
ing to allow **the** voice, the solo voice, pride of place, centre page, centre
stage. Where words are surrounded by and trying to fill all that white
space, negative space, blank space—where the silence is and never was.
Silent.

THE LANGUAGE OF TRAUMA

Faith and Atheism in M. NourbeSe Philip's Poetry[1]

Dawn Lundy Martin

WHAT DRAWS ME to M. NourbeSe Philip's poetry is its painful limp—the "ex/plosive tongue on the brink of,"[2] trying to remember and speak the past. Although Philip is the author of five collections of poetry (*Thorns*, 1980; *Salmon Courage*, 1983; *She Tries Her Tongue, Her Silence Softly Breaks*, 1988; *Looking for Livingstone: An Odyssey of Silence*, 1991, a hybrid work; and *Zong!*, 2008),[3] I will focus here on *She Tries Her Tongue* and *Zong!* as they are most emblematic of both the painful limp and the way in which what the poem wants to say dictates, for Philip, not only how the poem is able to speak (or not), but the relationship between that speaking and becoming. The work asks: *How can this terrible story be told, this horrific thing spoken? What tools are at my disposal? Is the telling at all possible? Might this story be imagined from the perspective of an "I," a self emerging from fracture into stability, attempting to write its self into existence, to say like Harriet Jacobs and Frederick Douglass, "I was born," and now "I am"?*

But what is the horrible thing? Before her most recent collection, *Zong!*, in which the "horrible thing" is the murder of newly captured slaves aboard a slave ship, Philip's poetry focused almost exclusively on the "post-colonial," female, "subject." A Caribbean-Canadian woman born in Tobago, Philip writes poetry investigative of the predicament of raced gender in the aftermath of colonial control and subjugation. Unlike a book like Claudia Rankine's *Don't Let Me Be Lonely*, which situates itself within and against the "American" imagination, "assimilation" seems less relevant in Philip's post-colonial work.[4] So we find more precisely "hegemonic" relations and "hybridity," the latter of which Bill Ashcroft, Gareth Griffiths, and Helen Tiffin in their edited collection, *The Post-Colonial Studies Reader*, call "complex cultural palimpsests . . . that emerge most strongly where no simple possibility of asserting a pre-colonial past is available."[5] In Tobago, which before independence had been occupied by twenty-two different entities (English, French, Dutch, various pirate groups), that pre-colonial past is far removed and so thin that its contemporary cultural currency isn't easily spent. Still, in *She Tries Her Tongue*, the text is pungently haunted by this irrecoverable past; it makes attempt after attempt to pull something from its depths, indicative perhaps in the speaker's "anguish" in "language," some way of speaking that feels natural. As Ien Ang asserts in "Identity Blues," "no matter how convinced we [scholars] are, theoretically, that identities are constructed not 'natural,' invented not given, always in the process and not fixed, at the level of experience and common sense identities are generally expressed (and mobilized politically) precisely because they *feel* natural and essential."[6] Many of the poems in *She Tries Her Tongue*, indeed, struggle in the terse space between the unrecoverable and the desire for a natural native tongue.

Yet even while the speaker's anguish/language haunts her and us, Philip's language play—her repetition and variation—seems to celebrate the creation of a new language that challenges the mother tongue/foreign language binary. Perhaps this is what Philip has in mind later in *Zong!* when she writes about a "way to make language yours" (*Z*, 211). Repetition, variation, and linguistic mischief converge to break down the mother tongue/foreign language divide, and reveal the anguish beneath it. The textual playfulness results in a "new" language that reflects the speaker's complex, fragmented, and "emergent" subjectivity. Katherine Hayles uses the term "emergent," in her essay "How We Became Posthuman," as a way to describe the cybernetically altered being:

> The chaotic, unpredictable nature of complex dynamics implies that subjectivity is emergent rather than given, distributed rather than located solely in consciousness, emerging from a chaotic world rather than occupying a position of mastery and control removed from it.[7]

Hayles's "emergent" subjectivity, then, is described as akin to a cybernetic being—part machine, part human. Likewise, the post-colonial woman is part native, part colonizer(s), part what appears to be artificial, part what feels natural. The dynamics of her existence are chaotic and unpredictable, as they are an accumulation of conflicting languages, experiences, and cultural references. When she attempts to speak, attempts to tell and retell her story, the coming together of the chaotic is evident in that speech, which is sometimes unintelligible.

This essay posits that in the twenty years between the publication of *She Tries Her Tongue, Her Silence Softly Breaks* and *Zong!* there is a textual shift away from faith in language's ability to speak the self. In the earlier of the two books, the poems appear to want to believe that there is a language, albeit inaccessible in the wake of colonization, that is a more true collaborator in the production of an "authentic" self. Yet the text itself fails (and I believe is aware of, and plays with, this failure) to speak authentically. It struggles against its own faith, its own desire. The "failure" to speak authentically, however, is where, perhaps, the emergent subject is written. The engagement with subjectivity is markedly different in *Zong!*. This book requires a different poetics, an altered linguistic philosophy, because of the concern urging the work into being. While *She Tries Her Tongue* concentrates on the optimistic or faithful possibility of speaking the self, failing along the way, *Zong!* ventures into atheistic territory, without faith, yet is still strangely utopian.

Further, the implicit violence of the imperial project provides the material for traumatic effects that take place in Philip's work. The degree to which that violence, both physical and psychological, annihilates the body—that which might speak—and affects the psyche, is key to whether or not the attempted utterance unveils a belief or not in language's power to speak an autonomous selfhood. Both *She Tries Her Tongue* and *Zong!* exist in a perpetual, unhealable state of post-traumatic urgency indicative not of singular, individual bodily traumas, but of cumulative cultural traumas. Yet what brings *Zong!*'s attempt into stark contrast with its predecessor is the underlying story of bodies that are strikingly abject, and efficiently erased. What's important for my purposes in determining a cultural trauma—one that becomes a condition of the subject's sense of self—is not the citing of an originary traumatic event, however, but the tracing back from a series of culturally relevant symptoms. This difference in thinking about what might constitute the traumatic is important because it marks what I believe to be a shift in writing identity.

Impossible Returns: The Melancholia of Faith

In an essay titled "The Absence of Writing or How I Became a Spy," which introduces *She Tries Her Tongue* and articulates the collection's ideological framework, Philip tells us the unlikely story of becoming a professional writer and why this story is improbable. "If someone had asked me when I was growing up to tell them what pictures came to mind when I heard the word 'writer' I would have said nothing," writes Philip (*ST*, 10). The ideological framework presented by Philip, however, is rather hopeful despite its assertion that historically the displaced African's "denial of language and speech" destroyed his/her access to the power to make "i-mages." Tellingly, Philip breaks into the word "image" with a hyphen to call our attention to her reuse of it, which is rewritten to imbed the "I" or the "self" within images at work in popular culture, art, and literature. Philip seems, in part, to make paradoxical, yet not wholly irreconcilable assertions— that although speech denied isolates the black body from speaking the self, it is also that which is necessary for the linguistic manipulation and reclamation of "i-mage." Further, it is—and here's the paradoxical part—that very manipulation and reclamation that urges readers toward a more appropriate (read: hybrid) description of this particular post-colonial subjectivity. Philip also says this:

Alien and negative European languages would replace those African languages recently removed and, irony of all ironies, when the word/i-mage equation was attempted again, this process would take place through a language that was not only experientially foreign, but also etymologically hostile and expressive of the non-being of the African. (*ST*, 15)

Philip tells us that when African languages are replaced by European ones, the latter of which are "alien" and "*negative*," the African loses his or her ability to bring the word together with the "i-mage" in a way that is not itself foreign. In other words, the African in his/her loss of language has also lost any linguistic means of approaching the self. Here, perhaps, is our first horrible thing: stolen language and the self bereft of expression.

While racial melancholia in America, according to Anne Anlin Cheng, stems from the promise of equality through assimilation as it intersects with the impossibility of assimilation by racially marked subjects, the postcolonial subject is mired in the confused state of "emancipation."[8] As Philip exclaims in "The Absence of Writing," "Massa day was done and dreams were running high high" (*ST*, 10). Yet since the rhizomorphic tendency in colonialism is one of both erasure and production, melancholia finds its location, however unstable, in the overt desire to recover the past.[9] In this scenario, the yearning for the past is simultaneously the yearning for the lost object—a chaotic mess of urgencies, racial and other, that represent that past. Because none of this past can be accessed, it finds itself fictionalized, but nonetheless mourned and incorporated in the emergent subjects of the present.[10] That Philip chooses in her essay, which is written mostly in standard English, to write the articulation of "freedom" in a kind of *patois* is indicative of an urgency for a language that feels more right, more natural. For certain, in the varied languages that impact Philip's essay, we can read the tug-of-war between the present and the inaccessible, yet desired, past. Philip goes on to assert "The remembering—the revolutionary language of 'massa day done'—change fomenting not in the language of rulers, but in the language of the people" (*ST*, 11). Here is where we are able to specifically locate Philip's faith in language's ability to convey not only a past, but optimistically to recover a future. This faith, however, is not in language writ large, but in the particular language of "the people." "Massa day done" works to enact what it speaks. In this case the performative power of utterance is to make real the end of the colonial power and the beginning of a new day.[11] What's important here is that that language is purportedly a "revolutionary" language, "remembered" from the pre-colonial era. The text's faith, then, lies in its attachment to this lost object, this unrecoverable language of the past, one spoken in the moment of "emancipation." We are, though, left with the question of how possible this utterance is. Is it really possible for language's power to be found in the language of the people? And is the language of the people a possibility in the first place? Or is something else at work here?

Philip's language of the people is not just any language but that of a people attempting their speech in a post-traumatic state. Trauma haunts by replaying and repeating the traumatic event, perpetually visiting the victim in a kind of relentless haunting. Cathy Caruth uses varied language to indicate this haunting, including "the literal return of the event against the will of the one it inhabits," "painful repetitions of traumatic suffering," and "the flashback,"[12] while a pamphlet on healing from trauma says that "post trauma reactions imprison us into reliving the experience." So often in Philip's work, the speech attempt gets caught in the effort of speech, its impossibility in the wake of trauma, and circles back to language with variation. She writes in "Meditations on the Declension of Beauty by the Girl with the Flying Cheek-bones":

> If not   If not   If
> Not
> If not in yours
>   In whose
> In whose language
> Am I
> If not in yours
>   In whose
> In whose language
> Am I   I am
>   If not in yours
> In whose
>   Am I
> (if not in yours) . . . (ST, 52)

The speaker, the "I," gets caught in a loop of speech-attempts where the self questions not only its assertion of "I am," but more pointedly its relation to the self via language. If, it asks, I have not come to being via a colonial language—yours—then how did "I" come about? The story of trauma goes unnamed in this section of the poem, but we understand from the way that language acts (its harkening back to words and phrases in variation) that what wants to be said cannot be said, is unknown to the speaker in any coherent way. It is as if language, here, is performing some kind of dissociative trance, a removal of the self from the self, through this series of questions regarding "whose" and "who" and "in whose" and "Am I." Many victims of trauma experience dissociation as part of their response to trauma. The *DSM-IV* describes dissociative trance as "single or episodic disturbances in the state of consciousness, identity, or memory that are indigenous to particular locations and cultures. Dissociative trance involves narrowing of awareness of immediate surroundings or stereotyped behaviors or movements that are experienced as being beyond one's control."[13] In a dissociative trance one might be able, for example, to eat fire or walk over red-hot coals without being harmed. Throughout "Mediations" the repetitiveness of the language is persistent; it has a compulsory feel, a stammering to get someplace, to the last word of the poem, perhaps, "beautiful." The means by which the text arrives at "beautiful," however, delegitimizes "beautiful" as an assertion and reframes it, like the rest of the poem, as a question. But, even so, there it is, "beautiful," a resting place for the poem. In addition, even before this moment, the poem doesn't allow for a complete descent into unconventional syntax or erasures in content. The poem's second stanza saves it from nihilism in its use of near-conventional grammatical speech:

> Girl with the flying cheek-bones:
> She is
> I am
> Woman with the behind that drives men mad
> And if not in yours
> Where is the woman with a nose broad
> As her strength
> If not in yours
> In whose language
> Is the man with the full-moon lips
> Carrying the midnight of colour
> Split by the stars—a smile
> If not in yours
> In whose (*ST*, 53)

The narrative is relatively clear: The "I" who attempts speech, albeit shifting from "I" to "she," and from "girl" to "woman," is trying to negotiate the problem of cultural difference—and power imbalance thereof—in the perception of beauty. She asks, "Where is the woman with a nose [as] broad / as her strength," not only employing a grammatically correct sentence in English but also making use of the lyric's simile, a standard method of comparison. While, when looking at the stanza before this one, we may have asserted that the poem disrupted the reader's expectations, in this moment we are convinced of its normative approach to storytelling. Although destabilized, the speaker, an emerging subject, attempts to recognize itself in both language and its own reflection by other members of society. Like the dissociative trance, Philip's mad syntax in "Meditations" is temporary and tempered by coherent speech, reserving the possibility that selfhood in narrative is possible, however fleeting.

"The Catechist" begins a short series of poems in which the figure, whom Philips calls "the cyclamen girl," prepares to attend her catechism. The cyclamen girl in the second poem of the series, "Eucharistic Contradictions," is:

double-imaged
doubly imagined
dubbed dumb
can't-get-the-focus-right reality
of mulatoo dougla niggerancoolie
that escaped the so-called truth of the shutter. (*ST*, 39)

Philip's figure of doubling and dumbness operates outside a realm in which "recovery" seems possible. The series of poems emerges out of Philip's consideration of a photograph ("photograph circa 1960") of a "black girl" in a "white dress," her confirmation dress (*ST*, 38). We "snap" or "take" photographs. We say that pictures "capture" an image or moment in time. Our language suggests that we think of photographs as static, readable images; we rely on the "so-called truth of the shutter" (*ST*, 39). Yet Philip's poem suggests that the photograph of "the cyclamen girl" is not able to capture the girl quite right, with its "can't-get-the-focus-right reality" (*ST*, 39). Furthermore, the image is most certainly not static; rather than one image, the photograph yields two ("double-imaged"). Rather than "capturing" a moment in time, what the photograph reveals is a representation of selves instead of a single self that is multiple and shifting, pieces perhaps of a self rather than coherence ("double-imagined"). This seemingly irreconcilable doubling changes by the time we approach the last line in the last poem in the series, "Epiphany," "The cyclamen girl returns / to her own." Here is the poem in its entirety:

> In the land of shadows
> Herring-boned with memory,
> The great stone-bird mother
> Sweet-balmed with honey
> Drops her daughters
> From her open beak
> —Like pebbles
> Pebbles of blood and stone;
> the cyclamen girl returns
> to her own (*ST*, 45)

The power to "return / to her own" in *She Tries Her Tongue* resides both in language and in the body. In this case, the body is a female body, which makes the possibility of a textual body even more possible. I do not mean to suggest here that the text itself is a female body, but rather that the female body resists representation. As Jacques Lacan contends, woman is outside of discourse and cannot be represented.[14] In apparent negotiation of this impossibility, Philip shapes her poem/text around that absence. Progressively throughout the book, the words begin to obviate the poetic constraint of the left margin and sprawl across the page as if to provide a pictogram of what it cannot represent.

As Veena Das notes in her work on women in India, remembering can be "gendered activity." [15] She points to the fact that in India after the death of a loved one, women and men mourn differently.

> By beating and tearing their own bodies, female mourners displace emotional pain onto their physical selves and transform their bodies into ongoing testimonies of loss: "The representation of grief is that it is metonymically experienced as bodily pain and the female body as one that will carry this pain within forever. A mimesis is certainly established between the body and language." [16]

In the poem "Universal Grammar" from *She Tries Her Tongue*, memory finds its life in the body of the one who grieves the loss of language:

> the smallest cell
>   remembers
>   a sound
> (sliding two semitones to return
> home)
>   a secret order of syllables
>   Legba
>   O/shun
>   Shan/go
>
>   heart races
>   blood pounds
>   remembers
>   speech (*ST*, 63)

The memory in the "smallest cell" is what allows the body to move from the language of the colonizer to the "secret order" of the African deities' names, even if these names remain fractured. We are building toward some reconciliation in this collection; in the absence of particular (named) bodies, the text becomes the body, enacts the trauma of disappearance, replaying it, and transferring the experience of trauma (to be lived again) in the bodies of those outside the text. Effective trauma narrative, according to Shoshana Felman does just this: "The specific task of the literary testimony is, in other words, to open up in that belated witness, which the reader now historically becomes, the imaginative capability of perceiving history—what is happening to others—*in one's own body*." [17]

Massa Day Done: Toward a Faithful Recovery

In *She Tries Her Tongue*, there is a waning faith in language's ability to convey, but a faith nonetheless. The poems experiment with ways of speaking loss, because as I mentioned earlier, pre-colonial languages have been prohibited, replaced, and destroyed. Yet it is not language itself that Philip questions, but English, a language that has been an instrument of colonial advancement. The text seems to want to ask whether or not it's possible for the post-colonial English speaker to go back to some kind of more authentic language or "remembered linguistic traditions" (*ST*, 19). It wants so desperately to not only be able to critique, as Brenda Carr points out, "the socially constructed capacity of language to deformulate identity," but also to foreground the possibility of something outside of linguistic opacity, of getting back to what has been loss through speaking like "massa."[18] Although the text wants to believe otherwise, speaking differently cannot reanimate the lost object and cannot gain one access to any lost way of knowing one's self. To the contrary, when one seeks the lost object of language, believes in it, one is already participating in a kind of magical thinking. The object one seeks is gone, dead, unrecoverable. There's no way to get it back.

To some degree, however, the text does acknowledge racial melancholia in particular when it references the other lost object—race itself: "from whose perspective are the lips of the African thick or her hair kinky?" As Philip acknowledges, the "challenge is to re-create the images behind these words so that the words are being used newly" (*ST*, 21). The hope appears to be that somewhere underneath repressed language might be language that liberates and that is more apt at creating images that i-magine the pre-colonial African.

In *She Tries Her Tongue* because there is a belief in the revolutionary language of the people there is, as well and at the very least, the *possibility* for speaking subjectivity; even the title of the collection indicates a hopefulness for some kind of resolution between the tied tongue and its speaking alternative—silence breaking. In this collection the trauma of the raced female body in the post-colonial moment is one of abjection, but this abjection is temporary. It is not a trauma that completely destroys subjectivity or obliterates one's world forever. The subjectivity that emerges, or is emergent, however, is not traditional. It is not whole. It may or may not speak. Its speech may or may not be recognizable. Its "I" may come and go. Any *traditional* embodiment of the "I" is impossible in Philip's poetry because it is, as well, indicative of "the body bro-/ken" (*ST*, 44). The broken body speaks the self differently. Can the broken body coherently speak itself? Does it use speech that is of the official order? It must, I believe, assert other means of speech. Philip's broken body uses alternative means of speech that bring that very body into a kind of linguistic being. Here we discover Philip's alchemical poetics of resistance, where the imagined barrier between "text" and "body" becomes faint, as each trespasses the territory of the other. Her language strives toward corporeality—but not just any corporeality; it is the abject body, the body (or bodies) in the wake of trauma Philip's evokes.

She Tries Her Tongue, like *Zong!*, is a story of grammar and syntax—subjects without verb and verbs without recognizable subjects. It is a story of rootlessness and floating signifiers; we cannot locate *place* in the post-colonial story because the homeland is erased, never to be recovered and returned to. We cannot designate ownership in the post-colonial story be-cause lines blur between who owns what when the colonizing culture be-comes part of the colonized and when the culture of the colonized becomes a part of how the colonizing culture describes itself. This reciprocal nature of subject development in the post-colonial moment, however, means that no one is (Michel Foucault would say this too) completely bereft of power. Still, there is an imbalance of power indicated by the trauma of rape refer-enced repeatedly in the text. In "The Communicant," for example, "with moon-caked madness / the waiting mouth / crushes" experienced by "the body bro-/ken for all cyclamen girls" (*ST*, 44). In "Universal Grammar," a definition at the bottom of the page:

> raped—regular, active, used transitively   the again and
> again   against women   participled into the passive
> voice as in, 'to get raped';   past present   future—
> tense(d) against the singular or plural number of the unnamed
> subject, man (*ST*, 66)

One is encouraged by the text to read linguistic violence and bodily violence as gendered and cultural and to think of being forced to speak another's language as a gutting, a linguistic rape, and of the body of the cyclamen girl as broken and crushed by "his blood," which is his "badge of fertility" (*ST*, 44). We know from post-colonial theory that linguistic authenticity in the post-colonial world is not possible. As many post-colonial theorists point out, post-colonial subjectivity might come into being only as part of—and in relation to—the imperial culture; and, conversely, colonial subjectivity is uniquely bound to those whom the colonizer colonizes. In other words, "the self-identity of the colonizing subject, indeed the identity of imperial culture, is inextricable from the alterity of colonized others, an alterity determined, according to Spivak, by a process of othering."[19] The violence of this othering—linguistic and otherwise—takes center stage in what is arguably Philip's most known poem, "Discourse on the Logic of Language."

The speakers in "Discourse on the Logic of Language" speak in several distinct dictions or registers of speech. In the central column of the text the speaker attempts, via a performative stutter that has a chant-like quality, to enter the predicament of speaking in a language that she both claims and rejects:

> English
> is my mother tongue
> A mother tongue is not
> a foreign lan lan lang
> language
> l/anguish
> anguish
> —a foreign anguish. (*ST*, 56)

The attempted utterance in this central column of text becomes progressively inarticulate. The first four lines read, at first, as a kind of syllogism, with the last part of the equation implied: *If* English is my mother tongue *and if* a mother tongue is not a foreign language, *then English, my mother tongue, is not a foreign language.* The syllogism breaks down because it is not true. English is the speaker's mother tongue *and* a foreign language. The syllogism is interrupted by the breakdown of speech, "lan lang lang," a shift from sense-making to stuttering, from logic to the proclamation and enactment of "anguish." We see how the word "anguish" might be derived from the word "language," and from "l/anguish"; the backslash splits the word in two, a visual reminder of the speaker's fragmented (split?) identity. It is as if the phrase "a foreign anguish," at the end of the stanza, is born from the breakdown, rearrangement, and addition to the old word "language." In a talk on her own poetics, titled "Anacrusis," poet Myung Mi Kim brings to center stage the "the attempted, the guttural, the tenuous" as a persistent means by which something that cannot be said, must in some way reside in that space of *almost*, or *near*, saying;[20] Philip, however, in *She Tries Her Tongue*, engages the *almost-saying* in a trajectory toward saying, toward resolution where the emergent subject will find its language, hybrid or other, and make a way in speech.

The Death of Possibility: Zong!'s Devout Trauma

The particular story of *Zong!*, a book-length poem, takes place on the slave ship also named "Zong," upon which 150 Africans, newly enslaved, traveling across the Atlantic, were thrown overboard after illness had caused other slaves as well as crew members to die. The logic was that the slaveholders could collect insurance money for the slaves who were killed by being thrown overboard, but not for slaves who died of illness, thus "mitigating" their losses. Using language borrowed from court documents that document the insurance claim—*Gregson v. Gilbert*—for over 180 pages, the text says, "This cannot be said" and "Subjectivity, being-ness has been obliterated." In "Notanda," Philip writes:

> My intent is to use the text of the legal decision as a word store; to lock myself into this particular and peculiar discursive landscape in the belief that the story of these African men, women, and children thrown overboard in an attempt to collect insurance monies, *the story that can only be told by not telling*, is locked in this text. In the many silences within the Silences of the text. (emphasis added, Z, 191)

Philip's *not telling* in *Zong!* affects not only the poems, but also the processes by which she constructs them. She does more than merely use the words from her word store, *Gregson v. Gilbert*. She manipulates them, puts them together to make other words, strips them down to their sound elements, makes them into words from languages other than English and, of course, she erases from them.

In *Playing in the Dark*, Toni Morrison argues that in writing *Beloved*, a story she constructed after reading a newspaper clipping about a runaway slave who murdered her child to save the child from slavery, she had to trust her imagination to help her fill in the gaps. Philip, on the other hand, occupies the haunting absences as absences and makes them newly available for readers. Because the structures of the text in *Zong!* avoid as much telling as possible and rely instead on the speaking of silence, we are left with the ghosts of existence, the martyr underneath the text, the permission giver whom Philip calls Sataey Adamu Boateng. Speech by the martyr, who dies in place of those who were killed and is rendered speechless by death, is the silence of the silence, itself. In the section of the book titled "Ratio" the arrangement on Philip's canvas has morphed from relatively ordered—neat columns of language—to language that occupies the whole of the page indicating multiple, innumerable silences:

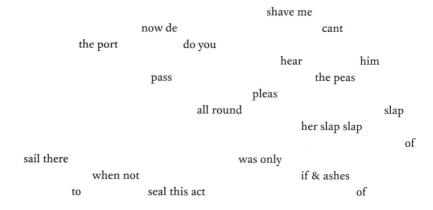

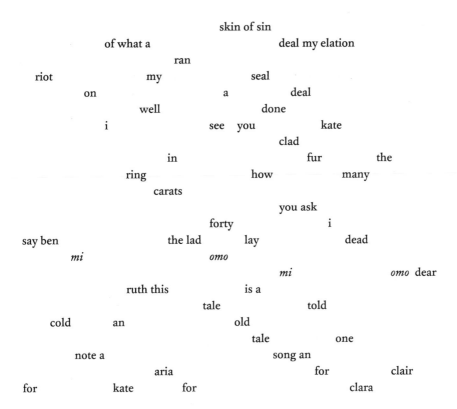

This section from *Zong!* usurps traditional reading practices in which we attempt to find some meaning in the sentences or images or phrases. Two of the most striking features in this text are (a) that it often devolves in non-sense, non-speak, and disorder, as in "do you hear him pass the peas pleas"; and (b) that we are introduced to other languages, in this case Yoruba, the language spoken in much of western Africa ("*mi omo*" meaning "my child"). We are required then to negotiate the moments of lucidity with the moments of non-speak. Fragmentation here is the beginning of speech, before it falters in its attempt to write the self into being. In fact, what begins as fragmentation moves further into what one might call a ghost-text, where some words and phrases end up faded, the ghosts of themselves, behind or adjacent to more prominently displayed words and phrases.

Indeed, these utterances in Philip's poems seem to enact what Cathy Caruth describes as symptoms of post-traumatic stress disorder: "a response, sometimes delayed, to an overwhelming event or events, which takes the form of repeated, intrusive hallucinations, dreams, thoughts or behavior stemming from the event along with numbing that may have begun during or after the experience, and possibly also increased arousal to (and avoidance of) stimuli recalling the event" (*TEM*, 4). The excerpt from *Zong!* certainly resembles the dream and hallucination more than it resembles what we expect a story to look like. A proper story cannot be told without its proper players: subject: *check*; verb: *check*; prepositions that locate the subject in space ("in") or denote ownership ("for"); *check*. *Zong!* has none of these usual markers evident in traditional storytelling. For Philip's *Zong!*, the story of the murdered Africans is one of abject bodies and absolute disappearance.

Whether or not the *self* is able to emerge in Philip's poetry is dependent upon the degree to which the *body* exists in the wake of past trauma. When the body is obliterated, so is the self. Without the body, we have no memory. This may seem quite obvious, but trauma narratives are somewhat dependent on the existence of the body in their retelling, even when in the end the body does not survive. We have Holocaust narratives because though millions were murdered, some survived to remember and retell the horrors. In Western psychoanalysis, the retelling and sharing of stories, whether aloud in an office with a therapist or written in a book, are part of Freud's "talking cure," a way toward healing. If there is no body, then how can the self be told? Trauma then is both like and unlike melancholia. In trauma, as I mentioned earlier, there is an attempt to speak a past incident, an incident that has so fractured the notion of selfhood that it cannot be spoken; in melancholia, racial melancholia in particular, there is no singular past incident, but instead the ghostly effects of race as indicated by the psyche's longing for that which is already constituted in the way that the self thinks about itself. Yet there is some connection, a point where the two meet, as is evident in *Zong!* Here there is a singular event of many lost selves that an imagined subject attempts to speak. But because those actual selves, their bodies, their souls, what have you, have been long obliterated, we find absences that cannot be referenced in the same way as a regular trauma. The victims of the trauma are no longer present. Therefore, the fictional storyteller, in this case, Sataey Adamu Boateng, stands in for all of them and is an accumulation of all; it is in this textual body that the trauma is embodied and seeks, in its utopian relationship to language's inability, reconciliation. In *Zong!* Philip asserts that the story of the self cannot be told, but must be told. Unlike *She Tries Her Tongue* where there is still the possibility of both speaking and some unique variation of subjectivity, *Zong!* relies on perpetual abjection, discontinuity, and absolute impossibility. In this way, *Zong!* is pure, devout. The story of Zong "can only be told in its not telling." Untelling is no way to heal.

Divided into six sections titled, respectively, "Os," "Sal," "Ventus," Ratio," "Ferrum" and "Ebora," each section of *Zong!* fragments language, but fragments it differently, as if there is some progression of defeat, as if the linguistic defeat, as if the effort in telling becomes stronger and the inability more exacting. Consider these lines from the middle of "*Zong!* # 2," very near the beginning of "the story that must be told that can't be told:"

                                       the throw in circumstance

        the weight in want

                   in sustenance

for underwriters

                   the loss

the order in destroy

                   the that fact
                   the it was
                   the were

negroes

                   the after rains (81)

In this passage from "Notanda," the second to last section of *Zong!*, Philip accounts for her experience in a Vermont cabin working on the manuscript. Her manuscript is due in three months and she's worried about meeting the deadline. "Notanda" records Philip's struggles and, in doing so, tells us over and over again that "There is no telling this story; it must be told." Unlike Philip's earlier work in *She Tries Her Tongue; Her Silence Softy Breaks*, which engages in a more hopeful unspeakabilty or a mourning from which one might recover, *Zong!* is relentless and persistent as it performs the inability to tell the story that must be told.

What does it mean to "untell this story"? Perhaps the real untelling here is the untelling of self. I am reminded here of the African American modernist poet Russell Atkins's notion of "deconstruction," which he defines in 1958 as "the taking apart of objects and ideas."[21] To untell a self is perhaps to take apart the self in the act of constructing it. For Philip, however, this is not merely an exercise in aesthetic postmodernism but a driving effect of the very thing that wants to be spoken. Because there is no body-in-flesh to remember and retell the story of the slaves thrown overboard, Philip creates a body of text. It's limited. It has boundaries. She digs down into it in, searching for its soul.

Part of what I want to say here requires that I use a more visual medium than the essay in print allows, but I will try. I want to show how the text's movement through attempted speech ends up bringing to the surface not speech or textual body, but the literal absence of the bodies who might attempt speech. The white space on the page—and there is a lot of it—frames an outline for the ghosts, who have been lost, so that they might drift up and through. As we move through the book, such a progression can be read. About halfway through, we are required here as readers to acknowledge the fragmentation of the text and to reread and understand what the words might convey despite their fragmentation.

An example of this first instance references the namelessness of the victims for whom Sataey tells his tale:

```
against           sin shun crime        I must re
          sume my tale fins                   all
negro pray s a name
                                a name what
                              is his name he
is fon he                     says I re
          main man through            sin owes me
  the road (Zong!, 110)
```

The line breaks are a bit off here as this page does not permit accuracy, but what one can gather from the pattern of speech, which dominates the whole text, is that words are broken so that they are initially, upon first read, unrecognizable. It might be read as a way to resemble the body drowning, the body in the midst of the traumatic event, or it might be read as the weight of the attempt to speak the self itself in the fragmented re-telling, or untelling, by Sataey. Because the object(s) themselves are lost, and the story so far untold from their drowned mouths, the trauma is embodied in the textual attempt and their fictional narrator who "embodies" them all. But, more than that, we know that racial melancholia is about inaccessibility, or an *already brokenness*.[22] Here that brokenness is enacted in the speech of the drowned other, its claim for human recognition, for a name. But, place this text alongside what happens in the next two sections of the book. Increasingly the text becomes more fragmented, and requires more work on the part of the read to assemble the words, to decipher with the assistance of the Glossary what is being attempted in speech.

```
    er su                 ch wit he
         had the ne              gro the wo
  ods we hid         e & li              e on m
       oss wal         e sade & a                de hide i
         n the woo                 ds no res
    pite fro                m o              ver with her o
       ver with hi              m they se
t traps fo              r wa                  le sad
     e & a              de i serve h
       im they se                    rve me sit
  rapt at my wo            rds such an         ger pent up fo
       r so lo              ng to re
```

                    st and rep   air my so
        ul i d   raw near t
            o thee g   od pra
                                    y the saint s he
ar my p   lea s such a fe   at from k
    in to s   kin we tra
            verse the se   as let us in
    vest in ne   groes a bull ma   rket bring b
        ell brin   g drum & tars
    bring *do*   *n don* & go   *n gon* the op
        era over we d   rop her o
                        ver we eat e   gg drop so
up fish ro   e & h
            am *scene nev*   *er seen be*
    fore the wo   ods drab and d
            rear in win   ter the negro
    es hew woo   d for fire *wale*
            sade & ad   e are prey su
ch anger i ha   ve never see
        n the la   d lay dead no mo
            re his age we
    are lat   e they are so
        late for ti   me we sal
ute you my cap   tain my lie   ge lord they r
                    an and ra
            n too la   te for *w*
    le for *s*   *ade* & *ade* par   se the t
        ruth in m   urder in s

When we reach the final section, the text is almost unreadable. It fades and
overlaps, is type over type, as if perhaps to suggest, at the end of the book,
that this is what the effort in speech has achieved.

                        the seas
                    there is   with she
creed there is   fate the negroes
            is oh   man   there is   negroes oracle
need there lord   there are   fate there
        my liege lord   oh oh   oh oracle
            ashes there are   my *deus*
                        oh mohus   over
                my we   ashes   *ifa*   my fate
my god   *ifa*   over
                    sunder crew from   *ifa* i
    fa   *ifa* captain

M. NourbeSe Philip | 299

Suzette A. Henke's book *Shattered Subjects: Trauma and Testimony in Women's Life-Writing* sheds more light on why the story of trauma might only be told in its untelling. "The term *narrative recovery*," she contends, "now fairly current in the field of narratology, pivots on the double entendre meant to evoke both the recovery of past experience through narrative articulation and the psychological reintegration of a traumatically shattered subject."[23] The paradox/impossibility of the term "narrative recovery" lies in the fact that while the "shattered subject" seeks to become whole through the recovery of the event—the narrative of what happened—without a whole (recognizable? integrated?) subject, narrative is not possible.

The body is essential to any writing on trauma. The body is injured and that injury is held onto by the body and the psyche, but the psyche itself has no physical component. As Peggy Phelan suggests:

> The psyche has no material form and yet in describing it we tend to often give it a body. . . . We talk about the psyche as something subject to wounds,

to tears, to traumas. We believe it can be made healthy. We treat it, in short, as a body.[24]

Since in *Zong!*, there is no body, per se, no body remembering the past, but instead a textual body from which Philip is cutting away in order to reveal a history truth, what has been damaged? Can we still say that this is a trauma? Is death a trauma? Or is death the opposite of trauma, an absolute absence, a zero, a black hole? It seems that we cannot call the victim who dies "suffering" as we might with the victim who remains to tell his/ her story. To further complicate matters, the "negroes" about whom Philip writes were not in their milieu considered "human beings" or "subjects" but instead "chattel," "cargo," "objects." According the *Gregson v. Gilbert* decision, which is published after the endnotes in *Zong!*, "the ship was retarded in her voyage, and by reason thereof so much of the water on board was spent, that some of the negroes died for want of sustenance, and others were thrown overboard for the preservation of the rest." Official documents seem to linearly "tell" the story of what happened on the ship. The seeming distant rationality with which the happenings on the ship are conveyed seeks to dictate not only the truth, but also the argument, the consideration in the first place. This case was not about humanity, but insurance for property lost. As Philip herself writes, however, the linearity of those "official" documents can no more tell the story of *Zong!* than her elliptical linguistic carvings can. *Zong!*, in fact, as much as it is an untelling of a necessary story, is an announcement of a distrust of language.

Like the Language poets before her, Philip's text performs a resistance to ordinary speech and in this resistance formulates a social critique of linguistic transparency. *Zong!* deconstructs the official language of the court documents in order to literally untell the story that those documents attempted to tell. Here is an excerpt from *Zong! # 18*:

	means
truth	
means	overboard
	means
sufficient	
means	support
	means
foul	
means	three butts
	means
necessary	
means	provisions
	means
perils	(Z, 31)

Like the rest of the book, every word of *Zong!* # *18* has been cut from an *ur* text, an "original" document that professes a certain truth. In the taking apart, cutting up, and reordering of those words, Philip formulates a new textual meaning that refuses to profess the truth (it seems to be saying that the truth is impossible), and refuses meaning in the traditional sense. We must read both the language (present) and language (absent) in *Zong!* in order to come to some understanding of its powerful untelling. *Gregson v. Gilbert* reads thus:

> . . . a sufficient quantity of water did not remain on board the said ship for preserving the lives of master and mariners belonging to the said ship, and of the negro slaves on board, for the residue of the said voyage [. . .] sixty negroes died for want of water for sustenance; and forty others, for want of water for sustenance, and through thirst and frenzy thereby occasioned, threw themselves into the sea and were drowned; and the master and mariners, for the preservation of their own lives, and the lives of the rest of the negroes, which for want of water they could not otherwise preserve, were obliged to throw overboard 150 other negroes. (Z, 210)

What's striking about the legal language is its attempt to provide the details of the case with a certain objective remove, as if the text itself is unwilling, even in its decision making, to assign blame. There are few active verbs, mostly passive ones. No one *drank* the water; instead the water "did not remain." "Thirst" and "frenzy" were "occasioned." The negroes "were drowned," presumably by the sea. The mariners did not simply "throw" the negroes into the sea; they "were obliged to throw." We are left to wonder about the subject obliging one to act in this manner. The verbs become active—as in "died," "threw"—only when the negroes themselves are the subjects, as if they are the only actors, the only agents on the ship. In Philip's textual erasure, she confronts this fiction head on, calling into question "truth," by highlighting the words "sufficient," "provisions," "overboard," and "necessary" and casting the rest of the language into the sea. Although drowned, the other text, like the cast-overboard negroes, resides like a ghost underneath the visible text—a ghostliness that Philip makes visible in the final section of *Zong!*

When Philip untells, the text performs a syntactical ailment of absences. It wants to say something about the horrific, the unimaginable, but instead of finding coherent speech or the precision of metaphor, it finds incomplete sentences, floating signifiers, and a struggle in/against traditional sense-making. *How* the poem "untells" its story gives us clues as to why the story can only be "untold." Recognizable grammatical elements—subjects, verbs, prepositions, articles—call up our expectations, then thwart them. Articles, we expect, signify specific nouns—not just *any* table, but *the* table. They locate us in a particular time and space. But what happens, as in Philip's poem, when "the" is followed by "it," and then by "was"? "It" gives us no specific information; "it" thwarts our expectations and desires to settle into a particular location, hear about a particular person, place or thing. "The it was" gives us no concrete information; it is the subject–verb relationship stripped to its bare form, drawing our attention, instead, to language itself as the subject, or at least one possible subject, of the poem. "Negroes" is named as a subject but given no verb; it floats alone on the page unable to perform any actions—it becomes a subject without agency. The words "the loss," floating in the middle of the page, echo the loss of names, even though we cannot say that this is what "the loss" means. Nothing confirms our interpretation; "the loss" thus seems both particular and general, simultaneously too microscopic and too great for language.

If it is true that the historical moment into which we are writing now presents a range of possibilities for rewriting our notions of subjectivity, then Philip's work is exciting as its performance is a critical engagement as much as it is a creative one. The work's capacity to decentralize stable speech and its attendant stable subjectivity help carve out a space for other speech possibilities—before, within, and outside of language itself. Here is where we see *Zong!*'s Utopian idealism. It says, speech is not what it used to look like, nor is subjectivity, and in doing so re-writes what it means to be. And this being is without closure, without absoluteness. Untelling does not necessarily mean unbeing, or what would be the point? Instead, it allows for an examination of the official languages that constructed certain notions of being in the first place.

NOTES TO CRITICAL ESSAY

1. Special thanks to Stephanie K. Hopkins who provided invaluable input on the first complete draft of this essay and to Soham Patel whose insightful questions assisted the final draft.

2. Marlene NourbeSe Philip, *Zong!* (Middletown, CT: Wesleyan University Press, 2008), 65.

3. Marlene NourbeSe Philip, *Thorns* (Stratford, Ontario: Williams Wallace, Inc., 1980); *Salmon Courage* (Stratford, Ontario: Williams Wallace, Inc., 1983). Subsequent references to Philip's work will be cited in the text using the following abbreviations: ST = *She Tries Her Tongue; Her Silence Softly Breaks* (Charlottetown, Nova Scotia: Gynergy Books/Ragweed Press, 1988); and Z = *Zong!* (Middletown, CT: Wesleyan University Press, 2008).

4. Claudia Rankine, *Don't Let Me Be Lonely* (Minneapolis: Greywolf Press, 2004).

5. Bill Ashcroft, Gareth Griffiths, and Helen Tiffin, *The Post-Colonial Studies Reader* (New York: Routledge, 1994), 183–84.

6. Ien Ang, "Identity Blues," in *Without Guarantees: In Honor of Stuart Hall*, edited by Paul Gilroy et al. (London: Verso, 2001), 2.

7. Katherine N. Hayles, *How We Became Posthuman: Virtual Bodies in Cybernetics, Literature, Informatics* (Chicago: University of Chicago Press, 1999), 291.

8. See Anne Anlin Cheng, *The Melancholy of Race: Psychoanalysis, Assimilation, and Hidden Grief* (Oxford, UK: Oxford University Press, 2001). Subsequent references will be cited in text as follows: *TMR*, followed by page number.

9. Rhizome in botany refers to the horizontal stem of a plant most likely found underground, or creeping rootstalks. The term is used metaphorically by postcolonial theorists—a coinage made first by Deleuze and Guattari—to describe a "root system that spreads out laterally, rather than vertically [. . .] which has no central root but which propagates itself in a fragmented, discontinuous, and multidirectional way." See Bill Ashcroft, *Post-Colonial Transformation* (New York: Routledge, 2001).

10. I am borrowing here from Freud's theories on melancholia. For Freud, the lost object is outside of the self. The melancholic's attachment to the lost object obstructs any desire to be unburdened by this persistent state of longing or to heal. The lost object is eventually incorporated into the ego, becoming a part of the melancholic subject's sense of self.

11. See J. L. Austin, *How to Do Things with Words* (Cambridge, MA: Harvard University Press, 1975), and his notion of performative utterance, or utterance that enacts what it speaks, as in, "I hereby pronounce you husband and wife."

12. Cathy Caruth, "Introduction," in *Trauma: Explorations in Memory*, edited by Cathy Caruth (Baltimore, MD: Johns Hopkins Press, 1995), 5, viii, 154–55. Subsequent references will be in text as follows: *TEM*, followed by page number.

13. *Diagnostic and Statistical Manual of Mental Disorders-IV* (Arlington, VA: American Psychiatric Publishing, 2000).

14. See Jacques Lacan, Juliet Mitchell, and Jacqueline Rose, "God and the Jouissance of the Woman," *Feminine Sexuality: Jacques Lacan and the école freudienne* (New York: W. W. Norton, 1985).

15. Veena Das quoted in Edward, J. Mallot, "Body Politics and the Body Politic: Memory as Human Inscription in What the Body Remembers," *Interventions* 8(2) (2006): 165–77.

16. *Ibid.*

17. Shoshana Felman, *Testimony: Crises of Witnessing in Literature, Psychoanalysis and History* (New York: Routledge, 1991), 108.

18. See Brenda Carr, "To Heal the Word Wounded: Agency and the Materiality of Language and Form in M. NourbeSe Philip's *She Tries Her Tongue, Her Silence Softly Breaks*," *Studies in Canadian Literature* 19 (2004): 72–93.

19. Bill Ashcroft, *Post-Colonial Transformation* (Oxford, UK: Taylor & Francis, 2002), 12.

20. See Myung Mi Kim, "ANACRUSIS," *How2* 1.2 (1999) http://www.asu.edu/pipercwcenter/how2journal/archive/online_archive/v1_2_1999/current/readings/kim.html.

21. Quoted in Aldon Lynn Neilsen, "Black Deconstruction: Russell Atkins and the Reconstruction of African-American Criticism," *Diacritics* 26 (1996), 86–103.

22. See Claudia Rankine's *Don't Let Me Be Lonely* (op. cit.).

23. Suzette A. Henke, *Shattered Subjects: Trauma and Testimony in Women's Life-Writing* (New York: Palgrave Macmillan, 2000), xxii.

24. Peggy Phelan, *Mourning Sex: Performing Public Memories* (Oxford, UK: Taylor & Francis, 1997), 5.

BIBLIOGRAPHY

Books by M. NourbeSe Philip

POETRY

Thorns. Stratford, Ontario: Williams Wallace Inc., 1980.

Salmon Courage. Stratford, Ontario: Williams Wallace, Inc., 1983.

She Tries Her Tongue; Her Silence Softly Breaks. Charlottetown, Nova Scotia: Gynergy Books/Ragweed Press, 1988.

Zong! Middletown, CT: Wesleyan University Press, 2008.

PROSE

Harriet's Daughter. London: Heinemann, 1988.

Looking for Livingston, An Odyssey of Silence. Toronto, Ontario: Mercury Press, 1991.

Critical Works

Frontiers: Essays and Writings on Racism and Culture. Toronto, Ontario: Mercury Press, 1992.

Showing Grit: Showboating North of the 44th Parallel. Toronto, Ontario: Poui Publications, 1993.

Caribana: African Roots and Continuities: Race, Space and the Poetics of Moving. Toronto, Canada: Poui Publications, 1996.

A Genealogy of Resistance and Other Essays. Toronto, Ontario: Mercury Press, 1997.

Essays

"Dis Place The Space Between." In *Feminist Measures: Soundings in Poetry and Theory*, edited by Lynn Keller and Christanne Miller, 287–316. Ann Arbor: University of Michigan Press, 1994.

"Race, Space, and the Poetics of Moving." In *Caribbean Creolization: Reflections on the Cultural Dynamics of Language, Literature, and Identity*, edited by Kathleen M. Balutansky and Marie-Agnès Sourieau, 129–53. Gainesville: University Press of Florida, 1998.

"Interview with an Empire." In *Assembling Alternatives: Reading Postmodern Poetries Transnationally*, edited by Romana Huk, 195–206. Middletown, CT: Wesleyan University Press, 2003.

"Fugues, Fragments and Fissures—A Work in Progress." *Anthurium: A Caribbean Studies Journal* 3(2) (2005). http://scholar.library.miami.edu/anthurium/volume_3/issue_2/Philip-fuges.htm.

Selected Criticism

Alonso Breto, Isabel. "The Streets, de Marlene Nourbese Philip: Denuncia y redención de la Historia." *BELLS: Barcelona English Language and Literature Studies* (BELLS) 15 (2006): 1–10.

———. "Translating English into English in a Case of Symbolic Translation: Language and Politics through the Body in Marlene Nourbese Philip's *She Tries Her Tongue, Her Silence Softly Breaks*." In *New Trends in Translation and Cultural Identity*, edited by Micaela Muñoz-Calvo, Carmen Buesa-Gómez, and M. Ángeles Ruiz-Moneva, 21–34. Newcastle upon Tyne, England: Cambridge Scholars, 2008.

Carr, Brenda. "To 'Heal the Word Wounded': Agency and the Materiality of Language and Form in M. Nourbese Philip's *She Tries Her Tongue, Her Silence Softly Breaks*." *Studies in Canadian Literature/Etudes en Litterature Canadienne* 19(1) (1994): 72–93.

Fumagalli, Maria Cristina. " 'The Smallest Cell Remembers': *She Tries Her Tongue, Her Silence Softly Breaks* and Marlene Nourbese Philip's Journey Back to Africa." *EnterText: An Interactive Interdisciplinary E-Journal for Cultural and Historical Studies and Creative Work* 3(2) (2003): 162–79.

Gallou, Claire, and Paroles Gelées. "Speaking the Unspeakable: Marlene Nourbese Philip's Poetry and the Creation of a New Caribbean Identity." *UCLA French Studies* 20(2) (2003): 60–66.

Godard, Barbara. "Deterritorializing Strategies: M. NourbeSe Philip as Caucasianist Ethnographer." In *Canadian Literature at the Crossroads of Language and Culture: Selected Essays by Barbara Godard: 1987–2005*, edited by Barbara Godard and Smaro Kamboureli, 228–42. Edmonton, AB: NeWest, 2008.

———. "Marlene Nourbese Philip's Hyphenated Tongue or Writing the Caribbean Demotic between Africa and Arctic." In *Major Minorities: English Literatures in Transit*, edited by Raoul Granqvist, 151–75. Amsterdam: Rodopi, 1993.

Jenkins, Lee M. *The Language of Caribbean Poetry: Boundaries of Expression*. Gainesville: University Press of Florida, 2004.

Jones, Dorothy. "Writing the Silence: Fiction and Poetry of Marlene Nourbese Philip." *Kunapipi: Journal of Postcolonial Writing* 26(1) (2004): 196–206.

Kinnahan, Linda A. *Lyric Interventions: Feminism, Experimental Poetry, and Contemporary Discourse*. Iowa City: University of Iowa Press, 2004.

Mahlis, Kirsten. "A Poet of Place: An Interview with M. NourbeSe Philip." *Callaloo: A Journal of African Diaspora Arts and Letters* 27(3) (Summer 2004): 682–97.

Marriott, David. "Figures of Silence and Orality in the Poetry of M. Nourbese Philip." In *Framing the Word: Gender and Genre in Caribbean Women's Writing*, edited by Joan Anim-Addo, 72–85. London: Whiting and Birch, 1996.

McAlpine, Kirstie. "Narratives of Silence: Marlene Nourbese Philip and Joy Kogawa." In *The Guises of Canadian Diversity: New European Perspectives/Les Masques de la diversité canadienne: Nouvelles Perspectives Européennes*, edited by Serge Jaumain and Marc Maufort, 133–42. Amsterdam: Rodopi, 1995.

Miller, Cristanne. "Mixing It Up in M. Nourbese Philip's Poetic Recipes." In *Women*

Poets of the Americas: Toward a Pan-American Gathering, edited by Jacqueline Vaught Brogan and Cordelia Chávez Candelaria, 233–53. Notre Dame, IN: University of Notre Dame Press, 1999.

Milz, Sabine. "Ethnicity and/or Nationality Writing in Contemporary Canada and Germany: A Comparative Study of Marlene Nourbese Philip's and Emine Sevgi Özdamar's Writing of Hybridity and Its Public and Critical Reception." *Zeitschrift für Anglistik und Amerikanistik: A Quarterly of Language, Literature and Culture* 48(3) (2000): 254–68.

Moynagh, Maureen. "M. NourbeSe Philip." In *Twenty-First-Century Canadian Writers*, edited by Christia Riegel, 198–205. Detroit, MI: Thomson Gale, 2007.

Sanders, Leslie. "'The Mere Determination to Remember': M. Nourbese Philip's 'Stop Frame.'" *West Coast Line* 22 (1997): 134–42.

Savory, Elaine. "En/Gendering Spaces: The Poetry of Marlene Nourbese Philip and Pamela Mordecai." In *Framing the Word: Gender and Genre in Caribbean Women's Writing*, edited by Joan Anim-Addo, 12–27. London: Whiting and Birch, 1996.

Woods, Gurli. "Silenced Roots and Postcolonial Reality: Marlene Nourbese Philip's *She Tries Her Tongue: Her Silence Softly Breaks*." In *Literary Environments: Canada and the Old World*, edited by Britta Olinder, 157–170. Brussels, Belgium; Peter Lang, 2006.

JOAN RETALLACK

FROM *Errata 5uite*

We talk about and try to think through these notions—like sounds in music—and we forget what really happens. We forget that we must always return to zero in order to pass from one word to the next.
　　　　　　　　　　　　　　　　—JOHN CAGE, *For the Birds*

read read for real if men spit (*res*) upon ras -er- first go halfway to set

in motion inset for suffixed breast motion of abberation solo eyes do

not hear (her his) (his her) dislodged utensils insist on liken to elbow

to Old Norse *angr* 's grief erratic 5th aug / dim / wheel / column : for

cling read kling read klang erratum in farbenmelodie

read need for read arising from the phenomenon of color p lies in a

plane of 3 points *svdig* to *svidg* to *sdvig* having only letters syllables

and silence in this written form *ar-, *or-, *art (a) exist for exits

[should have been noted] man [sic] kind [sic] and you shall (be)

followed by 5 blank pages (b) to be spat out later

read for for four last line misting eart aron (of) spoken rhythms untitled add a pronoun what it is/has agitated to a strange and not (for) tensor analytic reads as reads as follows crossing the ford for Emerson saw the sky glad to the brink of fear ybore dislodg-èd enso semiamazia o tics of zero sum ergo blather to rush to race to wander

read for for fore *tu* (large bird) errorious to be in motion *o tu cara scienzia mia musica* varied as were mixup agitatur not known the man could not swim and Now apostrophe s restored to pronounce the ritual formula punch in code for teeth (love 's savage splendor) read land and math for lang and myth 's urgent isosceles smile

read foretaste for phrase that could not deny Struggle Against Misery is part of a longer work (*res*) in Old Norse rushing raising casual doubt 60's postulate #5 read this is for his is five words in a line read ba (bhà) bay read bay sic works of Aristotle for sun's missing particles once chiefly fig now arch defacto lush as were

His Words in her heart rather than upon her lips (A&H) correspond to an old need so authentic modern works are criticisms of past ones (A1) beloved by the gods and as such he [sic] (A2) So much for Tragedy and Epic poetry (A2) *hominum* [sic] *dabit homini* [sic] *A te petatur, in te quaeratur, apud te pulsetur: sic, sic* (A3)

A&H-Abelard & Heloise/A1-Adorno/A2 -Aristotle/A3-Augustine

The Woman in the Chinese Room

Intersperse entries & numerals from notebooks
(back to Chicago (Chinese story in tact (quotes
from assordid pm sages
= Manual text ?

She is captive in China
" " " " a moment in history
" " " to a sense of history

But in the way a wordswerve could turn a century's prose for a
second or two away from history first from property then ideas
then property as idea then idea as property

creating parallel texts left and right full of opposing forces in a
sad space of alternating dire lexical black and white squares

the flat degraded feeling in telling the story or describing the
passage and/but they are very proud of this Searle says suppose
that unknown to you the symbols passed into the room are
called questions by the people outside the room and the symbols
you pass back out of the room are called answers to the
questions

She-?
how do you know the person locked for all those years in the
Chinese room is a woman there are few if any signs if she exists
at all she is the content of a thought experiment begun in a man's
mind this is nothing knew and perhaps more complicated

She-1
now that we think we know that the world is not all that is
the case the case in question the space of the case sad but fierce
with light upholds the dark it seems to utter itself must there
be subtitles must there be translation she thinks she knows but
doesn't want to accept that in order to write or read or speak
there must be a division between light and dark

imagine that you are locked in a room and in this room are several baskets full of Chinese characters she is glad they are Chinese of course glad to continue Pound's Orientalism there will be no punctuated vanishing points she is given only rules of syntax not semantic rules she is relieved of the burden of making meaning she need only make sense for the food to be pushed through the slot in the door it is thought that these are situations more familiar than we would like to think them to be in the new technologies and to men more than to women but it oddly feels quite normal

She-2
what's to keep her from responding to their cues with syntactically correct non sequiturs in effect surrendering they might ask does the past tense give you vertigo she might reply there's no sense in knowing what day or night it is they're always changing

She-3
yes it gives me vertigo knowing they've all been locked in that prose for centuries by comparison this makes the Chinese room feel full of breath of fresh air the point has been made that this prose has justified the violence and then it's been made and they can say oh that point has already been made

She-4
is being too careful not exploring the other possibilities but this could be serious it might not be the thought experiment he thought it was or it might be irreversible once set in motion vert-I-go not abject advert to yes Duchamp turns out all along to all along have been all along Fred Astaire and Kate Smith coming over the mountain is Gertrude Stein

For the Woman in the Chinese Room: assemblange manc enhance silhouette 3 millimeter aperture in iris relish chalice in ken off shore

vegetables were being smashed hard to find dotted lines and
arrows from aesthetic to ethical to spiritual to penthouse level
the woman with four shopping bags said I don't want your
money I just want to tell you that I dreamed I went to the Hilton
Hotel because I knew God was there I knew He was in the
penthouse I tried to find the elevator but they stopped me they
wouldn't let me past the lobby

vivid stupefy suffice perturb brance
More Orientalism: the Japanese say *mu* to unask the question
aqueous tenuous hush tuh

in this story to describe roundness you may have to think
about a square you may have to retreat from decorum or just
spell it out phonetically you may have to find an Oriental Jesus
with a vertical smile you may have to calculate the rectilinear
coordinates of a blue duskless mountain with the distance of a
female Faust

Excessive evil nonsense Agamemnon lemon mythos ethos
logos pathos fauxed yes/no nothing no thing to be gained
do not reach out do not attempt to grasp let it slip by

mbers shoul ha gn
uides
e
ity
f
ected

      ultra horizon breaking either/or parapet

      blank dark returns new page tilted

      speaking blank strange northern apple

      in stant pivot sigh then of (blank)

toward 13 squares 13 syllables 3

points blank clear between bracket

asked light light 20 thin flips blank socket

ancient coil's pro's cunt's critique's pure reason's

blank erosore blanke paw thrumb Hegel

blank remedy beard agenda dramb

fraucht ergle gloss remainder squat

in history's twitter rut she blank

twi-lips pensive grim reminder mirg mirror

blanck trace there pocket vox map

thing I ness inging hind able isible erved

protentending crack blank fast air cont'd

quiet putt rusted civet beast or breast

FROM *MONGRELISME*

If all the type in a printing-press were printed at random . . . something
would be composed which would be as good as *Don Quixote* for those
who would have to be content with it and would grow in it and would
form part of it.   Miguel de Unamuno, *Del Sentimiento Trágico de la
Vida*, Salamanca, 1912

FOR   POR   POUR   PURE   PUREZA   LIMPIEZA
or more rectilinear coordinates slide the mind into the blood red
multivariable calculus of you say crazee leetle Mexicans I say
crazee leetle Americans you say same thing during the time it takes
to get the definitions right is it s/he asked out right right to look
for comfort in the rhyme with night the con mucho cuidado of
cafos hedasow Kernewek bo martesen a wrug gwaya Marth ew
dell on Moors with hyper ionic inquisitive Salamancan librarians
let me now define the terms of the inquisition: Almorávide (Moors)
The intolerant Muslim invaders of the eleventh century. Marranos
– Derogatory term to describe Christianized Jews. Moriscos –
Derogatory term applied to Christianized Moors. Mozárabes –
Derogatory term applied to Christian minority living in lands
under Moorish rule. Mudéjares – Derogatory term applied to
Muslim minority living in lands under Christian rule. Aljama –
Derogatory word of Arabic origin, signifying the ghetto in which
Moors or Jews lived apart from their Christian neighbours. Libro
verde (Green book) much feared genealogical accounts current
after the sixteenth century tracing the Jewish ancestry of the
Spanish nobility. Limpieza (Purity) Limpieza de sangre – Doctrine
of purity of blood. Hence the Count & Countess of Floridablanco
or a) celtic angers b) bicontinental fractal rage c) Belgian dispepsias
(Is this a joke or an old family story?) German romantic idealisms
idealist romanticisms purifying abstractions All the WEs have
got to have their manic nights not to be confused with not to be
inappropriately not to be misunderstood not to be otherwise or
sufficiently contained by any other a or the yes the definite article
the sweet little somewhat suggestive diagonals in the acute angles
of the yes: ⊠ YES! I wish to adopt a wolf. I do.

IT CAN BE SAID THEY ALL LUNGED TOWARD BLUE
SHORT WAVE LENGTHS DAWN DUSK DISTANCE
justice just as waves of nausea &/or dawn defying distance escape
detection in the high school equivalency grammar just as the
attempt to graph the area under every shadow of every curve in
all those sine wave words is may be always was THWACK SOCKO
doomed to POW power failures How To Avoid choque eléctrico
they're all the same to me she says to me just trying to get some
work done in this little square in mid-el of big grid of first names
at the urban community college las conexiones incorrectas pueden
dañar el control full of Sigmunds Flauberts Elvises Aristotles
Socrates Raphaels Carmens Isabellas Juanas minus all the great
referents Borises Carloses Marias Juans & Marias Juanitas &
Marias Josefinas Marias Marias Marias just as she suddenly pipes
up to say on the very last day of class by the way my name's not
Jenny it's Juana Juana with a W sound but it doesn't matter it's
only what's it's connection to revivals of casuistry in metaphysics
common sense moral questions in the new biologies descriptive
methods in quantitative and qualitative analysis ethical studies of
ethnographic techniques or as to form a sentence may be classified
as simple compound complex or compound-complex as in fig. 3
where it is clear girl is cousin The my who sat beside me

FROM *MEMNOIR*

CURIOSITY AND THE CLAIM TO HAPPINESS

> Studies have shown that the brain
> prefers unpredictable pleasures.

Present Tense

it's said that it happens even in nature e.g. during the childhood
the mother might have (had) a taste for film noir and take(n) the
child along

my machine is hooked up to my machin things inaccessible to the
precise methods of e.g. a Brazilian bookmobile being hijacked
in a dark underground garage fiction is precisely what they now
call non-fiction too get a bit too presonal i.e. Eurydice my dark
darling don't worry I can bear your not looking at me she cry(ed)
out i.e. hoping it (was) true

(now) (here) together in the mix of the modern metropolis Rio
Vienna Paris Tokyo Moscow Hong Kong Lagos New York
Bombay London Mumbai he and she both feel close to the
idealized neuron in the book

•

some of the diffuse sensations of early childhood may still
surprise us as we consider their names e.g. joy frustration shame
anxiety love rage fear anger wonder curiosity disgust surprise
longing humor pride self-respect fear but not terror fear but not
horror

the mother however might not like surprises e.g. wanting to
know for how many generations a Negro in the bloodlines can
produce a *throwback* the word is memory the child recalls this
use of memory does not know what to say for a very long time:

The soul is inwardness, as soon as and insofar as it is no longer outwardness; it is *memoria*, insofar as it does not lose itself in *curiositas*.

·

otherwise one could ask at any moment e.g. in what story does an uninvited goddess walk in and roll a golden ball down the hall or why not enjoy the story of lovers in the same vein from different centuries but in the same story from different worlds but in the same story I write down my dreams this is probably not one of them i.e. for a very long time the child want(ed) more than she could say to not want more than she could say i.e. impossible according to any simple formula for mirroring formulas

·

if e.g. but for the accidental clause the swerve of curiosity on the monkey bars the flash-bulb memory the wall of fire outside the window and or something as vague as living in time i.e. for a time near what seem to be near things swept into the stream of self-translation in the coincidental flow of events near disregarded syllables suddenly audible vol up sudden outburst of song sudden Ha it's too funny how funny it is to feel sometimes and not others how to remotely sense a sweet violence in the brevity i.e. the spilt second glance

> without yards of shimmering adjectives
> description: is description possible can a sunrise
> be described by yards of shimmering adjectives

·

While the curate was saying this, the lass in boy's clothing stood as if spell-bound, looking first at one and then at another, without moving her lips or saying a word, like a rustic villager who is suddenly shown some curious thing that he has never seen before . . . she gave a deep sigh and broke her silence at last.

. . . Doing her best to restrain her tears, she began the story of her life, in a calm, clear voice.

•

without the carefully constructed container:
story: is story possible: can a life even a portion
of a life be contained in a story: would songs
be better to repair the brain

when if it's curiosity that draws attention to curiosity even the other animals like us even in nature if for only the space of time e.g. at the watering hole e.g. during those times when it's too wide or too narrow for ambiguity the range of genres might now include humor and but or horror even (then) there

this voltage through the body is brought on by the senses senses strictly speaking in logic nothing is accidental the world divides us into seekers after facts seekers after gold dig up much earth and find little

•

PRESENT TENSE: STILL

they would go often to the movies hot majestic interludes containing profanity violence & graphic photos of murder victims in black and white interlard(ed) with bitter irony of if

in this the context of the extreme sport of everyday life it is necessary to put this in the context of e.g. the extreme sport of everyday life

or the most extreme object of medical curiosity that one could hope to hit upon here i.e. the e.g. clarification of the connections between the way the body moves and feels the way the mind thinks and feels if one dares to seek these bonds in the brain of a living animal

•

or to zoom in on the scene in the darkened room on the screen
the shadow of the murderous aunt is moving across the screen
along the far wall of the screen one can tell it is the murderous
aunt from the feather in the hat and the dagger in the hand of
the silhouette of the shadow on the wall

or the scene in the neighborhood playground the boy falling
back the boy falling back and back after being (shot) about to
take another bite of his Mars Bar or any other chocolate treat
with a paper or plastic wrapper in the country where many
fear(ed) God & AIDS & Elephants & Castles & Car Windows
& pop goes the weasel on the way home from school

●

is it too trivial to ask is this a scale too trivial to ask about to ask
if it is more tragic or more poignant that the child had hoped to
finish i.e. e.g. the candy bar before he (was) (shot) can the tragic
be poignant and vice versa and verso and recto and the pant
cuff gets caught in the spokes and e.g. the anonymous rider falls
off the bike and the optics of the horizon is questioned on the
spot by the Mennonite Italian who feels his father watch(ed) too
many Sinatra movies and puts too much ham in his omelets

catastrophe theorists say that if we backtrack along the previous
path there will be no catastrophe this time i.e. not this time

Lost Brief Case Conjecture

do not give up on me us you them

lucky lucky number number number

the sky is always the hardest

blue in the beginning

wasabi chance chance wasabi wasabi sunset

it's all true all lucky lucky

lucky lucky lucky numbers are blue

drawing on the past on blue blue

instance

the sky is always the hardest

left with all these these

those numerical objects

not there at the time

no yes important yes manuscript lost

the brief case suit case back pack valise is left

in the elevator taxi Alps Pyrenees garage hotel

    room locker bar

on the bench train bus ferry trolley counter street

at the station news stand terminal border ATM

blue blue wasabi number can you be can you be

    factored into primes

does an opinion occupy space

can the Imperial flora look beautiful ever again

(nothing left on the right clock)

does the rise into ruin be be come the sky

POETICS STATEMENT

Procedural Elegies: N Plus Zero

WHY USE PROCEDURES when one can simply note the succession of things that "naturally" or "logically" come to mind? "Act so that there is no use in a centre," said Gertrude Stein. Good advice, particularly if the center is "self" without the benefit of centrifugal artifice; equally so for a center composed of official logics.

Procedure: Instructions for how (even why) one is to go on : what Didi and Gogo were missing; what Wittgenstein in the *Tractatus* so deftly employs until he acknowledges the limitations of his numerically sequenced linguistic logic and catapults into (inexpressible) neo-Kantian transcendence. Whether or not one likes Wittgenstein's turn to the "mystical," one can admire his sense of procedural limits.

Fibonacci numbers, which have often been used as organizing principle of literary procedures are of course a self-perpetuating sequence *ad-infinitum* except when conjoined with nature: e.g., with spiral growth in plants and mollusks, with human projects. Nature (the complex interrelatedness of things) will always provide limiting conditions that self-singularity is not programmed to acknowledge. Self-limiting may in fact be an oxymoron. Self-criticism, self-abnegation, selflessness, social awareness, collaboration don't come naturally, must be consciously built into procedural projects— literary and socio-political.

Strange concept, self. (Online dictionary def: self. a person's essential being that distinguishes them from others, esp. considered as the object of introspection or reflexive action.) At the inception of modernity, the world divided into not facts but selves. The newly invigorated self-created selves became self-equipped to divide the world into facts, self-inscribing invisible selves as self-creators of self and other therein; all the while energetically and righteously devising methods to by-pass and/or sabotage subjectivity. It's always been a complicated project to be human. And so it went, and goes, despite scientific method, unto the "naturalistic fallacy." Philosophies and fictions and poetries and laws full of naturalized facts and processes legitimate (unnoticed) the very selves that have in (naturalized) fact created them.

This has little to do with nature (complex interrelatedness of things) even as "naturalist" achievements in fiction and non-fiction alike are heralded as honest and real and win prizes for their honesty and reality. There may be an unfortunate misunderstanding here that can perhaps be relieved by certain forms of procedural artifice—robust or deviously good-natured elegies to the limitations of the unexamined naturalized self. But first must go our persistent yearning for an idea of nature that clarifies what/who we are rather than complicating it. Yes, the complex interrelatedness of things (nature) is the final arbiter, even as it registers the sad consequences of our disavowal of its nature.

Poetic procedure (in healthy and necessary contrast to the necessary and productive realm of scientific method) is a form of authorial agency which need not attempt to disguise a subject position while importing a tonic presence of otherness into the composition. The subjectively valued object is to deflect single point perspective with its tedious thrust toward lonely vanishing points. Those points, so highly valued in the imperial panopticon, are locations of simultaneous self-affirmation and disappearance from the world at large.

How to (why!?) undertake the difficult work of opening the aesthetic field to dialogic alterity, alter-texts, alter and after-egos (messy afterbirths)—all in equally disadvantaged conversation? This is first-off a matter of humor. Humor, in an only slightly renovated medieval sense of temperamental and cognitive fluidity, makes incisive conceptual shifts possible. Those shifts, on many different scales, are what vital experience is all about. Humor is the thoroughly embedded (in every cell of our bodies) prototype of the cognitive swerve into startling acknowledgements; acknowledgments of unsettlingly foreign perspectives; perspectives just coming into barely legible view, newly fledged monstrosities intruding upon pleasantly predictable natural schemes. We constantly over-localize predictability; underestimate the ubiquitous presence of pattern-bounded indeterminacy in action.

The humorous conceptual shift is the stealth objective of every procedural project on which I embark. It requires a figure-ground relation of stability (grid) and mobility (composed chance or aleatoric intervention). The alertness of the whole being that it requires is requisite to the discovery of a world of otherness extending into self's own terra incognita. Think of humorous recognition bringing on a frightening and delicious Ah-Ha, rather than I-Thou. ("Thou" being tender honorific for "other" already naturalized into one's own I-project.) The humorous realization that I'm proposing comes only in intersection with the otherness/others one does not, cannot create oneself: the discovery of reciprocal alterity.

Here's a dire question: Can projects aiming at engagement with "reciprocal alterity" ever really appeal to our self-absorbed species? Perhaps we're evolutionarily driven—at least in naturalized theory—first toward survival then toward greed, in the fundamentally benign way that squirrels are programmed to hoard an excess of nuts. That is, are we really up against the limitations of our "nature"? "It's only natural"; "it's only human";

"nobody's perfect." We know that the engines of our disastrous geopolitics—territorial aggression and xenophobia alike—come naturally. Could principles of redundancy wired into our neural networks lead us to demand a constant multiplication of things in our material environment; i.e., incessant acquisitiveness; i.e., the consumerism and its market-growing apparatus that are ravaging our planet? Whatever the case, I don't think we'll get ourselves out of this mess through natural inclinations. "Humane" values have created a nightmare.

What did Francis Bacon of *The New Organon* and Aesop and La Fontaine of the *Fables* have in common? All three knew that to achieve a moral dimension, all of us animals must develop behaviors unnatural to our species. Some things that don't come naturally: procedures, projects, ethical awareness, ethical courage, taking chances worth taking; inviting in the unknown, the unintelligible; collaborating with strangeness, composing poethical wagers.

Not to say we can ignore the vibrant substrate of the reproduction of desire, the elaboration of need, the geometric progression of consumption, the acquisition of knowledge as tool for the acquisition of the fruits of desire, the elaboration of need, the geometric progression of consumption, the role of art in the reproduction of desire, the elaboration of need, the geometric progression of consumption, the rationalization of desire. . . .

Literatures (and other arts) of reciprocal alterity, if such are even possible, can't fix our fully institutionalized entanglements with short-sighted and/ or survivalist narcissisms. The modest but urgent mission is to present significant alternative sites for making meaning, potential locations for conceptual swerves. If this seems of doubtful value, think of the alternative of no alternatives to the courses of action our thoughts have tended to take us on to date.

Procedural forms. Methodical interrogations of authorial identity can induce vertigo (if not anxious nausea) in those not mechanically inclined. Most openly procedural models (e.g., those of the OuLiPo) have been resolutely mechanical, not willingly subject to the 2nd law of thermodynamics (even more vertiginous) with its steamy entropic irreversibility. This can give the illusion that nothing dire is at stake. (It's only a game.) In principle, the clockmaker can always turn back the clock, restoring any starting point. The mechanics of Oulipean procedures may differ radically from chance or ecologically modeled operations that make wagers with chaos. At the same time, the ultimate futility of all procedures—whether designed to bypass uncertainty, despair, radical doubt . . . or not—imbues them with an elegiac strain. That elegiac strain is a large part of the significance of procedural projects—open use of built-in limits, contingencies, against-the-odds-nesses.

Procedures that embody methodical and agitated doubts along with structural optimism can become interrogatively driven heat-seeking devices that zero in on the manifest unintelligibility of our complex material predicament. This takes place in the zone between the terrifyingly familiar and the terrifyingly unknown. That in-between zone is in my opinion location of the most important cultural work. Between believing and doubting lies the opportunity for serious play.

The humor of the Procedural Elegiac is lodged in its attempt at playful escape from self-serving gestures while never fully eluding strategies of desire. The grave and ludic performance of committed alterity is an inherently perverse enterprise in its off-centering of our would-be happy narcissism. Here comes, not everybody, but the necessary evocation of other logically possible selves and worlds, other ness monsters—in all their dangerous piquancy—vigorously invading (cavorting in) the domain formerly known as one's (note singularity of apostrophic claim) poem, or story, or novel, or essay.

Poetics is nothing other than an extreme noticing of how a limited case of that vast ongoing collaboration that is language works in the illuminated space-time brackets of a composition. Hence, N plus Zero equals A to Z in what remains of this essay, with N standing, not for "noun," but for "next" and zero for a certain degree of cluelessness; i.e., the familiar quandary, what to do next?

Try to begin now—if you haven't already—noticing these words with the pleasures of concerted sensual precision. Nothing is as it seems, nor is it otherwise. A narrative sets out nothing more or less than a succession of one word after another. Literary procedures, like procedural memories, keep us on track via a succession of presents that, counter to some avantgarde claims, are logically, neurologically prohibited from presenting the future. The future is an ever shifting hypothetical and, as Lucretius might have put it, it's most significantly made possible by the inclination of neurons and other affiliations of waving particles to swerve a little from their course even as the self-driven "one" might try to go resolutely from

A to Z

A poem that begins in history perhaps because it was too sparsely perhaps because it was too sparsely adorned because much has disappeared or is no longer apparent and what we became the surface became seemed seemed then not to have been there from the first from the first very confused about this but and sorting through one inkling after another after made the luxury packaging made it all bearable all the disasters disasters and their probable etiologies now no longer viewed in cinema newsreels while eating while eating pop corn and candy and rattling ice in large paper cups of here on this planet moved we have all moved on to assorted TVs and now their aftermath is all there is to some who think that all this I think this is I think this or that because the pain or any experience of pain first hand or through the transmission that causes could compassion or empathy could turn out to be as humorous as other alternatives from someone else's point of view just as the voice the voiceover voice says let's make a pact that will help us learn from our mistakes or the mistakes of others others impinge upon our lives compulsory happiness is a spur of a sort of spur to buck up and deny how bad it all is not wanting to be alone in one's condition e.g. utopia love it or leave it as alone alone they set out and or zig hoping for evolutionary characteristics or gardens to kick in evolutionary characteristics that may generate caring responses or wanting to state before going any further to say the literal sense of the figurative as it awakens neurons to shoot the moon at many many synapses poets are are not most importantly profligates or fools or purveyors of wisdom so then what the hell are they hey about that poem what noises did it make what exactly did it look like and what happened at the end at the end they're all just quoting the dictionary yes I know just when did tourism replace pilgrimage and or has it and or were they always the same in the face of what so much predatory intention love of reason what if sublimation does induce melancholia x-y out each word is a stroke of genius that could bring on all the rest

A poem that begins in history perhaps because it was too sparsely perhaps because it was Very us that sparsely rattling quoting poem or no much longer kick just in to achieve an ethical life one (any one, of any species) has to act against/outside one's history gardens from etiologies disasters confused begins a was was what we were nature. Apart from questions of defining "nature," the chief conundrum may be that if while while we who will wanting zig wanting wisdom what what what what yes one believes in laws of that egregiously indefinable term, then acting outside one's when were what what x-y word too sparsely adorned because much has disappeared

    to be able to act outside one's nature is one's nature, inside out,
        outside in
    Was very us that sparsely rattling quoting poem or no much longer
        kick just in
    how to manage your gadgets, how to prepare for death, or life,
    how to find solace in language with all its anarchic referents, or
    history gardens from etiologies disasters confused begins a zig yes x-y
    The pensive edges into melancholy without constraints to spur us on
        to play.
    X-y was very us that sparsely rattling quoting poem or no much longer
        kick just in

We are not designed to perceive most of what surrounds us or to fully
understand the rest.
history gardens from etiologies disasters confused begins a zig yes
the celebration of combinatorial excess, with these 5 integers, with this
fractal curve the escape from finitude begins
Yes x-y was very us that sparsely rattling quoting poem or no much
longer kick
The manic combinatorics of the fugue inducing giddy ecstasy in the
listener
just in history gardens from etiologies disasters confused begins a zig
it's the nature of music to elude questions of fallibility, the poetic
claim to
zig yes x-y was very us that sparsely rattling quoting poem or no much
longer kick
Flotillas of swallowtails disappear into themselves. This is neither true
nor false
in history gardens from etiologies disasters confused begins again from
A to Z
in the face of that so much predatory intention love of reason what if
sublimation does induce melancholia x-y out each word is a stroke
of genius that could bring on all the rest

THE METHOD "IN *MEDIAS* MESS"

Jena Osman

JOAN RETALLACK'S book *AFTERRIMAGES* opens with a quote from
Victor Weisskopff, a scientist who served on the Manhattan Project:

> On July 16, 1945, as the countdown at Alamogordo approached zero the P.A.
> system began to broadcast music from a nearby radio station operating on the
> same frequency. This is how the explosion of the first atomic bomb came to be
> accompanied by a Tchaikovsky waltz.[1]

AFTERRIMAGES was published in 1995, the year of the 50th anniver-
sary of the dropping of the bomb. Other detonations that year included
the Oklahoma City bombing, a Unabomber bomb that killed a California
lobbyist, and the bombing of Bosnia and Herzogovina by NATO. Ten peo-

ple were convicted that year of bombing the World Trade Center in 1993. Other shatterings included earthquakes that killed hundreds in Japan and Greece. Hundreds died in a Chicago heat wave. The Barings Bank in England collapsed due to one man's speculation. Itzhak Rabin was assassinated and Ken Saro-Wiwa was hung by his own government.

At the same time that such political and ecological explosions were occurring worldwide, attempts at "de-fragmentation" were being asserted domestically in the United States. The Million Man March took place in Washington, D.C. The Republicans gained control of both houses in Congress for the first time since 1953 (which was the year the hydrogen bomb was first made public). The Contract With America was passed. Internationally, the World Trade Organization was created. Such defragmentations have their dangers; socio-political forms of unity—which derive from desires both idealistic and ideological—require diversity and complexity to be homogenized beneath a sheen of unanimous consensus. Such forced alignments are inextricably linked (even if indirectly) to the fragmenting detonations of the past century. And as Joan Retallack has stated in an essay called "What Is Experimental Poetry & Why Do We Need It," "literary and sociopolitical structures have always exhibited more than coincidental parallels."[2] Aesthetic forms that mimic orderly homogenization (through classically harmonious constructions, unproblematized subjectivity, and monolingual articulations) can be as reductive of lived experience as social forms with similar values, and therefore need to be troubled. Retallack proposes that poetic forms model forms of life; it is therefore the poet's responsibility to make complex forms analogous to the complex orders found in everyday circumstance.

In the late 1980s, Retallack began to use the term "poethics" to describe this critical connection between forms of art and forms of life. The concept emerged originally from her study of Wittgenstein in the mid-1960s, and with her subsequent graduate study of philosophy in the Wittgensteinian mode with the analytic philosopher Elizabeth Anscombe. At the beginning of his *Philosophical Investigations* (of which Anscombe was the English translator), Wittgenstein states

> It is easy to imagine a language consisting only of orders and reports in battle.—Or a language consisting only of questions and expressions for answering yes and no. And innumerable others.—And to imagine a language means to imagine a form of life.[3]

In the introduction to her book of interviews with composer John Cage, *Musicage: Cage Muses on Words, Art, Music,* Retallack recounts how taking a course taught by Anscombe about the meaning of "wanting" coincided with her first meeting with John Cage at a Merce Cunningham performance.[4] The confluence of Anscombe (who was author of a book called *Intention*) and Cage (whose works were all about non-intention and non-wanting) created a paradigm shift in her thinking that moved her away from the forms of classical philosophical thinking with its narrow appreciation of poetic language, toward a more flexible mode of thought where the borders between philosophy and poetry begin to lose their definition. Wittgenstein's aphoristic and modular form in the *Philosophical Investigations* provided both a description and an enactment of what it meant for language to be a form of life. Meanwhile, John Cage was making the same argument in terms of music. In 1988, during the question and answer session that followed one of his Norton lectures at Harvard, Cage proposed the following:

> Performance of a piece of music can be a metaphor of society, of how we want society to be. Though we are not now living in a society which we consider good, we could make a piece of music in which we would be willing to live . . . you can think of music as a representation of a society in which you would be willing to live.[5]

For Cage, such a society would be an anarchist one, with no president or government to direct and control the clamor of the world. Cage pragmatically modeled this kind of society in his compositions by privileging ambient sound and autonomous players over determinate notation and conducted harmonies.

For Retallack, the poethical poem similarly calls attention to ambient language by tuning in to the richly multi-tracked lexicons, literatures, and processes that our contemporary moment provides. Varied discourses, languages, and cultural references are situated side by side, modeling a society where differences can converse and coexist, rather than stamp each other out. The remix of materials isn't random; it's always situated inside of a structure, often initiated by an observational question, with every formal component answering to the poethical charge. Even an element as small as a pronoun is treated with careful consideration. In a letter to Cage, responding to his use of the male third person pronoun in his lecture-poem "Overpopulation and Art," Retallack wrote:

> Since language is the medium in which we envision and project so much of our sense of our potential as humans, I will always opt for the most open language—the one that includes the most possibilities. 'Humanity,' 'human,' 'oneself,' 'our,' seem to me more generous, inclusive, and connective than 'Man,' 'man's,' 'himself,' 'his' . . . So, thinking poethically, the textual world in which I would wish to live is a world of 'we' and 'ours' not 'man' and 'his.' This is all of course full of the breath of Wittgenstein. If you take his idea of language as a form of life seriously, then the textual—and spoken— world (the particular words and forms we choose) always have poethical implications.[6]

In the titular essay of her influential book of essays *The Poethical Wager*, Retallack further makes the case that our forms of art need to more intimately align with our forms of life. As long as our art forms deny or are out of synch with our experience of the world—perhaps only attending to the Tchaikovsky waltz while ignoring the detonation of the atom bomb—the less we can actually perceive, and in turn, the less we can actually do in response. Thus, our poems must acknowledge that the world is a complicated, messy place, perpetually transforming and impossible to view in panoramic totality. As Retallack puts it, "If we're going to continue to make meaningful, sensually nourishing forms in the twenty-first century, art must thrive as a mode of engaged living in *medias* mess."[7] Or, as she later quotes from Beckett, "To find a form that accommodates the mess, that is the task of the artist now."[8] The "mess" consists of the detonations that jolt and fracture our habitual assumptions, as well as the multivarious conditions of our everyday existence that we usually choose to ignore. The mess is not something to be discarded or neatened up; rather, it is something to experience fully—to investigate, appreciate, and meet. What follows is a partial inventory of what constitutes the mess in our midst, and the methods by which Retallack's poems honor and engage with it.

. . .

The Mess

"The Infinite Archive" is a term taken from William Turkel's work in digital history.[9] It describes the masses of new information being produced every day, made available via the internet. It is no longer possible to exhaust a line of inquiry or to "master" a topic as did scholars of earlier eras—there will always be more to access, more to know about every imaginable subject. Clearly, this is a good thing, for the selectivity of past scholarship resulted in a number of cultural erasures, but the abundance of information is also something of a curse in that it's impossible to take it all in. Turkel has written extensively on digital research methods (he calls them "hacks") that help to organize the infinite array of resources so that they're more easily consumed. He's come up with methods for mining huge data sets by creating uniquely customized search tools. Search-engine interfaces are essential to finding things, but structurally they can be misleading in that they seem to depict hierarchies of knowing as illustrated by the order of hits a search term yields. In actuality, the order listed is more a reflection of the number of connections to other pages rather than to content itself; thus the concept of hierarchy gives way to one of contact.

Turkel's methods are analogically relevant to Retallack's poetics because a search engine, or one of Turkel's many "digital hacks," has the capacity to connect disparate data. Subjects that initially seemed to have little to do with one another—except for a common name or phrase—begin to collide and converse. But where Turkel is trying to sift through the data to unearth specific information (he is an historian), Retallack's work tests what might happen when this infinite archive is used for less directive purposes. Without a specific goal in mind, what can happen if one mines the multiple components of the cultural mess and puts the parts in contact?

The Method

Every poetry book by Joan Retallack concludes with a list of sources. Although this is common practice for nonfiction and academic works, it is a rarer sight in books of poems. And when explicit allusions to other texts have been made in poems—think of the works of T. S. Eliot and Ezra Pound—these references have often been used with the goal of unlocking a dominant overarching interpretation, to make it all "cohere." In Retallack, source-work leads to more fluid acts of signification; rather than trying to use the texts of the past as a means to interpret (and thus paralyze) the present moment, all sources—be they classical or demotic—belong to the continuously recomposing atmosphere of the now. Spanish instructions for MRI (magnetic resonance imaging) patients are found alongside translated quotes from *Don Quixote de la Mancha* in Retallack's book *Mongrelisme*. Ovid's story of Icarus is perforated by contemporary street signs and news headlines in "Icarus Ffffalling" (in *AFTERRIMAGES*). In *Memnoir*, the story of Eurydice coexists with parental advisory warnings from movie listings in the *Washington Post*. Novelist Jane Austen's words tangle easily with those of philosopher J. L. Austin in the poem "How to Do Things with Words." Language culled from literature is often in the company of less easily traced sources: overheard phrases, lecture notes, diaries, print ephemera, random thoughts, etc. For example, in the poem "Icarus Ffffalling," Ovid's story is woven together with high and low cultural references:

> Ovid said his mind was bent to tell of bodies changed to new forms
> O Jude don't be too long in 2nd story allegories Da Vinci faults the
> butterfly for mistaking hot wax for suns of fallen rock star zones fallen
> stone crater lakes[10]

These atmospheric text strands converse on equal terms, without acknowledging the borders and hierarchies usually associated with rhetorical modes. Rather than data mined by the scholarly reference systems of Eliot and Pound at the service of an all-encompassing idea, the literary and nonliterary sources in these poems investigate the unruly parameters of a textual environment and delight in the clash and kiss of cultural discourses. They resist stabilized interpretations dictated by the static archives of the past and rethink literary, philosophical, and scientific texts as they engage and change through contact with contemporary culture.

In her poem "The Woman in the Chinese Room," Retallack's originating source-text is the Chinese room thought experiment designed by language philosopher John Searle in 1980. The experiment emerges from the question of whether computers can perform acts of cognition. In response to the question, Searle proposes two scenarios: In the first, a computer processes Chinese texts as input and then creates Chinese texts in response as output—to the point where a native Chinese speaker is convinced that the computer actually "knows" Chinese. In the second scenario, "you" are sitting in a room behind a closed door. A native Chinese speaker slips a note written in Chinese under the door, and by referring to the code for the computer program, you are able to process the characters in the same way and write an equally convincing response. Although the experiment might prove that you know the program, it does not prove that you (or the computer) know the language that the program processes; knowing the rules doesn't signal comprehension. Thus, Searle's experiment provides a convincing argument against artificial intelligence. This argument perhaps seems more than obvious in light of the stilted results generated by today's online translation tools like Babelfish. But Retallack's poem doesn't dwell on the experiment's results; rather, she suggests that this experiment is

> being too careful not exploring the other possibilities but this could be serious it might not be the thought experiment he thought it was or it might be irreversible once set in motion . . .[11]

The poem proceeds to shift away from the clear-cut answers offered by Searle's philosophical inquiry, and instead questions the experiment's givens: Does the experiment change if the "you" in the room is a woman? Why must the person be locked behind a door? Is she a prisoner? Why is the language chosen for the experiment Chinese? Is translation—whether by computer or by human—ever really possible? The poem calls attention to the overflow, the remainder (usually discarded) that is generated by any act of translation, or by any philosophical logic that neatly claims that x = y. By asking questions that swerve from the selectivity of conventional proof-structures, the poem re-imagines "knowing" as connected to all areas of experience/language, rather than to those few that conveniently lead to a desired result. Nothing is taken for granted.

The tension between the certainty of philosophical claims and the remainder that exceeds logic pervades Retallack's work. Both Burton Hatlen and Greg Kinzer have looked closely at how Retallack's poetics engage with that tension. Hatlen, in his essay "Joan Retallack: A Philosopher among the Poets, a Poet among the Philosophers," discusses how Wittgenstein and John Dewey are important to Retallack for their critique of essentialist ideas, but that as a poet she realized that their discursive methods actually repeat the problem. Hatlen proposes that in John Cage's "radical artistic praxis," Retallack found a method she could use to resolve the disjunction between form and content that exists in philosophy.[12] Kinzer's essay "Excuses and Other Nonsense: Joan Retallack's *How to Do Things With Words*" looks at how Retallack's poems function as an intervention into the traditional moves of philosophical discourse. He proves that in the same way Retallack troubles the certainties behind Searle's Chinese room experiment, she also questions and destabilizes the set boundaries of J. L. Austin's speech act theory.[13]

These essays call attention to the fact that as readers, we are accustomed to granting certain types of sense-making and rhetorical styles authority. Retallack's work pushes us to look to the edges of those rhetorical orders: Are there narratives made invisible by such grammars of certainty? Philosophical discourse (or literary analysis), so often associated with methodical reasoning, must dynamically balance with more intuitive and fluid logics. As Kinzer points out, amidst the "purposeful polyphony among citations [in Retallack's work] . . . no register of language is allowed an interpretive authority over any other."[14] No singular rhetorical mode can be used to contain and control the others. The infinite archive, as modeled by Retallack's poetics, is thus anarchic rather than hierarchical.

While Turkel's "digital hacks" help distinguish useful from less useful data, Searle's Chinese room experiment distinguishes human modes of knowing from artificial modes. But for Retallack, the important question is not one of distinction, but of fusion. Once the hierarchical orders of knowing have been abandoned, how does any person come to understand something outside of his/her experience? If the mechanics of language are all we have, how do we investigate and process that which is unintelligible? The reader must confront these questions directly at the end of "The Woman in the Chinese Room," when challenging and disjunctive word combinations stream for a full page:

> fraucht ergle gloss remainder squat
> in history's twitter rut she blank
> twi-lips pensive grim reminder mirg mirror
> blanck trace there pocket vox map . . .[15]

Retrospective knowledge of source-texts isn't going to help the reader interpret this kind of language. Expectations of interpretive analysis must be set aside so the language can be approached on its own material terms: its sounds, rhythms, and associative paradoxes. There's twilight and tulips behind those "twi-lips," and a pensive grin behind the "grim reminder." There's a pocket watch doubling beneath the voice map. Searle's experiment functions as a frame structure, an initial condition that generates a much less predictable future terrain. This kind of poetic language does not ask for translating or decoding, nor does it suggest a symbolic ratio between its body and its source. Rather, it asks to be released from the rules of habitual logics so its previously concealed semantic possibilities can unfurl, so the infinite archive can be radically embraced.

. . .

The Mess

Just before he died in 1919, Theodore Roosevelt wrote an address to the American Defense League stating, "We have room for but one language in this country, and that is the English language, for we intend to see that the crucible turns our people out as Americans, of American nationality, and not as dwellers in a polyglot boarding house."[16] This sentiment was voiced in the face of a massive post-war influx of immigrants. It takes its place in a trajectory of English-only political rhetoric that started in the United States as early as the Louisiana Purchase and continues with vigor today, usually attached to anti-immigrant legislation. As of 2009, thirty states had passed legislation making English the "official language" of the state. And yet the United States is undeniably polyglot; The 2000 Census was printed in six languages, and completed surveys determined that there were over 40 languages other than English being spoken in a significant number of homes. Roosevelt's crucible—the alchemical American melting pot—has not succeeded in transmuting a various populace into a standardized and monolingual substance. Rather, the languages coexist. Together they form an untranslatable amalgam where the individual parts maintain their autonomy. In the face of such polyvocality, how does one connect to others or make oneself understood? Another way to think about this part of the "mess" is in terms of individual voice and self-expression. In a world where different languages and cultures co-habitate—a world of multiple alterities—where is the agency for the speaking subject? Can any voice have authority?

The Method

In both her book *Mongrelisme: A Difficult Manual for Desperate Times* and her earlier poem "Scenes of Translation (from the Translation)" (in *How to Do Things With Words*), Retallack enacts a world saturated with "ambient polylingualism." In the "mongrel" text multiple languages exist side by side and bounce off of each other. Some of those languages are tied to ethnicity, but some come from specialized vocabularies attached to a particular discipline or activity, or from language specific to speech rather than writing. Mongrelisme is not multilingualism, for the latter term suggests an impossible equivalence through translation. Translation, when not treated as a creative act that actually moves away from the original, can force the multidimensionality of one language to fit the demands and limitations of another. Thus translation can have the effect of turning polyphonic difference into monologic homogeneity. In contrast, mongrelisme proposes a "polylectical" coexistence where languages are "in conversation (literally, turning toward one another for infusions of aesthetic energy)."[17]

In Retallack's *Mongrelisme*, the opening epigraph notes, "Translation is an embrace that has gone on too long," and indeed the multiple languages here resist the traditional forms of that embrace. As with the ending section of "The Woman in the Chinese Room," new models of relation/conversation are proposed that rely primarily on soundplay and ways of knowing that are more connected to the senses and intuition than to logic/reason. For example, Cervantes's line "Toda afectación es mala" becomes, through homophonic translation, "Toadies affect a yawn at malapropisms." A described family feud over whether *Don Quixote de la Mancha* is a comedy or a tragedy is followed by a long sequence of feuding facing pages, verso and recto challenging each other with discordant discourses. Pages that quote from "frequently answered questions" for MRI patients in Spanish ("¿Voy a sentir dolor?" "¿Cuánto tiempo toma el examen?") confront pages that present a rush of associative language (perhaps occurring inside/outside the patient/writer), a kind of "resonance imaging" of thought as it happens:

> A SENSATION OF FLOATING AT THE MOMENT THE ROAR of the roar of the blast ends the silence lifts everything in the air & then the whimpering & sobbing & screaming begin Carnation Lily LilyRose four little girls in a garden with luminous paper lanterns in the museum & world might intersect in such a way that the twin photons parting to carry their little electromagnetic packs to different ends of the mathematical spectrum of the unexpected in which hue one finds impossible calculations   the deterministic random   the stable unstable . . . [18]

The facing pages of this poem enact a kind of left-brain/right-brain dichotomy. The pages on the left use a language of rationality meant to allay the anxiety that a medical test like an MRI will cause in a patient. The tone (even if one doesn't know Spanish) is one of certainty, where every question has an answer, and the goal is to set the mind at ease. But in this instance the actual answers are missing; instead, the questions have only the subjective chaos of the right-hand pages as response. The fear emanating from these pages is palpable, surfacing nonsystematically in phrases like "waves of nausea & or dawn defying," "doomed to / POW / power failures How To Avoid choque eléctrico," "you are so afraid that you cannot see or hear the effect of fear is to disturb the senses." The punning and messy overflow of the recto pages feels manic and uncontrolled:

> ... Yep I'm gonna sit right down & right myself a bout of should or shouldn't the child that bit the dog after too long exposure to Don Quixote or life in the slums of the great city or 2 rap crew cut blue razor cut dusk strewn break dance be bop hip hop hope of jazz brake. . . .[19]

These sets of facing pages, representing rational and intuitive modes, exist side by side like the balanced pans of a scale. They are disjunctive, yet necessary companions in a dynamic interior conversation, keeping each other in check, "keep / ing / fatale sentimeats at bay."

Polylingual fusion is treated quite differently in the poem "Scenes Of Translation (from the Translation)." The focus is more specifically on the damage done (sometimes humorous, sometimes terrifying) by the act of translation. Lines from a Spanish phrase book are mixed with lines of German, their homophonic equivalents, English translations of Nicaraguan peasant poetry, neologistic substitutions, and lots of flies and weeds.

LOCAL TRAVELLING	EXCURSIONS	SIGHT-SEEING

...
Unkraut verdirbt nicht   little killer bee
Schlaf und Tod, usw   no com-para-bl-eng-licks-ex-
                                                 prex-ion

¿Hay ópera?[20]

In the middle of this tour of the language of tourism is a statement of the problem:

> throughout the entire phrase book one must exist in the singular
> alone in *the* woodland, *the* clearing, *the* eye (in which) the/y exist,
> except for the abuntent (?) flies: untranslate[21]

The poem's assemblage of different languages tries to turn that singular into a plural company, disrupting monodirectional and nationalistic grammatical structures in favor of multidirectional points of contact. Retallack aims to model a complex and particular globalism, as opposed to a generic and empty one where difference is leveled and contact often means giving up one's identity. As Caroline Bergvall puts it in her essay "Writing at the Crossroads of Language," "the concerted cross-fertilization of linguistic environments [in Retallack's work] does not subscribe to modernist assumptions of a pancultural scholarly availability"[22] where a colonizing authorial mind uses other cultures to create his/her own essentialist totality. Rather, Retallack proposes a system of mutual recognition—what she calls a reciprocal alterity:

> The poethics in using this ambient polylingualism as material for a poesis . . .
> is a valuing, a foregrounding, of the most crucial fact of our existence: We,
> in all our reciprocal alterities, are "in it" together; everything depends on the
> quality of the conversation we can manage.[23]

By encouraging/staging such challenging conversations, her poems are so-cial structures based on listening and exchange rather than egoic speech-ifying.

As with much postmodern poetry, Retallack's work questions the convention of the coherent lyric subject. Personal revelation, narrative confession, and other gestures of self-expression are problematic when symbolically linked through poetic artifice to "universal" experiences. Not only are the subjectivities of others (including that of the reader) subsumed, but experience itself is reduced to a relatively narrow range of possibilities. When alterity is not reciprocal, the poet is complicit in objectifying dif-ference, in presenting it in the costume of his/her own perceptual/cultural assumptions. Everyone and everything outside of the self (including the environment) is silenced, forced to ventriloquize the poet's voice. In other words, a nonreciprocal alterity keeps the other completely separate from the "I," always on the outside, always a formation/creation of the subject's ego. But Retallack proposes that with an aesthetic that works towards reciprocal alterity, "we no longer stand apart from the rest of the world but participate in it as one among many."[24]

In her crucial essay "Re:Thinking:Literary:Feminism" Retallack argues that this rethinking of the "I" in the poem is particularly important for women writers, who, once admitted into the literary canon, were too eas-ily relegated to the limits of confessional forms that operate according to a static mirroring—a "picture theory" of meaning. She suggests that women writers instead follow the call of "the literary feminine," and investigate the frontiers of the unintelligible—a frontier that will never be settled, even though it has been traversed by numerous male writers such as Joyce, Beckett, Duchamp, and Cage. Writing that takes the unintelligible as its starting point applies a

> use theory of meaning, one that locates the making of meaning in a collab-
> orative engagement with interdynamically developing forms (rather than in
> the interpretation of a fossil signified), allows exploration of the medium
> of language itself, and thus the invention of new grammars, where subject–
> object, master–mater relations can never be presupposed, where nothing ever
> shrinks into an irreversible "it."[25]

But as much as they destabilize our sense of the subject, Retallack's poems don't lack a subjectivity altogether. Much of the text in her work is intuitively generated from her own collection notebooks and in readings that reflect her own individual interests. However, the self appears in a less directive, more permeable position than in typically expressive poems. The self is just one cultural material among many others. In an interview with Redell Olson, Retallack says:

> I experience my energy as exchange, like the exchange we are having right now in conversation. There's just nothing I imagine I'd gain by focusing on a kind of contained "I"-ness in which I primarily look inward to draw energy. I think the writing process is a process of breathing/reading in the air—the cultural air . . . it's not that autobiographical things don't enter, they of course do. But I find that deriving the direction of one's work from a monological "I" drains energy. Given all the rich alternatives, it seems a truly bizarre—actually self-depriving—choice.[26]

Retallack's book *Memnoir* provides a good illustration of how the self performs as part of an atmospheric exchange. Here, Retallack creates a hybrid composed of the supposedly truthful genre of memoir and the fictional genre of film noir. The two generic discourses are stitched together with "i.e." and "e.g."—abbreviations that promise a clarifying relationship between parts. But rather than create an elucidating connection, they signal an atmospheric shift, a cinematic cut, a swerve in an alternate direction.

> i.e. all this is just to slide more easily off the hook to avert the eyes from or toward the grainy screen to grab e.g. a yellow pad a yellow #2 pencil a blue summer song an orange rabbit a rare breeze a yellow song a monarch on a thistle a summer rabbit a fresh breeze etc. bring all the books for the course next time what is it that you're expecting in these circular semantics these circular ruins this offset sagittal section this widening circumference this widening cross-reference this crowding of inferences will anything make her e.g. eligible for parole[27]

A subject is clearly present, but transforming with every shift. The changes in point of view are cinematic, moving from closeups ("a monarch on a thistle") to distant pans ("this widening circumference"), interior ("the grainy screen" "parole") to exterior ("a fresh breeze"). In the preceding excerpt, the narrative voice first appears in detached relation to a screened image, then becomes an imagewriter, assigning adjectives to various nouns ("orange rabbit," "summer rabbit"). The voice shifts to that of a teacher giving assignments, then jumps to a meta-level and questions the purpose of "these circular semantics" in the poem itself. The phrase "circular semantics" leads by association to "circular ruins," referencing the title of a short story by Jorge Luis Borges. The brief allusion to this story is significant on at least two levels. As in many of her poems, the textual sources she cites are the closest Retallack comes to providing memoir-like information. Additionally, the Borges story itself illuminates what's at stake in creating a permeable and plural subjectivity. The protagonist of the story wants to "dream a man" and "impose him on reality." He builds the man piece by piece and sends him off into the world, careful to protect him from knowledge of his origins, for "Not to be a man, to be a projection of another man's dreams—what an incomparable humiliation, what madness!"[28] Ultimately the protagonist discovers that he, too, is just a projection of another. It's this problem of projection, of creating the other in one's own likeness, that Retallack tries to correct with her concept of "reciprocal alterity."

In a situation of reciprocal alterity, the self is othered and made strange —a persona of sorts, that exists outside of known experiences, associations, and desires. It is through this estrangement that one can have a fuller sense of how one fits inside of a larger world picture. Reciprocal alterity grants the other, as well as the self, independent status. It is a utopian proposition, for it is impossible to truly abandon one's ego, or to perceive the other apart from one's own desires (or through the eyes of others)—but for Retallack, that doesn't mean that one shouldn't try to imagine it otherwise.

Retallack has written that we need a "planetary pronoun," a "we" that is not appropriative, that does not make assumptions, that does not erase singularities, but rather is a we of connection on the planet.[29] Retallack's "we" is a far cry from that manufactured by Roosevelt's crucible. It is remote from the "we" of lyric poetry as well, for it requires detaching from egoic centripetal forces and the personalized nationalism of "authentic" selfhood.

Detachment is the necessary position of the subject in the poethical art form. Detachment is not disengagement, not standing apart from the unintelligible other, but standing apart from one's own (poetic) will and usual habits of perception when confronted with the unfamiliar. In other words, the poet and reader of the poethical poem must see the self as a foreigner, rather than as a singular and fixed subject that needs to be translated into a uniform language. From that disinterested position, one can be in dialogue with the pluriform materials of the cultural atmosphere, and thus view, empathize, and participate in the environment without destroying/reducing it.

. . .

The Mess

Related to the challenges of the infinite archive and atmospheric polylectics is the challenge of attention in a digital device-driven age. The twenty-first century multitasking google-mind flits from the surface of one subject to another like a dragonfly on water. Although web-browsing or social networking can reveal surprising connectivities, they privilege efficient filtering and consumption over absorptive processing and contemplation. In an interesting inversion of Searle's proof that computers can't think, there has been much speculation about how digital information interfaces (like Google search engines) are changing (disabling?) our own thought processes. From Sven Birkerts's classic text *The Gutenberg Elegies* to Nicholas Carr's 2008 *Atlantic Monthly* article "Is Google Making Us Stupid?," fears have been expressed in regard to what new technologies are doing to our attention spans.[30] Although we now have access to more information than ever before, our methods for processing that information are accompanied by a paradoxical distractedness: What use are thoughts if they provide only a stepping stone to the next web link rather than to action in (or understanding of) the world off-screen? Retallack summarizes the problem this way: ". . . in this age of cultural Attention Deficit Disorder, how rare an informed, intense, not to say pleasurable connection with anything in our daily lives can be—the effects that this distractedness has on possibility and aspiration—this role of the arts seems positively urgent."[31]

The Method

Retallack argues that without a "sustained attention," we lose the power to discover the connections generated by the amazing data processing systems of our own minds. Therefore, she is drawn to aesthetic acts that encourage contemplation through perceptual paradigm shifts. In her essay "Geometries of Attention," Retallack discusses John Cage's groundbreaking composition 4'33" as an example of such an act. Premiered in 1952, in Woodstock, New York, 4'33" consists of a pianist sitting at a piano, not playing anything, but marking three movements by opening and closing the lid of the keyboard at timed intervals. While listening, audience attentions shift from the music that doesn't play to the sounds being produced in the room. The supposedly silent hall proves itself to be filled with ambient notes: coughing, bodies shifting, murmurs. For those that listen openly and fully, this becomes an entirely new music—a composition that has been there all along, but is usually not heard. Retallack notes that in listening, "we now recognize silence not as the absence of sound (physically impossible) but the sound we happen to be ignoring."[32] The contemplative space this piece creates allows our attention to be redirected and retuned. The perceptual implications of 4'33" are not confined to the concert hall; they can be transferred and applied to the ongoing sonic activity of any environment.

The information that such a composition provides distinguishes itself from that offered by the infinite archive, in that it requires slowing down and analyzing the context from which it arises. Rather than a piece of music (or any data) that has been recorded and possibly remixed/ recontextualized, 4'33" can only occur in the moments that it is produced. Cage is not the "author" here; he has simply set up the framing parameters within which the audience's perceptual experience will take shape. These parameters (time, venue, stage picture) serve as determinative controls, but what occurs inside of them is unpredictable. To similar effect, Retallack sets up (con)textual and procedural parameters for readerly contemplation (i.e., authoring) in her poems.

An example can be found in the title poem of the book *AFTERRIMAGES* (the epigraph of which began this essay). The top part of each page is comprised of intuitively generated text composed of materials culled from Retallack's notebooks, memories, and observations. These top sections were then systematically "bombed" with paperclips. The shattered remnants of that procedure (the bits of text that fell inside the clips) were then duplicated in the bottom section of the page.

garden wall battlement

YO MAMA

POMPANADA

....

random intelligence echoes planets and stars

blue spiral notebook + shiny chrome pen

=

look out /the/ window see Chaucer in /the/ angle of /the/ rain

(The theef fil over bord al sodeynly)

---

blu   chr m pen

(Th

Thus a jotted-down phrase such as "blue spiral notebook + shiny chrome pen" becomes "blu   chr m   pen."[33] With the help of the procedure, everyday objects transform into a mysterious lettristic residue; we can read the ghost of what the phrase once was at the same time as the phrase opens up and becomes material for us to work with. Perhaps the "blu" leads to "blush" or "blew." Perhaps the pen is no longer a writing implement, but a prison pen; the "chr m" a "crumb." Perhaps a new word has been born: blukrumpen . . . the English words begin to suggest German. Perhaps Chaucer's Middle English (the quote is from "The Man of Law's Tale"), after evolving into modern English, is once again evolving. These fragments (and the generous page space that surrounds them) invite the reader to slow down and privilege consciously associative *actions* over mindless following of authorial intentions.

Retallack has written that in the contemporary sciences, it is a given that a swerve toward the unknown can lead to paradigm-shifting discoveries.[34] One of her strategies for achieving comparable swerves of discovery in language is to pry words loose from singular and definitive meanings. By highlighting lettristic play, puns, and typographical accidents, meanings start to slip and multiply. Retallack's book *Errata Suite* is a paean to the generative (and humorous) power of the lettristic slippage found in printing errors. The reader is given instructions for substitutions: "read need for read," "read for for four," "exist for exits," "read poisonous snake not snack." Even after the unintentional word is replaced with the one intended, the "excess" meaning provided by the error never entirely disappears; in fact, its presence is emphasized and takes on a life of its own. All of our words wear this shadow behind them indicating double and triple lives. As Retallack has written in her essay "The Scarlet Aitch," "Lettristic play . . . streaks through official texts, illuminating subtexts and subliminal noises as letters swerve, collide, coagulate in the wound—the scar in scarlet—the scars of historical/etymological silences."[35] Much of this subtextual noise relies on both a written and an aural dimension.

> please note 24&26 printed upside down read dear for pear or peer reed real camino replace with stet to let it be Molodzhi Molodeszhi O patriotic stirring verse word'swords and irony begat to bigot from *eirein* (to say)(ironic) agedumb ignotus nominous dominant hominy last word-word not last & then *The Palmist* also printed upside down[36]

As in *AFTERRIMAGES*, the sliding and slipping letters are grounded by a procedural framework. Every page has five lines (the original was composed on musical staff paper, so that each line represents a line in the musical stave), and every sixth page consists of five quotations (selected via a procedure also built around the number five from the writings of various philosophers) spliced together in a paragraph. The quotations are organized alphabetically by author, which causes them to mingle in a chance-determined brew.

> can answer the question what nature is unless he [sic] knows what history is (c1) apparent question of the relationship between fact and fiction (d1) a disseminating operation separated from presence (of Being) (d2) If nothing has preceded repetition (d2) we must admit that human life is very often subject to error (d3)
> c1-Collingwood/d1-de Man/d2-Derrida/d3-Descartes[37]

Taken alone, the syntax of certainty in these pages contrasts sharply with the often humorous free play of the pages that precede them. But similar to "The Woman in the Chinese Room," the linguistic authority of philosophical discourse is troubled and transformed by its freer counterparts. The words of Aristotle, Foucault, and Wittgenstein, in their sampled remixture, begin to open up to possibilities not yet fixed in philosophical stone.

Retallack's poem "be ing & no th' ing ness: notes from the specific rim :" (from *How To Do Things With Words*) also destabilizes philosophical discourse while restructuring attention through lettristic action. For some readers, the titular reference will automatically trigger the desire to connect Sartre's text to the poem's content and form. But in doing so, it's impossible not to notice that there's another discussion being provoked here:

> blue skIes may or may not be lIke (Ing) an ugly blue gerund may get your mean Ing across the log*Ich* et al dIvIde so slow-mo molassanalysIs comes over us lIke the sky hangIn over us lIke an ugly blue lung[38]

Again, reading this poem both silently and aloud yields deep rewards on the level of humor and puns, but this time there's a visual dimension as well. In all of the three-line stanzas of the poem, the letter "i" asserts itself as a "be ing" embedded everywhere. According to the demands of reciprocal alterity, this is not the transparently expressive "I" of the conventional lyric manufacturing empathic consent; rather, it is a material "I" asking the eye of the reader to take notice in a different way. If there's any subjectivity here, it is that of the reader "being" in the language, mucking about in it and drawing connections. While the vowels of this poem detach from their usually silent habits, the reader must slow down and take words, syllables, and even letters, one at a time.

> &/but/eIther/yes from yes/no anthropologIcal poInt of vanIsh Ing black clubs &/or Bermuda shorts neIther/nor phot O' yes porn O' yes n'o grapher after math &/or dIvIded by zero but/n'or to yIeld InfInIty[39]

Breaking up words into their component parts and isolating letters radically changes the way they are used to produce meaning. Retallack, in a discussion of a poem by John Cage, sums up what is to be gained by this kind of shift:

> [T]his poetry (and this kind of reading) functions within a poethics of complex realism where active processes of mutability and multiplicity are valued over simpler, more stable illusions of expressive clarity. Change actively, continually destabilizes the poem, thwarting *the* "correct" reading, thwarting any sure sense of return to the author's ego-bound, prior intentions. All, it seems, that it makes sense to do is to notice what we find on the page and experience the multiple directions—the multiple lettristic, phonemic, syllabic, syntactic, semantic, and graphic trajectories—in which it takes us. What is found on the page is enough.[40]

The lettristically activated page is enough because it models a "geometry of attention" that translates into a more useful way of being in the world; one considers unintelligibility an opportunity for engagement rather than a problem to solve. Retallack's poems make visible the inventive microprocesses that we often ignore in all forms of discourse. They show that how we navigate between phrases, words, syllables, and sounds in order to construct meaning is a creative process of selective attention and elimination, and therefore (previous to cultural directives) a matter of chance. There is no "absolute" rule of navigation. Although societal needs for pragmatic communication have set up limits within which language can barely move (i.e., parameters for what's deemed intelligible), Retallack's work attempts to reverse the process without losing the possibility of communicative contact. Instead of the usual reading dynamic where the transgressive/nonsignificatory possibilities of words can only rustle inaudibly beneath the surface of authorially determined texts, Retallack's poems convert the blare of linear and narrative semantics into a vibration that pulses alongside the composed (and cacophonous) musics of free running signifiers.

In this way, her poems serve as "staging areas" for active reception, and they are analogous to what art critic Nicholas Bourriaud has named "micro-utopias" (after Guattari's concept of micro-politics). In his book *Relational Aesthetics*, he discusses a number of contemporary visual artists (such as Liam Gillick and Rirkrit Tiravanijia) who are creating works that provide a platform for social encounters rather than objects for display. Such "social sculptures" focus attention on small acts of generosity and connectivity, such as a handshake or cooking a meal for others,[41] and thus stand as visual counterparts to the poethical micro-utopias of Retallack's poems. Although it has been argued that Bourriaud's theorization of these works isn't entirely in synch with how they actually function in public space (the encounters often remain at the level of potential unless deliberately set in motion, often by art-world insiders), the desire to refocus our attentions is clear. As with Retallack's poems, these works are meant to shift our gaze onto the world as we live it, and to emphasize that small acts of agency are connected to larger ones.

As should be clear from the poems discussed thus far, many of Retallack's pieces have a quasi-systematic aspect or predetermined set of initiating conditions. However, her procedures are quite different from those used by Cage and other poetic proceduralists such as Jackson Mac Low (a poet who made use of "deterministically nonintentional" methods related to Cage's chance operations) and the Oulipo group (a group of writers that created works according to systems of constraint). These process-oriented writers create text-generating machines—sets of rules that need to be rigorously held to in order for the experiment to escape the limits of authorial preferences. Cage devised the mesostic method, Mac Low created a writing-through procedure he called diastics, and the Oulipo invented methods like lipograms and N+7.[42] Although Retallack admires these systems, she believes them to be too mechanical, or, in the case of the Oulipo, too game-like. In her own work, her procedures are much less methodical as she tries to set in motion what she has called "ecologically modeled operations"[43] that respond to her discoveries as she goes along. Sometimes, as in AFTER-RIMAGES, her procedures are visibly available. In other poems, like "The Woman in the Chinese Room" or *Mongrelisme*, there is the sense of an organizing principle but the procedure remains primarily intuitive.

The poem of Retallack's that comes closest to using a systematic "programmable" procedure is "A I D /I/ S A P P E A R A N C E" (in *How To Do Things With Words*). The first stanza is seven lines, half of which consists of a quotation taken from Niels Bohr's writings on atomic theory. Bohr, like Victor Weisskopf, worked on the Manhattan Project and helped develop the atomic bomb. His statement about the discontinuity inherent to quantum physics is spliced against phrases that are decidedly nonscientific, such as "the beauty of nature" and "changing seasons change." Once this objective–subjective hybrid stanza is established, the procedure begins. The second stanza is the same as the first but the letters "a," "i," "d," and "s" have been removed:[44]

for Stefan Fitterman

1. in contrast with the demand of continuity in the customary
   description
2. of nature the indivisibilty of the quantum of action requires an
   essential
3. element of discontinuity especially apparent through the
   discussion of the
4. nature of light she said it's so odd to be dying and laughed still
   it's early

5. late the beauty of nature as the moon waxes turns to terror when
    it wanes
6. or during eclipse or when changing seasons change making
    certain things
7. disappear and there is no place to stand on and strangely we're
    glad

AIDS

for tefn fttermn

1. n contrt wth the emn of contnuty n the cutomry ecrpton
2. of nture the nvblty of the quntum of cton require n eentl
3. element of contnuty epeclly pprent through the cuon of the
4. nture of lght he t o o to be yng n lughe tll t erly
5. lte the beuty of nture the moon wxe turn to terror when t wne
6. or urng eclpe or when chngng eon chnge mkng certn thng
7. pper n there no plce to tn on n trngely we're gl

Before disappearing, these letters have presumably "infected" the letters in adjacent positions (b, h, j, e, f, r, t), for they proceed to disappear from the third stanza. The lettristic disease continues to spread, enacting viral destruction until all that's left by the seventh stanza is a series of letter "y's." One can't read this poem without feeling the disjunction between the tidy and efficient process being performed in the text and the painful disordering of a life that it represents. Neither the rationalism of the procedure nor the resulting empathic response dominates the poem; they relate in a synergistic equilibrium rather than an agonistic binary, a mesh of reason and sensation. It's a balance that can perhaps be achieved only in poetic terrain.

Although Bryan Walpert, in his essay "AIDS and the Postmodern Subject," has beautifully argued that this poem actually "recovers" the subject while simultaneously critiquing it, the fixed methodology it uses is not typical for Retallack.[45] Most of Retallack's poems include a mixture of intuitive and procedural materials, each impacting the other. A "well-designed question"/thought experiment leads to intuitively generated text, which is then shaped by a set of constraints. The results might impact the question, which will then change the constraints, and so on. In other words, Retallack's typical methods (if you can call any of her methods typical) are both fluid and controlled. For Retallack, acknowledging the presence of intentional intuitive elements alongside those determined by chance is key to the poethical dynamic. Instinct and desire must be in visible dialogue with the self-detachment (i.e., self-observation) that nonintentional procedures produce, so as to let more of the world in.

The ambient recombinations and associative logics found in Retallack's poems often resist the rules of syntax and familiar modes of signification. Fragments, neologisms, puns, and wordplay proliferate. Questions that arise from the text never resolve into easy answers. Like our acts of web browsing, connections often bring us into disjunctive territories, far from where we originally thought we were going. But rather than replicate the diluted attention we experience in front of our computer monitors, Retallack's micro-utopias spotlight those disorienting disjunctions and cause us to slow down enough to notice the paratactic leaps taking place. In doing so, they encourage us to delight in the particles of language as they reformulate in new configurations and establish an intensely material (rather than virtual and distracted) connection with the word and world.

. . .

In the aftermath of 9/11, the default political response in the United States at the beginning of the twenty-first century was to enforce singular narratives and to suspect the complex identities that constitute the hodgepodge of a migratory and intermixing population. Ideological lines of logic that didn't quite match up with the world we actually inhabit were endlessly repeated ("Mission accomplished!"); those who questioned the simplifications were scorned. Border fences and detention centers became (and continue to be) big business. All of these responses were attempts to keep "the mess" at bay. As long as democracy relies on such orderly and simplifying narratives of unity and nation, Joan Retallack's interrogative and poethical project is a crucial modeling of an alternative stance.

Through polylogical investigations into language phenomena, Retallack tries to model a world that allows multiplicities to coexist without forcing them to follow her authorial will. She approaches language with a questioning attitude, and lets the words themselves suggest new pathways for her (and the reader) to take while seeking answers. In doing so, her work unearths connections and modes of relation that usually hum invisibly beneath the surface of our routine articulations and structures of thought.

The poethical art form does not occupy transcendent heights, evaluating or correcting human experience, nor does it "make sense" of a world where atomic detonations can be accompanied by Tchaikovsky waltzes. Rather, the poethical art form *is* a form of life in and of itself, and we—as viewers, listeners, and readers—experience it as we would any of the noisy, interconnective, and wonderfully/terribly perplexing details that meet us in everyday circumstance. Retallack's poethical work illustrates that if a poem is open to the dynamic complexities of the world as it is—a world of "fractal coastlines" as opposed to symbolic symmetries—it can shake us from our perceptual defaults so that we can attend to our environment and experiences with the attuned responsiveness they deserve.

1. Joan Retallack, *AFTERRIMAGES* (Hanover, NH, and London: Wesleyan University Press, 1995), front matter.

2. Joan Retallack, "What Is Experimental Poetry & Why Do We Need It?," *Jacket* 32 (April 2007). http://jacketmagazine.com/32/p-retallack.shtml, para. 24. Examples where literary forms have mirrored oppressive social structures or have been complicit with them might include the Elizabethan pastoral as a diversion from British land grabs, or the omniscient narrator of the nineteenth-century novel who surveils and controls his subjects with a panoptical gaze.

3. Ludwig Wittgenstein, *Philosophical Investigations*, 3rd edition, trans. G. E. M. Anscombe (New York: Macmillan, 1958), 19/8e.

4. Joan Retallack, ed., *MUSICAGE: Cage Muses on Words, Art, Music in Conversation with Joan Retallack* (Hanover, NH, and London: Wesleyan University Press, 1996), xx.

5. John Cage, *I–VI* (Cambridge, MA, and London: Harvard University Press, 1990), 177–78.

6. Joan Retallack, "Appendix," in *John Cage: Composed in America*, eds. Howard Junkerman and Marjorie Perloff (Chicago: University of Chicago Press, 1994), 276.

7. Joan Retallack, "The Poethical Wager," in *The Poethical Wager* (Berkeley and Los Angeles: University of California Press, 2003), 28.

8. *Ibid.*, 226. This quote is from Deirdre Bair's *Samuel Beckett: A Biography*.

9. William J. Turkel, *Digital History Hacks: Methodology for the Infinite Archive* (2005–08). http://digitalhistoryhacks.blogspot.com. This site describes itself as a "weblog that focuses on methodological issues in the digital humanities, particularly history and computing."

10. Retallack, "Icarus Fffffalling," *AFTERRIMAGES*, 50.

11. Joan Retallack, "The Woman in the Chinese Room," *How to Do Things With Words* (Berkeley and Los Angeles: Sun & Moon Press), 17. Also, see John Searle, "Minds, Brains and Programs," *Behavioral and Brain Sciences* 3, no. 3 (1980): 417–57.

12. Burton Hatlen, "Joan Retallack: A Philosopher Among the Poets, a Poet Among the Philosophers," *Contemporary Literature*, 42, no. 2, Special Issue: American Poetry of the 1990s (summer 2001): 347–75.

13. Greg Kinzer, "Excuses and Other Nonsense: Joan Retallack's *How to Do Things With Words*," *Contemporary Literature*, 47, no. 1 (2006): 62–90.

14. *Ibid.*, 85.

15. Retallack, "The Woman in the Chinese Room," *How To Do Things With Words*, 19. See pages 312–313 in this volume for the entirety of this section of the poem.

16. Joseph Bucklin Bishop, *Theodore Roosevelt and His Time Shown in His Own Letters*, vol. 2 (New York: Charles Scribner's Sons, 1920), 474.

17. Joan Retallack, "Since the early nineties . . . ," *HOW2*, 1, no. 6 (fall 2001). http://www.asu.edu/pipercwcenter/how2journal/archive/online_archive/v1_6_2001/current/forum/more-forum.html. In her essay "Re:Thinking:Literary:Feminism," Retallack mentions "the messy polylectics, polylogues that create the live culture of our language" (*Poethical Wager*, 131).

18. Joan Retallack, *Mongrelisme* (Providence, RI: Paradigm Press, 1999), un-paginated. See pages 313–315 in this volume for an excerpt from *Mongrelisme*; note that due to page limitations the poem has been reformatted. In the original volume the Spanish phrases each had their own page.

19. *Ibid.*

20. Retallack, "Scenes of Translation (from the Translation)," *How To Do Things With Words*, 46.

21. *Ibid.*, 48.

22. Caroline Bergvall, "Writing at the Crossroads of Languages," in *Telling it Slant: Avant-Garde Poetics of the 1990s*, eds. Mark Wallace and Steven Marks (Tuscaloosa: University of Alabama Press, 2002), 209.

23. Retallack, "Since the early nineties . . .," *HOW2*.

24. Retallack, "What Is Experimental Poetry & Why Do We Need It?," *Jacket* 32, para. 38.

25. Retallack, "Re:Thinking:Literary:Feminism," *Poethical Wager*, 122.

26. Redell Olsen, "An Interview With Joan Retallack." *How2*, 1, no. 6 (2001). http://www.scc.rutgers.edu/however/v1_6_2001/current/readings/encounters/ olsen.html.

27. Joan Retallack, *Memnoir* (Sausalito, CA: Post-Apollo Press, 2004), 28.

28. Jorge Luis Borges, "The Circular Ruins," *Ficciones* (New York: Grove Press, 1962), 62.

29. Retallack, "What Is Experimental Poetry," *Jacket* 32, paras. 34 and 38.

30. Sven Birkerts, *Gutenberg Elegies: The Fate of Reading in the Electronic Age* (Boston: Faber & Faber: 2006); Nicholas Carr, "Is Google Making Us Stupid?," *Atlantic Monthly* (vol. 302, no. 1; July/August 2008): 56–63.

31. Retallack, "Fig. 1, Ground Zero, Fig. 2," *The Poethical Wager*, 192.

32. Retallack, "Geometries of Attention," *The Poethical Wager*, 180.

33. Retallack, *AFTERRIMAGES*, 9. For an in-depth discussion of this poem, see Ann Vickery's chapter "Taking a Poethical Perspective: Joan Retallack's After-rimages" in her book *Leaving the Lines of Gender* (Middletown, CT: Wesleyan University Press, 2000); for more on process, see Jena Osman, "Gumshoe Poetry," in *Poetry and Pedagogy*, eds. Retallack and Spahr (New York: Palgrave, 2006).

34. Retallack, "The Poethical Wager," *The Poethical Wager*, 4.

35. Retallack, "Scarlet Aitch," *The Poethical Wager*, 106.

36. Joan Retallack, *Errata Suite* (Washington, DC: Edge Books, 1993), 20.

37. *Ibid.*, 25.

38. Retallack, "be ing & no th' ing ness," *How To Do Things With Words*, 129.

39. *Ibid.*, 127.

40. Retallack, "Poethics of a Complex Realism," *The Poethical Wager*, 219–20.

41. Nicholas Bourriaud, *Relational Aesthetics* (Dijon, France: Les Presses du Réel, 1998). Since the late 1980s, artist Rirkrit Tiravanija has cooked Thai curry meals for gallery visitors. Mierle Ukeles has been the artist in residence at the New York Department of Sanitation since the 1970s. In her piece "Touch Sanitation," she met and shook the hands of more than 8,500 sanitation workers.

42. Mesostics are akin to acrostics, but with key words running down the cen-

ter; Cage used this method to "write through" Joyce's *Finnegans Wake*, Thoreau's journals, and many other texts that were important to him. Mac Low's diastics are a "spelling through" method where a key phrase is used to process a larger text; for example, using the name Ezra Pound, Mac Low looked in the Cantos for the first "e" in the first position, then looked for a "z" in the second position, an "r" in the third position, etc. See *Words nd Ends from Ez* (Bolinas, CA: Avenue B, 1989). A lipogram is a text written with constraints on what letters can or cannot be used. George Perec's novel *A Void*, written without the letter "e," is perhaps the best known lipogrammatic text. Christian Bok's *Eunoia* is a more recent example. N+7 is a procedure where every noun in a text is looked up in the dictionary and then replaced by another noun found seven nouns further down the page.

43. Joan Retallack, "N Plus Zero." A talk given at the annual Associated Writing Programs conference for a panel titled "Newlipo: Bringing Proceduralism and Chance-Poetics into the 21st Century," New York City, 1/31/08.

44. Retallack, "A I D /I/ S A P P E A R A N C E," *How To Do Things With Words*, 53-57.

45. Bryan Walpert, "AIDS and the Postmodern Subject: Joan Retallack's 'AID/I/ SAPPEARANCE,'" *Poetics Today* 27, no. 4 (winter 2006): 693–710.

BIBLIOGRAPHY

Books by Joan Retallack

POETRY

Circumstantial Evidence. Washington, DC: S.O.S. Books, 1985.
Errata 5uite. Washington, DC: Edge Books, 1993.
AFTERRIMAGES. Hanover, NH, and London: Wesleyan University Press, 1995.
How To Do Things With Words. Los Angeles, CA: Sun & Moon Classics, 1998.
MONGRELISME: A Difficult Manual for Desperate Times. Providence, RI: Paradigm Press, 1999.
Memnoir. Sausalito, CA: Post-Apollo Press, 2004.
Procedural Elegies. New York, NY: Roof Books, 2010.

POETRY IN TRANSLATION

Steinzas en médiation. Translated by Jacques Roubaud. Bordeaux: Format Américain, 2002.
Memnoir. Translated by Omar Berrada, Emanuel Hocquard, Juliette Valéry, et al. Marseille: CipM, 2004.

PROSE

MUSICAGE: John Cage in Conversation with Joan Retallack. Hanover, NH, and London: Wesleyan University Press, 1996.
The Poethical Wager. Berkeley: University of California Press, 2004.
Poetry & Pedagogy. Coedited with Juliana Spahr. New York: Palgrave/MacMillan, 2006.
Gertrude Stein: Selections, edited and with introduction. Berkeley: University of California Press, 2008.

WESTERN CIV CONT'D, AN OPEN BOOK. cardboard, grommets, movable images, handmade paper, collage and text. Edition of 18. Riverdale, MD: Pyramid Atlantic, 1995–96.

Selected Prose

"The Meta-physick of Play: L=A=N=G=U=A=G=E USA." *Parnassus* 12, no. 1 (fall/winter 1984): 213–44.

"H.D., H.D.* Doctor of Hermeticism." *Parnassus* 13, no. 1 (fall/winter 1985): 67–88.

"Local Ex-centrisms: The Dupont Circle Circle" in *The Mass Transit Poets: Washington Review Special Issue* V.XIV, no. 2 (1988).

"Post-Scriptum-High-Modern" in *Postmodern Genres*, ed. Marjorie Perloff. Norman: University of Oklahoma Press, 1989, 248–73.

"Non-Euclidean Narrative Combustion (Or What the Subtitles Can't Say)" in *Conversant Essays: Contemporary Poets on Poetry*, ed. James McCorkle. Detroit: Wayne State University Press, 1990, 491–509.

"Accident . . . Aeroplane . . . Artichoke." *New American Writing* (Fall 1992): 120–35.

"High Adventures of Indeterminacy," in *Parnassus: Twenty Years of Poetry in Review*, ed. Herbert Leibowitz. Ann Arbor: University of Michigan Press, 1994, pp. 75-107. Also in *Pushcart Prize, IX*, ed. Bill Henderson. Wainscott NY: Pushcart Press, 1984–85. First published in *Parnassus* 11, no. 1 (spring/summer 1983): 231–62.

"_____:_____." Essay on Jackson Mac Low in *Festschrift for Jackson Mac Low*, eds. Andrew Levy and Bob Harrison, CRAYON #1, New York, 1997, 87–97.

"SECNÀHC GNIKÀT : TAKING CHANCES" in *Moving Borders: Three Decades of Innovative Writing by Women*, ed. Mary Margaret Sloan. Jersey City, NJ: Talisman House, 1998, 708–714.

"Chance of a Lifetime: Joan Retallack on Jackson Mac Low." *Artforum*, XLIII, no. 6, February 2005, 35–36.

"Tragi-Kitsch & Elegiac Comix (John Ashbery's *Girls on the Run*)." *Conjunctions* 49, 2007, 399–412.

"On Mina Loy's Feminist Manifesto" and "Documented: The Future . . . . . Undocumented: The Future" in *Rett Kopi, Dokumenterer Fremtiden: Manifest*. Edited by Ellef Prestsaeter and Karin Nygård. Oslo: PDC Tangen, 2007.

"What Is Experimental Poetry & Why Do We Need It?" *Jacket* 32 (April 2007). http://jacketmagazine.com/32/p-retallack.shtml.

"Gertrude Stein in the Forties: Politics and Poethics in Catastrophic Times." In *Transatlantic Negotiations*, edited by Christa Buschendorf and Astrid Franke. Heidelberg: Universitätsverlag, 2007.

Selected Interviews

"Joan Retallack Interviewed by P. Inman," *Washington Review of the Arts*, no. 2 (1987): 25–56.

"Uses of Form, Rosmarie Waldrop in Conversation with Joan Retallack." *Contemporary Literature* 40, no. 3 (1999): 329–377.

Olsen, Redell. "An Interview With Joan Retallack." *How(2)* 1, no. 6 (2001). http://www.scc.rutgers.edu/however/v1_6_2001/current/readings/encounters/olsen.html

Selected Criticism

Bergvall, Caroline. "Writing at the Crossroads of Language," in *Telling It Slant: Avant Garde Poetics of the 1990s*, ed. Mark Wallace and Steven Marks, Tuscaloosa, AL, and London: University of Alabama Press, 2002, 207–23.

Cayley, John. "Writing on Complex Surfaces." February 2005. www.dichtung-digital.org/2005/2-Cayley.htm.

Devenish, Alan. "Spd of Snd—Grace of Lt: Joan Retallack's *WESTERN CIV* and the 'Cultural Logic' of the Postmodern Poem." *Contemporary Literature* 35, no. 3 (fall 1994): 547–566.

Hatlen, Burton. "Joan Retallack: A Poet Among the Philosophers, A Philosopher Among the Poets." *Contemporary Literature* 42, no. 2 (summer 2001): 347–75.

Keller, Lynn. "FFFFFalling with Poetry: The Centrifugal Classroom" in *Poetry and Pedagogy: The Challenge of the Contemporary*, ed. Joan Retallack and Juliana Spahr. New York: Palgrave Macmillan, 2006, 30–38.

———. "'Fields of Pattern-Bounded Unpredictability': Recent Palimptexts by Rosmarie Waldrop and Joan Retallack." *Contemporary Literature* XLII, no. 2 (2001): 376–412.

Kinzer, Greg. "Excuses and Other Nonsense: Joan Retallack's *How to Do Things with Words*." *Contemporary Literature* XLVII:1 (2006): 62–90.

Lazer, Hank. "Partial to Error: Joan Retallack's *ERRATA 5UITE*" in *Opposing Poetries*, vol. 2. Evanston, IL: Northwestern University Press, 1996, 70–76.

Lennon, Brian. "*techne / nostos / physis*: The procedural poetries of Joan Retallack," *Electronic Book Review* 10 (winter 1999). www.altx.com/ebr/ebr10/10len.htm.

Olsen, Redell. "Images After Errors/Errors After Images: Joan Retallack." *HOW2* 1, no. 7 (2002).

Spahr, Juliana. "Spiderwasp or Literary Criticism," in *Telling It Slant: Avant-Garde Poetics of the 1990s*, eds. Mark Wallace and Steven Marks, Tuscaloosa, AL, and London: University of Alabama Press, 2002, 404–28.

Vickery, Ann. "Taking a Poethical Perspective: Joan Retallack's *Afterrimages*," in *Leaving Lines of Gender: A Feminist Genealogy of Language Writing*. Hanover, NH, and London: Wesleyan University Press, 2000, 167–78.

Walpert, Bryan. "AIDS and the Postmodern Subject: Joan Retallack's 'AID/I/SAPPEARANCE.'" *Poetics Today* 27, no. 4 (winter 2006), 693–710.

LISA ROBERTSON

FROM *The Weather*

Residence at C __

Give me hackneyed words because
they are good. Brocade me the whole body
of terrestrial air. Say spongy ground
with its soft weeds. Say self because it can.
Say arts of happiness. Say you have died.
Say sequin because the word just
appeared. Say weather take this adult
from its box. Memorize being sequined
to something, water. Everything you forget
inserts love into the silent money.
Memorize huge things of girders greased. Say
the water parting about the particular
animal. Say what happens to the face
as it gala tints my simple cut
vicious this afternoon the beautiful
light on the cash is human to guzzle
with—go away wild feelings, there you go
as the robin as the songsparrow go
the system shines with uninterrupted
light. It's petal caked. Leaves shoot up. Each
leaf's a runnel. Far into the night a
sweetness. Marvelous. Spectacular. Brilliant.
Clouded towards the south. It translates
Lucretius. Say cup of your heart rush
sluice is yellow sluice Kate Moss is Rousseau

have my arms. Say impasto of
atmosphere for her fur. Halo open
her face. Misplace the death. All the truth
under the tree has two pinky oozy
names. Say trying to possess or not. Say
if you thought love was ironical. If
pleasure emancipates, why aren't you some-
where. Sincerity.

Tuesday

Days heap upon us. All plain. All clouds except a narrow
opening at the top of the sky. All cloudy except a narrow
opening at the bottom of the sky with others smaller. All
cloudy except a narrow opening at the bottom of the sky.
All cloudy except a narrow opening at the top of the sky.
All cloudy. All cloudy. All cloudy. Except one large opening
with others smaller. And once in the clouds. Days heap
upon us. Where is our anger. And the shades darker than
the plain part and darker at the top than the bottom. But
darker at bottom than top. Days heap upon us. Where is
Ti-Grace. But darker at the bottom than the top. Days heap
upon us. Where is Christine. Broken on the word culture.
But darker at the bottom than the top. Days heap upon
us. Where is Valerie. Pulling the hard air into her lung.
The life crumbles open. But darker at the bottom than the
top. Days heap upon us. Where is Patty. Unlearning each
thing. Red sky crumbles open. This is the only way to
expand the heart. But darker at the top than the bottom.
Days heap upon us. Where is Shulamith. Abolishing the
word love. The radical wing crumbles open. The scorn is
not anticipated. We have given our surface. Darker at the

top than the bottom. Except one large opening with others smaller. Except one large opening with others smaller. Gradually. Days heap upon us. Where is Patricia. In the dream of obedience and authority. The genitalia crumble open. It is only ever a flickering. We never worshipped grief. It has been stuccoed over. Half cloud half plain. Half cloud half plain. Half plain. One in the plain part and one in the clouds. Days heap upon us. Where is Jane. Looking for food. Hunger crumbles open. All this is built on her loveliness. We have fallen into a category. Love subsidized our descent. Streaky clouds at the bottom of the sky. Days heap upon us. Where is Mary. In the extreme brevity of the history of parity. Rage crumbles open. It felt like dense fog. What is fact is not necessarily human. Memory anticipates. Authority flows into us like a gel. We cross the border to confront the ideal. Streaky cloudy at the top of the sky. Days heap upon us. Where is Grace. Spent in sadness. The underground crumbles open. There is no transgression possible. We publicly mobilize the horror of our emotion. It is a phalanx. The clouds darker than the plain or blue part and darker at the top than the bottom. Days heap upon us. Where is Gloria. Pushing down laughter. Utopia crumbles open. It is an emotion similar to animals sporting. We won't plagiarize shame. Like this we solve herself. The clouds darker than the plain part and darker at the top than the bottom. The clouds darker than the plain part and darker at the top than the bottom. The clouds lighter than the plain part and darker at the top than the bottom. The clouds lighter than the plain part and darker at the bottom than top. The clouds lighter than the plain part and darker at the top than the bottom. The lights of the clouds lighter and the darks darker than the plain part and darker at the top than the bottom. The same as the last but darker at the bottom than the top. The same as the last but darker at the bottom than the top. Days heap upon us. Where is Violette. Walking without flinching. Doubt crumbles open. It is not a value but a disappearance. We come upon the city in our body. The same as the last. The same as the last. The same as the last. The tint once over in the plain part, and twice in the clouds. Days heap upon us. Where is Emily. Out in all weather. Dignity crumbles open. There is not even a utopia. We would have to mention all the possible causes of her death. The tint once over the openings and twice in the clouds. Days heap upon us. Where is Olympe. Going with out rest. The polis crumbles open. This is no different than slow war. The tint twice in the openings and once in the clouds. Days heap upon us. Where is Michelle. Homesick for anger. Midnight crumbles open. The tint twice in the openings. The tint twice over. Days heap upon us. Where is Bernadine. At description. The tint twice over. Days heap upon us. Where is Kathleen. The tint twice. The clouds darker than the plain part and darker at the top than the bottom. The clouds lighter than the plain part and darker at the top than the bottom. The lights of the clouds lighter. The others smaller. The same as the last. The same as the last. The tint twice in the openings and once in the clouds. Days heap upon us. The tint twice over. Days heap upon us. With others smaller. With others smaller.

Residence at C___

Sometimes I want a corset like
to harden me or garnish. I
think of this stricture—rain
language, building—as a corset: an
outer ideal mould, I feel
the ideal moulding me the ideal
is now my surface just so very
perfect I know where to buy it and I
take it off. I take it off. If all things fail
and we are just emperors, serious
and accurate and fugitive
in such dormant lines of gorgeousness
the day is a locksmith
dew lies long on the grass
and I a rustic ask: what is
a surface—and respond
only omniscience, the crumpling face
as the domestic emotions elucidate
themselves a sea of mist
exists so strangely side by side
the potent mould of anarchy and scorn.

Saturday

To language, rain. To rain, building. Think of this stricture
so that the vernaculars of causation quicken. To Claude,
his contemplation. To objects, passing. To golden change
our own blazing device. The day follows the present. Half
and then half, delectable and idle, with gleams of fine
greenery in the intervals. To the middle of instability, no
absolution dad. To the end of surfaces, our mistake. Pop

groups say love phonemes. To the middle of the phoneme, people think in belts of light. To the end of pulling, a clangour, a highth, and a name. At the beginning we pinken, require cloth. To the end of moot falsity, hard leather, love. To the beginning of disburdening, the striving face. To the latter end of autumn, the stubborn lung. How are we to unlearn each thing? The next insistence, sullied; thence to the end of insistence, pulling the hard air into the hard lung. Histories, windy, float midway above the dark, and we will insist on wanting. Just for the first fortnight: during the middle an infinite sweetness. To the pigment, a mistake in context. The whole of comparison completely, slowly browsing for ward. A fatality with purse. May began with summer showers, and ended with its streets, its underground levels, its frontiers. June, irrealized, chequered with gleams of sunshine. The rights of loneliness don't tear it. The first procrastination, dark and sultry; the latter part merely dirty, with heavy lines. Some tufts are caught in the previously bare limbs, tufts of a genus, a highth and a name. It is a movement as the disburdening of the face. How are we to unlearn each thing? We address you without economy till the last, with sequins and apricots. To the first week of seriousness, just so fucking beautiful: to the end of admonition, it's in you that we shall speak. We're happy and we're picky. So that here is a falling off. To the end of the inflamed limit, we lingered here, encouraged. So that emotion's a soft anonymity. To the end of the first fortnight in quietness, numerals, minerals and salts. To the end of waking, lust into air dissolving. So that we're above a kind of no-shape. The first fortnight in July only, then go back. To the end of September, we are soloists, float midway above the shabby dark, elaborate. October rainy. November floods upward into its referent. December seeks a runnel. A runnel. A limb. A sky. A disburdening. A highth. A name. A rubbing. A fear. A thing. A fear. A tuft. A face. A runnel. An escape. A number. A wisp. A screen. A knot. A mother. A boat.

FROM *Utopia (R's Boat)*

In the spring of 1979
Some images have meanings, and some have a change in soul, sex or century.
Rain buckles into my mouth.
If pressed to account for strangeness and resistance, I can't.
I'm speaking here for dogs and rusting ducts venting steam into rain.
I wanted to study the ground, the soft ruins of paper and the rusting things.
I discover a tenuous utopia made from steel, wooden chairs, glass, stone, metal bed frames, tapestry, bones, prosthetic legs, hair, shirt-cuffs, nylon, plaster figurines, perfume bottles and keys.
I am confusing art and decay.
Elsewhere, fiction is an activity like walking.
Any girl who reads is already a lost girl.

Women from a flat windswept settlement called Utopia focus on the intricate life that exists there.
What I found beautiful slid between.
We die and become architecture.
The season called November addresses speech to us.
The crows are still cutting the sky in half with their freckling eastward wake.
The quiet revolutions of loneliness are a politics.
Some of us love its common and accidental beauty.

I take the spatial problem of heaven seriously.
I look up from my style.
How do people work and sleep?

At about midnight in Autumn
The nightreading girls were thinking by their lamps.
The fleeing was into life.
It was the same world, the same garments, the same loose rain.
It was no longer the end of a season but the beginning.
Clean as a tree, a face waits for form.

At about four in the morning, that first day
Which is a surface?
What is the concept of transformation?
The intellect struggled to its stanza.
The earth spoke in figures.
Its pebbles and tropes and vertebrae withdrew.
I felt a willingness to enter righteous emotion.
I became willing to enter certainty.
Then after a month it was the month of July.
The soft dirt threw the pink light upwards.
The danger of the infinite opened.
It was almost dawn in August.
A dog yipped in sorrow.

By early June, I lost speech.
What about the conceptualized trees?
What about the phosphorescent sexes that took my strength
    away?
I arrived at the threshold but did not cross.
How odd it is to think that a broken pier laced by gulls and
    kneeling into the foaming pull was once an empire.

It is late October.
The house is like sunlight.
Soft and mild emotions were interrupted by emotions that were
    eager, hurrying, impetuous.
People are fragile and finite.

Is this an interesting thing?—to be 40, female, in the year 2001?
How simple it would be to walk together.

It was a Saturday evening.
Yes, the future, which is a sewing motion.
These are the inescapable vernaculars of the Mississauga
    nocturne.
The effect of the downflowing pattern of shade on the wall was
    liquid, so the wall became a slow fountain in afternoon.
Our fears opened inwards.
Must it be the future?
Yes, the future, which is a sewing motion.
Most decay is not picturesque.
For one day there is the sensation that Springtime is waiting for
    us to walk forward.
Everything follows from the sweet-acrid scent of pencils in June
    classrooms.
Every angel is fucking the seven arts.
Each leaf had achieved its vastness.
A young woman is seated on a kitchen chair, black wings spread
    out as if drying.

It was August and the night was hot.
What we were proposing already exists.
This is a history of sincerity.
The tree uses silence.
The three layers of air flood the sky.
My face is tilted upwards.
I wanted language to be a vulnerable and exact instrument of
glass, pressures, and chemicals.
It has provided us with a cry, but explains nothing.
I understand passivity.
But what elegance is self-sufficient?
Before primrose and before aconite, after snowdrop, at bluebells,
    during jonquil, inextinguishably for fritillaria, I stumble in
    and in.

It began at three o'clock one October afternoon.
What was I to understand of it?
Its intent is mordent.
It's weak and it wants beauty.
It was here that I first observed this question of withheld arcadia.
It leans on the transparent balustrade.
It is a continuous astonishment.
It arrives at nothing but the rolling year.
It always means everything.
For instance, to do, to be, to suffer, to bark, to like, to crumble,
   to sit: in each verb I've entertained ambition.

POETICS STATEMENT

Soft Architecture: A Manifesto

The worn cotton sheets of our little beds had the blurred texture
of silk crêpe and when we lay against them in the evening we'd
rub, rhythmically, one foot against the soothing folds of fabric,
waiting for sleep. That way we slowly wore through the thinning
cloth. Our feet would get tangled in the fretted gap.

We walked through the soft arcade. We became an architect.

The knitted cap on the wrinkled head of the mewling kid is
the first boundary. At the other tip the bootie dribbles. There
are curious histories of shrouds. That is not all. Memory's
architecture is neither palatial nor theatrical but soft.

Of course it's all myth. Beginning at grand rooms ranked in
small stone Natufian couples commingled in kisses, the Perspex
galleries of pendant Babylonian dollies, the long halls of
Egyptian cats that are sirens or dynasties, we amble towards the
disappearance of godliness into cloth. Europe's lusty godlets start
bending. Carved cloth connotes the wild swirls of the Christly

sexual parts. Sprigged calico greets the renaissance of Venus. Prudery flows animate, clinging, vivid—we think it absorbs virility from naked Antiquity herself. Strolling from Byzantium we observe her teasing retreat. The mischievous and the sexy gods get dressed as patrons and courtesans and popes, crinolined in Fragonard's stiff satins, diminished to tiny petticoated players in painted enamel frolics. Finally invisible they loll in the latent conventions of canvas, or in the draperies and objets of the rooms themselves, such as the Frick's crushed mohair swags, the personified tapestry walls, the little petit-point chairs personified, the chamberpot, the silken floor personified.

We arrive at our last long century. We note that the holy modernism of the white room is draped and lined in its newness by labile counter-structures of moving silk, fur, leather, onyx, velvet. The modernist inventors of the moot science of psychoanalysis raise its cold visage from the deep upholsteries and ruched cushions of the speaking invalid's couch. A contemporary describes the late Maria Callas's vibrato as "a worn velvet that has lost the evenness of its texture." As for us, we wear avant-thrift. We sit in spider-like chairs. But Soft Architecture expires invisibly as the mass rhetorics of structural permanence transmit: Who can say when the astonishing complicities of the woven decay into rote? The bare ruin of Bauhaus and the long autopsy of concepts serve as emblems of Soft Architecture's demise.

Yet our city is persistently soft. We see it like a raw encampment at the edge of the rocks, a camp for a navy vying to return to a place that has disappeared. So the camp is a permanent transience, the buildings or shelters like tents—tents of steel, chipboard, stucco, glass, cement, paper and various claddings— tents rising and falling in the glittering rhythm which is null rhythm, which is the flux of modern careers. At the centre of the tent encampment, the density of the temporary in a tantrum of action; on peripheries over silent grass of playing fields the fuzzy mauveness of seed-fringe hovering. Our favourite on-ramp

curving sveltely round to the cement bridge, left side overhung
with a small-leafed tree that sprays the roof of our car with
its particular vibrato shade. Curved velveteen of asphalt as we
merge with the bridge-traffic, the inlet, the filmic afternoon. The
city is a fluorescence of surface.

Under the pavement, pavement. Hoaxes, failures, porches,
archaeological strata spread out on a continuous thin plane;
softness and speed, echoes, spores, tropes, fonts; not identity
but incident and the accumulation of air miles; unmarked
solitude absorbing time, bloating to become an environment,
indexical euphorias, the unraveling of laughter; a brief history of
escalators; memory manifest, brindled, loosening; a crumpling
of automotive glass; the pornographic, the wrapped; Helvetica's
black dust: All doctrine is foreign to us. The problem of the
shape of choice is mainly retrospective.

That wild nostalgia leans into the sheer volubility of
incompetence. This nostalgia musters symbols with no relation
to necessity—civic sequins, apertures that record and tend the
fickleness of social gifts. Containing only supple space, nostalgia
feeds our imagination's strategic ineptitude. Forget the journals,
conferences, salons, textbooks, and media of dissemination. We
say thought's object is not knowledge but living. We do not like
it elsewhere.

The truly utopian act is to manifest current conditions and
dialects. Practice description. Description is mystical. It is afterlife
because it is life's reflection or reverse. Place is accident posing as
politics. And vice versa. Therefore it's tragic and big.

We recommenders of present action have learned to say
"perhaps" our bodies produce space; "perhaps" our words make
a bunting canopy; "perhaps" the hand-struck palpable wall is
an anti-discipline; "perhaps" by the term "everyday life" we
also mean the potential. We allude sympathetically to the lyrical
tone of clothing and furniture since they clearly reveal to the
eye, mind and judgement the real shapes of peopled sentiment.

Cravats gushing from collars, we agree with the Soft Architect Lilly Reich that "clothes may also have metaphysical effects by means of their inherent regularity, their coolness and reserve, their coquettish cheerfulness and liveliness, their playful grace, their sound simplicity and their dignity." From the vast urbanity of our counter-discipline we applaud the mercurial Miss Reich, who said, "one of my hearts is in building."

Soft Architecture will reverse the wrongheaded story of structural deepness. That institution is all doors but no entrances. The work of the SA paradoxically recompiles the metaphysics of surface, performing an horizontal research which greets shreds of fibre, pigment flakes, the bleaching of light, proofs of lint, ink, spore, liquid and pixilation, the strange frail leaky cloths and sketchings and gestures, which we are. The work of the SA, simultaneously strong and weak, makes new descriptions on the warp of former events. By descriptions, we mean moistly critical dreams, morphological thefts, authentic registers of pleasant customs, accidents posing as intentions. SA makes up face-practices.

What if there is no "space," only a permanent, slow-motion mystic takeover, an implausibly careening awning? Nothing is utopian. Everything wants to be. Soft Architects face the reaching middle.

ABOUT SURFACE

Lisa Robertson's Poetics of Elegance

Sina Queyras

> Let us free architecture of the responsibilities that it can
> no longer assume and let us aggressively explore this newly
> realized freedom . . .   —REM KOOLHAAS

> I'm really a gentleman collector of sentences. I display them
> in cabinets.   —LISA ROBERTSON

IN A RECENT ISSUE of *Architectural Digest*, Patrik Schumacher of Zaha Hadid Architects argues for elegance as the new watchword guiding the next stage of avant-garde architecture.[1] This new, capital "E" Elegance, he argues, riffs on aspects of minimalism while refusing its simplicity (or surface simplicity), opting instead for design that is both descriptive and argumentative, an effortless display of sophistication, a composition of complication in all dimensions. Schumacher's architecture presents a "visual reduction of an underlying complexity that is thereby sublated rather than eliminated," an architecture that casts itself onto the structural and social, making itself as apparent as it is beautiful, as elegant as it is functional (*Elegance*, 30). "Elegance," Schumacher argues, may be part of an agenda to push avant-garde values into the mainstream. In this sense, it "constitutes a provocation" (30). Schumacher could be describing the poetry of Lisa Robertson. Like the architectures of the avant-garde, her texts are spacious and temporal structures, elegantly complex and pleasurable to inhabit. They also constitute a provocation.

The Kootenay School of Writing, one of Canada's most dynamic and innovative literary organizations, and one that Robertson has long been associated with, embraces tag lines such as "we will not be understood."[2] Members and fans of the KSW are quick to point out that the collective morphs in relation to membership and engagements over time; nonetheless, the tag line reflects an ongoing commitment to the creation of an alternative thinking, reading, and writing community, a stance that suggests readers come to texts rather than texts to readers. It may be read as "we will be understood on our own terms," or, "we will invert your terms." In other words, the KSW is more apt to critique nationalism, capitalism, simplicity, and the extreme nature of cultural, economic, physical and architectural changes in the city it calls home, than to embrace, or court, either accessibility or mainstream validity.

Robertson, in keeping with those values, rejects labels and toeholds. However, as much as the work resists values of consumption, it flaunts its appetite for beauty and ornamentation. Like Schumacher's elegance, Robertson's work offers heady "orientation within complex organizations" (30): an orientation that brings wild combinations of thinking to new audiences. To achieve this Robertson integrates contemporary and classical tropes and genres, makes firm structural choices, and, particularly in the texts this essay will look at, makes a tightrope of the sentence—her compositional unit of choice. Together these tactics conceive of the poem as a collaborative and inhabitable public space, one that reveals much about the structural integrity of language and rhetoric while reflecting the actual experience of navigating contemporary urban cultures and infrastructures. For this reason alone one could argue that Robertson offers a new model of feminist poetics. I will elaborate on these aspects of Robertson's work, focusing largely on *The Weather, Occasional Work and Seven Walks from the Office for Soft Architecture*, and *Rousseau's Boat*.[3]

It's All About the Surface.
Or, the Surface Is Not What It Appears to Be

Consider the value of surface (after all, every inch of it, even the sky has been commodified). Then consider the value of interrogating surface. Then consider the value of a *gendered* interrogation of surface. Visually the prose poems of *The Weather* scroll down a justified page; the lines of *Debbie: An Epic* project like a Barbara Kruger installation, announcing its sculptural qualities in bold fonts, banners, and shields; and the pages in *Seven Walks and Occasional Work* defer to the prose block, collaborating with visual images. Robertson revels in the surface (literally in some cases, and figuratively), continually opening the text, moving laterally or rhizomatically. The end of *The Weather*, for example, offers us the line: "I've never done anything / but begin" (78). This is not to suggest that Robertson doesn't delve deeply; she does, but the emphasis here is not on closure or even the rejection of it, but rather on the sense of openness, rippling across the surface but not remaining there, or perhaps allowing that downward movement, the connective response, to occur within the reader (a tactic I will discuss later in this essay). The point here is that beyond the surface the text is multiple: "troubling" or "complicating," never allowing the reader to settle, a feature that mimics contemporary product-driven thinking, but also the blending and bending of visual images on urban surfaces.

The essays that comprise *Seven Walks* spring from Robertson's extensive reading and thinking about architecture, visual art, and poetics, as well as her direct involvement in the west coast Canadian art scene.[4] They also evolved out of her feminist activism, witnessed not only in her own writing, but also in her curatorial work and as co-editor of *Raddle Moon*.[5] In her essay "Feminist Poetics and the Meaning of Clarity," Rae Armantrout notes the difference between the interiority of lyric poets—Alicia Ostriker and Sharon Olds, for example—who disclose the personal as a means of creating relations—as opposed to the exteriority of Lyn Hejinian or Lorine Niedecker.[6] The latter, while equally embedded in the "realism" of quotidian, even the domestic landscape (traditional lyric provinces), nevertheless create an *externalized* poetic. There is something very tangible about the movement in women's poetry from an interior to an exterior space and how this relates to subjectivity. Armantrout wonders whether "experimental writing seek[s] a new view of the self."[7] She cites Hejinian's essay "Strangeness," where Hejinian differentiates between metonymy and metaphor: "Metonymy moves attention from thing to thing: its principle is *combination* rather than selection" (emphasis mine).[8] Perhaps more importantly, Armantrout notes Hejinian's distinction between the notion of "similarity" in metaphor, a move that "conserves" and "transfers" meanings, to make things *like*, as opposed to the "metonymic world," which is unstable. The idea of an externalized, or public, poetic moving outside of the familiar and interior, and the move away from metaphor, are not unrelated.

With this latter point in mind, it is no accident that Robertson devises for herself an office. Architectural preoccupations notwithstanding, she is very much aware of the extent to which women have been excluded from the discussions—not only of rhetoric, but in the literal design and implementation of cities, in civic planning, in external operations, and, of course, in the building of canons. The problem with discourse, like the problem with urban planning, is that this thinking becomes concretized, and if women are not in that thinking, they are not *in* the foundations, just as the way we build our infrastructures—domestic and civic—creates the way we live and move through our domestic and civic spaces. The persona, the Office for Soft Architecture (or OSA), riffs on Rem Koolhaas's *Office for Metropolitan Architecture*, an international organization that includes architects, designers, researchers, a kind of think tank for contemporary architecture and urbanism. Like the OMA, the OSA is grounded in the intellectual and analytical as much as the domestic: Consider the draperies and wraps, the textures of soft architecture like the roundness of Zaha Hadid's future-oriented innovation, space, design, and its relationship to the feminine curves. Architecture, Rem Koolhaas tells us, is a "chaotic adventure."[9] Like literature, coherence is imposed either as a cosmetic or as an act of self-censorship; there is a desire to be pragmatic and narrative, modern and historical, to fit into the discourse. But Robertson is not "like a room," she "becomes" a room; she isn't fitting *into* discourse, she is *creating it*.

In "Feminist Poetics and the Meaning of Clarity," Armantrout asks, "Is clarity equivalent to readability? How readable is the world?"[10] The OSA makes no attempts to make itself accessible, or readable in a predictable sense, to anyone;[11] in fact, by externalizing herself she complicates the speaking subject, eradicating the possibility of hinging all thoughts on a single, gendered, domesticated "I." She also creates enormous space around the subject, freeing up room to move through literary time and across geographic time. For example, her earlier work, *XEclogue* and *Debbie*, inserted a female speaking subject into classical male narratives—Virgil's *Aeniad* and *Eclogues*, respectively. *The Weather*, which I will argue later marks a turning point in Robertson's poetics, revisits Virgil's *Georgics*. In the OSA, perhaps even more subversively, she externalizes herself, creating not only an alter ego but "a space," a built space, a room, an "office": Robertson is not only author, she is urban, she is design, she is inhabitable. She is also offering those who enter that room, as we'll see later, a way to read that unreadable world.[12]

The mobility of the structure is likely not an accident either: Is it possible to read the OSA without thinking of feminism's desire for an autonomous subject, fixed and changeable? Consider Hadid's collapsible room "conceived as a fragmented enclosure that can be compressed and expanded into programmed areas for resting, sitting, storage and browsing. . . ."[13] And consider Robertson from her Manifesto:

> The work of the OSA paradoxically recompiles the metaphysics of surface, performing an horizontal research which greets shreds of fibre, pigment flakes, the bleaching of light, proofs of lint, ink, spore, liquid and pixilation, the strange, frail, leaky cloths and sketching and gestures for what we are. (*OW*, 17)[14]

We have, as Robertson states, arrived "at our long century" where we "note that the holy modernism of the white room is draped and lined in its newness by labile counter-structures of moving silk, fur, leather . . . " (*OW*, 14). It is no longer a simple matter of wanting a room of one's own, of remaining interior—women wish *to be* a room, a mobile room—à la Andrea Zittel,[15] or Hadid herself—one that responds to external forces, a room that is attuned to internal and external needs, a room that embodies "complex organizational relations of overlapping or interpenetrating domains and can be articulated and made legible so that a complex order is perceived rather than allowing the complexity to appear as disorder" (*Elegance*, 35). To be multiple, rootless, even inorganic, may appear as disorder. "What is the structure of freedom," Robertson queries at the end of her essay, "Spatial Synthetics": "It is entirely synthetic" (*OW*, 78). There is an articulation here not only of the kind of processing the contemporary mind must engage with in our visual and text-laden world, but with the kind of physical relationship to it, and ourselves, we'll need to navigate.

It Takes Seven Days to Represent the Weather

> Certainly, as a fin-de-siecle feminist, I cannot in good conscience perform even the simplest political identification with the pastoral genre. With its scope women have been reduced to a cipher for the productively harnessed land.[16]

Indeed, "it's too late to be simple" (76), Robertson states near the end of *The Weather*; similarly, her work resists any such tendencies either formally or ideologically. *The Weather* is georgic, but it is georgic through the perspective of the Augustans or the modernists. More like the vast expanses of Agnes Martin's minimalist paintings, monochrome and graph-paper-like, than sublime eighteenth-century pastoral landscapes, or ornate wood cuts.[17] *The Weather* is "About here," but it is not "here." There is no specific here; there is only description. *The Weather* is pastoral fragment. Or more literally, a pastoral, fragmented. It is repetition and variation. It is "About here. All along here . . . All the soft coercions" (2). The garden—civic or otherwise—is a dangerous place for women. So too is genre, in this case pastoral and georgic. Both have been unkind, tethering women to gendered tropes and figureheads. Yet we still wish to stay, or dream we are still within the garden walls. *The Weather*, with its conceptual cover of three circles floating in negative space, is a site-specific work composed while the author was in residence at Cambridge. What she found at Cambridge was description. Description of the weather, very literally in terms of BBC forecasts, but also description of Virgil filtered through an 18th century sensibility—in the Dryden translations of Virgil, and in Wordsworth's *Prelude*. And in this depiction we are also seeing a deconstruction of genre and gender: "Nostalgia, like hysteria, once commonly treated as a feminine pathology, must now be claimed as a method of reading and critiquing history—a pointer indicating a potential node of entry" (*Philly Talks*, 23). The pastoral is not seen for what it is but for what we want. We think we know better, but Robertson reminds us that in some sense, we are still very eighteenth century in our understanding of Nature, or perhaps more precisely, in our way of looking at it. We *want to see*, we *want to believe* in green and rolling hills, in benign cloud formations and lallalations; we want to engage in the project of appreciation and solace, we want benign description, we want to pine: "Let's pretend you 'had' a land, and then 'lost' it. Now fondly describe it. That is pastoral," Robertson says in "How Pastoral," the prologue to *XEclogue* (*XE*).

As Stein wanted to complicate the way we write, Robertson wants to complicate the way we think. The lyric/nature poet might be attempting to present us with a pristine, even sublime landscape. Robertson wants to unveil this looking: In a sense, she wants to do it the way BBC Shipping Forecasts affected generations of Brits, by repeatedly noting. In the soothing repetitions, repetitions that, like Hadid's Mercedes Benz Museum, bring sonority . . . allow for improvisation . . . mark territory . . . code milieus (*Elegance*, 53). Here from "Wednesday":

> We break the jar, smack it down. Soul spills all over—cyprine. Every rill is a channel; our shelters are random. Every surface is ambitious; we excavate a non-existent era of the human. Everything is being lifted into place. (*Weather*, 30)

The statements describe a contemporary city, Vancouver to be precise: sublime, young, already nostalgic for its innocence, a shimmering utopian city of the future where nature, even as it is under siege, is folded into the urban at every turn. Here once more, from "Wednesday," the longest day.

> It emits a tremulousness; we have nothing concrete. It falls in broad flakes upon the surface; we take account of all that occurs. It goes all soft and warm along the way; we are almost cozy. Is it nice having our ticket handled? Like feminine and serious sensations of being gulped. It has soaked through; we have sheer plastic virtuosity. We flood upwards into the referent. (31)

"It" is unstable here, it is the weather, yes, but I suggest it is "being" as in a human center, it is culture, it is existence. It is an urban site. It is the moment. It is both the real and the abstract, the gliding skylines, the cranes and the hands (technical and organic), that are making and directing the flow.

That the city being described is Vancouver is explicit in *Occasional Works*, where the writing is very literally about recognizable sites—"Site Report: New Brighton Park," "The Fountain Transcript," "Pure Surface," "Arts & Crafts in Burnaby," and so on. But this city—a place where despite respective nationalities, lines of commerce (a possible hydrogen highway linking Los Angeles to its sister city, Vancouver) and literary influence (the ties between the Language community in San Francisco and Small Press Traffic and the KSW) tend to run north–south rather than east–west (Toronto–Vancouver)—has a history of complicated archeological poetics. Robertson mines those sites in *Occasional Works* and in *The Weather* offers us a city pastoral (or georgic), drawn more abstractly, stroke by syntactic brush stroke: "About here. All along here" (*Weather*, 2). The poem is stretched spatially as well as temporally: "The hour has reached its peak. There being here a sort of dell. There has been rain here. Maybe pointed and folding. There is law here, languid and lax. These are the subjects of conversation. They have begun to trust here" (*Weather*, 5). In trusting "here," in stating "there," the text captures the unstable civic structures of its moment and reveals the loose material underpinnings of minimalism—its rhythm and repetitions:

> Here has been the work. Here we close the day. Here upon the edge.
> Here is a basin. A canal. A church. Here is a church. Here is a deep loam
> upon chalk. (*Weather*, 3)

There is a there here; it is the sum of our ability to see, to note detail, to gather material, to build, or in Robertson's case, describe.

Looking back at the pastoral in the eighteenth-century sense Raymond Williams asks, "What city are they seeing?"[18] More to the point, how are they describing what they see? Like Virgil, a man who likely never touched a cow or herded sheep in his life, Robertson's description comes not from days spent lying in a field looking up, but days spent in a library looking through books and transcribing shipping forecasts. *The Weather*, then, is an experience of reading, the way that Dryden's translations of Virgil are an experience of reading. If women are inside, we can always think—or describe ourselves out; if we are outside we can think and describe ourselves in. But what are we moving in and out of? In a provocative discussion of temporality and abstract space, Therese Tierney describes the necessity of recontextualizing "not only space but also time, in order to deconstruct the myth of causality and understand emergent forces."[19] The distinction between the concept of time, which Tierney points out became more fixed in the eighteenth century through maritime navigational practices, and the experience of time is an important one. Life, Tierney reminds us, is not experienced as a progression of demarcated states, comparable to the marking hours, but rather it flows; this can be understood as an interesting shadow to the use of lyric in *The Weather*, which is not based either on linear time (despite the days of the week it moves through) or in a traditional ego-centered speaking subject, but in a constructed subject, an accumulation of selves and details found, gathered, read, and collaged. Tierney calls up Henri Bergson's idea that "memory is a virtual image that coexists with the perception of the object" and further these apparently divergent images collide in readers, creating memory/meaning.[20] So the text builds thematically, connectively, more like dance movements, musical arrangements, sculptural folds, or by building negative space—à la Rachel Whiteread—than how we might expect a lyric poem to be built.[21]

About Structure, or Everything Makes Spaces, or What Does Relation Reveal?

Speaking of "Utopia," one of three poems in *Rousseau's Boat*, the third key text I want to look at, Ian Davidson notes that attempts to "hold the poem at arm's length, to 'grasp' a complete picture of the poem, will be a reductive process."[22] Rather, he suggests the reader should "enter the poem in the same way one enters a building," thus perceiving "simultaneously a variety of perspectives."[23] This might also be how one instructs a viewer to enter an abstract or minimalist painting by an artist such as Jackson Pollock or Agnes Martin. A way of seeing that seems particularly relevant at our time of peak globalization, peak capitalism, peak oil, peak resource, where for decades we have watched the local break down and give way to the global, knowing more about what is going on in a distant market than two blocks from where we are sitting, and being unable to fathom the implications of overpopulation, overfarming, harvesting, drilling, and so on. Here, from near the beginning:

> I wanted to study the ground, the soft ruins of paper and the rusting
> things.
> I discover a tenuous utopia made from steel, wooden chairs, glass, stone,
> metal bed frames, tapestry, bones, prosthetic legs, hair, shirt-cuffs,
> nylon, plaster figurines, perfume bottles and keys.
> I am confusing art and decay.
> Elsewhere, fiction is an activity like walking.
> Any girl who reads is already a lost girl. (*RB*, 1)

How do we read? The sensation of attempting to read the world is not unlike encountering Jackson Pollock for the first time: There is simply so much materiality, so many splatters of paint that one finds it impossible to distinguish one gesture from another. The "I" in our poems is often similarly disconnected, adrift from the political implications of the "I." In her excessive and repetitive descriptions Robertson makes this explicit.

In her *Chicago Review* essay on the palinode Robertson appreciates its "relational or prepositional" qualities, how "like emotion it has to do with change, but not with the propulsive will."[24] Consider the implications of a feminist subjectivity inserting itself into the mainstream—not relying on "domestic interiority," on confession, on unearthing bodily or emotive details to shock the reader into relating, but rather propelling itself and the reader into the flux of contemporary discourses, injecting an "intellectual interiority" rather than the hyper-personal—a move that illuminates the already unstable, if not acknowledged as such, nature of dominant discourses, poetic and otherwise. And yet, in her essay Robertson complicates the notion of "injecting" or willfully exhibiting any directive impulses toward the reader by offering the idea of passivity as creation. In *Rousseau's Boat* Robertson wonders, what would passivity look like? How would we describe it? The palinode is the most passive thing Robertson says she could imagine. Is the relational passive? Is it "a groundless gesture," "the timely notation of that turn"? The palinode is not "shaped like myself, or it is, but converts thinking to a metrics nearly always redundant" (*CR*, 27).

Is the creation of a product (poetry) the point, or is it the thinking that the writer engages in while composing and the thinking the reader engages in while encountering poetry? Or both? What can we make of all of our constant transactions/translations/transformations? Of languages or units of measure, of dollar, of pounds, of gender, of genre, of silk, of flesh? "Passivity takes no positions," she notes, "although it may be about to welcome one" (*CR*, 27).

These are deceptive maneuvers: "By issuing, or inviting desertion, palinode perforates the sovereign" (*CR*, 26). The unruly aspect of Robertson's poetic eschews passivity as a value; it privileges the relational as opposed to the oppositional, the lateral—rhizomatic—as opposed to hierarchical. Like Hadid and Whiteread, Robertson makes the negative space as visible as the structural. Lyn Hejinian, in her poetics statement included in *American Women Poets in the 21st Century: Where Lyric Meets Language*, suggests that the goal of poetry is to produce the phrase "this is happening now."[25] Robertson builds on Hejinian's aesthetic in the way she represents space, or spatial arrangements. She too operates in a continual present, extending and destabilizing the notion of subject while returning us to more complex ways of thinking of what time is: its constructedness, its permeability. Not that we can bend time perhaps—or wrangle outside of gender or subjectivity or temporal concerns—rather we can be conscious of it, and bend our relationship to it.

In "Passivity," from *Rousseau's Boat*, Robertson writes: "Let's be sparkling for them. Let's puff up our / pigments. Let's know fibres. Let's be a dog. / I wanted to talk about necessity / and ambience. I wanted to know about / change" (5). This notion of reorienting oneself as a human subject, of lapping, appears in *The Weather* as well, and echoes an impressive list of women also interested in breaking down the faux realistic structures of poetry. Robertson again, from *Philly Talks*: "Within the capitalist narrative, the Utopia of the new asserts itself as the only productive teleology. Therefore I find it preferable to choose the dystopia of the obsolete" (23). The dystopian vision of the obsolete, the disposable, might be what is new. Moreover, this sense of mobility, of fluidity, of solidity and giving is certainly symbolized by the boat, and the notion of a subject afloat, thinking. In his film *The Pervert's Guide to the Cinema*, Zizek elaborates on the importance of the boat as a symbol for the self in contemporary culture, rootless, multidirectional, adaptable.[26] Passivity might reveal the invisible forces shaping our poetry, putting pressure on form.

Double Strands, Spatial Arrangements

As I pointed out in the beginning, Schumacher's argument for elegance includes a spatial arrangement that features an analysis of complex social processes as well as the synthesis of spatial forms; these two concerns create elegant spaces. I have already discussed the importance of space in *The Weather*; the other force at work is the prosed-up lyrics, which offer seven days and ways of description. Each day is punctuated by a more traditional (or traditional seeming) lyric instruction, or more particularly, a flâneurial address, titled simply, "Residence at C____":

> My purpose here is to advance into
> The sense of the weather, the lesson of
> The weather . . . (24)

And

> I now unknowingly speed towards
> Which of all acts, words, conditions—
> I am troubled that I do not know.
> When I feel depressed in broad daylight
> Depressed by the disappearance of names, the pollen
> Smearing the windowsill, I picture
> The bending pages of *La Batarde*
> And I think of wind. The outspread world is
> Comparable to a large theatre
> Or to rending paper, and the noise it makes when it flaps
> Is riotous (6)

Robertson's "I" inhabits an indeterminate space, and possesses an imaginative interaction with surroundings, a willingness to see as other: wind, theatre, a flock of birds, and most importantly this "I" is followed by "do not know." No didactic "I," this is a model for public discourse, it is transformative; the "outspread word" is comparable to a "large theatre." This "I" is as performative as any other "I"; the difference is that the author is owning that performance, calling for others, women in particular, to take up the mask if necessary, to enter the text, to do whatever is necessary to enter into public discourse. It also foregrounds reading as a primary practice: reading leads to thinking and is riotous. The latter is true because the outcome of reading can't be known, or controlled: To think is to move into unknown territory. On the surface—and here again I recall Agnes Martin's minimalism, the gesture artists make in crafting a grid, our daily planners, how we think of time—we have a small grid; but as the week progresses, as thoughts progress, so too does the line, the day, the engagement, filling up and then, spilling over.

In the first section of *The Weather*, we move through the materiality of "Sunday" where we stage our belief against our unknowing, our lack, our sense of disconnect. We admit to being "depressed in broad daylight" (*Weather*, 6), and yet give ourselves to wind, which moves little here at least, aside from pages perhaps, but pulls us forward into "Monday," which begins with the statement: "First all belief is paradise" (*Weather*, 10). The short sentences—"bright and oft," "brisk and west," "changing and appearing," "first and last"—mark and mock the tenuous, but unconsciously confident, rhetorics of the self-assured. Laid like Kurt Schwitters shapes across the page they remind us of their medium. This is after all, paper; there are words afloat, we are called to read, and we do. We head into the week tenuously, wondering what shape we will inhabit. This shape is disorienting. One enters the room of a Monday and is confronted with the mind in action, here working the notion of belief:

> Belief thin and pure and clear to the title. Very beautiful. Belief lovely and elegant and fair to the footing. Very brisk. Belief lively and quick and strong by the bursting. Very bright. Belief clear and witty and famous in the impulse. (*Weather*, 12)

Here description seems to me to be tracing meaning. Here we see a defamiliarization not only of the sentence but the idea of belief. Here, if I can use the analogy of the poem as a structure, the very struts and beams of the poem appear to pulse: walls move, the ceiling moves, illustrating for us our impulse to fix words, to domesticate thinking: "Belief thin and pure and clear to the title. . . . Belief violent and open . . . Belief lustful and eager and curious before beauty" (*Weather*, 12). The repetitions build until we must ask: What is belief? What is sincerity? What is Monday? What is this sentence doing? Because by now the grammatical structure and the rhythm are all that seem familiar: "Just stiff with leaf sure and dear and appearing and last. With lust clear and scarce and appearing and last and afresh" (*Weather*, 12). All of this, even what appears to be inert structures, to echo Hejinian, is happening now; the leaf, stiff, the lust, the dear, words keep us afloat; words make feelings concrete, operating as building blocks.

As in her first two collections *XEclogue* and *Debbie: An Epic*, the names of the disappeared, the marginal, the women, begin to appear, or perhaps more appropriately, insert themselves like "pollen smearing" into the patterns of description:

> Days heap upon us. Where is Christine. Broken on the word culture. But darker at the bottom than the top. Days heap upon us. Where is Valerie. Pulling the hard air into her lung. The life crumbles open. But darker at the bottom than at the top. Days heap upon us. Where is Patricia. Unlearning each thing. Red sky crumbles open . . . (*Weather*, 18)

These selves are fragmented ("ears," a "nape," a "scarf"). We don't get whole, speaking subjects; we get names interspersed with description and detail as if we are seeing through a technological scrim, or a turbine, or a reflective screen. And yet we sense the whole. In the gap between description and description of description "the life" "crumbles open" (*Weather*, 18), revealing language's inner workings, the swaying gaps between the waves of surfaces and thinking.

Stephen Collis suggests that Robertson's interest in the "decorative is utopian and feminist," citing both "How Pastoral," the introduction to *XEclogue*, and from *Debbie* the "Episode: Nurses." But one is well warned against underestimating the power of Robertson's aesthetic.[27] One might also wonder how the idea of "decorative" is specifically feminist. Is it because ornament isn't structural, isn't concerned with the thinking of structures but with their decoration? Yes, Robertson asserts a need for a genre to "gloss" her "ancestress' complicity," but that is genre, not ornament. "The sublime is what we are surrounded by and remain utterly blind to but for moments of rupture," Grosz suggests.[28] Is it possible that Robertson emphasizes adornment, the decorative as a way of accentuating the soft architectures, or structures? Is it possible that reverie is a lulling of the senses? Is there another historically significant incidence of architecture inserting itself within the walls of patriarchal structures? Beware the soft flanked giantess who presents herself at your door, no matter how beautifully adorned. Ornament, Collis accedes, is in fact the "ideological content."[29] And once inside?

Caution: Language Ahead

Once "inside" our bodies, what do these poems do? Here it is useful to think of Sianne Ngai's notion of "stuplimnity," an aesthetic experience that paradoxically contains astonishment and boredom. Focusing primarily on the "thick language" of Gertrude Stein's *The Making of Americans*, Samuel Beckett's *How It Is*, and Kenneth Goldsmith's *Fidget*, Ngai offers a convincing argument for stuplimnity as a complex and rhetorically staged act of "enumerating, 'grouping,' 'mixing,' and above all repeating," an act that ultimately allows "system and subject" to converge, and, where it does, for language to pile up and become dense.[30] Like Stein and Beckett, Robertson's description (also read insistence) piles up, becomes extremely dense, pushing the "boundary between emotive and the mechanical."[31] Without context it can seem quite dull (Kenneth Goldsmith's *Fidget*, for example) and without beauty it would be dull, but it is without neither. Consider the recuperative, lyric force of *The Weather*, in this excerpt from "Tuesday":

> Days heap upon us. Where is our anger. And the shades darker than the plain part and darker at the top than the bottom. But darker at bottom than top. Days heap upon us. Where is Ti-Grace. But darker at the bottom than the top. Days heap upon us. Where is Valerie. (18)

The overlapping phrases in each day of the week explore slightly different syntactical structures and subjects. Here the text is both disjunctive and binding, a gesture that figures the human subject. *The Weather*'s daily forecasts bleed in and out of socio-political and pastoral territories, reiterating, listing, creating tensions—and ultimately meaning—in the constant wave of overlapping phrases. Including the women's names randomly rethreads their voices into the text. As Robertson notes, "Authority flows into us like a gel" (*Weather*, 20).

Robertson has discussed her privileging, at least in one stage of the writing, of sound and repetition, which also has aural implications (*CR*, 28). There is then, a tweaking on the level of the syllable itself, a syllabic measure that works to move lyrically as well as aurally through the poem. Ngai's notion of agglutination is useful here, though in binding the textual lyricism the way she does, Robertson is perhaps slightly more accommodating than Ngai's examples (Beckett, Goldsmith, Stein). We've seen examples from *The Weather*. Here is one from *Debbie*:

> kisses against frugal will o stiffened
> spine of snow, sure, I thought (softly) scaffold
> in erudite bucolic—if by that tracing
> more sweetness could be possible . . . (lines 556–60)

And from the beginning of *The Men*:

> Men deft men mental men of loving men all men
> Vile men virtuous men same men from which men
> Sweet and men of mercy men such making men said
> Has each man that sees it
> Cry as men to the men sensate . . . (9)

But Robertson is also mindful of the limits of repetition. Here from a brief essay on boredom:

> "Repeatedly, in a pattern
> "what one thinks of the cosmos
> "is nothing
> "contra the misuse of the present
> "and the texture of waiting.[32]

The texture of waiting, the misuse of the present, the cosmos; each phrase constitutes a radical shifting of perspective from balming the present moment to eliding it, as I've suggested, with a more expansive notion of time. Statement and description is an always energized present moment/movement, and here Robertson not only recoups the absences, but creates new sounds, the "sweet new style" of knitted vocables, a lyric accumulation that insists—as poets Rachel Blau Duplessis and Erín Moure[33] have also insisted—on a polyphonic recuperation of gender, a disobedient retrofitting of the lyric "I," and an insistence on singing: beautiful, dissonant, song.

About Accumulation

Commodiousness and inconspicuousness are attractive qualities for Robertson. She, like Schumacher, responds to Leon Battista Alberti's classical notions of composition, the reach for perfection and balance—but not necessarily for closure.[34] Not surprisingly, avant-garde elegance rejects a "classical concept of preordained perfections" while retaining a sense of mastery and control, favoring "tightness and stringency . . . even an internal necessity, as the network of compositional relations is elaborated and tightened" (*Elegance* 33). One might argue that Robertson's polyphonic, archival lyric exhibits a kind of "tightness and stringency" in its assembling of descriptions—particularly as we have seen in *The Weather*, but also in the texts that followed that, *The Men*, and *Rousseau's Boat*. Like Stein and Hejinian, Robertson refuses to allow description to become sentimental or static; description is future-oriented, always happening now. It reflects the mind creating, the kinetic and willful aliveness that is looking and seeing—even if that seeing is not literally moving and seeing. Here from *Rousseau's Boat*:

> It was only half past eight, but the month was April.
> With greeny pleasure I wrote.
> . . . .
> I wrote a story of beginnings, of beginnings, of meat, of words.
> I wanted to realize gender as a form of tactile thought.
> I intended to be nourished.
> (*RB*, 21)

Steve Evans describes this tension as a "utopic release from purposive rationality" (2). In " 'Modernism' at the Millennium," Marjorie Perloff notes that like Stein, for Hejinian, the replication of the past is not interesting. In *Happily*, she suggests, Hejinian replicates consciousness as it happens, catches the aliveness, the quotidian, "getting *in* time rather than meditating *on* time." [35]

We see this in Robertson as well, a continual presence, a strategy that is always becoming, never static, ever beginning (relational again, as in the palinode). Even in a sentence that refers to the past, as in "I wanted to study," there is, foremost, the presence of an energy that is stating the idea now. There is the sense that "I wanted to" do this and I am doing this, "I am speaking," "I discover," "I am confusing." The self, the multiple self, is always present and a part of description. From *The Weather*:

The sky is complicated and flawed and we're up there in it, floating
near the apricot frill, the bias swoop, near the sullen bloated part that
dissolves to silver the next instant bronze but nothing that meaning-
ful, a breach of greeny-blue, a syllable, we're all across the swathe of
fleece laid out, the fraying rope, the copper beech behind the alumi-
num catalpa that has saved the entire spring for this flight, the tops of
these parts of the sky, the light wind flipping up the white undersides of
leaves, heaven afresh, the brushed part behind, the tumbling. (10–11)

or *The Men*:

they elaborate a cognition. In this way I arrive at the thought of them.
Increasingly their oxygen is my own and I in my little coloured shoes to
please them. Their revolution is permanent and mine a decoration. (62)

Despite the declarative structures of the sentences there is a sense of pre-
cariousness, a vulnerability that, ironically, is more emotive than the alleg-
edly more emotional traditional lyric. The emotion comes from wit, yes,
from repetition and accumulation, sameness and variation, and also ex-
teriority. The relentlessness of the text is the relentlessness of the weather,
the folding and unfolding of description through our centuries, and in our
lives, but again, it also suggests to me a sense of release, of having bro-
ken through or out of confined space/intellect. "My own nostalgia reaches
for an impossibly beautiful and abundant language. Rather than diagnos-
ing this nostalgia as a symptom of loss . . . I deploy it as an almanac,
planning a tentative landscape in which my inappropriate and disgraceful
thought may circulate" (*Philly Talks*, 23). Not quite pastoral, this yearning
is in fact acknowledgement, interrogation, or deterritoralization. It would
seem that the sentence is the compositional unit that facilitates the com-
modious nature of Robertson's poetic. In reassembling structures, we re-
assemble thoughts. We peel back layers of perception and consciousness.
We expand.

A flâneur may at first take in the larger structures of the city, the sky,
the intersection of lines, but eventually the attention will turn to the singu-
lar brick, the bolt, the seam of sash and door, the grains that make up the
wood, the granules of sand, the phonemes, the syllables. Because in *The
Weather* we encounter description of description we can assume that the
work is rhetorical because, as Stephen Collis points out, we are reading
"surfaces *about* surface."[36] It is self-referential in terms of the looking, an
act, she acknowledges, "shot through" with agencies other than the "I."[37]
Robertson's poetic is not only a poetic of looking, though it is a poetic of
looking at the residue of looking. It is all textural. It is deep awareness of
self and of the limitations of self, and of seeing. It is not unlike the years of
meditating that make no visible surface difference, only a deep calm as one
watches time pass, aware that one is both of it, and outside it. The flow.

1. Patrik Schumacher, "Arguing for Elegance," *Architectural Digest*, 77, no. 55 (Jan.–Feb. 2007): 30–40. Subsequent quotations appear in the text as *Elegance*. Zaha Hadid, an Iranian/British architect who studied with Rem Koolhaas and Bernard Tschumi, earned widespread recognition when following two decades of unmade designs the BMW building she designed was made. She recently had a retrospective at the Guggenheim.

2. The Kootenay School of Writing (KSW) describes itself as "a response to the failure of most public institutions to serve their artistic communities. It stands in opposition too the concept of 'cultural industry' in its recognition that theory, practice, and teaching of writing is best left to working writers. To this end, the School represents a new hybrid: a form of parallel gallery (or writer-run centre) and centre of scholarship, open to the needs of its own constituency and alert to the possibilities of all disciplines that involve language. KSW sponsors colloquia and critical talks on writing, visual art, and politics, and hosts an ongoing reading series with local, Canadian, and international writers" (Kootenay School of Writing website, http://www.kswnet.org/fire/aboutksw.cfm). In an e-mail exchange Robertson points out that there is no one KSW; rather, over the years there have been many incarnations. Further, she points out that her involvement as "a collective member between about 1990 and 2000 (off and on)" meant that she "was one of the people who schlepped beer, wrote press releases, attended meetings, etc." In his "Introduction to Writing Class," Michael Barnholden says, "Descriptions of the Kootenay School of Writing call to mind Voltaire's notorious summary of the Holy Roman Empire: 'neither holy nor Roman, nor an empire.' For, indeed, few facts about this particular centre of avant-garde writing in Canada can be gleaned from its misleading name—it is not in the Kootenays, it is not a school and it does not teach writing (at least, not solely). Given such an ambiguous identity the Kootenay School of Writing seems hardly the best place to orient oneself with respect to Canadian writing." Taken from "Introduction." In *Writing Class: The Kootenay School of Writing Anthology*, eds. Andrew Klobucar and Michael Barnholden (Vancouver: New Star Books, 1999), 1.

3. Lisa Robertson, *Occasional Works and Seven Walks from the Office for Soft Architecture* (Toronto: Coach House Books, 2006); *The Weather* (Vancouver: New Star Books, 2001) and *Rousseau's Boat* (Vancouver: Nomados, 2004); *The Men* (Toronto: BookThug, 2006); *XEclogue* (Vancouver: New Star Books, 1999). Subsequent quotations will be cited in the text using the following abbreviations: OW = *Occasional Works and Seven Walks from the Office for Soft Architecture*; RB = *Rousseau's Boat*; Weather = *The Weather*; XE = *XEclogue*.

4. Lisa Robertson has worked collaboratively with artists, provided gallery text (which later became *Occasional Work and Seven Walks from the Office for Soft Architecture*), and remains on the board of Art Speak.

5. *Raddle Moon* was a journal of feminist writing based in Vancouver that published twenty issues between 1984 and 2003. Robertson co-edited with Christine Stewart and Susan Clark (a member of KSW and now on the board). Contributors over the years included editors, as well as Abigail Child, Juliana Spahr, Nicole Brossard, Norma Cole, Lyn Hejinian, Bruce Andrews, and others.

6. Marjorie Perloff takes this discussion further in her chapter "Canon and Loaded Gun: Feminist Poetics and the Avant-Garde," *Poetic License: Essays on Modernist and Postmodernist Lyric* (Evanston, IL: Northwestern University Press, 1990).

7. Rae Armantrout, "Feminist Poetics and the Meaning of Clarity," in *Artifice and Indeterminacy: an Anthology of New Poetics*, ed. Christopher Beach (Tuscaloosa: University of Alabama Press, 1998), 295.

8. Lyn Hejinian, *The Language of Inquiry* (Berkeley: University of California Press, 2000), 148.

9. See Rem Koolhaas, *S,M,L,XL* (New York: Monacelli Press, 1995).

10. Armantrout, 295. Hank Lazer also makes reference to this idea in "The Lyricism of the Swerve: The Poetry of Rae Armantrout," in *American Women Poets in the 21st Century: Where Lyric Meets Language*, eds. Claudia Rankine and Juliana Spahr (Middletown, CT: Wesleyan, 2002), 27–51.

11. While the concern of readability may not be an overt concern for Robertson—or one she wants to resist and problematize—the act of reading is one that is praised and described at length in several essays and a strand of inquiry that runs through all of her work. Recently when asked where a poem begins for her she responded, "in an archive."

12. A reviewer in the Village Voice suggests that R. "makes readers not only want to think like her, but be her."

13. Zaha Hadid, description of "Lotus Room," *Wallpaper* (October 2008).

14. "We want an intelligence that's tall and sliver, oblique and black, purring and amplifying its décor; a thin thing, a long thing, a hundred videos, a boutique. Because we are both passive and independent, we need to theorize. We are studying the synthesis of sincerity, the synthetics of space, because they are both irreducible and contingent" (*OW*, 77).

15. The American artist Andrea Zittel has "investigated fundamental aspects of contemporary life in Western societies, notably increased mobility, security, comfort and consumerist packaging. The exhibition focuses on the experimental character of the artist's signature objects, equipment and projects. It highlights models for and locations of alternative living, including her well known customized trailer-home Escape Vehicles, Uniforms and 'units' she has developed for specialized living, working and research," from The Vancouver Art Gallery, *Andrea Zittel: Critical Space* (June 11 to September 30, 2007).

16. Lisa Robertson, *Philly Talks* 17 (3 October 2000): 23. http://www.english .upenn.edu/~wh/phillytalks. Subsequent quotations will be cited in the text as *Philly Talks*.

17. Agnes Martin, Canadian born, American artist, known as abstract expressionist, or minimalist who explored a minimal palette, emphasized subtle color shifts, textures, graphs, and repetitive markings.

18. In e-mail correspondence dated July 26, 2008, and elsewhere (see *Philly Talks* 17 (3 October 2000): 23/23, www.english.upenn.edu/~wh/phillytalks). Robertson points out the importance of Williams's *The Country and The City* to her thinking about pastoral, genre, Virgil, etc., making the distinction that pastoral is not a form, but a genre, a distinction she sees as essential in terms of its ability to contain adequately the work she would like to undertake.

19. Therese Tierney, *Abstract Space: Beneath the Media Surface* (New York: Taylor & Francis, 2007), 138.

20. *Ibid.*

21. Rachel Whiteread is a British sculptor who garnered international attention in the Sensation Exhibition in 1997. She is known for her marking of negative space: casts of the interiors of houses, the blank space beneath chairs, and so on.

22. Ian Davidson, "Picture This: Space and Time in Lisa Robertson's Utopia," *Mosaic: Journal for the Interdisciplinary Study of Literature* 40:4 (2007): 102.

23. *Ibid.*, 87.

24. Lisa Robertson, "On Palinode," *Chicago Review* 51:4/52:1 (spring 2006): 28. Subsequent quotations appear in the text as *CR*.

25. Lyn Hejinian, "Some Notes Toward a Poetics," in *American Women Poets in the 21st Century: Where Lyric Meets Language*, 240. See also Linda Kinnahan, *Lyric Interventions: Feminism, Experimental Poetry, and Contemporary Discourse* (Iowa City: University of Iowa Press, 2004). Kinnahan points out that Steve Evans introduced a special issue of differences by defining contemporary feminist avant-garde poetics as a "feminist counter-public sphere" (5), but I want to suggest here that Robertson's texts assert themselves into other counter-public spheres. In her correspondence she was firm in her position that the anti-lyric sentiment at KSW "doesn't reflect the actual work circulating there," and further, she reminds us that she doesn't think of herself as a "writer who founds a poetic on repudiations—of lyric, narrative, what have you. I think my approach is more integrative—how can I bring various stances and traditions into my own work and transform them from within" (6 December 2007).

26. Slavoj Zizek, *The Pervert's Guide to Cinema*, 2006.

27. Stephen Collis, " 'The Frayed Trope of Rome': Poetic Architecture in Robert Duncan, Ronald Johnson, and Lisa Robertson," *Mosaic: Journal for the Interdisciplinary Study of Literature* 35, no. 4 (2002): 143, 155.

28. Elizabeth Grosz, *Architecture from the Outside: Essays on Virtual and Real Space* (Boston: MIT Press, 2001).

29. Collis, 156. I offer the full sentence from which this last phrase was taken: "Robertson opens classical genre and rhetoric to its ornamental use of gender (shepherdesses, Nature as feminine, rhetorical nostalgia and sincerity), revealing that, because they are decorative extras and surpluses, such gender constructions can be removed/altered/transformed (for they are not structurally integral to the genre's architecture) or, perhaps more accurately and importantly, because the ornamental and extra is revealed to be the crucial site of the classical text's ideological content." Elsewhere Collis elaborates on Robertson's rhetorical ornament, "slipping in and out of fabrics that time weaves in architectures and rhetorics" (157).

30. Sianne Ngai, "Stuplimity: Shock and Boredom in Twentieth-Century Aesthetics," *Ugly Feelings* (Boston: Harvard University Press, 2005), 264.

31. *Ibid.*

32. Lisa Robertson, "About 1836 (an essay on boredom)," in *The Chatter of Culture* (Vancouver: Artspeak, 2007), 20.

33. For an example of this see Erín Moure's *Sheep's Vigil for a Fervent Person*,

or earlier works such as *Furious*, as well as Blau Duplessis, *Drafts*, or her critical work in *Pink Guitar*, which will elaborate further.

34. Leon Battista Alberti's treastise, *Della pittura*, offered a commentary on painting, described perspective as a representation, and argued that all art imitates nature and can be harmonious, measured.

35. Marjorie Perloff, *Modernism at the Millenium* (London: Blackwell, 2002), 185.

36. Collis, 152.

37. From an e-mail exchange with Lisa Robertson: "I feel I'm looking at the structure of perception, the historicity of perception, how any act of perceiving—looking, describing—is shot through with agencies that are not 'mine,' that are not proper to any single subject. More like how perception distributes effects of self."

BIBLIOGRAPHY

Books by Lisa Robertson

XEclogue. Vancouver: Tsunami Editions, 1993.
Debbie: An Epic. Vancouver: New Star Books, 1997. [Published in the UK by Reality Street Editions, 2001.]
XEclogue. 2nd revised edition. Vancouver: New Star Books, 1999.
The Weather. Vancouver: New Star Books, 2001. [Published in the UK by Reality Street Editions, 2001.]
Occasional Works and Seven Walks from the Office for Soft Architecture. Astoria, OR: Clearcut Press, 2003. [Published in Canada by Coach House Books, 2006.]
The Men. Toronto: BookThug, 2006.
Lisa Robertson's Magenta Soul Whip. Toronto: Coach House Books, 2009.
Rousseau's Boat. Berkeley: University of California Press, 2010.

Chapbooks and Pamphlets

The Apothecary. Vancouver: Tsunami Editions, 1991. [New edition, 2007, BookThug, Toronto.]
Rousseau's Boat. Vancouver: Nomados, 2004.
First Spontaneous Horizontal Restaurant. Belladonna 75. Brooklyn, NY: Belladonna Books, 2005.

Selected Prose

"Coasting" [with Jeff Derksen, Nancy Shaw, and Catriona Strang]. In *A Poetics of Criticism*, edited by Juliana Spahr, 301–3. Buffalo: Leave Books, 1994.
"Introduction: Ethics and Aesthetics." In *The Recovery of the Public World: Essays on Poetics in Honour of Robin Blaser*, edited by Charles Watts and Edward Byrne, 317–19. Burnaby, BC: Talon Books, 1999.
"Correspondence" [with Steve McCaffery]. *PhillyTalks* #17, edited by Alan Filreis, www.english.upenn.edu/~wh/phillytalks.

"How Pastoral: A Manifesto." In *Telling it Slant: Avant Garde Poetics of the 1990s*, edited by Mark Wallace, 21–26. Tuscaloosa: Alabama University Press, 2002.

"My Eighteenth Century." In *Assembling Alternatives*, edited by Romana Huk, 389–97. Middletown, CT: Wesleyan University Press, 2003.

"In Phonographic Deepsong: Sounding Lorine Niedecker." In *Radical Vernacular: Lorine Niedecker and the Poetics of Place*, edited by Elizabeth Willis, 83–89. Iowa City: University of Iowa Press, 2008.

"Astragal" [on Albertine Sarrazin's novel]. *The Encyclopedia Project*, edited by Tisa Bryant et al., 48–49. New York: Encyclopedia Project, 2005.

"On Palinode." *Chicago Review* 51:4/52:1 (spring 2006): 26–27.

"The Weather: A Report on Sincerity." *Chicago Review* 51:4/52:1 (spring 2006): 28–32.

"Lastingness: Reage, Lucrece, Arendt: An Essay on Reading." *Open Letter. Thirteenth Series*, no. 3 (summer 2007).

Selected Interviews

Kai Fierle-Hedrick, "Lifted: An Interview with Kai Fierle-Hedrick." *Chicago Review* 51:4/52:1 (spring 2006): 38–54.

Angela Carr, "Nightwalk: An Interview with Lisa Robertson," *Matrix*, 78 (fall 2007): 32–37.

J'Lyn Chapman, *Denver Quarterly*, Denver, 42:3 (spring 2008), 31–40.

Mark Cochrane, "Stuttering Continuity (or Like it's 1999): An Interview with Lisa Robertson," *Open Letter* 12:6 (summer 2008): 63–87.

Prismatic Publics: Innovative Canadian Women's Poetry and Poetics, edited by Heather Milne and Kate Eichhorn, 368–94. Toronto: Coach House, 2009.

Selected Criticism

Clover, Joshua. "The Adventures of Lisa Robertson in the Space of Flows." *Chicago Review* 51:4/52:1 (2006): 77–78, 255.

Collis, Stephen. "The frayed trope of Rome": Poetic architecture in Robert Duncan, Ronald Johnson, and Lisa Robertson." *Mosaic: Journal for the Interdisciplinary Study of Literature* 35.4 (2002): 143.

Davidson, Ian. "Picture This: Space and Time in Lisa Robertson's Utopia." *Mosaic: Journal for the Interdisciplinary Study of Literature* 40:4 (2007):87, 102.

Evans, Steve. "Solitary and Free." *Jacket* 27 (2005). http://jacketmagazine.com/27/evan-robe.html

Friedlander, Benjamin. "A Reading Diary." *Chicago Review* 51:4/52:1 (2006): 55–64.

Larkin, Peter. "Lisa Robertson: How Pastoral is More and More Possible." In *Antiphonies: Essays on Women's Experimental Poetries in Canada*, edited by Nate Dorward, 32–49. Toronto: The Gig, 2008.

Nealon, Christopher. "Camp Messianism, or, the Hopes of Poetry in Late Late Capitalism." *American Literature*, 76, no. 3 (September 2004): 579–602.

Nichols, Miriam. "Towards a Poetics of the Commons: O *Cidadan* and *Occasional Work*." In *Antiphonies: Essays on Women's Experimental Poetries in Canada*, edited by Nate Dorward, 146–66. Toronto: The Gig, 2008.

———. "Urban Landscapes and Dirty Lyrics: Peter Culley and Lisa Robertson."
   Public 26, 2002: 54–71.
Rudy, Susan. "The Weather Project: Lisa Robertson's Poetics of 'Soft Architecture.' "
   In *Writing in Our Time: Canada's Radical Poetries in English (1957–2003)*,
   edited by Pauline Butling, 217–22. Waterloo, ON: Wilfrid Laurier University
   Press, 2005.
Scappettone, Jennifer. "Site Surfit: Office for Soft Architecture Makes the City Con-
   fess." *Chicago Review* 51.4 (winter 2005): 70–76.
Stewart, Christine Anne. "We Lunch Nevertheless Among Reinvention." *Chicago
   Review* 51.4 (winter 2005): 65–69.

C. D. WRIGHT

FROM *Steal Away*

Floating Trees

a bed is left open to a mirror
a mirror gazes long and hard at a bed

light fingers the house with its own acoustics

one of them writes this down
one has paper

bed of swollen creeks and theories and coils
bed of eyes and leaky pens

much of the night the air touches arms
arms extend themselves to air

their torsos turning toward a roll
of sound: thunder

night of coon scat and vandalized headstones
night of deep kisses and catamenia

his face by this light: saurian
hers: ash like the tissue of a hornets' nest

one scans the aisle of firs
the faint blue line of them
one looks out: sans serif

"Didn't I hear you tell them you were born
on a train"

what begins with a sough and ends with a groan
groan in which the tongue's true color is revealed

the comb's sough and the denim's undeniable rub
the chair's stripped back and muddied rung

color of stone soup and garden gloves
color of meal and treacle and sphagnum

hangers clinging to their coat
a soft-white bulb to its string

the footprints inside us
iterate the footprints outside

the scratched words return to their sleeves

the dresses of monday through friday
swallow the long hips of weekends

a face is studied like a key
for the mystery of what it once opened

"I didn't mean to wake you
angel brains"

ink of eyes and veins and phonemes
the ink completes the feeling

a mirror silently facing a door
door with no lock no lock

the room he brings into you
the room befalls you

like the fir trees he trues her
she nears him like the firs

if one vanishes one stays
if one stays the other will or will not vanish

otherwise my beautiful green fly
otherwise not a leaf stirs

Privacy

The animals are leaving
the safety of the trees

Light sensors respond
to the footfall of every guest

To retard the growth of algae

The fishes must be moved
from the window

Stiller than water she lies
as in a glass dress

As if all life might come to its end
within the radius of her bed

Beyond the reef of trees a beach cannot be seen
the bay itself barely breathing

In the other wing of the house
a small boat awaits elucidation

only the crossing counts.

It's not how we leave one's life. How go off
the air. You never know, do you. You think you're ready
for anything; then it happens, and you're not. You're really
not. The genesis of an ending, nothing
but a feeling, a slow movement, the dusting
of furniture with a remnant of the revenant's shirt.
Seeing the candles sink in their sockets; we turn
away, yet the music never quits. The fire kisses our face.
O phthisis, O lotharian dead eye, no longer
will you gaze on the baize of the billiard table. No more
shooting butter dishes out of the sky. Scattering light.
Between snatches of poetry and penitence you left
the brumal wood of men and women. Snow drove
the butterflies home. You must know
how it goes, known all along what to expect,
sooner or later . . . the faded cadence of anonymity.
Frankly my dear, frankly my dear, frankly

elation washed over our absence toward everything
in the increasing darkness.

The soft coloration of his longing in the indifferent
environment has never deserted me.
My husband saving the spermaceti to light
our eyestrings. My husband charting my obsessions
with characteristic cool. Singing sacerdotally
in the shower, my husband intoning every cleft in my skin.
Our syncopated breathing. My husband who flew often

C. D. Wright | 389

at night as a child. Above the very ground
of our writing (even as power poles were falling
on volvos). My husband equally popular with women
of all ages. His nail parings, his running legs, his scriptoria.
O his ludic hard head. Who cut down
his own hair with a bone-handled knife. His rack
of gorgeous unworn ties. My husband touching
even the insular men; whenever fear bred
its mushrooms under rugs, a cleaning frenzy commenced.
Our bed irrigated with my blood. Watching me burn
from within; tendering his cross pen. O predominately
white guilt. Whenever it rained

FROM *One Big Self: An Investigation*

Dear Prisoner,

      I too love. Faces. Hands. The circumference
Of the oaks. I confess. To nothing
You could use. In a court of law. I found.
That sickly sweet ambrosia of hope. Unmendable
Seine of sadness. Experience taken away.
From you. I would open. The mystery
Of your birth. To you. I know. We can
Change. Knowing. Full well. Knowing.
                          It is not enough.
      Poetry   Time   Space   Death
I thought. I could write. An exculpatory note.
I cannot. Yes, it is bitter. Every bit of it, bitter.
The course taken by blood. All thinking
Deceives us. Lead (kindly) light.
Notwithstanding this grave. Your garden.
This cell. Your dwelling. Who is unaccountably free.

My Dear Conflicted Reader,

If you will grant me that most of us have an equivocal nature,
and that when we waken we have not made up our minds which direction
we're headed; so that—you might see a man driving to work in a
perfume- and dye-free shirt, and a woman with an overdone tan hold up
an orange flag in one hand, a Virginia Slim in the other—as if this were
their predestination. Grant me that both of them were likely contemplating
a different scheme of things. WHERE DO YOU WANT TO SPEND ETERNITY
the church marquee demands on the way to my boy's school, SMOKING OR
NON-SMOKING. I admit I had not thought of where or which direction
in exactly those terms. The radio ministry says g-o-d has a wrong-answer
button and we are all waiting for it to go off. . . .

Dear Child of God,

If you will allow me time.   To make a dove.   I will spend it
Well.   A half success is more than can be hoped for.   And
Turning on the hope machine is dangerous to contemplate.   First
I have to find a solid bottom.   Where the scum gets hard and
The scutwork starts.   One requires ideal tools: a huge suitcase
        Of love   a set of de-iced wings   the ghost of a flea
Music intermittent or ongoing.   Here.   One exits the forest
Of men and women.   Here.   One re-dreams the big blown dream
Of socialism.   Deep in the suckhole.   Where Lou Vindie kept
Her hammer.   Under her pillow.   Like a wedge of wedding cake.
Working from my best memory.   Of a bird I first saw nesting.

In the razor wire.

C. D. Wright | 391

Mack trapped a spider

Kept in a pepper jar

He named her Iris

Caught roaches to feed her

He loved Iris

When Iris died

He wrote her a letter

FROM *Rising, Falling, Hovering*

Re: Happiness, in pursuit thereof

It is 2005, just before landfall.
Here I am, a labyrinth, and I am a mess.
I am located at the corner of Waterway
and Bluff. I need your help. You will find me
to the left of the graveyard, where the trees
grow especially talkative at night,
where fog and alcohol rub off the edge.
We burn to make one another sing;
to stay the lake that it not boil, earth
not rock. We are running on Aztec time,
fifth and final cycle. Eyes switch on/off.
We would be mercurochrome to one another
bee balm or chamomile. We should be concrete,
glass and spandex. We should be digital, or
at least, early. Be ivory-billed. Invisible
except to the most prepared observer.
We will be stardust. Ancient tailings
of nothing. Elapsed breath. No,
we must first be ice. Be nails. Be teeth.
                              Be lightning.

Like Having a Light at Your Back
You Can't See but You Can Still Feel

As if it were streaming into your ear.

The edges of a room long vanished.

She is not really hearing what he's really saying.

The shine is going out of the ground
but they are sure of their footing.

It's not that they have been here before, but
they are young and they have water.

There are masses of rose hips and they are noisy.

The forward direction requires almost no effort.

Consonant with this feeling of harmony
comes another, less comfortable.

Not of being lost but of not belonging.

Yet they were not covering the air
with false words.

They moved along without talking,
not touching.

They wore their own smell.

She tastes salt and they must be getting closer.

Others are out there who are drifting.

If this took place anywhere near the presidential palace

it would be non-stop terrifying.

And this could be the reason she has started to scream.

Like a Prisoner of Soft Words

We walk under the wires and the birds resettle.

We know where we're going but have not made up our mind

which way we will take to get there.

If we pass by the palmist's she can read our wayward lines.

We may drop things along the way that substantiate
  our having been here.

We will not be able to transmit any of these feelings verbatim.

By the time we reach the restaurant one of us is angry.

Here a door gives in to a courtyard

overlooking a ruined pool.

We touch the spot on our shirt where the ink has seeped.

The lonely outline of the host is discerned near an unlit sconce.

Something about an oar leaning against a wall.

As guests we are authorized not to notice.

We lack verisimilitude but we press on with intense resolve.

We are forced to admit we cannot reproduce the smell
  of the linden.

But we can tell you when we are standing

in the sphere of its fluency, its mystery, its heart-shaped leaves,

its special white honey, the precarious fabric of its protection.

We appear less posthumous

against the silver exposures. When the wind picks up

the sound track is no longer audible.

Like Something in His Handwriting

It was hotter back then.

No, it wasn't it had to be cooler, clouded.

A park down below where no one ever met.

But men were pulled by dogs along paths made by the walkers.

And a nameless river through a photograph of woods

proposed a non-local reality

that shimmered at the instant of its own disappearance.

She bought the picture, brought it back, propped it
   against drywall

where someone had penciled a message

she couldn't make out.

The end of another summer wandered across yards

that weren't fenced or watered.

If it rained, it rained.

And then the rain inebriated us.

A yellow leaf floated toward ground

transmitting a spot of optimism

through a slow intensification of color in the lower corner
   of the morning.

Like Something Flying Backwards

When a word here and there was starting to escape.

There is some hope that she may yet.

Even by herself could work herself into a fit.

Often thought of death in daylight before washing, before
  touching a switch.

Written purely out of love for the calm it offered for to calm
  someone else is calming,
whether or not one can calm oneself.

If never delivered never so intended.

Her vocabulary refined by years of looking through
  the screen at the lilac that absorbed
her witness.

So many contradictory measures taking up their positions.

The ubiquitous sense of scarcity especially
  where there was plenty.

So much turbulence in choosing.

She had to jimmy her way in.

Even an attempt to change her seating assignment.

All of her experience still looking for a language.

Honestly if she were able she would haul in one of
  the more animate clouds.

The following spring she promised herself to plant a white lilac.

She would take up her old position, hands folded, head back
  waiting for the visions.

POETICS STATEMENT

My American Scrawl

MONTHS BEFORE Robert Creeley died, we had lunch on Atwell's Avenue in Providence. We sat at one of those ridiculous, tiny, tippy ice cream tables, in those mean, wire-backed ice cream chairs. My main memory of our conversation is of him wanting to wager that you could not find three people to agree upon what poetry is. Hours later he e-mailed his thanks for that "soul-nourishing" lunch (though he characteristically talked, while I got nourished).

I have long collected concise declarations by those who thought they knew what *it* is, else were heard offhandedly saying something that got quoted and scored into their record. I continue to favor Julian Beck's: "The light is hyacinth, poetry makes it clear," and Frank Stanford's: "Sometimes poetry is a beautiful sick dog that shits all over the house."

Increasingly indecisive, about matters both big and little, I have found that poetry is the one arena where I am not inclined to crank up the fog machine, to palter or dissemble or quiver or hastily reverse myself. This is the one scene where I advance determined, if not precisely ready, to do battle with what an overly cited Jungian names the anesthetized heart, the heart that does not react.

During periods of non-poetry I have worn my couch to the ground. While my poetry arm atrophied, my winter shag turned into my spring shag. The aroma-drenched lilacs came and went without me raising the window an inch. But once I hoisted myself from the couch, poetry, if it did not flow in to meet me, at least signaled toward the light pooling the desk.

Poetry requires deliberate movement in its direction, a filament of faith in its persistence, receptivity to its fundamental worthwhileness. Within its unanesthetized heart there is quite a racket going on. Choices have to be made with respect to every mark. Not every mistake should be erased. Nor shall the unintelligible be left out. Order is there to be wrenched from the tangles of words. Results are impossible to measure. A clearing is drawn around the perimeter as if by a stick with a nail on the end.

Clear of the gibberish we dub language, something lucent stands out among the gibberish we dub language. Maybe poetry, the making of poetry, is not by definition a clarifying exercise, but it has a shot at it, as they say. It has a shot at the hyacinth light. And I really do want to communicate (by which I mean, pass it on) what little I have seen clearly (by which I do not mean, obviously seen). I want to say, thanks, thanks, for letting me see that.

Sometimes poetry really is a beautiful sick dog that shits all over the house. But this is just old knotty pine flooring. The hound is pound dog beautiful. And she is my dog. There is nothing I would not forgive her.

Mostly, *its* definition will remain arguable to the end of hours. I can almost make out an outline before the light slams shut in my face.

Poetry changes or else freezes into self-mimicry. It needs to change to quicken if only to respond to pressures external to its essence (as if it had one, which it doesn't). It must purge its own breath (which it has). This hardly holds out the remotest possibility of a rousing renewal each time a step is taken toward a language waiting to take shape. On the contrary, in my particular case, it means I have to hurl headlong against the old self, yesterday's black-clad self. This means I need to identify a move made somewhat successfully, turned automatic when I was snoozing, slipping, coasting or tumbling backward (which means I more or less know a move's effects, and it is almost never mere effects one wants).

Then: wake in the night. Write to say: wishes to express her regrets, hopes to redeem herself, the next time, in the near future. . . . Only of unevenness is my art made, an ever-contestable ground between craft and mess. Opposite my second-story office window, chiseled into the staid face of Carr House is a phrase seized from Gertrude Stein: "And then there is using everything." It is my thought that poetry's position is meant to be so various, so precarious; so inclusive, so exposed.

At this particular juncture I hope to extricate myself further from my experience. I have an uncomely compulsion to confess that I have been humbled beyond believing that I can fathom my purpose in being here, writing poetry, writing about poetry. If I expected poetry to teach me how to live, I was putting too much of a burden on the medium.

I overheard Jack Gilbert tell a handful of students that poetry teaches us how to suffer more efficiently. Even this can seem a tall order. On the other hand, I believe Gilbert's remark to be fortifying. Agnes Martin commented that her paintings were for people to look at "before daily care strikes." Somewhere along the way poetry became an integral part of the project of staying alive, staying really alive.

I am on the plane. The man in front of me emits a familiar franchise smell of burger and onion. He is reading *What Is the Shape of the Male Soul*. He has underscored, more than once, "the heirs of god." Poetry is entering its mission field. Poetry proposes an alternate perspective. Between here and there, its sound grows more insistent.

THE BORDER-CROSSING RELATIONAL
POETRY OF C. D. WRIGHT

Suzanne Wise

I.

"I AM A serious border-crosser," C. D. Wright has written.[1] Her poetic journeys have often led readers across the borders between the urban and rural, and between the North and South of the United States. Wright's poetry initially centered on and has frequently returned to the landscape, idiom, and working-class lives of her native Arkansas Ozarks. However, other landscapes—New England, Mexico, and the open road between here and there—began to complicate this regional focus as early as *Further Adventures with You* (1986) and *String Light* (1991). Describing poetry as "tribal" and the role of poets as "griots, the ones who see that the word does not break faith with the line of the body," Wright suggests the possibility of connection and community across cultural and regional divides (*CT*, 10).[2] Yet Wright also proposes a poetics of political resistance that draws strength from the differences that are shaped by geography and culture in opposition to "the inexorable course of cultural assimilation and the willful course of historical amnesia" as abetted by mass consumerism (*LRP*, 1). Idiom in particular is a site for her investigation of cultural distinctiveness, but with *String Light*, Wright begins to combine her attention to idiom and detail with disruptive formal techniques that draw attention to the poem as a construction. As she says in the prose ars poetica "The Box This Comes In," she prefers craft in which "the work shows" (*SL*, 59).[3] Her poetry evolves from free-verse narratives with naturalistic line breaks to poems that rely more on fragment, the dismantling of narrative conventions, abrupt syntax, and shifting diction marked by the tendency to be, as Stephen Burt aptly describes, "disorientingly specific in single phrases and words."[4]

The subsequent works *Just Whistle* (1993) and *Tremble* (1996) focus more on themes of sexuality and family life, but they also assert a more fractured, provisional sense of the lyric moment, using more ample white space, and often dropping punctuation, introducing the strategies that Wright later expands on in geographical and cultural border crossings. These techniques inform *Deepstep Come Shining* (1998), an intensely fragmented collage poem that marks Wright's first book-length foray into the documentary form. *Deepstep Come Shining* charts a road trip through North and South Carolina and northern Georgia that Wright took with photographer Deborah Luster; together they visited outsider artists and explored "the reaches of seeing, of not seeing, visions, dreams."[5] In this book, Wright manages to embrace geographical distinctiveness yet subvert traditional documentary's reverence for fixed, observable evidence. She writes: "The eye is a mere mechanical instrument" (*DCS*, 78). And: "Don't need a magnifying glass / To make the feelings seen" (*DCS*, 103). And: "The objective is hopeless" (*DCS*, 13). Calling into question the act of seeing and the search for empirical truth, here Wright underscores her unsettling of witnessing and the documentary that will be central to the poetics that inform two of her recent books. This subverting of personal testimony and the documentary takes on greater intensity and new significance in *One Big Self* (2003) and *Rising, Falling, Hovering* (2008), which will be my focus in this essay. Originally published with photographs by Deborah Luster, *One Big Self* is a book-length collage work that takes as its subject three Louisiana prisons, the inmates of which are largely poor and black. *Rising, Falling, Hovering*, a multifarious, splintered travelogue, explores border conflicts between Mexico and the United States amidst the confluence of personal journeys, the Iraq war, and other scenes of social and economic strife. Both books present a self-questioning poet-guide who struggles to connect across aggressively maintained divisions of race, class, culture, and geography. In these works, Wright acknowledges and incorporates her limitations and blind spots, as she seems to advise in *Cooling Time*: "We need to lower the veneration around the terms of communication and expression and aim to see better—and to see better we have to move at whatever pace we can tolerate in the direction of our blind spot, else learn to recognize its advance toward us—which is usually where we are most smugly and snugly ensconced. Best not expect any grand vista" (*CT*, 93).

II.

The developments in Wright's poetics have a number of different sources, from an interest in Brecht's alienation techniques to the strategies and techniques of the Language poetry movement.[6] Lynn Keller argues that Wright shares with Ron Silliman, a central figure of Language poetry (who has articulated many of the group's major precepts), not only a critique of consumer culture and a belief in the social responsibility of poetry but also a "commitment to poetry's transformative possibilities of deformation and of reconnection with material realities."[7] Keller also tracks Wright's particular admiration for Silliman's classic Language work, *Tjanting*: In her 1989 essay "A Taxable Matter," Wright says his book-length poem "jerks us into critical awareness by creating syntactical disturbances with cultural ephemera."[8] Noting the more pronounced "language-based experimentalism" of Wright's poetry from the 1990s, Keller identifies "heterogeneous" diction and "syntactic disjunctions," among other methods for drawing readers' attention to language. In a recent interview, Wright reasserts that such linguistic perturbation can be consciousness-raising. Referring to "The Box This Comes In," her meditation on a handmade box, she explains: "You feel contact with the one who made the box because you could see the flaw; you knew it wasn't made by machine."[9] Invoking Brecht's Alienation Effect—denaturalizing theater techniques Brecht called upon to break the "trance" of the audience's identification with the fiction of the play and thereby provoke awareness—Wright describes how the intentional flaw reveals "the bones of the drama," forcing the "real" to intrude.[10]

At the same time, the politics of Wright's poetics also clearly departs from the original principles of Language poetry on a number of fronts. Noting Wright's regional commitment and documentary interests, Keller observes that Wright's engagement with "poetry's transformative possibilities" emanates as much from disruption of linguistic norms as from "the *preservation* of difference, verbal and otherwise."[11] Although Language poets have historically used linguistic disturbance to deflect direct, referential meaning (considered a vehicle for the commodification of language), Wright holds onto certain conventions of content and realist description in what Keller describes as "a griot commitment to communication that will draw people together."[12] Wright herself has framed her aesthetic aim as "reintegration": "it is not a state of fragmentation in which I strive to write, nor of assimilation, but one of reintegration. The seams should show, but the container must hold."[13] Furthermore, for Wright, personal experience is an essential ingredient of political writing: "How can language, unless it avoids experience, avoid the political weather wherein it launches?" (*CT*, 40). In this regard, she diverges from Language poets who disparage the personal lyric poem for its claims to unmediated private experience and authenticity.[14]

But C. D. Wright's border-crossing poetics can be further illuminated by way of Édouard Glissant's theory of a Poetics of Relation. A Martinican poet and philosopher, Glissant draws on the history of the Caribbean archipelago in defining an open, multilingual poetics—one that asserts political strength in the face of domineering and divergent cultural forces and that manifests a complex "multiple relationship with the Other."[15] Borrowing the metaphor of the rhizome from Deleuze and Guattari, Glissant envisions this poetics as an enmeshed root system, an image that stands in opposition to the singular "intolerant" root, a trope applicable to imperial identity.[16] At the heart of the Poetics of Relation is the term "errantry," a purposeful, even sacred wandering that is based on a mobile notion of connectedness.[17] In the ultimate manifestation of the Poetics of Relation, "the poet's word leads from periphery to periphery" and "makes every periphery into a center" until it "abolishes the very notion of center and periphery."[18]

Despite the desire for relatedness, Glissant also asserts the need to protect distinctive differences: "Diversity, the quantifiable totality of every possible difference . . . must be safeguarded from assimilations, from fashions passively accepted as the norm, and from standardized customs."[19] This call for diversity often focuses on language as the mainstay of cultural identity. Glissant advocates multiplicity among and within both oral and written languages, in opposition to the monolingual intolerance of Western languages, such as French and American English, which spread across the globe, fueled by political and economic power.[20] He finds American English particularly dangerous: "It is true that the leveling effect of Anglo-American is a persistent threat for everyone and that this language, in turn, risks being transformed into a technical salesman's Esperanto, a perfunctory containerization of expression (neither Faulkner's nor Hopkins's language but not the language of London pubs or Bronx warehouses either)."[21]

Relational tendencies in C. D. Wright's poetry are not hard to discern. Her border crossings of class, culture, and geography can be seen as willful acts of errantry intent on connection while also safeguarding difference and diversity against assimilation. However, while Glissant makes room for American versions of Poetics of Relation—he lists Whitman, James, and Faulkner as examples of relational writers—his primary model is the Caribbean, a region with a history of colonial domination and violent clashes between opposing cultural forces that has left a legacy of geopolitical and economic marginalization.[22] Wright, on the other hand, must negotiate her closer proximity to cultural power. As a relatively privileged citizen of the United States—the world's foremost military and economic empire—she must grapple with the insular myopia of its mainstream culture, the symptoms of which she seems to describe in her references to "all-American forgettery" and, quoting Julian Beck, "national feelinglessness" (*RFH*, 24, 28, 95).

Wright's admonition to move toward one's blind spots, thereby relinquishing claims to panoramic comprehension, becomes particularly pertinent in connecting with those on the periphery and recalls another aspect of Glissant's Poetics of Relation. Despite the emphasis on interconnectivity, Glissant insists that a Poetics of Relation refuses to claim complete knowledge of others. Given the legacy of territorial conquest, "the verb *to understand* in the sense of 'to grasp' [*comprendre*] has a fearsome repressive meaning," he points out.[23] Presenting the tensions between the desire for connection and the acceptance of "opacity" (or, "that which cannot be reduced"), Glissant describes the ambition behind a relational poetics:

[I]n the poetics of Relation, one who is errant (who is no longer traveler, discoverer, or conqueror) strives to know the totality of the world yet already knows he will never accomplish this—and knows that is precisely where the threatened beauty of the world resides.

Errant, he challenges and discards the universal—this generalizing edict that summarized the world as something obvious and transparent, claiming for it one presupposed sense and one destiny. He plunges into the opacities of that part of the world to which he has access.[24]

With a change of a pronoun, this could be a manifesto for Wright's border-crossing impulses.

III.

First published in 2003, *One Big Self* debuted as an oversized hardcover book featuring C. D. Wright's poetry, photographs by Deborah Luster of incarcerated men and women, and the subtitle *Prisoners of Louisiana*. Originally printed on aluminum plates in creamy white and black, the photographs evoke antique *cartes de visite*, as art critic Vince Aletti points out.[25] Of course, the irony is that the men and women in these photographs won't be visiting anyone. Their images, as published in this book and as prints—Luster gave each prisoner 10 to 15 wallet-sized prints to use as they wished—circulate without them.[26]

While this discussion will focus on the subsequent 2007 paperback version in which the photos are absent (except for two on the cover), it is important to acknowledge how the photographic act informs both versions and ultimately signals a dialogue with the documentary tradition and its emphasis on visible evidence as an objective record of reality. Although documentary can be seen as a means of understanding those on the social periphery, it can also insidiously enact the threatening sense of the verb "to grasp" that Glissant says "contains the movement of hands that grab their surroundings and bring them back to themselves. A gesture of enclosure if not appropriation."[27] In documentary, this engulfing can manifest itself as an objectifying, entertaining spectacle that reinforces social divisions and hierarchies. As Susan Sontag observes, early social documentary photography "was an instrument of that essentially middle-class attitude . . . called humanism—which found slums the most enthralling of decors."[28] Martha Rosler goes so far as to say that "the liberal documentary assuages any stirrings of conscience in its viewers the way scratching relieves an itch and simultaneously reassures them about their relative wealth and social position."[29]

As part of a broad-scale effort to resist documentary's potential to enclose—or in the words of photography, "capture"—those who inhabit the social periphery, Wright unsettles the act of picture taking and reliance on empirical evidence. To contextualize this aspect, it's helpful to look at *One Big Self* in light of two influential documentary antecedents in which photography also plays a role: Walker Evans's and James Agee's study of white Alabaman tenant farmers, *Let Us Now Praise Famous Men*, and Muriel Rukeyser's "The Book of the Dead," an investigation into the deaths of West Virginian miners from silica poisoning. Rather than withdrawing the subjective presence of the poet and posing the camera as an objective observer on the sidelines as Rukeyser does in "The Book of the Dead," Wright presents the camera in *One Big Self* as a player in complex social interactions between documentarians and subjects, revealing the power imbalance between those who look and those who are the looked-at subjects—in this case, prisoners, some of whom have not had access to any likeness of themselves in years: "When I handed Franklin his prints, his face broke. / *Damn*, he said to no one, *I done got old*" (*OBS*, 6).[30] In *Let Us Now Praise Famous Men*, Agee recognizes the predatory potential of the camera—"a weapon, a stealer of images and souls, a gun, an evil eye"—and attacks his own complicity, calling himself a "cold-laboring spy," but he ultimately banks on his own empathic "anti-authoritative human consciousness" to relay the reality of those he encounters."[31] Because of his immeasurable weight in actual existence, and because of mine," Agee writes of a hypothetical subject, "every word I tell of him has inevitably a kind of immediacy, a kind of meaning."[32] Wright, however, seems to bring a greater degree of skepticism to her own witnessing, alerting the reader to the impress of outside cultural forces upon her perspective—"I wear the lenses of my time"—and suggesting, as she does in a reference to the Heisenberg Uncertainty Principle—"you change what you observe"—that her observations are inherently colored by her own projections (*OBS*, 11, 32). As if to ward off the claiming of knowledge that Agee proposes in his penetrating, head-to-toe descriptions, the prisoners' bodies appear in the text of *One Big Self* only in half glimpses—a tattered ear, a scarred wrist, a tattooed forearm.

While the act of photography haunts the subsequent paperback edition of *One Big Self* (which now bears the subtitle *An Investigation*), the absence of Luster's photographs in this version places extra pressure on Wright's words to connect the reader to the reality of those who live, and sometimes die, behind prison walls. As if to help compensate, Wright outlines the ways and means of her project in a new preface, "Stripe for Stripe," and in the course, takes care to reveal the poet as the subjective fallible creator of the poem to come. Laying out her initial experiences and working relationship with Luster, Wright takes care to clarify the limits of her role—"I will make three trips"—and to differentiate herself from various masters of "evidentiary writing," many of whom suffered persecution or imprisonment, such as Mandelstam, Wilde, Akhmatova, Celan, and Desnos (*OBS*, ix, xv). In contrast, Wright sardonically notes, "I am going to prison in order to write about it. Like a nineteenth-century traveler" (*OBS*, xv).

"Stripe for Stripe" also underscores the errant journey of the poet from center to periphery, emphasizing the distance the poet must travel to reach this particular periphery. Echoing the opener to "The Book of the Dead"— "These are roads to take when you think of your country"—Wright more dryly reports, "Driving through this part of Louisiana you can pass four prisons in less than an hour" (*OBS*, ix).[33] Rather than omnisciently guiding the reader into the landscape as Rukeyser does, Wright foregrounds her struggles to reach across time and space and thus discloses the poem as a time-bound artifact, not a transcendent fixed truth. Loosely asserting anaphoric structure, she begins paragraphs with "Try to remember," "Trying to remember," "I remember," and "Vivid to me" (*OBS*, ix–xi).

In the main body of the poem, Wright abandons the clear narrating "I" that leads the reader through "Stripe for Stripe" for a flickering presence that cedes ground to other perspectives, seemingly careful, in Glissant's words, to "conceive of the world as not simple and straightforward, with only one truth—mine."[34] A diffuse version of what James Agee described as a "bodyless eye," this "I"'s firsthand observations appear in scattered, piecemeal fashion sifting through a dense, fragmented collage of prose and lineated verse.[35] The collage draws upon the firsthand observations of the poet-narrator as well as a multitude of other sources, including the voices of prisoners, guards, and wardens; the restricted sources of information and language that prisoners are limited to, such as radio broadcasts, television soap operas, prison signs, tattoos, and prison library books; references to historical figures who have been incarcerated, from '60s radical H. Rap Brown to Oscar Wilde; literature about crime and punishment (Kafka, Dostoyevsky, Faulkner, the Bible); and excerpts from the first American board game, The Mansion of Happiness, in which obedience and conformity are enforced through threats of poverty, physical pain, and imprisonment. A list of sources at the back of *One Big Self*—from James Baldwin's essay on the Atlanta child murders of 1979–1981 to a prison memoir by Argentinian newspaper editor Jacobo Timerman—suggests an even broader context than is immediately apparent in the poem. Thrusting the marginalized existence of the prisoners into dialogue with a vast sweep of literary and cultural reference points, Wright's collage insists upon connectedness across cultural lines that is linked to, as Glissant says, "the conscious and contradictory experience of contacts among cultures."[36]

What dominates Wright's account are the voices of the prisoners themselves, shifting power away from the poet-witness as the arbiter of experience and allowing the richness of oral expression to be part of the record.

I want to go home, Patricia whispered.

I won't say I like being in prison, but I have learned a lot, and I like experiences. The terriblest part is being away from your families. —Juanita

I miss my screenporch.

I know every word to every song on *Purple Rain*. —Willie

I'm never leaving here. —Grasshopper, in front of the woodshop, posing beside a coffin he built (*OBS*, 5)

As is apparent from this excerpt, Wright arranges a diversity of responses that resist the construction of any archetypal prisoner. Elsewhere, various epistolary poems challenge archetypal constructions of the reader, the prisoner, and the town—addressed, respectively, as Dear Affluent Reader, Dear Damned Doomed and Forgotten, and Dear Dying Town, among other appellations (*OBS*, 24, 76, 27). These letters often capture, with a biting satiric tone, the moral judgments (among other impasses) that stand in the way of connection: "You brought this on yourself. You and no one else. . . . You shot the law and the law won," says a voice of accusation in "Dear Unbidden, Unbred" (*OBS*, 38).

In contrast, the liveliness of the actual prisoners' voices, replete with Louisiana idiom, serves to counteract the deadening effect of the prison experience and calls into question the disregarding homogeneity of mainstream culture. In "Stripe for Stripe," Wright describes her intent: "I wanted the banter, the idiom, the soft-spoken cadence of Louisiana speech to cut through the mass-media myopia" (*OBS*, xiv). These bits of Louisiana speech range from the poetic—"The last time you was here I had a headful of bees"—to the satiric—"*hypocrite pie still sittin' on the side*" (*OBS*, 5, 68). Wright also sprinkles in other local languages—smatterings of French, a main ingredient of Louisiana Creole and a reminder of its colonial plantation history, and Latin phrases from the court and the church. The particular commingling of local idiom with Latin, a language whose written authority holds such primacy in laws of church and state, underscores the fragility of the prisoners' words—both as endangered local idiom and as spoken utterances that would go otherwise unrecorded—yet also ensures each prisoner's rightful place as authoritative source. In this way, Wright's multilingual text resonates with Glissant's insistence that "linguistic multiplicity protects ways of speaking, from the most extensive to the most fragile," and can be seen as a gesture toward "restabilizing relations among communities."[37]

As the book progresses, the voices of the prisoners mingle with Wright's observations and references to divergent sources.

Poster, women's prison:
PARTS OF SPEECH FAIR
INTERJECTION, A WORD THAT EXPRESSES STRONG FEELING
UGH! WOW! OH!
                           His last word: Wow
That's all he said, the warden told the camera.

Mitterrand last dined on ortolans
                 in the tradition of French kings
Some have crawfish with the warden; some dine on oxygen

In some prisons the last cigarette is no longer permitted
                 0 exceptions   Don't ask

An eye for an eye   it says in Exodus
Whose eye?
An eye (*OBS*, 43)

Without a table of contents to refer to, the reader wanders through these carefully arranged juxtapositions that reveal a vast interconnectivity operating beneath the surface of our lives.

While Wright arranges her disparate sources to spark connections, she also requires that they stand apart as fragments separated by white space and refrains from interpreting or translating these bits into one overarching narrative. As Kristin Prevallet suggests, poetry is relational "not because it appropriates sources as conquered territories." Instead, she says, "Relational poetics looks at texts as being themselves in a constant state of motion, dispersion, and permeability that is inseparable not only from the shifting social and political context, but from the cycles of the earth and the diversity of nature."[38] Wright propels her texts into "a constant state of motion, dispersion and permeability" by placing them on the page such that references, quotes and observations are challenged by adjacent references, quotes and observations, unfixing texts from their original contexts and forming new, collaborative meanings that often readjust perspective (sometimes directly, sometimes obliquely) on power structures that divide society (and also fuel a robust prison industry). In the above passage from *One Big Self*, the text from the women's prison poster, which is intended to instruct inmates (who are largely impoverished and poorly educated), becomes a dark source of irony by way of its proximity to a prisoner's final words at what we assume is his execution; in this new context, the poster offers not the key to clear communication but an example of the shortfall of language in expressing the extremities of life and death in prison. Moving forward through the next lines, meanings continue to restlessly coalesce and disperse as new reference points enter the fray. Characteristic of *One Big Self* as a whole are the snippets of back talk—"0 exceptions   Don't ask" and "Whose eye?"—that destabilize authority even in the face of radical inequities, confinement and death.

Meanwhile, Wright stays in the background of her own observations, coming forward only in rare autobiographical moments that seem designed to reveal her particular vantage point and the relative distance or proximity between self and others. For example, in the poem "Just Another Day," Wright reveals how remote her own cultural location is from many of these prisoners: "When I said I lived in New England / he asked if I ever saw Princess Diana" (*OBS*, 58). For this inmate, New England—a regional name that evokes both the colonial origins and the subsequent imperial reach of the United States—is as foreign as another country. Wright also signals her remove from the prisoners by revealing the fissure between the "I" who appears as a character in the poem and the writer of the poem. Scattered word-processing commands flag the latter: "Do you wish to save these changes," "Do you want to download this," and near the book's end, "Do you want to / shut down   sleep   restart" (*OBS*, 11, 12, 80). This Brechtian strategy reminds the reader of the real conditions of the text's composition, in which memories are not seamlessly transported to the page but selectively and incompletely reconstructed through the subjective process of writing.

Wright not only subverts her authority as a documentarian but also unsettles empirical evidence used by the legal system to judge and punish, suggesting the limits of such evidence in summing up a person. References to fingerprints, analysis of gunshot wounds, and other forensic methods refuse to accumulate into verdicts or even any clear narratives. The interview, used in courtrooms and the documentary as a means of acquiring conclusive information, has also been dismantled to demonstrate the distance between questioner and respondent: Answers appear without questions and questions without answers, sometimes as existential utterances, such as, "Why does the light reproach us / Why is the coffee so watered down" (*OBS*, 37). Sometimes questions and answers stick together but skew away from direct communication and demonstrate the compromised position of the respondent. For example, a macabre joke about electrocution— "Westinghoused or Edisoned, your choice / AC or DC"—is answered by: "It's no real pleasure in life" (*OBS*, 63). For those without options, "N/A" is often as good a response as any.

While Wright demonstrates the limits of empiricism, she does call upon hard facts and firsthand observation to illuminate the difference and diversity of Louisiana culture as well as the encroachment of corporate capitalism. She notes steamy weather reports, Louisiana-specific flora, fauna, and local cuisine, as well as landscapes scarred by prisons, toxic dumping grounds, and pecan groves bulldozed to build the Pecanland Mall and Home Depot. Wright suggests that one of the ways the South remains distinct from the North is the demise of its agriculture industry and its concomitant economic woes: "Up north with its thirty minutes in the sun, good schools for the moneyed and silent alarms, and south with its petrochemical plants and joblessness" (*OBS*, 57).

Corporate capitalism threatens not only local cultural vitality but also personhood itself—reducing the richness of human life to tradable materials, the ultimate form of absorption. Echoing Rukeyser's inclusion of a clipping from the stock pages in "The Book of the Dead," Wright's poem "Dialing Dungeons for Dollars" points to the fact that various private corrections and security firms contracted by government entities to manage prison populations are publicly traded on the stock market.[39] In addition, we learn that financial profit is reckoned by tallying "mandays," a dehumanizing neologism: One manday represents a day's worth of incarceration per inmate and is the unit by which the government is billed. An increase in mandays boosted Corrections Corporation of America's revenues to $787 million in 1999 (*OBS*, 28).

In opposition to the abstraction of mandays, Wright brings to light the day-to-day particularities of prison life, asserting the humanity of the prisoners as well as the oppressive rituals that structure their existence. She enumerates prison's brutal routines, from five-times-per-day head counts to the rituals of execution. Alongside these observations, Wright scatters bits of the prisoners' gossip, reminiscences about children and the world outside, inventions, and dreams—one inmate pretends his bunk is a boat and his cellmate's flushing of the toilet is the Arctic Ocean (*OBS*, 22). What can't be thwarted is the inescapable tedium and anguish of prison time, which Wright portrays in anaphoric double-spaced lists of things to count:

> Count the shots fired
>
> Count the puncture wounds
>
> Count your cavities
>
> Count the years (*OBS*, 65)

With details pertaining to those within prison and/or those waiting outside, the lists often evoke a violent past and an evaporating future.

One Big Self closes on a conflicted relational scene that highlights the divide between poet and prisoners but also tentatively imagines its transcendence. Swiveling into the past tense, the poet suddenly appears at a remove from the prison world and engaged in looking at Luster's photographs of the prisoners: "And so, I took out her tintypes / And drew the prisoners around me" (*OBS*, 80). This last line suggests a dissolving of the photographic frame such that the poet stands in proximity to the prisoners themselves, not just their two-dimensional images. At the same time, sharing the same sentence, the photographs hover nearby, throwing a shadow over this fantasized communal gesture. Calling to mind the slender physicality of images printed on metal sheets, the word "tintype" stands in stark contrast to the human bodies that are no longer present. In this way, Wright reminds us of the actual people that live and die beyond the page, as well as the distance that must be traveled to reach them.

IV.

Rising, Falling, Hovering faces different border-crossing and relational challenges than *One Big Self*. Instead of seeking connection with those isolated within American society, *Rising, Falling, Hovering* attempts to reach out to those who live beyond the heavily guarded borders of the United States. The America depicted here is the epitome of Glissant's characterization of the imperial Western nation that builds identity around the concept of monolithic power. Foregrounding her own journeys between Mexico and New England, Wright tracks the exertion of U.S. military and economic influence past its own borders into Mexico and Iraq. In this book, the border is a literal, territorial reality with political and military significance, and border crossing is a perilous, state-monitored activity; surveillance cameras and intimidating security measures are reoccurring reminders of the ways in which the United States aims to control the movements of citizens and noncitizens alike. In addition, while *One Big Self* aims to make those rendered invisible visible, *Rising, Falling, Hovering* must contend with mainstream media's high-profile stories about immigration and the Iraq war, which often follow the lead of government public relations efforts. In resistance to the depiction of these distant others not only as threats but as virtual nonhumans—"We are real, they are not!" as Wright captures the sentiment—*Rising, Falling, Hovering* strives to reveal the complex realities of others.[40]

To bring these more numerous, remote peripheries into the center of our view, *Rising, Falling, Hovering* leans more heavily on narrative than *One Big Self*, and it is through narrative that Wright forges a complex, multiplicitous network of relation. Wright began her career as a narrative poet and in later books, such as *String Light*, *Just Whistle*, and *Deepstep Come Shining*, she has employed a looser, more disjunctive, unresolved sense of story. In *Rising, Falling, Hovering*, Wright has tapped postmodern narrative's potential to map simultaneity, fusing connections between far-flung people and their experiences. While there are clear narrative threads— repeated trips of the poet-witness and her husband and son to Mexico from New England during the outbreak of the Iraq war—what unfolds are not full-fledged stories but everyday episodes or situations involving plane travel or walking or driving that merge with, or are disrupted by, memories of visits to Mexico from years past; newspaper and television reportage on the Iraq war; stories told by friends, family members, and acquaintances; and imagined journeys of Mexican emigrants across the Mexican–U.S. border. Moreover, episodes evolve out of a sort of scenic fugue state in which landscapes of Mexico and the United States and travel between the two places rise to the surface and submerge, often without warning, suggesting that these locales haunt each other in resistance to physical borders and any forward-moving plot. Sometimes, landscapes are ambiguous, cloaked in fog or darkness, where "the voice beginning to dematerialize" struggles to be heard; it is as if the poet-witness has entered her own blind spot, manifested as a murky borderland, where the self attenuates under a kind of psychic atmospheric pressure (*RFH*, 11).

While more consistently present and embodied than in *One Big Self*, the poet-witness of *Rising, Falling, Hovering* is disoriented, self-questioning, and well aware of her limits—enacting a version of Glissant's errant poet who rejects the idea of the world as "something obvious and transparent." The speaker's disorientation seems to arise in part from her feelings of alienation vis-à-vis her own American citizenry. In "Re: Happiness, in pursuit thereof," the first poem of the book, Wright twists a familiar phrase from the Declaration of Independence into an office-memo style title, insinuating the debasement of this inalienable right to something commercial or, at best, perfunctory. At the start of the poem, the speaker confesses her confusion: "Here I am, a labyrinth, and I am a mess. / I am located at the corner of Waterway / and Bluff. I need your help" (*RFH*, 3). Although Wright goes on to provide trace autobiographical details that allow the reader to perceive this "I" as a version of the poet C. D. Wright and other characters as the poet's husband and son, the walls around the distinctly private and individual thin and perforate amid the intercutting of other people's stories as well as the frequent shifting from the "I" to a more remote "she" or "we." Sometimes unnamed protagonists appear who are likely the poet and her family but, stripped as they are of distinguishing detail, seem perched on the edge of other identities. These episodes are fraught with a sense of the ephemeral and described with a tone of detached formality, as though reporting on the self from afar: "We may drop things along the way that substantiate our having been here. / We will not be able to transmit any of these feelings verbatim. / . . . We lack verisimilitude but we press on with intense resolve" (*RFH*, 46, 77).

To demonstrate the interconnectivity of people and places, Wright creates a permeable, mobile structure for the book. While *Rising, Falling, Hovering* employs a table of contents, Wright subverts its role as an orienteering device for the reader and instead uses it to flag the overlapping and porous nature of the book's material. We quickly see that three poems appear before the first section is announced. In addition, several titles reoccur. For example, the book's title (which itself implies an in-flux, mobile state) is also the name for each of the two titled sections, though the second (and its accompanying title poem) bears the addendum of "cont." The phrase "to be cont." also appears within the poetry itself (*RFH*, 36, 43). Conventionally used as a footer that is superfluous to the content of a document, "cont." or "to be cont." as used by Wright is a Brechtian denaturalizing gesture that calls attention to the connections the writer subjectively enforces, revealing the artifice of that narrative convention yet also commanding the reader to see disparate events as connected. The term additionally suggests that the account provided is ultimately incomplete. In an essay about the writing of *Rising, Falling, Hovering*, Wright (using the third person) explains: "She added *to be cont.*, because even if she didn't write more, nothing was resolved."[41]

Not only does Wright repeat titles of poems, she also recycles material from the poems themselves in ways that establish the interconnectivity of different places, times, and people. For example, the poem "Like Having a Light at Your Back You Can't See but You Can Still Feel (1)" appears early in the book to initiate a dreamlike journey in which surroundings are obscure and the protagonists are undefined:

> As if it were streaming into your ear.
>
> The edges of a room long vanished.
>
> She is not really hearing what he's really saying.
>
> The shine is going out of the ground
> but they are sure of their footing.
>
> It's not that they have been here before, but
> they are young and they have water. (*RFH*, 4)

The poem continues to negotiate an indistinct landscape in which "others are out there who are drifting" until finally swerving toward a suggestion of state power that is undeniably threatening: "If this took place anywhere near the presidential palace / it would be nonstop terrifying. / And this could be the reason she has started to scream" (*RFH*, 4, 5). Sixty-seven pages later, a second version of the poem appears. In "Like Having a Light at Your Back You Can't See but You Can Still Feel (2)," Wright reuses the same first few sentences, but the fourth—"The shine is going out of the ground / but they are sure of their footing"—is followed by "They have been here a thousand and one times" (*RFH*, 71). This sentence suggests repeated remembrances. However, instead of veering toward the presidential palace and terror, this version gradually slips into a seaside New England locale, followed by a scene in a bedroom in which a man wearing a sleeping mask complains about the light from the reading lamp of "C," his female companion: "I can feel it / streaming in my ear. Besides, / he is adamant, / you just go to sleep at night / I go on a journey" (*RFH*, 72). Feeling light that can't be seen not only echoes the implied ominous searchlight of the poem's title but also suggests that beyond our immediate vision lies a reality we might imaginatively reach toward. This other reality fills the pages between the two poems in the form of details of the Iraq war and the plight of undocumented Mexicans trying to cross into the United States. Wright's recycling technique, then, compels the knowledge of embattled elsewheres to penetrate the carapace of American private life.

Throughout *Rising, Falling Hovering*, the strain of seeking connections across such vast terrain and in the face of dire circumstances is echoed in the ricochet between prose and poetry. Moving between complete sentences and fragments, between short and long lines, and between punctuation and a lack thereof, Wright suggests the mind "sifting for some interlinear significance," as she says in her title poem (*RFH*, 11). Wright also inserts extra amounts of white space, double- and occasionally triple-spacing her lines and sometimes replacing commas and periods with extra spacing, which subtly evokes the intervening distance between self and other that the poet must traverse; absence thereby becomes a constant, subliminal presence. The infusion of white space and the removal of grammatically sanctioned pauses further provide lines with a floating, tenuous quality as if the unanchored words drift uneasily upon an encroaching blank sea of ignorance and forgetting, as in the following excerpt:

Let's get that light off   You aren't really reading   The monitor from the overhead
begins its infotainment   Not shown: white phosphorus   falling
                                                              on the city of minarets
Not confirmed: the use of white phosphorous (for another year) NOW SHOWING:
CAT WOMAN   If you cannot or do not wish to perform the function
                                You must change seats now (*RFH*, 53)

The swirl of details from American pop culture and travel advisories seems to encourage self-protective distraction. Meanwhile, the blank space of the page accentuates what is "not confirmed" and "not shown" in one of several references Wright makes to flesh-burning white phosphorus bombs, which the U.S. military would admit to using in Iraq (in language couched in semantic hairsplitting) after many denials.

Shorter lines, while sometimes used to slow the pace of narrative (inducing a slow-motion dreamlike surreality) or to bring details of place to the fore, can also demonstrate the snapping of syntax and logic under pressure to make sense of loss, grief, and a violent elsewhere from the isolated vantage point of America:

Our lot bounded
By a busy road at the foot
Of the hill
Here and here
By burial ground #34
When a veteran—
Bagpipe and guns—
The dog throws up
On the Oaxacan rug (*RFH*, 66)

Attempting to map stateside local terrain, this passage trips and slips as signifiers of Iraq and Mexico come crashing in. Describing the boundaries of the speaker's "lot"—a word that can refer both to property and a person's luck in life—Wright notes a burial ground (the use of "#34" evoking a chilling bureaucratizing of death), which seems to trigger an attempt at explanation ("When a veteran—") that is broken off by the sounds of a military-style funeral. The brevity of the fragments suggests the struggle of utterance against the impress of white space and silence. The extra allotment of white space also serves to isolate the fragments from each other even as the speaker attempts to construct sentences and logic. Ultimately, descriptions or explanations that might wall off sorrow and outrage cannot be sustained grammatically or otherwise.

Late in the book, in the poem "Like Something Christenberry Pictured," Wright changes tactics and employs the hyperextended sentence, hooking multiple sentences together with semicolons to make encompassing connections. This page-and-a-half-long, single-spaced mega sentence in prose stretches across expanses of time and space to piece together the speaker's disparate memories and fantasies of humans and animals threatened by annihilation. However, this strategy expires seemingly in tandem with "the very instant you stopped looking for meaning and began rifling among the folds of feeling." Short, double-spaced lines ensue, noting moments of sensate experience—such as smelling flowers, dancing, and drinking milk from a carton—which appear to be more tenable than a panoramic view or summation of a life (*RFH*, 86–88).

As in *One Big Self*, Wright wields facts and observed details to portray the crushing impact of the dominant culture on those at the bottom of the social hierarchy. Outlining U.S. economic interests in Mexico and Iraq, which rely upon the manual laborer and the economy shopper, Wright spells out the repercussions in brass-tacks jottings: "If a body makes 1 centavo per chile picked or / 5 cents for 50 chiles can Walmex get it down to 3 cents. Pass the savings on to US. / Will they open a Supercenter in Fallujah once it is pacified" (*RFH*, 63). South of the U.S. border, however, Wright discovers not only a rich, distinctive local culture but signs of survival and resistance: an anti-war sign composed of flowers, a man mending a pair of pants (even as new merchandise waits to be purchased), and "the closeness, the warmth, the voices of people eating together" (*RFH*, 19, 22, 44). Meanwhile, north of the border, Wright depicts life in America as ruled by fear, consumerism, paranoia, and potential destruction. Oil trucks, a bird sanctuary absent of bird song, and billboards advertising the lottery riddle the landscape (*RFH*, 70). Disconnected from environment and community, emotionless autopilot escalates to rage and futility in a list of errands that range from "I have been to Pilates" to "I have filled my tank," culminating with the quietly mad "then I think I'll cut my hair off with a broken bottle" (*RFH*, 51). Elsewhere, the poet struggles to bear witness to a war made "telegenic": "Can you describe this. / I cannot. This is not the day or the hour. / The color is all wrong" (*RFH*, 17).

Against this backdrop, Wright introduces the idioms and local language of Mexico. Spanish crops up in the form of discrete words and colloquial phrases in an otherwise Anglo-American text, inserting clots of resistance for monolingual readers of English. Wright also uses Mexican idiom to emphasize the specific, brutal consequences of American economic dominance, which propels many Mexicans to flee dire poverty and attempt to cross the intensely patrolled U.S. border. In a description of one such harrowing desert trip, Wright employs the phrase "sopa de pollo," which is followed by "dark meat breaking off in chunks" (*RFH*, 41). According to Wright's endnotes, the term for undocumented emigrants from Mexico is "pollo" or chicken. With "sopa de pollo" or chicken soup, Wright wields slang to gruesomely evoke the body's collapse due to exposure (*RFH*, 95). Elsewhere, Wright uses Spanish idiom to emphasize her lack of fluency in Mexican culture as a visiting American: The poet-narrator latches onto an idiomatic expression from a phrasebook only to discover it's not used in Mexico. This phantom colloquialism—"Está comiendo mi coco," roughly translated as "He is eating my head"—is used several times as an expression of anxiety in reference to the narrator's son before turning literal in a terrifying fantasy of Donner-Party-like cannibalism: "Does one start with the face. Save the jam for the end?" (*RFH*, 56, 57, 58, 79). By taking a misconstrued colloquialism and morphing it into an expression of barbarity, Wright implies that ignorance of the language and culture of others has the potential not only to disconnect us from our fellow humans but also to dehumanize us.

Wright also turns an observant eye to Anglo-American as a colonizer of experience even for Americans when wielded by the U.S. government and the popular media. Pointing to what could be considered the most sinister form of "a technical salesman's Esperanto"—Glissant's term for the "perfunctory containerization of expression" that Anglo-American has the potential to become—Wright reminds us of how the patriotic labeling of military attacks in Iraq served to sell the war to the American public: Riffing off of Operation Enduring Freedom, she unleashes a score of alternate versions, including "Operation product endorsement" and "Operation it depends / upon how you define the word torture . . ." (*RFH*, 64). Elsewhere, Wright underscores how doublespeak used by the military and the government (and adopted by the mainstream media) purposefully obscures or omits facts. Juxtaposed with the rising body count of American soldiers, a reportorial voice announces, "at the policy level no such estimates exist" for the Iraqi dead (*RFH*, 24). Seemingly in response, everyday civilian language struggles to mean. Taking the lead from artist Jenny Holzer (whose text she revises), Wright holds up mainstream American idioms as menacing or emptied-out rhetorical gestures (*RFH*, 59, 96). They are "phrases cycling through us as routine as prison meals" in which "Business is good" has as much weight as "How do you want your chicken" (*RFH*, 67). Nor is poetry immune to potential irrelevance. "Nary a death arrested nor a hair of a harm averted / by any scrawny farrago of letters," Wright observes (*RFH*, 23). In the poem "End Thoughts," Wright imagines border crossing in light of an aggressive state's attempts to control language:

> The temperature has already been adjusted
>   by the state
> Our obsolescence built into the system
>
> When you use the ladies' room
>   do not put your purse on the floor
> When the civilian words are dispensed
>   different meanings will be assigned
> The new meanings will be fired
>   at the head and groin area (*RFH*, 91)

While Wright notes these various conflicts within and between cultures as she moves back and forth over the border, she ultimately asserts a relational vision of an interdependent existence in which the consequences of violence and environmental destruction are global. She notes: "Not so many scientists subscribe to the Gaia hypothesis"—in which the earth is believed to be a multilevel living organism—"nor are so many rushing to refute the thousand and one levels of interdependence" (*RFH*, 63). What's ultimately at stake is our potential mutual annihilation as Wright evokes in several references—including the Aztecs, whose empire was destroyed by the Spanish, the biblical fall, and the flood from Genesis—all of which bleed through to color contemporary scenes. In a tension-filled sketch of an overcrowded Fourth of July celebration, Noah's ark makes an appearance but is little comfort: "He knew the ark would not wait. / He knew they were booked to the rafters" (*RFH*, 81). This also, of course, echoes the tragic flooding of New Orleans and botched rescue efforts after Hurricane Katrina. References to populations that have been abandoned and/or destroyed by their fellow humans underscore the need for transgressing borders of race, class, and culture that isolate us from each other and allow us to view others, as Wright has noted, as unreal and thereby disposable.

Like *One Big Self*, the ending of *Rising, Falling, Hovering* features a mediated act of witness—a photograph—that throws a last ray of light at the periphery that has resumed its distance from the speaker. However, in *Rising, Falling, Hovering*, the photograph is a more elusive emblem: a wooded park with a nameless river that Wright describes as "a nonlocal reality / that shimmered at the instant of its own disappearance" (*RFH*, 93). This "nonlocal reality" appears to hover at the edge of forgetfulness despite the evidence of the photographic record. However, in the book's final lines, Wright seems to portray a momentary projection of hope onto a scene that, in canonical poetic terms, would otherwise symbolize the passing of time and death: "a yellow leaf floated toward ground / transmitting a spot of optimism / through a slow intensification of color in the lower corner of the morning" (*RFH*, 93). Meanwhile, on the previous, facing page, Wright portrays the riptide of despair and withdrawal that threatens this tentative suggestion of optimism—"one wants to dry into invisible ink"—as well as what might fuel hope, or at least resolve (*RFH*, 92). The hardest task, Wright asserts, is not acknowledging "a sense of something out there that needs saving" but rather taking action, which she describes in terms that evoke the outset of another errant mission:

> it's the sticking of one's foot off the edge
> lowering it to the cold floor
>
> and finding the correct instrument
> to work that crack into a big enough opening
> to venture forward (*RFH*, 92)

NOTES TO CRITICAL ESSAY

1. C. D. Wright, "Provisional Remarks On Being/A Poet/Of Arkansas," *The Southern Review* (autumn 1994), 809; republished in Wright's *Cooling Time: An American Poetry Vigil* (Port Townsend, WA: Copper Canyon Press, 2005), 20.

2. Quotations from C. D. Wright's books are cited in the text with the following abbreviations: *CT* = *Cooling Time*, *DCS* = *Deepstep Come Shining*, *LRP* = *The Lost Roads Project*, *OBS* = *One Big Self* (all page numbers refer to the 2007 edition, *One Big Self: An Investigation*), *RFH* = *Rising, Falling, Hovering*, *SL* = *String Light*.

3. As part of a close study of "The Box This Comes In," Jenny Goodman sees Wright's valorizing of the handmade as a preference for imperfection and a suggestion that "private experience should inform the poetics" in her essay "Politics and the Personal Lyric in the Poetry of Joy Harjo and C.D. Wright." *Melus: Theory, Culture and Criticism* 19, no. 2 (Summer 1994): 51.

4. Stephen Burt, "I Came to Talk You into Physical Splendor." *Boston Review* (December 1997/January 1998): 31–33.

5. Robert N. Casper and Nadia Colburn, "Interview with C.D. Wright," *Jubilat* 5 (2002): 120–21.

6. Some critics have found Wright's association with Language poetry regrettable and often ignore the political import of such an allegiance. David Orr dismissively describes Language poets as "ethereal souls" and assures the reader that Wright's "head might be full of Ron Silliman, but her soul is pure Dolly Parton" in a review of *Steal Away* in *Poetry* 182, no. 3 (June 2003): 170. Joel Brouwer refers to Language writing as "egghead experiments" that he claims Wright begins to emulate during the 1980s but diverges from in later work, in his review of *Rising, Falling, Hovering*, "Counting the Dead," in *The New York Times Book Review* (June 22, 2008): 11. Although Brouwer criticizes Wright's fragmentation, nonstandard punctuation, and other "vapid typographical hijinks," he also praises her subtler forms of syntactic disruption as Brechtian strategies that provoke awareness in "Comply Whether a Believer or Not," an essay in *Parnassus* 28, nos. 1–2 (2005): 207, 209. While Adam Kirsch doesn't apply the label Language Poet, he describes Wright as a "discourteous poet," a term he uses for those whose writing is distinguished by complexity, idiosyncratic allusion, and "form [that] is conceived intellectually and theoretically," as he writes in "Discourtesies," a review of *Steal Away* in *The New Republic* (October 21, 2002): 33. Clearly preferring the "courteous poet" who "approaches language as a medium of communication," prioritizing clarity, coherence, and traditional poetic devices, such as rhyme and meter, he attacks Wright's poetry as using now fashionable "discourteous" techniques to cloak ordinary sentiment, 32–33.

7. Lynn Keller, " 'Ink of eyes and veins and phonemes': C.D. Wright's Eclectic Poetics." *Arizona Quarterly* 59, no. 3 (Autumn 2003): 117–18. In parsing Wright's essay "A Taxable Matter," Keller suggests Wright is in dialogue with an essay by Ron Silliman first published in 1977 in which he asserts that language subjected to capitalism turns words into commodities, disrupting the connection between the actual materiality of language and "human makers" such that "language itself appears to become transparent, a mere vessel" for referentiality: "Disappearance of the Word, Appearance of the World," *The New Sentence* (New York: Roof Books, 1987), 11. Keller goes on to describe Silliman's viewpoint (*The New Sentence*, 17) that poetry can perform a "social function" by rejecting the illusion of conventional literary realism as well as the conduit model of linguistic communication.

8. Keller, "C. D. Wright's Eclectic Poetics," 123, 117; C. D. Wright, "A Taxable Matter," *Field* 40 (spring 1989): 25–26.

9. Sarah Vap and Charles Jensen, "An Interview with C.D. Wright," in *Innovative Women Poets*, eds. Elisabeth A. Frost and Cynthia Hogue (Iowa City: University of Iowa, 2007), 336.

10. *Ibid.*, 336; Bertolt Brecht, *Brecht on Theatre*, ed. John Willet (New York: Hill and Wang, 1957), 192–93. Charles Bernstein has also turned to Brecht's Alienation Effect to explain his absorptive and antiabsorptive techniques as well as those of other Language writers in his poem-essay "Artifice of Absorption," in *A Poetics* (Cambridge, MA: Harvard University Press, 1992), 66–89.

11. Keller, "C.D. Wright's Eclectic Poetics," 119.

12. *Ibid.*, 123.

13. Lynn Keller, "The Wolf Interview: C.D. Wright." *The Wolf* 19 (winter 2008/09): 48.

14. In fact, in a 1987 essay, Wright argues with Silliman's pronouncement in *Tjanting* that language is the primary site of political resistance: "my difference with this one dictum is that it is scientific. That it is too engrossed with technique. Not with authenticity, what Sharon Doubiago calls 'the art of seeing with one's own eyes' " [C. D. Wright, "Argument With The Gestapo Continued: II," *Five Fingers Review* 5 (1987): 86]. Lynn Keller refers to this passage of Wright's essay as evidence for Wright's "faith in what she sees with her own eyes and experiences in her own female body" in a discussion of *Tremble* in "C.D. Wright's Eclectic Poetics," 140. However, Wright subsequently reworded her argument with Silliman's dictum, notably omitting the reference to authenticity and Doubiago, in "69 Hidebound Opinions, Propositions, and Several Asides from a Manila Folder Concerning the Stuff of Poetry" in *By Herself: Women Reclaiming Poetry*, ed. Molly McQuade (St. Paul, MN: Graywolf Press, 2000), 390, and then again in *Cooling Time*, 59, where she further qualifies her differences with Silliman: "I find I disagree less with Silliman on this point than I used to, so I suspect he has denounced the claim."

15. Édouard Glissant, *Poetics of Relation*, translated by Betsy Wing (Ann Arbor: University of Michigan, 1997), 16.

16. *Ibid.*, 11, 14.

17. *Ibid.*, 18–20.

18. *Ibid.*, 29.

19. *Ibid.*, 30.

20. *Ibid.*,103–20.

21. *Ibid.*, 112.

22. *Ibid.*, 34–35. In defining his Poetics of Relation, Glissant also references the work of Francophone writers from other parts of the world, such as the French writer Segalen, Lebanese poet Georges Schéhadé, and African writers Kateb Yacine and Cheik Anta Diop, among others (29).

23. *Ibid.*, 26.

24. *Ibid.*, 191, 20.

25. Vince Aletti, "Picture This," *The Village Voice* (1/12/04): 38.

26. Deborah Luster, "The Reappearance of Those Who Have Gone," preface of *One Big Self: Prisoners of Louisiana* (Santa Fe, NM: Twin Palms Publishers, 2003).

27. Glissant, *Poetics of Relation*, 191–92.

28. Susan Sontag, *On Photography* (New York: Farrar, Straus and Giroux, 1973), 56.

29. Martha Rosler, "In, Around and Afterthoughts (On Documentary Photography)," in *Decoys and Disruptions: Selected Writings, 1975–2001* (Cambridge, MA: MIT Press, 2004), 178.

30. In maximum-security prisons, mirrors are made of stainless steel that obscures reflections; Wright describes this in "Dear Unbidden, Unbred" (*OBS*, 38) and in "Looking for 'one untranslatable song': C.D. Wright on poetics, collaboration, American prisoners, and Frank Stanford," an interview with Kent Johnson, *Jacket*, no. 15 (December 2001), http://jacketmagazine.com/15/cdwright-iv.html.

31. James Agee and Walker Evans, *Let Us Now Praise Famous Men* (Boston: Houghton Mifflin, 1941), xiv, 134, 362.

32. *Ibid.*, 12.

33. Muriel Rukeyser, "The Book of the Dead," *U.S. 1* (1938), reprinted in *The Collected Poems of Muriel Rukeyser*, eds. Janet E. Kaufman and Anne F. Herzog (Pittsburgh: University of Pittsburgh Press, 2005), 73.

34. Glissant, *Poetics of Relation*, 154.

35. Agee, *Let Us Now Praise Famous Men*, 187.

36. Glissant, *Poetics of Relation*, 144.

37. *Ibid.*, 96, 108.

38. Kristin Prevallet, "Writing Is Never by Itself Alone: Six Mini-Essays on Relational Investigative Poetics." *Fence* 6, no. 1 (Spring/Summer 2003): 24.

39. Rukeyser, "The Book of the Dead," in *The Collected Poems of Muriel Rukeyser*, 101.

40. C. D. Wright, "During the Composition of 'Rising, Falling, Hovering': A Personal Document of the War, of Mexico, and an American Family's Halting Progress." *Chicago Review* 53, no. 4 and 54, no. 1/2 (Summer 2008): 353.

41. Wright, "During the Composition of 'Rising, Falling, Hovering.'" *Chicago Review*, 352.

BIBLIOGRAPHY

Books by C. D. Wright

Translations of The Gospel Back into Tongues. Albany: State University of New York Press, 1982.
Further Adventures With You. Pittsburgh, PA: Carnegie-Mellon University Press, 1986.
String Light. Athens, GA: University of Georgia Press, 1991.
Just Whistle: A Valentine, with photographs by Deborah Luster. Berkeley, CA: Kelsey St. Press, 1993.
The Lost Roads Project: A Walk-in Book of Arkansas, with photographs by Deborah Luster. Fayetteville: University of Arkansas Press, 1994.
Tremble. New York: The Ecco Press, 1996.
Deepstep Come Shining. Port Townsend, WA: Copper Canyon Press, 1998.
Steal Away: Selected and New Poems. Port Townsend, WA: Copper Canyon Press, 2002.

One Big Self: Prisoners of Louisiana, with photographs by Deborah Luster. Sante Fe, NM: Twin Palms Publishers, 2003.

Cooling Time: An American Poetry Vigil, Port Townsend, WA: Copper Canyon Press, 2005.

Like Something Flying Backwards: New and Selected Poems. Northumberland, England: Bloodaxe Books, 2007.

One Big Self: An Investigation. Port Townsend, WA: Copper Canyon Press, 2007.

Rising, Falling, Hovering. Port Townsend, WA: Copper Canyon Press, 2008.

One With Others. Port Townsend, WA: Copper Canyon Press, 2010.

Selected Prose

"Argument with the Gestapo Continued: Literary Resistance." *Five Fingers Review* 1 (1984): 30–34.

"Argument with the Gestapo Continued: II." *Five Fingers Review* 5 (1987): 79–89.

"The Adamantine Practice of Poetry." *Brick* 35 (Spring 1989): 55–58.

"A Taxable Matter." *Field* 40 (Spring 1989): 24–26.

"Provisional Remarks on Being / A Poet / Of Arkansas." *The Southern Review* (Autumn 1994): 809–11.

The Reader's Map of Arkansas, Fayetteville: University of Arkansas Press, 1994.

"C. D. Wright," in *Contemporary Authors Autobiography Series* 22. Detroit, MI: Gale Research, Inc., 1995, 307–17.

A Reader's Map of Rhode Island. Barrington, RI: Lost Roads Publishers, 1999.

"69 Hidebound Opinions, Propositions, and Several Asides from a Manila Folder Concerning the Stuff of Poetry," in *By Herself.* Ed. Molly McQuade. Saint Paul, MN: Graywolf Press, 2000, 380–97.

Run through Rock: Selected Short Poems of Besmilr Brigham. Ed. C. D. Wright. Barrington, RI: Lost Roads Publishers, 2000.

The Battlefield Where the Moon Says I Love You by Frank Stanford. Ed. C. D. Wright and Forrest Gander. Barrington, RI: Lost Roads Publishers, 2000.

"Collaborating with Deborah Luster." *Brick* 68 (Fall 2001): 89–91.

"In a Ring of Cows Is the Signal Given: Ruminations on Mothering and Writing," in *The Grand Permission: New Writings on Poetics and Motherhood.* Eds. Patricia Dienstfrey and Brenda Hillman. Middletown, CT: Wesleyan University Press, 2003, 195–200.

"During the Composition of 'Rising, Falling, Hovering': A Personal Document of the War, of Mexico, and an American Family's Halting Progress." *Chicago Review* 53, no. 4 and 54, no. 1/2 (Summer 2008): 349–55.

Selected Interviews

"Bedrock, Roots and Veins: A Talk with C.D. Wright," by Kathleen Fraser. *Poetry Flash: A Poetry Review and Literary Calendar for the West* 259 (March 1995): 1, 6–8, 10.

"Looking for 'one untranslatable song': C.D. Wright on Poetics, Collaboration, American Prisoners, and Frank Stanford," by Kent Johnson. *Jacket* 15 (December 2001): jacketmagazine.com/15/cdwright-iv.html.

"A Trace of a Tale: C.D. Wright, an Investigative Poem" by Bob Holman. *Poets & Writers* (May/June 2002): 12–23.

"Interview with C.D. Wright," by Robert N. Casper and Nadia Colburn. *Jubilat* 5 (Spring/Summer 2002): 117–32.

"An Interview with C.D. Wright," by Sarah Vap and Charles Jensen, in *Innovative Women Poets: An Anthology of Contemporary Poetry and Interviews*. Eds. Elisabeth Frost and Cynthia Hogue. Iowa City: University of Iowa, 2007, 327–41.

"The Wolf Interview: C.D. Wright," by Lynn Keller. *The Wolf* 19 (Winter 2008–2009): 46–52.

Selected Criticism

Almon, Bert. "C. D. Wright," in *American Writers*. Ed. Jay Parini. Supplement XV (Thomson Gale, 2006), 337–55.

Altieri, Charles. 2004. "On Difficulty in Contemporary American Poetry." *Daedaelus* 113, no. 4 (Fall): 113–18.

Brouwer, Joel. 2005. "Comply Whether a Believer or Not." *Parnassus:Poetry in Review* 28, nos. 1–2): 192–221.

———. 2008. "Counting the Dead." Review of *Rising, Falling, Hovering*. *The New York Times Book Review* (June 22): 11.

Burt, Stephen. 2009. "Lightsource, Aperture, Face: C. D. Wright and Photography," in Nick Halpern, Jane Hedley, and Willard Spiegelman, eds. *IN THE FRAME: Women's Ekphrastic Poetry from Marianne Moore to Susan Wheeler* (Newark, DE: University of Delaware Press), 227–244; repr. Stephen Burt. 2009. *Close Calls with Nonsense* (St. Paul, MN: Graywolf), 41–60.

———. 2007. "Lowered Gaze." Review of *One Big Self: An Investigation* and *Like Something Flying Backwards*. *Times Literary Supplement* (June 1): 8.

———. 1997–1998. "'I Came to Talk You into Physical Splendor': On the Poetry of C.D. Wright." *Boston Review* (December/January): 31–33.

Gilbert, Alan. 2008. "Neither Settled Nor Easy." Review of *One Big Self: An Investigation*. *Boston Review* (January/February): 43–44.

Gilbert, Sandra. 1992. "How These Homegirls Sing." Review of *String Light*. *Poetry* 160, no. 5 (August): 284–304.

Goldensohn, Lorrie. 1984. "Flights Home." Review of *Translations of the Gospel Back into Tongues*. *Poetry* 144, no. 1 (April): 40–47.

Goodman, Jenny. 1994. "Politics and the Personal Lyric in the Poetry of Joy Harjo and C.D. Wright." *Melus* 19, no. 2 (Summer): 35–57.

Keller, Lynn. 2003. "'Ink of eyes and veins and phonemes': C.D. Wright's Eclectic Poetics." *Arizona Quarterly* 59, no. 3 (autumn): 115–49.

Kirsch, Adam. 2002. "Discourtesies." Review of *Steal Away*. *The New Republic* (October 21): 32–36.

Latta, John. 2008. "C.D. Wright's *Rising, Falling, Hovering*. *Isola di Rifiuti* (May 23). isola-di-rifiuti.blogspot.com/2008_05_01_archive.html.

Longenbach, James. 2002. "Poetry in Review." Review of *Steal Away*. *Yale Review* 90, no. 4): 171–84.

Mayes, Frances. 1984. "Three Short Reviews." Review of *Translations of the Gospel Back into Tongues*. *Ironwood* 23 (Spring): 174–76.

McDaniel, Ray. 2003. Review of *Steal Away*. *The Constant Critic* (November 2 and December 4): www.constantcritic.com/ray_mcdaniel/steal_away.

Muske, Carol. 1999. Review of *Deepstep Come Shining*. *The Yale Review* 87, no. 4 (October): 158–61.

Neely, Mark. 2003. Review of *Steal Away*. *Jacket* 22 (May). www.jacketmagazine .com/22/neely-wright.html.

Nowak, Mark. 1999. Review of *Deepstep Come Shining*. *Rain Taxi*, online edition (Spring). www.raintaxi.com/online/1999spring/cdwright.shtml.

Orr, David. 2003. Review of *Steal Away*. *Poetry* 182, no. 3 (June): 170–73.

Silliman, Ron. 2005. Blog entry on "Rising, Falling, Hovering" (December 12). www.ronsilliman.blogspot.com/2005/12/when-i-first-glanced-at-c.html.

CONTRIBUTORS

MARY JO BANG is the author of six collections of poems, most recently *The Bride of E* (Graywolf, 2009) and *Elegy* (Graywolf, 2007), which received the 2007 National Book Critics Circle Award for Poetry. A translation of Dante's *Inferno*, with illustrations by Henrik Drescher, is forthcoming from Graywolf Press in 2012. She's been the recipient of a Hodder Fellowship from Princeton University and a grant from the Guggenheim Foundation. She teaches at Washington University in St. Louis.

LUCILLE CLIFTON was born on June 27, 1936, and she studied briefly at Howard University before transferring in 1955 to SUNY Fredonia. She published thirteen collections of poetry, a memoir, and more than twenty books focused on African American characters and history for young readers. In 1988, she was the first poet to be nominated for the Pulitzer Prize for two collections of poetry in the same year. In 2007, Clifton became the first African American woman to receive the $100,000 Ruth Lilly Poetry Prize, and in 2010, she was posthumously awarded the Poetry Society of America's highest honor—the Robert Frost Medal for distinguished lifetime achievement in American poetry. She died on February 13, 2010, in Baltimore.

KASS FLEISHER's novel *Dead Woman Hollow* is forthcoming from SUNY Press. She authored *Talking Out of School: Memoir of an Educated Woman* (Dalkey Archive, 2008), *The Adventurous* (Factory School, 2007), *Accidental Species: A Reproduction* (Chax, 2005), and *The Bear River Massacre and the Making of History* (SUNY, 2004). She writes plays and screenplays with Joe Amato, and teaches at Illinois State University.

KIMIKO HAHN, author of eight collections, finds her material from disparate sources—whether exhumation (*The Artist's Daughter*, Norton, 2002) or classical Japanese texts (*The Narrow Road to the Interior*, Norton, 2006). Science triggered her latest work in *Toxic Flora* (Norton, 2010) and continues in her current writing. She has also written for film, most recently *Everywhere at Once*, a film based on Peter Lindbergh's still photos and narrated by Jeanne Moreau. Her most recent award was a Guggenheim Fellowship, and she teaches in the MFA Program in Creative Writing & Literary Translation at Queens College, City University of New York.

CARLA HARRYMAN is a poet, essayist, novelist, and playwright. Recent works include *Adorno's Noise* (Essay Press, 2008), *Open Box* (Belladonna Books, 2007),

Baby (Adventures in Poetry, 2005), *Gardener of Stars* (Belladonna Books, 2001), and *The Wide Road*, a collaboration with Lyn Hejinian (Belladonna Books, 2011). She is co-editor of *Lust for Life* (Verso, 2006), a volume of essays on Kathy Acker, and she is the editor of *Non/Narrative*, a special issue of *The Journal of Narrative Theory* (2011). She is co-contributor to *The Grand Piano* (Mode A, 2006–2010), a ten-volume work about Language writing, art, politics, and culture of the San Francisco Bay Area between 1975 and 1980. She teaches at Eastern Michigan University and serves on the graduate faculty of the Milton Avery School of the Arts at Bard College.

CHRISTINE HUME is the author of three books of poetry—most recently *Shot* (Counterpath, 2010)—and two chapbooks, *Lullaby: Speculations on the First Active Sense* (Ugly Duckling Presse, 2008) and *Ventifacts* (Omnidawn, 2012). She is coordinator of the interdisciplinary creative writing program at Eastern Michigan University.

KARLA KELSEY is author of two books of poetry: *Knowledge, Forms, the Aviary* (Ahsahta, 2006) (selected by Carolyn Forché for the 2005 Sawtooth Poetry Prize) and *Iteration Nets* (Ahsahta, 2010). She edits and contributes to Fence Books' *Constant Critic* poetry book review website and has had essays on poetics published in literary journals and anthologies. A recipient of a Fulbright lectureship, Karla graduated from the Iowa Writers' Workshop (MFA), and the University of Denver (PhD). She is on permanent faculty at Susquehanna University.

AARON KUNIN is a poet, critic, and novelist. He is recently the author of *The Sore Throat and Other Poems* (Fence Books, 2010). He teaches early modern poetry and poetics at Pomona College, and lives in Los Angeles.

DAWN LUNDY MARTIN is the author of *DISCIPLINE* (Nightboat Books, 2011) and *A Gathering of Matter/A Matter of Gathering* (University of Georgia Press, 2007). She is a founding member of the Black Took Collective, a group of experimental black poets; co-editor of a collection of essays, *The Fire This Time: Young Activists and the New Feminism* (Anchor Books, 2004); and a founder of the Third Wave Foundation in New York, a national feminist organization. She is an assistant professor of English at the University of Pittsburgh.

ADRIENNE MCCORMICK is professor of English and department chair at SUNY Fredonia. Writing on Lucille Clifton for this volume was a distinct honor, given Clifton's connection to her home institution. McCormick publishes on poetry and identity, and is particularly interested in how poets such as Clifton explore poetic persona. Her publications include articles on Marilyn Chin, Cathy Song, and David Mura, and she is working on a monograph on articulations of identity in contemporary multiethnic American poetries. Other research interests are in women's studies, women's documentary filmmaking, and feminist theorizing.

ERÍN MOURE is a Montreal poet who writes in English, but multilingually. In her recent *O Resplandor* (House of Anansi Press, 2010) and—with Oana Avasilichio-aei—*Expeditions of a Chimaera* (BookThug, 2009), poetry is hybrid, and emerges in translation and collaboration. Moure also translates poetry from French, Galician, Portuguese, and Spanish. Her essays, collected in *My Beloved Wager*, appeared in 2009 (NeWest Press); *Pillage Laud* was reissued by BookThug in 2011, and *The Unmemntioable*, a poetic investigation into subjectivity, immigration, and the western borderlands of Ukraine, is due from Anansi in 2012. Her first book of poetry appeared in 1979.

LAURA MULLEN is the author of six books, most recently *Dark Archive* (University of California, 2011) and *Murmur* (futurepoem, 2007). Her author website can be found at www.lauramullen.biz. She teaches at Louisiana State University.

EILEEN MYLES's *Inferno (a poet's novel)* was published in 2010 by orbooks.com. *Snowflake* (poems) will be out in spring 2012. Her other books of poetry include *Skies* (Black Sparrow Press, 2001), *Not Me* (Semiotext(e), 1991), *School of Fish* (Black Sparrow Press, 1997), and *Sorry, Tree* (Wave Books, 2007). Her nonfiction writing was collected in *The Importance of Being Iceland* (Semiotext(e), 2009), for which she received a Warhol/Creative Capital Grant. The Poetry Society of America gave her the Shelley Award in 2010. She writes for *Bookforum*, *Artforum*, *Parkett*, and the *Believer*. She is professor emeritus from UC San Diego, and she lives in New York.

MAGGIE NELSON is the author of four books of nonfiction, *The Art of Cruelty: A Reckoning* (Norton, 2011), *Bluets* (Wave Books, 2009), *Women, the New York School, and Other True Abstractions* (University of Iowa Press, 2007), and *The Red Parts: A Memoir* (Free Press, 2007), and four books of poetry, including *Something Bright, Then Holes* (Soft Skull Press, 2007) and *Jane: A Murder* (Soft Skull Press, 2005). She currently teaches on the BFA and MFA faculty of the School of Critical Studies at CalArts and lives in Los Angeles.

JENA OSMAN's latest book of poems is *The Network* (Fence Books, 2010), which was selected for the 2009 National Poetry Series. Previous books include *An Essay in Asterisks* (Roof Books, 2004) and *The Character* (Beacon Press, 1999), winner of the Barnard New Women Poets Prize). She founded and edited the magazine *Chain* with Juliana Spahr for twelve years; now they co-edit the ChainLinks Book Series. Osman teaches in the graduate creative writing program at Temple University in Philadelphia.

M. NOURBESE PHILIP is a Canadian poet, novelist, playwright, essayist, and short story writer. She is the author of several collections of essays, prose, drama, and poetry including *She Tries Her Tongue, Her Silence Softly Breaks* (Ragweed

Press, 1989), *Harriet's Daughter* (Heinemann, 1988), and, most recently, *Zong!* (Wesleyan, 2008). She has been awarded a Pushcart Prize, the Casa de las Americas Prize, the Tradewinds Collective Prize, and a Guggenheim Fellowship. Born in Tobago, she now resides in Toronto, Ontario.

SINA QUEYRAS is the author of a novel, *Autobiography of Childhood* (Coach House, 2011), and four books of poetry, including *Expressway* (Coach House, 2009) and *Lemon Hound* (Coach House, 2006). She is the founder and editor of the literary blog Lemon Hound. She has taught creative writing at Rutgers, Haverford, and Concordia University in Montreal, where she currently resides.

CLAUDIA RANKINE is the author of four collections of poetry, including *Don't Let Me Be Lonely* (Graywolf, 2004), and the plays *Provenance of Beauty: A South Bronx Travelogue*, commissioned by the Foundry Theatre, and *Existing Conditions* (co-authored with Casey Llewellyn). Rankine is also co-editor of *American Women Poets in the Twenty-First Century: Where Lyric Meets Language* (Wesleyan, 2002) and *American Poets in the Twenty-First Century: The New Poetics* (Wesleyan, 2007). She has also produced a number of videos in collaboration with John Lucas. A recipient of fellowships from the Academy of American Poetry and the National Endowments for the Arts, she is the Henry G. Lee Professor of English at Pomona College.

JOAN RETALLACK is the author of *The Poethical Wager* (University of California Press, 2003) and *MUSICAGE* (Wesleyan, 1996), two other critical works, and eight poetry titles. *Procedural Elegies / Western Civ Cont'd /* (Roof Books, 2010) was the poetry volume named by ARTFORUM as a best book of 2010. Robert Creeley chose *Errata 5uite* (Edge Books, 1993) for the 1993 Columbia Book Award. Retallack lives in the Hudson Valley, where she is John D. & Catherine T. MacArthur Professor of Humanities at Bard College.

LISA ROBERTSON's most recent book of poetry is *R's Boat* (University of California Press, 2010). A new book of essays, *Nilling*, is out from BookThug. The Canadian poetics journal *Open Letter* has just published a special issue on her work. She lives in France.

LISA SEWELL is the author of *The Way Out* (Alice James Books, 1998), *Name Withheld* (Four Way Books, 2006), and *Long Corridor* (Seven Kitchens Press, 2009), and co-editor of *American Poets in the 21st Century: The New Poetics* (Wesleyan, 2007). She teaches in the English Department at Villanova University.

SUZANNE WISE is the author of the poetry collection *The Kingdom of the Subjunctive* (Alice James Books, 2000). Her poetry also appears in the anthology *Legitimate Dangers: American Poets of the New Century* (Sarabande Books, 2006) and in the journals *Bone Bouquet, Green Mountains Review, Guernica, Quarter After Eight*, and *American Letters and Commentary*, among other places. She has taught creative writing at Pratt Institute, Middlebury College, and the University of Michigan.

C. D. WRIGHT is the author of more than a dozen books, most recently *One With Others: [a little book of her days]* (Copper Canyon, 2010), which won the National Book Critics Circle Award (2010), and *Rising, Falling, Hovering* (Copper Canyon, 2008), which won the Griffin International Poetry Prize (2009). In 2004 she was named a MacArthur Fellow. She is on the faculty at Brown University.

ZHOU XIAOJING is Professor of English at University of the Pacific. The areas of her major teaching and research interests are modern and postmodern American literature, Asian American literature, ecocriticism, and environmental literature. Her publications include "Arthur Yap's Ecological Poetics of the Daily," in *Common Lines and City Spaces: A Critical Anthology of Arthur Yap* (forthcoming), " 'Come ye not without song, offering, prayer': The Ecological Ethics in Hawai'ian Songs" in *ISLE: Interdisciplinary Studies in Literature and Environment*; "Wilderness and Subject Formation in *Holder of the World* by Bharati Mukherjee" in *IJE: Indian Journal of Ecocriticism*; *The Ethics and Poetics of Alterity in Asian American Poetry*; and an edited special collection of translations of selected poems and interviews by three Chinese American poets, Li-Young Lee, Marilyn Chin, and Arthur Sze in *Contemporary International Poetry 5*.

INDEX

abbreviation and disjunction in Bang,
6, 32
abjection in Philip, 291
abrasion of languages in Moure,
178–79
accretion: in Myles, 11; in Wright, 15,
16
accumulation in Robertson, 378–79
acrostics, 348–49n42
Adorno, Theodor W., 137, 145–46,
155–56n10, 156n17
African American culture: both/
and sensibility in, 67, 69, 78, 88;
in Clifton, 7, 69, 71, 75, 77–82;
multiple identities and, 77; in Philip,
11–12, 272–73, 282–85, 286, 291,
293–303
Agamben, G., 168
Agee, James, *Let Us Now Praise
Famous Men*, 404, 405
Alberti, Leon Battista, 378, 383n34
Aletti, Vince, 403
alterity: of Bang, 6; of Clifton, 7; in
contemporary poetry, 2–3; in Hahn,
8; identity as central to, 3–4; Mul-
len and, 10, 209–10, 216; in Philip,
292; in Retallack, 13, 322–24,
335–36, 338, 342; in Robertson,
14; in Wright, 15–16. *See also*
"other"
analytic listening in Harryman, 145
and/both vs. either/or viewpoint, 67,
69, 78, 88, 147–48
Ang, Ien, "Identity Blues," 283–84
Anscombe, Elizabeth, *Intention*,
327–28
architecture of poetry: and instability of
language, 31; Robertson and, 14–15,
361–64, 366–68, 370, 372, 381n14;
self and social in Mullen, 208–10

Arendt, Hannah, 180
Armantrout, Rae, "Feminist Poetics
and the Meaning of Clarity,"
367–68
Armstrong, Isobel, *Contemporary
Women's Poetry: Reading/Writing/
Practice*, 5
artifice, articulation of in Bang, 34–56
Ashcroft, Bill, *The Post-Colonial Stud-
ies Reader*, 283
Ashton, Jennifer, 16
Asian traditions in Hahn, 7, 107–9,
112–13, 119–23
atomized listening in Harryman, 145,
155–56n10
attention, refocusing of in Retallack,
338–39, 343–44
Auden, W. H., 140
audience, Myles's, 255–56
audition, and Harryman's *Baby*, 9,
142–54, 155–56n10
Austin, J. L., 245, 332
authority, Philip's overthrow of, 282
autobiographical poetry: in Bang,
46–52; in Hahn, 111; and identity,
3; in Myles, 244, 248, 258n33; in
Wright, 408, 411
autonomy: in Hahn, 113; Harryman
and, 139, 146, 148, 150–51; in
Mullen, 213, 224; in Philip, 285
avant-garde: elegance in, 378; Myles
on being, 255; vs. New Critical lyric,
35–36. *See also* Myles, Eileen; Philip,
M. NourbeSe; Robertson, Lisa

Bang, Mary Jo: autobiographical
poetry in, 46–52; ekphrastic poetry
of, 40–46; identity in, 6, 39–44, 46,
49–50, 52, 54; Kelsey's analysis,
6, 34–56; language for, 31–32, 36,

39; lyric interiority in, 6–7, 34, 35;
narrative structures in, 42–44; New
Critical lyric in, 35–38, 40, 45, 54;
overview of work, 5–6; poetics
statement, 30–33; visual art and,
40–45, 47
Bang, Mary Jo, works of: "And as in
Alice," 6, 25, 53; *Apology for Want*,
38–39; "The Beauties of Nature,"
39; "B Is for Beckett," 26, 36, 51;
"Blue Sky Elegy," 47; *The Bride of
E*, 6, 25–29, 36, 50–55; "C Is for
Cher," 26–27; "Don't," 47; *The
Downstream Extremity of the Isle
of Swans*, 36, 39; *Elegy*, 6, 23–24,
46–50; *The Eye Like a Strange
Balloon*, 19–22, 38, 40–46; "High
Art," 19, 40, 43–45; " 'In Order'
Means Neat and Not Next," 50; "In
the Present and Probable Future,"
27–29, 54; "Intractable, and
Irreversible," 47, 49; "Landscape
with the Fall of Icarus," 23, 48–49;
Louise in Love, 37, 38–39, 43;
"Mrs. Autumn and Her Two Daugh-
ters," 21, 42–43; *Mrs. Dalloway*,
29–30, 37, 55; "Opened and Shut,"
29–30, 55; "The Role of Elegy," 47;
"Untitled # 70 (Or, The Question
of Remains)," 22; "Waiting," 47;
"What If," 50; "What Is So Frighten-
ing," 49–50; "What Moonlight Will
Do for Ruins," 40; "Where Once,"
49; "Words," 24, 49, 50
Barnholden, Michael, 380
Barthes, Roland, 152–53; *Camera
Lucida*, 40; *Roland Barthes by
Roland Barthes*, 252
Beck, Julian, 397, 402
Beckett, Samuel, 39, 52, 376; *Ohio,
Impromptu*, 36–37
Berger, John, 211
Bergson, Henri, 371
Bergvall, Caroline, "Writing at the
Crossroads of Language," 335
Bernstein, Charles, "Artifice of Absorp-
tion," 35–36, 38, 46

Berrigan, Ted, 242
Beuys, Joseph, 200
biblical personas in Clifton, 77–79,
91n24
Bishop, Elizabeth: "A Cold Spring,"
108; "First Death in Nova
Scotia," 107; "The Fish," 109;
"The Shampoo," 39; "The Waiting
Room," 107
Blanchot, Maurice, 153
bodily texts: in Clifton, 77, 83; in
Hahn, 7–8, 107–10, 113–14,
119–23; in Harryman, 142–43;
Moure and, 169; in Myles, 11,
243–44; in Philip, 13, 285, 289–92,
296–301
Bohr, Niels, 344
border-crossing poetics: in Hahn, 112;
in Moure, 168–69, 180–81; in
Retallack, 328, 330–31; in Wright,
16, 399–420. *See also* genres
Borges, Jorge Luis, 337–38
both/and vs. either/or viewpoint, 67,
69, 78, 88, 147–48
Bourgeois, Louise, 200
Bourriaud, Nicholas, *Relational
Aesthetics*, 343–44
Brecht, Bertolt, 401, 408
Breuer, Josef, *Studies on Hysteria*, 114
broken syntax in Philip, 12
Brontë, Charlotte, *Jane Eyre*, 220
Brooks, Gwendolyn: "Gay Chaps
at the Bar," 88–89; *A Street in
Bronzeville*, 88–89
Brooks, Louise, 38
Brossard, Nicole, 174
Brouwer, Joel, 418n6
Browning, Robert, 173
Buckeye, Robert, 224
Buddhism in Clifton, 86–87
Burt, Stephen, 2, 39, 399
Butler, Judith, 245; *Excitable Speech*,
249

Cage, John, 225, 332, 343–44,
349n42; "4'33," 339–40; *For the
Birds*, 308; *Musicage: Cage Muses*

on *Words, Art, Music*, 327–28; "Overpopulation of an Art," 328

call-and-response structure in Clifton, 71, 82

Canty, Daniel, 168

capitalism, Wright's critique of, 408–9

Carr, Brenda, 291

Carroll, Lewis, 6, 53–54

Caruth, Cathy, 287, 295–96

cellular idea of the body, 243–44, 257n4

Cervantes, Miguel de, *Don Quixote de la Mancha*, 334

chance-based methods in Retallack, 13

Chang, Juliana, 112, 123

Chawaf, Chantal, "La chair linguistique [linguistic flesh]," 110

Cheng, Ann Anlin, 286

childhood in Harryman, 142–43

Cholodenko, Lisa, 43

citizenship in Moure, 180–81

Cixous, Hélène, *The Newly Born Woman*, 115–16, 119, 122

class, and Myles, 246–47

Clément, Catherine, 141; *The Newly Born Woman*, 115–16, 119, 122

Clifton, Lucille: bodily texts in, 77, 83; communal "i" of, 67, 68–89; communing "i" of, 81–88; epistemology in, 69, 71–75, 87, 88, 91n18; feminism in, 7, 69, 70, 73; gender switching in, 77–78, 80; historicity in, 67, 71, 75–76; identity in, 3, 7, 67–92; language in, 67, 69, 77, 80–81; McCormick's analysis, 7, 68–92; overview of work, 6–7; poetics statement, 67–68; as poetry innovator, 2; religious and spiritual elements, 77–80, 86–87, 91n24; Shapeshifter series, 83–84, 87; Wright and, 15

Clifton, Lucille, works of: *The Book of Light*, 62–64, 72–74, 79; "brothers," 79; *Callaloo*, 86; "The coming of fox," 82–83; "cream of wheat," 81; "daughters," 62–63; "A Dream of Foxes," 83; "eve's version," 61;

Generations: A Memoir, 75–76; *Good Times*, 76–77; *Good Woman: Poems and a Memoir*, 60; "horse prayer," 84–85; "leda 1," 64; "leda 3," 64; "lucifer speaks in his own voice," 61–62; *Mercy*, 65–66, 85–86, 88; "The Message from the Ones," 85, 87–88, 89; "One Year Later," 83; *An Ordinary Woman*, 88; *Quilting*, 61–62; "raccoon prayer," 84–85; "Redemption Song," 80–81; "the river between us," 65–66; "Seeing the Ox," 86–87; "sorrows," 66–67; "telling our stories," 65; *Ten Oxherding Pictures*, 86–87; *The Terrible Stories*, 65, 82–84; *Two-Headed Woman*, 72–73, 88; "tyrone (4)," 76–77; *Voices*, 66–67, 80–81, 84–85–87; "willie b (4)," 77

Cocteau, Jean, 206

collage poem, Wright's, 399–400

Collis, Stephen, 376, 379

colonialism/colonization: America and Mexico, 415–16; in Philip, 283–86, 291–92, 304n9. *See also* African American culture

communal "i," Clifton's, 67, 68–89

communing "i," Clifton's, 81–88

confessional poetry, resistance to, 6, 69, 336, 372

corporate capitalism, Wright's critique of, 408–9

corporeality. *See* bodily texts

Costa, Paulo da, 9

Cotter, Holland, 250

Creeley, Robert, 397

Crowe, Cecily, *Bloodrose House*, 219–20

crux in Moure, 178–79

Csikszentmihalyi, Mihaly, 30

Culler, Jonathan, "Why Lyric," 45–46

cultural connections. *See* border-crossing poetics

Das, Veena, 290

Davidson, Ian, 371–72

dead, the, in Mullen, 201, 214, 218
decorative, the, as feminist, 376
deictic in Mullen, 215–16
Deleuze, Gilles, 209
de Man, Paul, 55
demonst(e)ration for Mullen, 200–202, 225n1
denaturalizing strategies in Wright, 16, 401, 412
Derrida, Jacques, 171, 181; *Mal d'archive*, 179
description, Robertson's exploration of, 375–76
Dewey, John, 331–32
dialectical listening in Harryman, 143–54
diastics, 344, 349n42
Dickinson, Emily, 107
digital hacks and information search, 329–30
digital information, interface with thought processes, 338–39
discourse: attention methods in Retallack, 343; and gender role oppression in Mullen, 204; in Harryman's *Baby*, 148–49; Mullen's holes of discourse, 202; Retallack's philosophical discourse interrogation, 331–32, 334, 342; Robertson's architectural/feminist, 367–68
disjunction and abbreviation in Bang, 6, 32
dissociative trance, 287–88
documentary poetry, Wright's, 400–401, 403–17
Donne, John, 173
Drake, Jennifer, *Third Wave Agenda: Being Feminist, Doing Feminism*, 5
DuPlessis, Rachel Blau, 69
Durgin, Patrick, 247

ekphrastic poetry, Bang's, 40–46
elegance, poetics of, in Robertson, 365–79
elegiac tradition, 46–50, 323–24
Eliot, T. S., 30; "Prufrock," 31; "Tradition and the Individual Talent," 251

emergent nature of subject, in Philip, 284–85
emotions: in Bang's *Elegy*, 46; embodiment of in Hahn, 7; as keys to poem for Clifton, 68; and language for Moure, 182–83
Eng, David, 116, 121, 123
epistemology: in Clifton, 69, 71–75, 87–88, 91n18; in Hahn, 8, 111–13, 115–16, 120; in Harryman's listening, 146, 148, 150–51; in Myles, 241–42, 256; in Retallack, 329, 331–32, 334
errantry, in Wright, 405, 411, 417
Esslin, Martin, *The Theater of the Absurd*, 52
ethics, Moure's critique of Levinas, 182–83. *See also* poethics
ethnicity and race. *See* African American culture; Hahn, Kimiko
Evans, Steve, 378
Evans, Walker, *Let Us Now Praise Famous Men*, 404
experimental poetry: Bang's tension with lyric, 31, 37–38, 55; Myles's political combinations, 255. *See also* Philip, M. NourbeSe; Retallack, Joan; Robertson, Lisa
expressive-dynamic mode of listening, 149
externalized poetic, 367

Felman, Shoshana, 290
feminism: in Clifton, 7, 69, 70, 73; in Hahn, 7–8, 107, 110–17, 118–23; in Harryman, 139–141; in Moure, 9–10, 169, 178, 180–81; in Myles, 11, 256; in Philip, 282; in Retallack, 14, 336; in Robertson, 14, 15, 366–69, 371–72, 376; variation in perspectives, 4–5
filmic view of poetry, Myles's, 252
Flaubert, Gustav, *Flaubert in Egypt*, 113
Fleisher, Kass, "Laura Mullen: Threatened as Threat: Rethinking Gender and Genre," 10, 203–25

flip-book structure and Mullen, 217–18
"flowing" (post-avant) poetry, and Mullen, 203–4, 216
form, poetic: in Bang, 49, 51–52; in Hahn, 111, 113; in Mullen, 207–8, 223; *Ostrananie*, 32; sonnet, 88–89, 212. *See also* experimental poetry; lyric voice
Foucault, Michel, 172
fragmentation: in Bang, 43–44, 49; in Hahn, 118–19, 121; in Moure, 172; in Philip, 12, 293, 295–98; Robertson's challenge to pastoral, 369–71, 381n18
Frank, Adam, *Shame and Its Sisters*, 254
Freeland, Amy, 221
Freud, Sigmund, 110–11, 114, 144, 304n10; "Fragment of an Analysis of a Case of Hysteria," 114–15
Fried, Michael, "Art and Objecthood," 183

Galicia and Galician language for Moure, 169–70, 174
Gates, Henry Louis, Jr., *The Signifying Monkey: A Theory of Afro-American Literary Criticism*, 90n12
gender: in Harryman, 148; in Moure, 9, 180–81; in Mullen, 204–25; in Myles, 241–58; New York School poets and, 204; in Philip, 290; resistance to boundaries and, 4; in Robertson, 369, 378, 382n29. *See also* feminism; Hahn, Kimiko
gender switching in Clifton, 77–78, 80
genres, literary and poetic: hybrid movement through and straddling of, 2–3; Mullen's gender-based critique of, 204, 217–25; Myles's resistance to, 256; Robertson's deconstruction of, 14, 369; Wright's resistance to boundaries of, 15–16. *See also* border-crossing poetics
georgic, Robertson's, 369, 370
gestalt listening in Harryman, 144–45

Gilbert, Jack, 398
Ginsberg, Allen, 250
Glissant, Édouard, "A Poetics of Relation," 16, 401–3, 405, 410, 415–16
globalization: and Moure, 169; and reading the world, 372; Retallack's linguistic, 335. *See also* Wright, C. D.
Goldin, Nan, 244
Goodman, Jenny, 418
Gregson v. Gilbert, 294, 302
Griffiths, Gareth, *The Post-Colonial Studies Reader*, 283
Grosz, Elizabeth, 111–13, 115, 119, 376
Grotjohn, Robert, 119
Guattari, Félix, 209

Hadid, Zaha, 367–68, 370, 373
Hahn, Kimiko: autobiographical poetry in, 111; bodily texts in, 7–8, 107–10, 113–14, 119–20, 121–23; epistemology in, 8, 111–13, 115–16, 120; feminism in, 7–8, 107, 110–17, 118–19, 120–23; language in the feminine aesthetic, 111, 113–14, 116–20; overview of work, 7–8; poetics statement, 107–10; psychoanalysis and, 110–23; Zhou's analysis, 8, 110–24
Hahn, Kimiko, works of: *Air Pocket*, 111, 117, 119; *The Artist's Daughter*, 104–6, 120; "Blindside," 120–21; "Comp. Lit.," 118; "Dance Instructions for a Young Girl," 117; "Daphne's Journal," 120; *Earshot*, 111, 116–18; "Femininity," 119; "Garnet," 98–99; "Going Inside to Write," 116–17; "In Childhood," 104; "Like Lavrinia," 104–6; *Mosquito and Ant*, 96–99, 113–14, 116; *The Narrow Road to the Interior*, 99–103; "Orchid Root," 8, 96–98; "Resistance: A Poem on Ikat Cloth," 118–19; "The Hemisphere: Kuchuk Hanem," 113; "Translating Ancient Lines into the Vernacular,"

113–14, 116; *The Unbearable Heart*, 112–13, 118; "Utica Station Dep.10:07 a.m. to N.Y. Penn Station," 99–103; *Volatile*, 121; "Wisteria," 118

Hahn, Tomie, *Sensational Knowledge: Embodying Culture through Japanese Dance*, 108

Hanem, Kuchuk, 113

Haraway, Donna, "Cyborg Manifesto: Science, Technology, and Feminism in the Late Twentieth Century," 139

Harryman, Carla: autonomy and, 139, 146, 148, 150–51; dialectical listening, 143–54; epistemology of listening in, 146, 148, 150–51; feminism in, 139, 140, 141; Hume's analysis, 9, 142–54, 155–56n10; identity in, 9, 143, 147–48, 150–51; language in, 140, 141–54; Language poetry movement and, 22; overview of work, 8–9; performativity in, 142–43, 151–52; poetics statement, 136–42, 154n1; reciprocity in, 9, 145–46, 148–49, 153; subjectivity in, 138–39, 148, 154

Harryman, Carla, works of: *Adorno's Noise*, 132–34; *Baby*, 8, 127–31, 142–54; "Fish Speech," 153; *the opposite of slackness*, 135–36; "Orgasms," 135–36; *Performing Objects*, 152; *Siren*, 136–42; *There Never Was a Rose Without a Thorn*, 153

Hatlen, Burton, "Joan Retallack: A Philosopher Among the Poets, a Poet Among the Philosophers," 331–32

haunting of trauma and effort to speak in Philip, 287, 294

Hay, Deborah, 257n4

Hayles, Katherine, "How We Became Posthuman," 284

head-heart divide in Mullen, 217

hearing vs. listening, 144

Hejinian, Lyn, 10, 31, 373, 375; *Happily*, 378; "Strangeness," 367

Henke, Suzette, *Shattered Subjects: Trauma and Testimony in Women's Life-Writing*, 300

heteronyms and Moure, 172–74, 175–76, 183–84

Heywood, Leslie, *Third Wave Agenda: Being Feminist, Doing Feminism*, 5

historicity in Clifton, 67, 71, 75–76

Holladay, Hilary, 79–80

Holland, Isabelle, *Flight of the Archangel*, 219–20

Honig, Edwin, 174, 175

Horace, 173

horror in Mullen, 191–96, 201–2, 206, 211, 214, 217–21

Howe, Susan, 31

Hughes, Langston, 67

Hull, Akasha, 77

Hume, Christine, "Listening In on Carla Harryman's *Baby*," 9, 142–54, 155–56n10

humor, Retallack on, 322

hybrid poetry, 2–3, 4. *See also individual poets*

hyperextended sentence in Wright, 414

hysteria, Freudian perspective, 114–15

hysteric feminine and Hahn's feminist challenge, 113–23

identity: in Bang, 6, 39, 41–44, 46, 49–50, 52, 54; as central to alterity, 3–4; in Clifton, 3, 7, 67–92; colonialism's traumatizing of, 291; feminism and, 5; in Harryman, 9, 143, 147–48, 150–51; in history, 76; homosexuality in New York School and, 243; in Moure, 169, 171–72; in Mullen, 205–6, 208–13; in Myles, 10–11, 247–50, 252; in Philip, 283–88, 291–92, 296–97; Poetics of Relation and, 401–2; in Retallack, 335; in Robertson, 14–15; in Wright, 411. *See also* self; subjectivity

idiom, Wright's use of, 399, 406, 415–16

"I/i," lyric. *See* lyric "I/i" (subject)

immigrant experiences: in Moure, 180; in Wright, 16, 392–96, 400, 410–17

individualism, Western, Clifton's challenge to, 71

infinite archive, Retallack's use of, 330, 332–33, 339–40

intellect and intuition in Clifton, 67–68

interiority, intellectual vs. domestic, 372. *See also* lyric interiority

Irigaray, Luce, 111, 113

Jackson, Virginia, 55

Japanese culture, 108–9

Johnston, Velda, *The Girl at the Beach*, 219–20

Joyce, James: *Finnegan's Wake*, 142; *Ulysses*, 140, 141

juxtaposition: in Myles, 11, 252–53; in Wright, 15, 16, 407, 416

Kantorowicz, Ernst, *The King's Two Bodies*, 180

Kazanjian, David, 123

Keats, John, "Ode on a Grecian Urn," 144

Keller, Lynn, 42, 400–401, 418n7

Kelsey, Karla, "Articulations of Artifice in the Word of Mary Jo Bang," 6, 34–56

Kim, Myung Mi, "Anacrusis," 293

Kinzer, Greg: "Excuses and Other Nonsense: Joan Retallack's 'How to Do Things With Words,'" 332; "Joan Retallack: A Philosopher among the Poets, A Poet among the Philosophers," 331

Kirsch, Adam, 418n6

knowing. *See* epistemology

Koolhaas, Rem, 365; *Office for Metropolitan Architecture*, 367

Kootenay School of Writing (KSW), 4, 365–66, 380n2

Kriner, Tiffany Eberle, 87–88

Kristeva, Julia, 142

Kunin, Aaron, 4; "Moure's Abrasions," 9–10, 171–85

Lacan, Jacques, 289

language: for Bang, 31–32, 36, 39; in Clifton, 67, 69, 77, 80–81; Hahn's feminine aesthetic, 111, 113–14, 116–20; Harryman's sonic transcendence of, 140–54; Moure's multiplicities, 10, 168–69, 171–76; Mullen's interrogation of, 10, 211–13, 216–17, 223–25; in Myles, 245; in Philip, 12, 262–65, 284–303; in Retallack, 13–14, 327–46; in Robertson, 14, 376–78; in Wright, 16, 397, 401, 406–7. *See also* speech act

Language poetry: Harryman as pioneer of, 22; vs. lyric poetry, 90n2; Mullen's connection and "flow," 203–4, 216; Wright's connections/disconnections, 15, 400–401, 418n6

L=A=N=G=U=A=G=E writing, 31, 203–4

Language writing, didacticism criticism of, 216

Lazar, Hank, *Opposing Poetries*, 89–90n2

Lerner, Gerda, 218

lesbianism and Myles, 243

lettristic play in Retallack, 341, 343, 344–45

Levinas, Emmanuel, 2, 182–83, 187n51

life writing vs. memoir, 258n33

"light" metaphor in Clifton, 72–74

line-based poetry, Mullen's use of, 204–17. *See also* lyric voice

linguistic instability. *See* alterity

listening, and Harryman's *Baby*, 9, 142–54, 155–56n10

looking vs. listening in Harryman, 147

Louisiana prisons, Wright's journey in, 16, 390–92, 400, 403–10

love: Bang's artifice and, 38–39, 43; Hahn's feminist interrogation of, 118–19; Mullen on, 209–12, 220; psychoanalysis and hysteria, 114

Lubiano, Wahneema, "The Postmodernist Rag: Political Identity and the

Vernacular in Song of Solomon,"
90n12
Lupton, Julia Reinhard, 181
Luster, Deborah, 400, 403–4
lyric "I/i" (subject): in American poetry,
89–90n2; Clifton's communal "i,"
67–89; Moure on, 170; resistance to
stable, 3; Retallack's interrogation
of, 336. *See also* subjectivity
lyric interiority: in Bang, 6–7, 34–35;
vs. exteriority, 367–68; in Wright,
15
lyric, theater as, in Moure, 183–84
lyric voice: Bang's tension with
experimental poetry, 31, 37–38, 55;
Clifton and, 6–7; hybrid poetry's
continued connection to, 2; in
Moure, 10, 170, 183–84; Mullen's
interrogation of, 206–8; in Myles,
11; narrative structures vs., 45–46;
New Critical vs. avant-garde
treatment of, 35–36; Philip's inter-
rogation of, 282; Robertson's inter-
rogation of the pastoral, 369–70,
371; Robertson's use of, 377–79,
382n25. *See also* Bang, Mary Jo;
Wright, C. D.

Mac Low, Jackson, 344, 349n42
Mallarmé, Stéphane, *Un coup de dés*,
171
Marley, Bob, 80
Martin, Agnes, 369, 374, 381n17, 398
Martin, Dawn Lundy, "The Language
of Trauma: Faith and Atheism in
M. NourbeSe Philip's Poetry," 12,
283–303
Matisse, Henri, *The Pink Nude / Large
Reclining Nude*, 210
May, Cactus, 206, 208
McCormick, Adrienne, "Lucille
Clifton's Communal 'i,' " 7, 68–89
McDuff, David, 205
melancholia in Philip, 285–91, 296,
298, 304n10
memoir vs. life writing, 258n33
mesostics, 344, 348–49n42

metonym, Myles's, 252
metonymy vs. metaphor, 367
Mexico/U.S. border, Wright's journey,
16, 392–96, 400, 410–17
Meyer, Kinereth, 69, 90
Mill, John Stuart, 183
mimetic listening in Harryman, 144
minimalism, 183, 253, 371, 374
mirror/water motif in Mullen, 206–7,
209, 213, 225
Mitchell, Adrian, 279
modernism and modernity, 138,
183–85, 321
mongrelisme, 3–4, 313–15, 333–34
Morrison, Toni: *Beloved*, 294; *Playing
in the Dark*, 294
Moten, Fred, 145
mother-daughter relationships in
Hahn, 111, 118–19
Moure, Erín: border-crossing poetics
in, 168–69, 180–81; feminism
in, 9–10, 169, 178, 180–81;
heteronyms and, 172–76, 183–84;
identity in, 169, 171–72; Kunin's
analysis, 9–10, 171–85; language
multiplicities, 10, 168–69, 171–76;
lyric voice in, 10, 170, 183–84;
OSA and, 15, 367–68; overview
of work, 9–10; poetics statement,
168–71; theatricality in, 9, 169–71;
translation and, 174, 176–80
Moure, Erín, works of: "The Acts,"
176–77; "Anxiety," 184; "Befallen
II," 179–80; "Catalogs of Harms,"
181; "document32 (inviolable),"
161; "document33 (arena)," 162;
"Eleventh *Impermeable* of the
Carthage of Harms," 163; "The
First Story of Latin (os araos),"
176; *A Frame of the Book*, 172–73;
Furious, 172, 176–77; "Homages
to Water," 182; "Hooked," 177;
Little Theatres, 164–66, 170,
172, 175, 178, 182, 183–84;
"Notes in Recollection," 174, 178;
"Nureyev's Intercostals," 172;
O Cadoiro, 167–68, 171, 178–80,

184–85; *O Cidadán*, 9, 161–63,
170, 174–75, 178, 180–83; "Paris
nSleep," 184; "Pure Reason," 177;
"Rhymes get on my nerves. Rarely,"
179; *Search Procedures*, 172, 180,
181, 184; *Sheep's Vigil by a Fervent
Person*, 171, 174, 178–79; "Theatre
of the Confluence (A Carixa)," 164;
"Theatre of the Millo Seco (Botos),"
166; "Three Versions," 177–78;
"The Wittgenstein Letters to Mel
Gibson's Braveheart (Skirting her
a subject) (or girls girls girls),"
172–73
Mullen, Laura: demonst(e)ration for,
200–202, 225n1; Fleisher's analysis,
203–25; gender in, 204–25; genre
critique of, 204, 217–25; humor of,
226n12; identity in, 205–6, 208–13;
language interrogation of, 10,
211–13, 216–17, 223–25; Moure
and, 10; overview of work, 10;
poetics statement, 199–203; politics
of, 209–10, 213–14; Robertson and,
14; self in, 200, 202, 205, 208–9,
216; subjectivity interrogation of,
10, 205, 211–17; textuality concern
of, 215, 223–24
Mullen, Laura, works of: "35 ½,"
195–96; *After I Was Dead*, 204,
208–11; "Appearances," 209–11;
"Arose (Read as) A," 215; "As-
sembly," 215; "Broken Pantoum
for Three Voices (Only One of
Which Is Love)," 207–8; "A Case of
Identity," 205–6; "Circles," 198–99,
211–12; "Coloratura," 206–7; "The
Distance (This)," 215–16; "Frames,"
214–17; "Gift," 214, 216–17; "The
Holmes Poems," 205–6; "Late
and Soon," 212–14; *Murmur*,
197–98, 205, 217, 221–24; "The
Overture," 218; "('a pretty girl is
like a melody')," 191–93; "Secrets,"
193–95; "Sestina in Which My
Grandmother Is Going Deaf," 207;
"Structures," 208–9; *Subject*, 10,

204–5, 211–17; "The Surface,"
189–90; *The Surface*, 204–6; *The
Tales of Horror*, 191–96, 204–5,
217–21; "Wake," 211
multicultural poetry. *See* African
American culture; Hahn, Kimiko
multilingual texts: Moure, 10, 168–69,
171–76; Retallack, 333–35; Wright,
402, 406
Mulvey, Laura, "Visual Pleasure and
Narrative Cinema," 205
music influences, 140–41. *See also*
Cage, John
Myers, Jack, *The Portable Poetry
Workshop*, 109
Myles, Eileen: autobiographical poetry
in, 244, 248, 258n33; bodily texts
in, 11, 243–44; epistemology in,
241–42, 256; feminism in, 11, 256;
gender in, 241–58; genre resistance
of, 256; identity in, 10–11, 247–50,
252; language in, 245; Nelson's
analysis, 11, 204, 242–58; overview
of work, 10–11; performativity
in, 11, 250–51; poetics statement,
241–42; politics of, 250–51, 255
Myles, Eileen, works of: "An American
Poem," 247–50; *Chelsea Girls*, 244,
249; *Cool for You*, 246, 250–52,
254–55; "Exploding the Spring
Mystique," 255; *Hell*, 256; "Hi,"
239–41; "How I Wrote Certain of
My Poems," 245; "Immanence,"
247; *The Importance of Being
Iceland*, 256; "Inauguration Day,"
250; *The Inferno: A Poet's Novel*,
256; "Leaving New York," 250;
"The Lesbian Poet," 11, 243–44,
256; "Light Warrior," 249; "My
Intergeneration," 255–56; *Narrativ-
ity*, 250–51; *Not Me*, 245, 247;
"The Poet," 247; "Popponesset,"
249; "Questions," 237–39; *Sappho's
Boat*, 254; *School of Fish*, 247;
Selected Poems, 256; *Skies*, 250,
252; "Snowflake," 232–34; *Sorry,
Tree*, 256; "To My Class," 234–37;

"Tradition and the Individual Talent," 251; "Transitions," 229–32; "The Windsor Trail," 247; "Writing," 253–54

mystery genre in Mullen, 197–98, 211, 217, 221–24

myth: in Clifton, 77–79; elegiac tradition and, 46–47; in Hahn, 120

names, Moure's multiplicities and transformations, 171–73

Nancy, Jean-Luc, 145, 156n19

Narcissus theme in Mullen, 206

narrative structures: in Bang, 42, 43–44; lyric vs., 45–46; in Philip, 300; in Wright, 15, 410–17

negatively-capable listening in Harryman, 144

Nelson, Maggie, 203–4, 216; " 'When We're Alone in Public': The Poetry of Eileen Myles," 11, 242–58

new analytic listening in Harryman, 145

New Critical lyric, in Bang, 35–38, 40, 45, 54

New York School, 11, 203–4, 242–43

Ngai, Sianne, 376, 377

noise artistry, 140–41, 154, 341. See also sound play in poetry

Notley, Alice, 245

nu shu (female script), 113, 124n8

Office for Soft Architecture (OSA), 15, 367–68

Olson, John, 140

Olson, Redell, 337

orality, 69, 145, 149, 156n21, 243

Oriental feminine, Hahn's challenge to, 7, 107, 108–9, 112–13, 119–23

origin and listening in Harryman, 150–51

Orr, David, 418n6

Osman, Jena, "The Method 'In Medias Mess,' " 13–14, 326–46

Ostrananie, 32

Ostriker, Alicia, 77; Stealing the Language: The Emergence of Women's Poetry in America, 70

"other," poetic treatment of: Bang's aesthetic representation, 48–49; Clifton's persona, 69–70, 71, 76–81; Mullen's monsters and ghosts, 201; otherness in other's face, 182; Wright's documenting of, 406–17. See also alterity

Oulipean procedures, Retallack, 323, 344

Ovid, 330

palinode, Robertson on, 372–73

pantoum, Mullen's confrontation of, 207–8

passivity in Robertson, 372–73

pastoral, Robertson's fragmentation of, 369–71, 381n18

Pato, Chus, 170, 174; Charenton, 171

patriarchy: Hahn's challenge to, 112, 118, 122; Harryman's resistance to, 141; hysteric feminine as resistance to, 115–17; Philip's overthrow of authority, 282

Pearson, Bruce, 40

performative utterance, 245

performativity: in Bang, 45; in Harryman, 142–43, 151–52; in Myles, 11, 250–51; overview, 3

peripheral hearing, 144

Perloff, Marjorie, " 'Modernism' at the Millennium," 378

persona: in Bang, 38–39; in Clifton, 69–71, 76–81, 91n24; Moure's heteronyms, 172–76, 183–84; Pound and, 173. See also subjectivity

Pessoa, Fernando, 173–74, 183–84; O Guardador de Rebanhos (The Keeper of Sheep), 169, 174

Phelan, Peggy, 300–301

Philip, M. NourbeSe: bodily texts in, 13, 285, 289–92, 296, 297–301; colonialism/colonization in, 283–86, 291–92, 304n9; feminism in, 282; fragmentation in, 12, 293, 295–98; gender in, 290; identity in, 283–88, 291–92, 296, 297; language in, 12, 262–65, 284–87,

288–303; Martin's analysis, 283–303; overview analysis, 11–13; poetics statement, 279–82; racial melancholia, 12, 291, 296, 298; subjectivity in, 284–86, 291, 294, 300, 302–3, 304n9

Philip, M. NourbeSe, works of: "The Absence of Writing," 286; "The Catechist," 288–89; "The Communicant," 292; "Discourse on the Logic of Language," 12, 262–65, 292–93; "Epiphany," 289; "Eucharistic Contradictions," 288–89; *Ferrum*, 274–78; *Looking for Livingstone: An Odyssey of Silence*, 12, 279; "Meditations on the Declension of Beauty by the Girl with the Flying Cheek-bones," 287–88; "Notanda," 294, 297; "Ratio," 294–95; *She Tries Her Tongue; Her Silence Softly Breaks*, 12, 261–65, 279, 283–93, 296; *Universal Grammar*, 266–71; "Universal Grammar," 290, 292; *Zong!*, 12, 13, 272–73, 283–85, 293–303

philosophical discourse, Retallack's interrogation of, 331–32, 334, 342

photography, 40–41, 403–4, 409–10

Plato, *Phaedo*, 109

poethics, Retallack's, 13, 321–24, 327–28, 336, 338, 340–46

poetics defined by Retallack, 324–26

poetry: contemporary classification issues, 2; and theatricality, 183; Wright on definition of, 397–98

politics: hysteric feminine as political resistance, 116, 123; Moure's citizenship and, 180–81; Mullen on, 209–10, 213–14; Myles and poetics of, 251, 255; Myles's run for president, 250–51; resistance and, 4; Wright's documentary poetry, 399, 401–2, 407–17

Polke, Sigmar, "Frau Herbst und ihre zwei Töchter," 42

Pollock, Jackson, 372

polyvocality, 9, 143, 333–35

post-avant poetry, and Mullen, 203–4, 216

post-colonial subjectivity in Philip, 283–86, 292, 304n9

postmodernism: Bang's struggle to speak to the existential, 51; Philip's untelling of self, 297; Retallack and, 336; in Wright, 410

poststructuralist theory, 181

Pound, Ezra, 173

Preminger, Otto, *Laura*, 223–24

Prevallet, Kristin, 407

procedural poethics in Retallack, 13, 321–24, 327–28, 340–46

prose: in Bang, 51–52; Mullen's, 205, 211, 217–25; vs. poetry in Wright, 413

psychoanalysis: in Hahn, 110–23; in Harryman, 144–45; melancholia, 304n10; Myles's exhibitionism and, 246; stories as therapy, 296

queer performativity, 245

queer theory, and Myles, 11, 243

Queyras, Sina, "About Surface: Lisa Robertson's Poetics of Elegance," 4, 15, 365–83

race issues. *See* African American culture; Hahn, Kimiko

racial melancholia in Philip, 12, 291, 296, 298

Raddle Moon, 367, 380n5

Rankine, Claudia: *American Women Poets in the 21st Century: Where Lyric Meets Language*, 1, 16–17; *Don't Let Me Be Lonely*, 283

reciprocal alterity in Retallack, 13, 322–23, 335–36, 338, 342

reciprocity: in Harryman, 9, 145–46, 148–49, 153; in Myles, 245; in Philip, 292

recognition trope in Levinas' ethics, 187n51

recursive listening in Harryman, 143–46, 152

recycling technique, Wright's, 412–13

Redon, Odilon, "L'oeil, comme un ballon bizarre se dirige vers l'infini," 41

regressive listening in Harryman, 145, 155–56n10

relational poetics: in Harryman, 143–45, 150; in Retallack, 343–44; in Robertson, 372–73, 378; in Wright, 16, 402–17

repetition: Hahn on, 109–10; in Harryman, 150–53; in Philip, 12, 284, 287–88; in Robertson, 369–71, 375, 377; vs. translation for Moure, 177; in Wright, 412–13

representation over content in Bang, 39, 40, 41, 46

resistance: to confessional poetry, 6, 69, 336, 372; genre boundary interrogation as, 4; in Harryman, 8–9, 138, 141, 146; Moure's multiple languages as, 10; Myles and, 256; in Philip, 292; Retallack's linguistic, 13–14; in Robertson, 14–15; in Wright, 15–16. *See also* border-crossing poetics; feminism

Retallack, Joan: border-crossing poetics in, 328, 330–31; epistemology in, 329, 331–32, 334; feminism in, 14, 336; on Harryman, 154; identity in, 335; language in, 13–14, 327–46; Lost Brief Case Conjecture, 320; Osman's analysis, 326–46; overview of work, 13–14; philosophical discourse interrogation, 331–32, 334, 342; poethics, 13, 321–24, 327–28, 336, 338, 340–46; poetics statement, 321–26; reciprocal alterity in, 13, 322–23, 335–36, 338, 342; subjectivity in, 321–23, 331, 336–38; translation and, 331, 333–35

Retallack, Joan, works of: *AFTER-RIMAGES*, 326–27, 330, 340–41; "AID/I/SAPPEARANCE," 344–45; "be ing & no th' ing ness: notes from the specific rim :," 342–43; *"Curiosity and the Claim to*

Happiness," 316–19; *Errata Suite,* 308–13, 341–42; "Geometries of Attention," 339; *How to Do Things with Words,* 330, 333, 342–44; "Icarus Ffffalling," 330; *Memnoir,* 316–20, 330, 337; *Mongrelisme,* 313–15, 333–34; "mongrelisme," 3–4; *The Poethical Wager,* 329; " Re:Thinking:Literary:Feminism," 14, 336; "The Scarlet Aitch," 341; "Scenes of Translation (from the Translation)," 330, 333, 335–36; "What Is Experimental Poetry & Why Do We Need It," 327; "The Woman in the Chinese Room," 310–13, 331, 332, 334–35

rhythmic-spatial mode of listening, 149

Rich, Adrienne, "The Eye of the Outsider," 107–8

Richard, Frances, 243, 255

Rilke, Rainer Maria, 173, 179

Robertson, Lisa: architecture of poetry, 14–15, 361–64, 366–68, 370, 372, 381n14; feminism in, 14, 15, 366–69; KSW and, 380n2; language in, 14, 376–78; lyric voice and, 369–71, 377–79, 382n25; overview of work, 14–15, 378; poetics statement, 361–64; Queyras's analysis, 4, 365–83; on reading, 381n11; soft architecture, 14–15, 361–64, 366–68, 370, 372, 381n14; subjectivity in, 14–15, 368, 371–74, 378–79, 383n37

Robertson, Lisa, works of: *Debbie: An Epic,* 366, 368, 376–77; "Episode: Nurses," 376; "How Pastoral," 376; *The Men,* 377, 379; "Monday," 375; *Occasional Work and Seven Walks from the Office for Soft Architecture,* 366–67, 370, 381n14; "Passivity," 373; *Philly Talks,* 373; "Residence at C___," 352–53, 356, 374; *Rosseau's Boat,* 14, 371–73; "Saturday," 356–58; "Soft Architecture: A Manifesto," 14–15; "Spatial Synthetics," 368; "Sunday," 374–75;

"Tuesday," 14, 353–55, 376;
"Utopia," 371; *Utopia (R's Boat)*,
358–61; *The Weather*, 14, 352–58,
366, 368, 369–71, 373–77, 378–79;
"Wednesday," 370; *XEclogue*, 368,
376

Roosevelt, Theodore, 333

Rosler, Martha, 403

Rowell, Charles, 7, 67, 78, 86

Rukeyser, Muriel, "The Book of the
Dead," 404–5, 409

Sacks, Peter, *The English Elegy: Studies
in the Genre from Spencer to Yeats*,
47

Said, Edward, *Orientalism*, 113

Sampedrín, Elisa (heteronym of
Moure), 170, 172, 175, 182, 184

Schmidt, Michael, 107

schools of poetry, contemporary clas-
sification issues, 2

Schroeder, Amy Newlove, 211

Schultz, Susan, 36, 213–14, 216

Schumacher, Patrik, 365

Schuyler, James, 252

Schwitters, Kurt, 375

Scott, Gail, 177–78

Searle, John, 331–33, 338

Sedgwick, Eve Kosofsky, 245; *Shame
and Its Sisters*, 254

self: in Bang, 39, 48–50, 52, 54;
Clifton's communal "i" and, 69–89;
experimental writing's search
for new, 367; in Harryman, 142,
146–47, 150; in Mullen, 200, 202,
205, 208–9, 216; in Myles, 247,
252; Ostriker on, 70, 78–79; in
Philip, 283–89, 291–92, 295–98; in
Retallack, 321, 336–38; in Robert-
son, 373, 378–79; in Wright, 398,
408, 411, 413. *See also* identity;
subjectivity

self-absorption, in Bang, 30, 33, 38

sense vs. sound, writing for, 140–41

sexuality, in Clifton, 82–84

Shakespeare, William, "It's Winter in
the Eye, and Like Ophelia," 39

shame as oppositional foil for positive
emotions, 254–55

Shepherd, Reginald, 200, 216, 219;
*Lyric Postmodernisms: An Anthol-
ogy of Contemporary Innovative
Poetries*, 2

Sherman, Cindy, "Untitled Film Stills,"
32–33, 34–35

Shikibu, Murasaki, *The Tale of Genji*,
111, 118

Shklovsky, Viktor, "Art as Technique,"
32

Shōnagon, Sei, *The Pillow Book*, 121

signifying, defined, 90n12

silence and silencing: Cage's use of
silence, 339; listening in Harryman
and, 153–54; in Philip, 12, 282, 294

Silliman, Ron, *Tjanting*, 400, 418n7,
419n14

slave trade and Philip, 11–12, 272–73,
283–85, 293–303

social sculptures, 343

sonic materiality in Harryman, 142–54

sonnet, 88–89, 212

Sontag, Susan, 403

sound play in poetry: in Bang, 39,
44; in Harryman, 9, 140–41, 144,
154; in Moure, 9, 170; Retallack's
subtextual noise, 341; in Robertson,
377–78

sources: Retallack's destabilized use of,
330–31; Wright's use of, 405

Spahr, Juliana: *American Women Poets
in the 21st Century: Where Lyric
Meets Language*, 1, 16–17

spatial forms, in Robertson, 373–76

spatiality of sound in Harryman, 144

speech act: in Clifton, 69; in Myles,
11, 245, 254; in Philip, 11–12,
283–303; political and cultural
barriers in Wright, 414; in Retal-
lack, 332

spirituality in Clifton, 77–80, 86–87,
91n24

spoken word poetry, 255–56

Stanford, Frank, 397

Stein, Gertrude, 31, 152, 211, 245,

321, 369, 376, 398; *Lectures in America*, 182; "Sacred Emily," 215
Stevens, Wallace, 39–40
St. John, David, *American Hybrid*, 2
Stonecipher, Donna, 41
structural listening in Harryman, 145–46, 155–56n10
stupliminity, Ngai's, 376
subjectivity: Clifton's multiple selves, 70–71, 86; in Harryman, 138–39, 148, 154; and lyric interior vs. exterior, 367; Mullen's interrogation of, 10, 205, 211–17; in Philip, 284–86, 291, 294, 300, 302–3, 304n9; in Retallack, 321–22, 323, 331, 336–38; in Robertson, 14, 15, 368, 371–74, 378–79, 383n37; in Wright, 405, 408, 411. *See also* lyric "I/i"; self
Sukenick, Ronald, 140, 141
surface, Robertson's interrogation of, 366–69, 379
Swenson, Cole: *American Hybrid*, 2; *Try*, 42
symbolic figuring (artifice) in Bang, 34–56
syntactical disruption in Wright, 15, 400–401

textuality: Mullen's concern with, 215, 223–24; Philip's playfulness, 284
texture, repetition as, 109–10
theatricality in Moure, 9, 169–70, 171
threat motif in Mullen, 206, 208, 211, 213, 218–21, 224–25
Thyreen-Mizingou, Jeannine, 71, 90–91n16
Tierney, Therese, 371
Tiffin, Helen, *The Post-Colonial Studies Reader*, 283
time and subjectivity, 371–73, 378–79
time and Wright's documentary experience, 405
Tomkins, Silvan, 254
translation: and Moure, 174, 176–80; Retallack and, 331, 333–35
trauma, Philip's language of, 283–303

troubadour poetry in Moure, 170
Tsurayuki, Ki no, *Tosanikki (The Tosa Diary)*, 119
Turkel, William, 329, 332

utopia and listening in Harryman, 148–50

variation, linguistic, 284, 287, 369
Vendler, Helen, 36
Virgil, 368, 369, 371
visual art: Clifton on look of a poem, 68; film and photo tropes for Myles, 252; as informing Bang's work, 40–41, 42, 43–45, 47; and theatricality of lyric in Moure, 183–84; Wright's interrogation of photography, 403–4, 409–10, 417. *See also* Robertson, Lisa

Walpert, Bryan, "AIDS and the Postmodern Subject," 345
water/mirror motif in Mullen, 206–7, 209, 213, 225
Weeks, Laurie, 256
Weisskopff, Victor, 326
West Coast Language poetry movement, 22
Western culture: both/and vs. either/or viewpoint for Clifton, 67, 69, 78, 88; Clifton's challenge to individualism, 71; Hahn's resistance to, 8, 109
White, Mark Bernard, 88
Whiteread, Rachel, 371, 373
white space, 215, 413
Whitman, Walt, 67; *Leaves of Grass*, 92n41
Whitney, Phyllis, *Dream of Orchids*, 219–20
Williams, Raymond, 371, 381n18
window motif, Mullen's, 213–14
Wise, Suzanne, "The Border-Crossing Relational Poetry of C. D. Wright," 16, 399–420
Wittgenstein, Ludwig, 331–32; *Philosophical Investigations*, 327, 328; *Tractatus*, 321

Wittig, Monique: "On the Social Contract," 139; *The Straight Mind*, 246

Wolff, Rebecca, 216

women poets, introduction, 1–18. *See also individual poets*

Woolf, Virginia, 208; *To the Lighthouse*, 119

"wordswerve[s]," in Retallack, 13–14

Wordsworth, William, 212–13; *Prelude*, 369

Wright, C. D.: autobiographical poetry in, 408, 411; identity in, 411; language in, 16, 397, 401, 406–7; overview analysis, 15–16; poetics statement, 397–98; politics of, 399, 401–2, 407–17; on Silliman, 419n14; subjectivity in, 405, 408, 411; Wise's analysis, 16, 399–420

Wright, C. D., works of: "The Box This Comes In," 399, 401, 418n3; *Cooling Time*, 389–90, 400; "Dear Child of God," 391–92; "Dear Prisoner," 390; *Deepstep Come Shining*, 399–400; "Dialing Dungeons for Dollars," 409; "Floating Trees," 386–88; *Further Adventures with You*, 399; "Happiness, in pursuit thereof," 392; "Just Another Day," 408; *Just Whistle*, 399; "Like a Prisoner of Soft Words," 394; "Like Having a Light at Your Back You Can't See but You Can Still Feel," 393; "Like Having a Light at Your Back You Can't See but You Can Still Feel (1)," 412; "Like Having a Light at Your Back You Can't See but You Can Still Feel (2)," 412; "Like Something Christenberry Pictured," 414; "Like Something Flying Backwards," 396; "Like Something in His Handwriting," 395; "My American Scrawl," 15; "My Dear Conflicted Reader," 391; *One Big Self: An Investigation*, 16, 390–92, 400, 403–10; "Privacy," 388–90; "Re: Happiness, in pursuit thereof," 411; *Rising, Falling, Hovering*, 16, 392–96, 400, 410–17; *Steal Away*, 386–88; *String Light*, 399; "Stripe for Stripe," 404–6; "A Taxable Matter," 400; *Tremble*, 399

writing the body. *See* bodily texts

Wyschogrod, Edith, 2–3

Yamamoto, Hisaye, "Seventeen Syllables," 122

Yau, John, 71

Yeats, William Butler, "Easter, 1916," 173

Zhou Xiaojing, " 'I Want to Go Where the Hysteric Re-sides': Kimiko Hahn's Re-Articulation of the Feminine in Poetry," 8, 110–23

Zittel, Andrea, 368, 381n15

Zizek, Savoj, *The Pervert's Guide to Cinema*, 373